THE POEMS OF
FRANCIS THOMPSON

THE POEMS OF
FRANCIS THOMPSON

A NEW EDITION

Edited by
Brigid M. Boardman

BOSTON COLLEGE

First published in 2001 by the John J. Burns Library,
Boston College, Chestnut Hill, MA 02467, USA

Edited, designed and produced by Haggerston Press, London
Printed in Spain by Grafos SA, Barcelona

ISBN 0-9625934-4-3

Copies may be ordered from

the John J. Burns Library,
Boston College, Chestnut Hill, MA 02467, USA

Frontispiece: Unpublished drawing of Francis Thompson, dated 1903,
attributed to Everard Meynell. (*Francis Thompson Collection, Harris Public
Library, Preston*)

*To the memory of
Charles F. Donovan, S. J.,
without whose initial support
and constant encouragement
this book could not have
been accomplished*

Pages from Thompson's last notebook showing his method of composition, here for the draft of an unfinished poem, together with other typical entries. (*Francis Thompson Collection, Boston College*)

*This publication has been made possible
by the generosity of the following:*

BENEFACTORS

Dane and Joella Baird in honor of Joseph and Eleanor Altobello
and Oliver and Catherine Baird
The Ian Anstruther Publication Fund of the John J. Burns Library
Mr and Mrs James (Alice Burns) Scanlon
Mr and Mrs Brian P. Burns

PATRON

Paul and Denise Delaney, Duxbury, Massachusetts

SPONSORS

Rev. Stuart W. Swetland, STD, Champaign, Illinois
Rev. Carl L. LoPresti, Chenoa, Illinois
Karen L. Ogorzalek, Monmouth, Illinois
Theresa D. O'Connor, Peoria, Illinois

Contents

List of Poems

PART ONE

POEMS PUBLISHED IN BOOK FORM

Poems (1893)

Sister Songs (1895)

New Poems (1897)

SIGHT AND INSIGHT

A NARROW VESSEL

MISCELLANEOUS ODES

PART TWO

POEMS PUBLISHED ELSEWHERE

Poems Published during Thompson's Lifetime

Poems Published after Thompson's Death

IN VARIOUS JOURNALS, 1907–35

ECCLESIASTICAL BALLADS

IN *THE LIFE OF FRANCIS THOMPSON* (1913)

IN *THE WORKS OF FRANCIS THOMPSON* (1913)

*AD AMICAM: FIVE SONNETS FROM THE AD
AMICAM NOTEBOOK*

IN *THE MAN HAS WINGS* (1957)

IN *STRANGE HARP, STRANGE SYMPHONY* (1968)

PART THREE
UNPUBLISHED POEMS

PART FOUR

Cricket Verse

Juvenile Poems

Acknowledgements

In the first place I wish to thank the British Academy and the Marguerite Eyer Wilbur Foundation for grants to enable me to study the Francis Thompson Collection at Boston College and to visit other locations in England and America with holdings of Thompson's manuscripts and papers. It has been a special pleasure to work on those still in the possession of the Meynell family, due to the hospitality and interest I have received from Wilfrid Meynell's granddaughters Elizabeth Hawkins and Alice Meynell. As the representative of the family's literary executors, Elizabeth Hawkins has given me full permission to use all the texts needed for this edition. The main collection is excellently housed at the Burns Library at Boston College, where the staff has given me the same unfailing help that I came to value highly while preparing the poet's biography. In particular I wish to thank Dr Robert K. O'Neill for combining friendship with his professional skills, and the same applies to John Atteberry.

I would have wished to add my special thanks to Charles F. Donovan S. J. for his constant encouragement and advice and it is a real sorrow for me that he did not live to see the outcome of the project he had so much at heart. It is therefore a privilege to dedicate this book to his memory. My gratitude to the College extends to other members of the Jesuit Community for similar support, notably Francis Sweeney and J. Robert Barth, while William F. Leonard has advised me on the pre-Vatican II liturgy and related topics.

The other libraries I have visited also gave me useful assistance. Here I wish to acknowledge permission to quote from manuscripts in the Ad Amicam Notebook at the Lilly Library, Indiana University, Bloomington, Indiana. I have had much support from the Lancashire County Library Service when working on the Thompson manuscripts in the possession of the Harris Public Library, Preston. The Ushaw College Library has given me permission to quote the manuscript of 'Nisi Dominus' and the first 45 lines of the ode 'To the English Martyrs', not hitherto published. In addition I acknowledge permission from the Harry Ransom Humanities Research Center, University of Texas at Austin, to publish the text of 'On the Threat of French Invasion', from the manuscript at the Center; also from the State University of New York at Buffalo to publish 'Canticum Novum' from one of the manuscripts held there.

Among the many individuals whom I have reason to thank two names stand out. Bernard Bergonzi's advice and criticism has been a constant support, together with his painstaking care in reading and commenting on the texts. Joseph Sendry's exhaustive appraisals of the manuscripts at Boston College set a standard of scholarship I can only hope I have maintained since. Others who have contributed in many different ways include Elnora Ferguson, with her specialist knowledge in the endnotes for the cricket verse; Dom Philip Jebb O. S. B. with translations of the titles of a number of poems and the Latin extracts and quotations from the Liturgy; Russell Kirk with his support and confidence in the outcome of my work, carried on since his untimely death by his wife Annette; Nicholas Lee with patient and faultless photocopying in the early stages of the book; Charles Praeger S. J. with valuable criticism and advice. Finally I must add special thanks to the publishers for their patience in correcting the manuscript and the care with which they have handled the project. Roger Hudson's determined following up of clues for the endnotes has added a richness to the whole in underlining the range and extent of Thompson's general and literary knowledge.

Abbreviations

AM	Alice Meynell
EM	Everard Meynell
FT	Francis Thompson
WM	Wilfrid Meynell
BMB	Brigid M. Boardman
TLC	Terence L. Connolly, S. J.

SOURCES

BC	Francis Thompson Collection, Boston College
EMH	Everard Meynell's Francis Thompson Collection now at the Harris Library, Preston, Lancs.
H	Francis Thompson Collection, Harris Library, Preston, Lancs.
M	Manuscripts and papers in the possession of the Meynell family
NB	Francis Thompson's Notebooks
WM Note	Wilfrid Meynell's notes made in his copy of *Selected Poems* (1908), lent to BMB by Sir Francis Meynell in *c.* 1970.

EDITIONS

Letters	*The Letters of Francis Thompson*, ed. John Evangelist Walsh (Hawthorn Books, New York 1969)
MHW	*The Man Has Wings: New Poems and Plays by Francis Thompson*, ed. Terence L. Connolly, S. J. (Hanover House, Garden City, N.Y. 1957)
TLC*Poems*	*Poems of Francis Thompson*, ed. with biographical and textual notes by Terence L. Connolly, S. J. (revised edn 1941, repr. Greenwood Press, Westport, Conn. 1979)
Works	*The Works of Francis Thompson*, ed. Wilfrid Meynell, 3 vols (Burns & Oates, London 1913)

OTHER WORKS

BHCC	Brigid M. Boardman, *Between Heaven and Charing Cross: The Life of Francis Thompson* (Yale University Press, New Haven and London 1988)

DR   *Dublin Review*

Life   Everard Meynell, *The Life of Francis Thompson* (Burns & Oates, London 1913). All references are to this edition, not to the second shortened edition published in 1926.

ME   *Merry England*

OED   *Oxford English Dictionary*, 2nd edn, prepared by J. A. Simpson and E. S. C. Weiner (Oxford University Press, Oxford 1989)

SHSS   John Evangelist Walsh, *Strange Harp, Strange Symphony*: *The Life of Francis Thompson* (W. H. Allen, London 1968)

Introduction

This edition originated a good many years ago in an informal discussion on late Victorian poetry. Someone observed how Francis Thompson's poem 'The Hound of Heaven' stands out from the rest—as indeed it can be said to stand out from any other poetic context. We agreed that this has been admitted by both Thompson's critics and his admirers, accounting to a large extent for his name being still remembered despite the neglect of his poetry as a whole. Then the question was raised: 'What kind of man and poet was he, who could write such a poem?' The question sent me back to re-reading 'The Hound of Heaven' and so to his other work. In looking for the answer I found it opened up a complex web of enquiries, leading me first to write the poet's biography.[1] During my research it became clear that a new edition of the poetry was essential for a full recognition of its range and variety, so far never properly presented, and this was confirmed by a number of the reviews when the biography was published in 1988.

About three-quarters of the published poems are available in manuscript, mainly forming the Francis Thompson Collection at Boston College, Massachusetts. In addition the Collection contains a sizeable number of unpublished manuscripts that contribute to the overall scope of Thompson's *oeuvre*. All the editions to date have been based on the *Works of Francis Thompson*, edited by Wilfrid Meynell, which appeared in 1913 (referred to hereafter as *Works*). Neither the two volumes of poetry nor the third of prose is anything like complete or representative of Thompson's work in either medium. Apart from the unpublished poems, there are many published ones which have remained uncollected, and among those which were published by Meynell in *Works* or elsewhere he made alterations to and deletions from the original texts that have so far gone unnoticed.

Part One of the present edition consists of the three volumes of poems published in Thompson's lifetime, until now not reprinted from the first editions as overseen by himself. Part Two starts with poems published in journals and other publications before and after his death, many not previously collected, in chronological order of appearance There are then separate sections for those first appearing in Everard Meynell's *Life of Francis Thompson* (referred to hereafter as *Life*) and in *Works*, the former also published in 1913. These are followed by poems from *The Man Has Wings* (referred to hereafter as *MHW*), the collection edited in 1957 by

Terence L. Connolly of Boston College and based on Thompson's note-book poetry. Part Two concludes with the five poems first published in 1968 by John Evangelist Walsh in his biography *Strange Harp, Strange Symphony*. Two of these, 'The Owl' and 'Nightmare of the Witch Babies', reveal much of Thompson's state of mind while on the London streets which until then had been all but suppressed. In Part Three the more important unpublished poems are supplemented by selected examples from the occasional poetry taken mainly from the notebooks that Thompson kept throughout his life, including some of the humorous verse; Part Four comprises his poems on cricket and his juvenile poems.

Each Part contributes towards the same end: to present for the first time the full range of his work. In addition to more distinctly religious poems there are hitherto uncollected or unpublished love poems and poems on children and childhood, together with others expressing his strongly-held views on social and political issues. Yet underlying his poetry as a whole there remains his conviction that he was to be 'the Poet of the Return to God';[2] but not, he was equally certain, in any narrow sense such as his contemporaries would have understood it and as it has been interpreted since. For him, the divine presence permeates all aspects of human experi-ence and it is this which the true artist is called upon to communicate, whatever the medium or outward subject matter. In this he was well ahead of his time, a fact of which he had a kind of prophetic awareness when he wrote in a late notebook: 'For me to write or to speak at all is to resign myself to the knowledge that I am, in the present, addressing very few. It would be almost impossible, because quite futile, for me to write were I not convinced that the few would one day be the many.'[3]

Changing religious and social attitudes mean that we are now in a posi-tion where we can better appreciate his aim, one which has directed my own in setting out to present his poetry as closely as possible to the way I believe he would have wished it to appear.

The chronological summary of his life following the Introduction includes the dates of his major poems. Bringing together the life of the man and the poet in this way is especially important for Thompson, whose poetry was notably influenced by his life experiences. In particular, his training for the priesthood at Ushaw College gave him his wide knowledge of Church his-tory and the Liturgy, while his familiarity with both the Old and New Testaments was outstanding for a Catholic layman at his time. The med-ical training that followed contributed to some of his most original and often gruesome imagery, to which was added the influences from his three years' homelessness on the London streets. These years also left him with his lifelong sense of outrage at contemporary society's treatment of the poor and the outcast. Although it must not be overlooked, the effect of his lifelong addiction to opium has been exaggerated by more recent critics.[4] It appears mainly in unfinished and fragmentary entries in the notebooks, whether poetry or prose, and the most that can be said of its influence on the overall character of his poetry is that it may have contributed to the exuberance and sometimes overblown wealth of his imagery.

People were no less influential than the circumstances of his life, and his poetic career can be said to have been generated through the encouragement of the unnamed prostitute who saved him from suicide and then cared for him through the last winter of his street life.[5] There followed the dramatic rescue when his poems were first recognised by the Meynells and he was accepted into their home. Subsequently, his three main creative periods were also the times when he enjoyed the warmth of sympathetic companionship, whether from the Meynell family or at Storrington or later at Pantasaph. In both of these places there was the added influence of outstanding beautiful surroundings, first on the Sussex downs and then among the Welsh mountains.

The biographical influences complement others more specifically related to the poetry and its composition. He possessed what must have been a remarkable memory, for although he never owned more than half a dozen books his sources include the classical writers of Greece and Rome, those of the medieval period and Dante as well as the Elizabethans and the seventeenth-century metaphysical poets. The presence of the metaphysicals is felt constantly and especially in the 'Love in Dian's Lap' sequence and other love poems. Yet in his own century Shelley is the only comparable figure, suggesting the truth of G. K. Chesterton's observation on Thompson's poetry: 'Perhaps the shortest definition of the Victorian age is that he stood outside it.'[6]

He was in the habit of adapting words from one part of speech to another: for example, by adding a suffix 'less' to form 'rebukeless', 'delimitless' and so on. Substantives can become verbs, as in 'empillared' and 'maenadize'. Another frequent habit is his use of obsolete words or archaisms such as 'brede', 'cestus', 'swart', 'assoil' and 'spilth'. Everard Meynell recalled that Thompson had no 'word lists' and never spoke of any conscious derivations or desire to collect samples from other poets.[7] His style was his own, evolved from his life's experiences and the reading that was aided by his prodigious memory.

Through his friendship with Coventry Patmore it appears that he knew of Gerard Manley Hopkins' poetry, some of which he may well have read in manuscript.[8] Despite obvious differences, Hopkins and Thompson shared a similar delight in the original use of words and images. They shared another characteristic in the strongly visual element in their poetry. In Thompson's case he was well aware of the influence of both painting and sculpture from the time of his earliest poetic efforts and his frequenting of the art galleries in Manchester during the years of his medical training. In particular, he was impressed by Dante Gabriel Rossetti's verse, though deriving as much from the painter as from the poet. This visual imagery that runs right through Thompson's work is carried on in his frequent use of synaesthesia, when words denoting colour or other visual effects appear where a non-visual word would normally be expected. He made a penetrating note on the relationship as he saw it: 'Colour, in the great masters, or at least the great imaginative painters, is an expression of the emotions like metre, to which it corresponds.'[9] It is worth adding an example here, from the 'Ode to the Setting Sun':

> Thy visible music-blasts make deaf the sky,
>   Thy cymbals clang to fire the Occident,
> Thou dost thy dying so triumphally:
> I see the crimson blaring of thy shawms!
>
>   (16–19)

In this, as in much else, he was closer to the poets of the seventeenth century than to those of his own day. After Coleridge he was in fact one of the first to seek a revaluation of their merits. Among his own contemporaries of the late nineteenth century Coventry Patmore was the only significant influence. Thompson himself readily admitted the debt: 'What I put forth as a bud, he blew on it and it blossomed. The contact of our ideas was dynamic: he reverberated my idea with such and so many echoes that it returned to me greater than I gave forth. He opened it as you would an oyster, or placed it under a microscope, and showed me what it contained.'[10] Yet he makes it plain here that the initial inspiration is his own. The similarities in their ideas only went so far, for Thompson was unable to accept the extent of Patmore's identification between divine and human love and so between the two worlds of supernatural and natural life they can be said to represent. But there were other ideas the two poets had in common. Apart from their shared preoccupation with the myths and symbols of the ancient world, they shared their preference for the so-called 'irregular ode' with its scope for experimenting and exploring themes beyond the normal poetic range, still within a structure that can claim descent from the poets of Greece and Rome. Yet Thompson discovered his preference well before Patmore's influence could account for it. The limits as well as the extent of the influences from Patmore need to be kept in balance for there has been a tendency to exaggerate their importance in Thompson's poetry.

For Thompson, if the ode satisfied the cosmic span of many of his longer poems, he found in the sonnet a containing framework to match other needs. Within its well-defined form a particular idea could be turned this way and that to display its many facets before closing in on itself in a conclusion which, in most of his sonnets, leaves the reader with the sense that it could not be completed in any other way.

Throughout, the uneven texture of his work is apparent. The wealth and originality of much of his imagery contribute to the success or failure of a poem according to the degree of control and appropriateness present. Where these are lacking, he can descend into mere flamboyance or crude banality very easily, often within a poem which in other places rises well above his average achievement. But having said this, his background and the experiences of his earlier years give rise to the liturgical and scientific images and symbolism that distinguish much of his best poetry. Taken with those inspired by mythology and pagan symbolism, they then contribute to what may be said to be the most outstanding feature of his work as a whole. He reaches out to the immensities of time and space with a daring that disturbed his contemporaries and added to his own self-doubts as a true 'Poet of the Return to God'. Yet the movement of expansion is most striking when the cosmic range of his poetic vision, expressed in passages from the 'Ode to the Setting Sun', 'The Hound of Heaven' and other longer poems, is contrasted with the delicate detail of many shorter poems such as 'To a Snowflake' or 'To Daisies', celebrating the wonders of the minutiae of creation. Nor must the poetry arising from the deprivations of the years on the London streets be omitted in this overall view. There is no doubt that poems written then are marked by his opium addiction in their frequent incoherence and excesses of language. But the excesses, occurring also towards the end of his life in a number of notebook drafts, only exaggerate what was his own particular approach to the mysteries and vagaries of life: the influences from his years on the streets were much more far-reaching than the effects of the drug. Now that his poetry can be responded to more fully than ever before, the range of his overall vision may be said to contribute to an opening up of the Christian world-view as it increasingly embraces the universality of human experience—confirming his belief that he wrote for a future generation rather than his own.

Apart from the changing religious and social attitudes noted above, there is another reason for the delay before a reappraisal of Thompson's work has been possible. A few days before his death he signed a will leaving all he possessed to his friend and patron Wilfrid Meynell. There were in fact virtually no personal possessions at his lodgings other than a battered tin trunk, some old tobacco pipes and the toy theatre he had played with as a child. But the trunk was found to contain almost forty years' accumulation of manuscripts and other papers, together with about a hundred and fifty notebooks—mainly cheap exercise books—where he recorded his thoughts and ideas as well as drafts for much of his poetry and other writings.

From the contents of the trunk it is clear that during his lifetime he made many drafts for the poems he decided to publish, and wrote much which has remained in manuscript. At his death in 1907 there would have been upwards of fifty of these unpublished poems and probably nearer a hundred unfinished drafts. During the next decade Wilfrid Meynell and his wife Alice prepared much of this material either for literary journals or, more often, for the Catholic monthly, the *Dublin Review* (now the *Wiseman Review*). After the first few years Meynell concentrated on editing the *Works*, which he prefixed with 'A Note from Francis Thompson's Literary Executor':

> In making this collection I have been governed by Francis Thompson's express instructions, or guided by a knowledge of his feelings and preferences acquired during an unbroken intimacy of nineteen years. His own list of new inclusions and his own suggested reconsiderations of his formerly published text have been followed in this definitive edition of his Poetical Work.

There is no reference in any of Thompson's many letters to the Meynells, or elsewhere among his papers, to such 'instructions' or 'suggested reconsiderations'. Furthermore, Everard Meynell's biography of the poet appeared the same year as *Works* and although he discusses the poetry, often at some length, he makes no mention of these provisions or of any exchange of the kind between Thompson and his father. Concerning the 'new inclusions', while there are several roughly made-out lists of poems that Thompson thought of submitting for a fourth volume to follow *New Poems*, he abandoned the idea before it had gone beyond that stage. As to the 'knowledge' based on years of friendship, although Thompson was usually politely submissive to the Meynells in his general dealings with them, where his poetry was involved he was determined to have his own way, and there are instances when he refused to agree to suggestions for alterations put to him by them. Nor is it at all likely that the many drafts could have been discussed between them—drafts which Meynell later apparently had little or no hesitation in editing to produce seemingly finished poems.

This was facilitated by Thompson's method of composition. On a single line he could accumulate a series of alternatives to a word or phrase, carefully bracketed together and then left for a subsequent selection to be made. These remain in the manuscripts of the unfinished poetry with hardly any deletions to indicate a preference that would account for the choices made by Meynell. In addition there are finished texts in manuscript that Meynell felt could be improved upon by incorporating words or phrases from an earlier version. Even in some poems published by Thompson he made similar alterations and deletions before reprinting them in *Works* or elsewhere in journals.

Meynell's editorial practices have so far gone unnoticed because, as stated earlier, his edition has been used as the basis for all subsequent editions and other publications of the poems. Although his conduct is undoubtedly open to criticism it did at times result in an improvement on the original text—as, for example, the effect of his deletions in 'Of Nature: Laud and Plaint' in shortening the poem as left in manuscript. But too often his deletions and adaptations served to weaken Thompson's purpose. In 'Assumpta Maria', for example, Meynell omitted four stanzas where the imagery from the pre-Christian past dominates the theme. Here it must be remembered that Meynell was not a scholar but a benefactor and friend who believed in what he was doing for his protégé as both man and poet. Thompson's later years coincided with the spread of the Modernist movement in the Catholic Church, and the Papal Encyclical *Pascendi Gregis*, with its stern condemnation of Modernism, was promulgated early in 1908, only a few months after his death. He had friends who were among the early supporters of the Modernists' more radical criticisms of the contemporary Church and although he did not adopt their views he could be outspoken in expressing his own on religious and social matters. Wilfrid Meynell and his wife Alice were aware of the possible danger to Thompson's reputation, promoted by themselves, as 'the poet of Catholic orthodoxy'.[11] They also believed that this procedure would confirm the position they were convinced he merited among the greater poets of the time. In fact it was to have the opposite effect in contributing to the decline of his reputation through the decades following the Second World War.

In America the decline has been slower, chiefly due to the transfer, during the 1930s, of the bulk of the manuscripts and notebooks to the library at Boston College. Here the Meynells' friend and colleague, the Jesuit Terence L. Connolly, set up the Francis Thompson Collection in a specially constructed room. He devoted much of his time to promoting Thompson and his work, his views on both being in accordance with those put forward by the Meynells. But in making the donation there were two conditions, subsequently recorded by Connolly: 'I was admonished that if I discovered anything unpleasant in the notebooks it should be burned, and again I was reminded that nothing second or third rate should ever be published.'[12] By 'unpleasant' Meynell appears to have meant anything that could detract from the image of orthodox piety he knew was endorsed by Connolly. Due to the number of mutilated notebooks and other manuscripts it is impossible now to assess how much may have been destroyed. Fortunately sufficient was either overlooked or spared to allow for a reappraisal first of Thompson's life and, now, of his poetry.

Like Meynell, Connolly had little or no hesitation in adapting and making changes in the texts, and his editing followed similar lines. His judgement, however, departed notably from Meynell's second injunction forbidding publication of anything 'second or third rate'. In *MHW* over two-thirds of the poems are put together from unfinished drafts, often very rough and often, too, of little poetic value. The drafts are of a kind such as any poet writes when experimenting with ideas and then abandons or develops elsewhere. Even when edited to form actual poems, in general they do little or nothing to enhance either the range or the quality of Thompson's poetry as a whole. Although Connolly has added brief notes to identify poems treated in this way, his notes are not always accurate and there is no indication of the extent of the editing process. In Part Two of the present edition the section for poems from *MHW* omits such edited poems but includes a generous selection of those for which there are final or near-final texts, which have therefore been followed. Similarly, for poems published elsewhere than in *Works* or *MHW*, those derived from incomplete manuscripts are omitted. An exception has been made for the poems first published in *Works* as they remain the most widely known from the subsequent editions. For this reason all such *Works* poems are included whatever the state of the original manuscripts. Where a manuscript survives with variants in the *Works* text the manuscript is followed with the variants given in the endnotes. In just three cases the poems have been so edited from an unfinished original that this procedure has not been possible. These poems are 'A Double Need', 'To Stars' and 'Peace' and they are distinguished by appearing in smaller print. Lastly, there are a few poems in *Works* and elsewhere for which no manuscripts exist and they have been reprinted from the text of their first publication.

Part Three consists of completed manuscripts of hitherto unpublished poems, followed by a small selection from the unfinished notebook poetry where the variants left by Thompson are not too difficult to reproduce. These spontaneous poems offer an insight into another aspect of his work in emphasising its outspoken social protest and therefore have a legitimate place in this edition. Mention should be made here of the article by Everard Meynell, 'The Notebooks of Francis Thompson', in the *Dublin Review* (January 1917). Except for a modern rendering of a medieval lullaby, all the poetry quoted by Meynell is from unfinished notebook drafts which are presented as finished poems that do not add anything significant to Thompson's work as a whole. In the present edition the only extensive omissions are two incomplete verse plays, attempted in his later years and abandoned when he found he had no aptitude in that direction. (It must be added that the preliminary work for this edition, including typescripts of the plays and other unfinished poetry, can be consulted in the archives at Boston College.)

It would do Thompson no lasting service to add the more extensive annotations that might be appropriate for a major poet. To assert that he is not of their number does not deny his unique if uneven voice, covering a wide range of human feeling and experience. Headnotes and endnotes are intended to confirm his position in this respect as well as providing, where necessary, information conducive to a fuller appreciation of the poems themselves. The headnotes give the date of composition, if known, and any relevant circumstances. For published poems the date and place of their first appearance is added and whether subsequently included in *Works* or elsewhere. The headnotes also draw attention to the presence of any substantive variants, which are given in detail in the endnotes. This applies mainly to the poems in Part Two edited by Meynell and Connolly. Endnotes in Part One, that is for poems published under Thompson's direction, do not include variants between the manuscripts and the published texts unless they throw some special light on the circumstances of the original composition and its revision (examples are 'To the Dead Cardinal of Westminster' and 'Any Saint'). Regarding his punctuation, in the case of poetry published in his lifetime the assumption is that he was happy with the way it was punctuated even if different from his manuscripts. His punctuation in the manuscripts is at times haphazard. Where this affects the meaning in the unpublished poems it has been altered, with the alteration mentioned in the endnotes to the poem in question. Otherwise, his original punctuation has been followed. In the posthumously published poems edited by Meynell or Connolly, they frequently change the punctuation, and as this makes for greater clarity their emendations have, in this instance, been followed. The endnotes provide glosses for most of Thompson's use of obscure or obsolete words and his occasional inventions. His extensive use of Biblical and classical sources often requires clarification, and where this occurs the general interpretation appears in the headnotes with more precise references in the endnotes.

For these references the debt to Connolly's research is considerable. His edition of Thompson's poems contains extensive notes which, when they elucidate such sources and also Thompson's use of liturgical imagery, have been of immense value. It should be added that in several places he refers to a 'catalogue' in preparation which it appears would have included original texts of poems he must have known had been edited by Meynell. But no further details are given and no record of such a catalogue has been found.

The titles of some poems published by Meynell and Connolly differ from Thompson's and occasionally they give titles to those with none. For poems with titles, Thompson's have been restored and the substitutes are added below. Untitled poems are given part of their first lines or their first lines as titles and these are enclosed in quotation marks. If given titles by Meynell or Connolly, their titles are likewise given below. Thompson made a number of translations which are clearly identified as such. Quotations and translations from the Divine Office are from the authorised texts in use before the Second Vatican Council and quotations from the Bible are from the translation from the Latin Vulgate known as the Douai Bible, the one he is known to have used. References to the Psalms therefore follow the Greek numbering based on the Vulgate.

Apart from the exceptions noted above where actual meaning is involved, his occasional inconsistencies in punctuation, capitals and the like in the manuscripts are retained but not the ampersand, which he used only to save time and space. His erratic quotation marks have been regularised as single quotes. He usually enclosed his own notes either in brackets or parentheses, and as brackets are used for the editorial notes his are distinguished by parentheses throughout. He rarely signed a manuscript and most are in pencil; so where one is signed that is noted, and also those that are in ink. All manuscripts and other papers are in the Boston College Collection unless otherwise stated.

1 Brigid M. Boardman, *Between Heaven and Charing Cross*, see Abbreviations: *BHCC*.

2 NB 21.

3 NB 24.

4 The influence of opium on Thompson's poetry is strongly argued by J. C. Reid, *Francis Thompson: Man and Poet* (Routledge, London 1959). In a review of Reid's book Geoffrey Grigson dismissed 'The Hound of Heaven' as the 'wild half-digested gush' of the drug addict dominated by 'indolence and self-delusion' ('Rags and Rubbish', *Catholic Transcript*, 31 March 1960).

5 See *BHCC*, pp. 89–90 and notes, p. 367.

6 G. K. Chesterton, *The Victorian Age in Literature* (Williams and Norgate, London 1913, reprinted 1920), pp. 202–3.

7 *Life*, pp. 154–6.

8 Hopkins' poem 'Heaven Haven' was published in *A Little Book of Life and Death*, an anthology reviewed by Thompson in *The Academy* on 19 July 1902, where he refers to it as 'a little poem by Father Hopkins'. As there is no reference to the poet being a priest and nothing else of Hopkins' work had been published, Thompson must have known of him and his poetry from their mutual friend Coventry Patmore. For this and other likely connections see *BHCC*, p. 382, n. 6.

9 NB 20A.

10 NB 21.

11 Alice Meynell, review of *Selected Poems of Francis Thompson* in *DR*, January/April 1909.

12 Terence L. Connolly, *Francis Thompson, In His Paths* (Bruce, Milwaukee 1944), p. 190.

Biographical Summary

THE MAIN EVENTS OF THOMPSON'S LIFE WITH DATES OF HIS MORE IMPORTANT POEMS

1859   Born 18 December, Preston, Lancashire.

1861   Sister, Mary, born.

1864   Second sister, Margaret, born.
       Family settles in Ashton-Under-Lyne, near Manchester.

1865   Begins long-lasting friendship with Canon John Carroll, later Bishop of Shrewsbury, who encourages Thompson's literary interests.

1870   Enrols at St Cuthbert's College, Ushaw, to prepare ultimately for the priesthood.

1876   Literary pursuits begin to be regarded as incompatible with a priestly vocation.

Poems in Ushaw College Notebook

1877   Leaves Ushaw.
       Enrols as medical student at Owens College, Manchester.

1879–80 Illness and death of Mrs Thompson (d. December 1880). Probable start of opium addiction.

1880–4 Frequents Manchester City Art Gallery and libraries as escape from medical studies.

c. 1882 'On the Anniversary of Rossetti's Death'

1884   Leaves Owens College after repeated failure in exams.

1885   Dr Thompson plans to remarry. Mary prepares to enter Presentation Convent, Manchester. Margaret engaged to Canadian. Thompson leaves home for London.

1886   Fitful employment leads to life on the streets.
       Autumn. John McMaster, churchwarden of St Martin-in-the-Fields, befriends him and takes him into the household.
       December McMaster arranges visit home which results in increased opium and departure from McMaster's (January 1887).

1887   February. Some contact with Canon Carroll who persuades him to submit poems and an essay for Catholic literary journal *Merry England*. MSS are lost at the journal office.
       Autumn. Suicide attempt, prevented by prostitute who shelters him through the winter.

1888   Wilfrid Meynell, editor of *Merry England*, finds MSS. Unable
        to trace Thompson, prints 'The Passion of Mary' in April issue
        of journal. Thompson hears of it through Canon Carroll.
        Late April–May. He meets Wilfrid and Alice Meynell. After
        deliberate disappearance of street girl he agrees to accept
        Meynells' hospitality.

1889   February. Meynells arrange period of recuperation at Praemon-
        stratensian (White Canons) Priory at Storrington, Sussex.

                                    May 'Ode to the Setting Sun'

                            Summer 'Song of the Hours', 'Daisy'

                            December 'Hound of Heaven' begun.

1890   March. Returns to London to lodgings in Kilburn.

                                    Finishes 'Hound of Heaven'.

        Assists Meynells with work on their journals.

                            'Love in Dian's Lap' poems begun.

                                Autumn 'Sister Songs' begun.

                            December 'Sister Songs' finished.

1891   Start of friendship with Capuchins at Crawley, Sussex.
        Initial enthusiasm for proposed 'system' of ideas on future of
        Church and Christianity.

                        Poems for 'Love in Dian's Lap' continued.

                                            'A Fallen Yew'

                                Autumn 'Sere of the Leaf'

1892   January. Death of Cardinal Manning.

                        'To the Dead Cardinal of Westminster'

                            Finishes 'Love in Dian's Lap'.

                                'A Judgment in Heaven'

        Feeling for Alice Meynell probable cause for tension with family.
        Return to opium. Meynells arrange visit to Franciscan Friary,
        Pantasaph, North Wales.
        December. Arrives Pantasaph. Lodges with Brien family at
        guest house.

1893   Friendship with Maggie Brien continues intermittently through-
        out Thompson's time at Pantasaph.

                                    'Narrow Vessel' poems

        Friendship with Capuchins continues the interest in their 'sys-
        tem' of ideas.
        November. *Poems* published.

                        Begins poems later to become 'Sight and Insight'.

1894   April. Father Angelo de Bary, leader of the Capuchin group,
        arrives at Pantasaph.

                            Easter 'From the Night of Forebeing'
                                Summer 'An Anthem of Earth'

        Autumn. Coventry Patmore visits Pantasaph. Friendship
        between the poets confirmed, following previous exchange of
        letters.
        October. Visit to Canon John Carroll and reconciliation with
        father.

1894–5 Gradual disillusionment concerning Patmore's 'philosophy' and
        link with ideas of Capuchin group.
        Final sublimation of feeling for Alice Meynell.

                                'Love Divided against Itself'

1895   Easter.   *'Orient Ode'*
        June. *Sister Songs* published.

1895–6 Preparation of *New Poems*. Acute sense of failure to achieve
        poetic goal as 'poet of the Return to God' with realisation that
        neither poetry nor its message will be understood by present
        age. Followed by growing certainty that both would be under-
        stood at a future time.

                                'Canticum Novum'

1896   April. Death of Dr Thompson.
        June. Visit to London. Meets Katherine ('Katie') Douglas King.
        July. Continued meetings with Katie and with her mother, who
        then frustrates final meeting before Thompson leaves London.
        27 July. Leaves for Pantasaph.

                                'A Lost Friend'

        August–October. Correspondence with Katie.
        October. Mrs Hamilton King forbids further contact with Katie.

            July onwards 'Ad Amicam' and other poems addressed to Katie

        November. Death of Coventry Patmore.
        December. Finally leaves Pantasaph for London. Lodgings in
        Elgin Avenue.

1897   Spring. Death of Canon Carroll, Coadjutor Bishop of Shrews-
        bury since 1893. Attends funeral at Stalybridge, Lancashire.
        Revival of friendship with Katie. Starts work reviewing for *The
        Academy* and other literary journals.
        May. *New Poems* published.
        June. Queen Victoria's Diamond Jubilee.

                    'Victorian Ode'. First of the 'public' odes

        Autumn. Fire at lodgings results in move to Goldney Road.

1899   Katie engaged to Rev. Godfrey Burr.
          Problems of health and work lead to change of lodgings to Elgin
          Avenue.

1900   June. Katie marries Godfrey Burr. Thompson attempts return
          to street life.
          Meynell restores his confidence and arranges more work. Prob-
          able return to opium during this year.

                                    Ode: 'The Nineteenth Century'

1901   January. Death of Queen Victoria.

                                                        'Victoria'

1902   March. Death of Cecil Rhodes.

                                              Ode: 'Cecil Rhodes'

1905   Monograph *Health and Holiness* published. Begins research for
          Saint Ignatius, rewritten from Stewart Rose's biography.

1905–6   Health deteriorates. Increasing friendship with Meynell's eldest
          son Everard. Shared enthusiasm for cricket.

                                    Probable dates for cricket verse

                              Probable date for 'In No Strange Land'

1906   Period of rest at Crawley, Sussex.

                                    Ode: 'To the English Martyrs'

1907   Easter. Returns to London to lodgings in Brondesbury Road,
          Kilburn.
          Health deteriorates further, diagnosed by Thompson as beri-
          beri.
          Meynells arrange rest period on Wilfrid Scawen Blunt's estate in
          Sussex.
          Blunt records these last weeks in his *Diaries*.
          October. Returns to London to enter Hospital of Sts John and
          Elizabeth.
          13 November. Dies at dawn.
          16 November. Buried at St Mary's Catholic Cemetery, Kensal
          Green.

PART ONE

POEMS PUBLISHED IN BOOK FORM

Poems (1893)

The poems are printed here in the original order in which they appeared in this first volume of Thompson's poems rather than according to their date of first publication. The 'Miscellaneous Poems' and 'Poems on Children' had already appeared in *ME*, except for the last, 'To Monica Thought Dying'. In the sequence 'Love in Dian's Lap', only two had also been printed in *ME*: 'To a Poet Breaking Silence' and 'A Carrier-Song'.

Dedication

To Wilfrid and Alice Meynell

If the rose in meek duty
   May dedicate humbly
To her grower the beauty
   Wherewith she is comely,
If the mine to the miner   5
   The jewels that pined in it,
Earth to diviner
   The springs he divined in it,
To the grapes the wine-pitcher
   Their juice that was crushed in it,   10
Viol to its witcher
   The music lay hushed in it,
If the lips may pay Gladness
   In laughters she wakened,
And the heart to its sadness   15
   Weeping unslakened,
If the hid and sealed coffer,
   Whose having not his is,
To the loosers may proffer
   Their finding—here this is;   20
Their lives if all livers
   To the Life of all living,
To you, O dear givers!
   I give your own giving.

LOVE IN DIAN'S LAP

These seven poems form the original sequence addressed to Alice Meynell. Five more were added by Meynell in *Works*, also addressed to Alice but composed later: 'Proemium', 'Domus Tua', 'In Her Paths', 'After Her Going' and 'Beneath a Photograph'. They therefore appear elsewhere in the present volume in accordance with their dates of first publication.

The connecting theme of the sequence as it appears in *Poems* is the attempted sublimation of a powerful physical attraction into an affinity of souls, a theme most fittingly dedicated to Diana as the goddess of chastity. Thompson takes as his models the metaphysical poets of the seventeenth century, who chose to conceal strong personal emotions within intellectual conceits. It is notable that three of the poems are concerned with portraits or other portrayals of the lady, the visual images creating safety valves for permissible emotions since she herself is not the direct object.

1 Before Her Portrait in Youth

In his own copy of *Selected Poems* Meynell noted that the portrait of Alice, the subject of this poem, was by Adrian Stokes (WM Note). It was painted in 1877 when Alice was already 30 years old. But that was 10 years before Thompson first knew her and it would appear comparatively youthful to him. In connection with their relationship it should be remembered that she was 12 years older than him.

> As lovers, banished from their lady's face,
>   And hopeless of her grace,
> Fashion a ghostly sweetness in its place,
>   Fondly adore
> Some stealth-won cast attire she wore,   5
>   A kerchief, or a glove:
>   And at the lover's beck
>   Into the glove there fleets the hand,
>   Or at impetuous command
> Up from the kerchief floats the virgin neck: 10
> So I, in very lowlihead of love,—
>   Too shyly reverencing
>   To let one thought's light footfall smooth
> Tread near the living, consecrated thing,—
>   Treasure me thy cast youth.   15
> This outworn vesture, tenantless of thee,
>   Hath yet my knee,

For that, with show and semblance fair
    Of the past Her
Who once the beautiful, discarded raiment bare,   20
      It cheateth me.
    As gale to gale drifts breath
      Of blossoms' death,
So dropping down the years from hour to hour
    This dead youth's scent is wafted me to-day: 25
I sit, and from the fragrance dream the flower.
      So, then, she looked (I say);
    And so her front sunk down
Heavy beneath the poet's iron crown:
      On her mouth museful-sweet   30
      (Even as the twin lips meet)
      Did thought and sadness greet:
        Sighs
      In those mournful eyes
    So put on visibilities;   35
As viewless ether turns, in deep on deep, to dyes.
      Thus, long ago,
She kept her meditative paces slow
Through maiden meads, with wavèd shadow and gleam
Of locks half-lifted on the winds of dream,   40
Till love upcaught her to his chariot's glow.
Yet, voluntary, happier Proserpine!
    This drooping flower of youth thou lettest fall
    I, faring in the cockshut-light, astray,
      Find on my 'lated way,   45
    And stoop, and gather for memorial,
And lay it on my bosom, and make it mine.
To this, the all of love the stars allow me,
    I dedicate and vow me.
    I reach back through the days   50
A trothed hand to the dead the last trump shall not raise.
    The water-wraith that cries
From those eternal sorrows of thy pictured eyes
Entwines and draws me down their soundless intricacies!

2   *To a Poet Breaking Silence*

ME, August 1893

The poem with which Alice Meynell broke her long silence as a poet was 'Veni Creator'. In a letter dated 12 August 1890, Thompson refers to 'an exquisite little poem by Mrs Meynell, the first she has written since her marriage' and adds, 'a long silence, disastrous for literature' (*Letters*, p. 43). Her poem had appeared in the *Scots Observer*, 2 August 1890.

Too wearily had we and song
Been left to look and left to long,
Yea, song and we to long and look,
Since thine acquainted feet forsook
The mountain where the Muses hymn   5
For Sinai and the Seraphim.
Now in both the mountains' shine
Dress thy countenance, twice divine!
From Moses and the Muses draw
The Tables of thy double Law!   10
His rod-born fount and Castaly
Let the one rock bring forth for thee,
Renewing so from either spring
The songs which both thy countries sing:
Or we shall fear lest, heavened thus long,   15
Thou should'st forget thy native song,
And mar thy mortal melodies
With broken stammer of the skies.

Ah! let the sweet birds of the Lord
With earth's waters make accord;   20
Teach how the crucifix may be
Carven from the laurel-tree,
Fruit of the Hesperides
Burnish take on Eden-trees,
The Muses' sacred grove be wet   25
With the red dew of Olivet,
And Sappho lay her burning brows
In white Cecilia's lap of snows!

Thy childhood must have felt the stings
Of too divine o'ershadowings;   30
Its odorous heart have been a blossom
That in darkness did unbosom,

Those fire-flies of God to invite,
Burning spirits, which by night
Bear upon their laden wing   35
To such hearts impregnating.
For flowers that night-wings fertilize
Mock down the stars' unsteady eyes,
And with a happy, sleepless glance
Gaze the moon out of countenance.   40
I think thy girlhood's watchers must
Have took thy folded songs on trust,
And felt them, as one feels the stir
Of still lightnings in the hair,
When conscious hush expects the cloud   45
To speak the golden secret loud
Which tacit air is privy to;
Flasked in the grape the wine they knew,
Ere thy poet-mouth was able
For its first young starry babble.   50
Keep'st thou not yet that subtle grace?
Yea, in this silent interspace,
God sets His poems in thy face!

The loom which mortal verse affords,
Out of weak and mortal words,   55
Wovest thou thy singing-weed in,
To a rune of thy far Eden.
Vain are all disguises! Ah,
Heavenly *incognita*!
Thy mien bewrayeth through that wrong   60
The great Uranian House of Song!
As the vintages of earth
Taste of the sun that riped their birth,
We know what never cadent Sun
Thy lampèd clusters throbbed upon,   65
What plumèd feet the winepress trod;
Thy wine is flavorous of God.
Whatever singing-robe thou wear
Has the Paradisal air;
And some gold feather it has kept   70
Shows what Floor it lately swept!

---

5 *The mountain where the Muses hymn* Parnassus. **11–14** The fountain that issued from the
rock of Horeb at the strike of Moses' rod is identified with Castalia, the sacred spring on

Parnassus. **23** *Hesperides* the maidens who guarded the golden apples given to the goddess
Hera at her marriage to Zeus. **27** *Sappho* the Greek poetess associated with illicit love. **28**
Cecilia a patron saint of chastity. **31–40** FT provides a gloss for these lines in an undated
letter to AM: 'The meaning (which I should have thought perfectly clear) is that flowers
which are fertilized by night-insects confront the moon and stars with a glance more sleepless and steady than their own. Surely anyone who knows a forest from a flower-pot is
aware, that flowers which are fertilized by night-insects necessarily *open at night*, and emit
at night their odours, by which those insects are attracted' (*Letters*, p. 101). **60** *bewrayeth*
reveals. **61** *Uranian House of Song* a derivation from Uranus, the god of the heavens whose
spouse is Gaia, the earth goddess. **64** *cadent* sinking. **65** *lampèd* shining. **66** *plumèd
feet* Hermes, the god of poetry, wore wings on his heels.

3 'Manus Animam Pinxit'

The title can be loosely translated as 'The Hand of Art Has Portrayed the Soul'.

> Lady who hold'st on me dominion!
> Within your spirit's arms I stay me fast
>   Against the fell
> Immitigate ravening of the gates of hell;
> And claim my right in you, most hardly won,   5
> Of chaste fidelity upon the chaste:
> Hold me and hold by me, lest both should fall
> (O in high escalade high companion!)
> Even in the breach of Heaven's assaulted wall.
> Like to a wind-sown sapling grow I from   10
> The clift, Sweet, of your skyward-jetting soul,—
> Shook by all gusts that sweep it, overcome
> By all its clouds incumbent: O be true
> To your soul, dearest, as my life to you!
> For if that soil grow sterile, then the whole   15
> Of me must shrivel, from the topmost shoot
> Of climbing poesy, and my life, killed through,
> Dry down and perish to the foodless root.
>
> Sweet Summer! unto you this swallow drew,
> By secret instincts inappeasable,   20
>   That did direct him well,
> Lured from his gelid North which wrought him wrong,
>   Wintered of sunning song;—
> By happy instincts inappeasable,
>   Ah, yes! that led him well,   25
> Lured to the untried regions and the new

Climes of auspicious you;
To twitter there, and in his singing dwell,
      But ah! if you, my Summer, should grow waste,
       With grieving skies o'ercast,   30
For such migration my poor wing was strong
But once; it has no power to fare again
       Forth o'er the heads of men,
Nor other Summers for its sanctuary:
       But from your mind's chilled sky   35
It needs must drop, and lie with stiffened wings
       Among your soul's forlornest things;
A speck upon your memory, alack!
A dead fly in a dusty window–crack.

       O therefore you who are   40
       What words, being to such mysteries
       As raiment to the body is,
        Should rather hide than tell;
       Chaste and intelligential love:
        Whose form is as a grove   45
Hushed with the cooing of an unseen dove;
Whose spirit to my touch thrills purer far
Than is the tingling of a silver bell;
Whose body other ladies well might bear
As soul,—yea, which it profanation were   50
For all but you to take as fleshly woof,
       Being spirit truest proof;
Whose spirit sure is lineal to that
       Which sang *Magnificat*:
       Chastest, since such you are,   55
       Take this curbed spirit of mine,
Which your own eyes invest with light divine,
For lofty love and high auxiliar
       In daily exalt emprise
       Which outsoars mortal eyes;   60
     This soul which on your soul is laid,
     As maid's breast against breast of maid;
Beholding how your own I have engraved
On it, and with what purging thoughts have laved
This love of mine from all mortality.   65
Indeed the copy is a painful one,
       And with long labour done!

O if you doubt the thing you are, lady,
    Come then, and look in me;
Your beauty, Dian, dress and contemplate   70
Within a pool to Dian consecrate!
Unveil this spirit, lady, when you will,
For unto all but you 'tis veilèd still:
Unveil, and fearless gaze there, you alone,
And if you love the image—'tis your own!   75

4 A Carrier-Song

ME, September 1893

I

Since you have waned from us,
    Fairest of women!
I am a darkened cage
    Song cannot hymn in.
My songs have followed you,   5
    Like birds the summer;
Ah! bring them back to me,
    Swiftly, dear comer!
      Seraphim,
      Her to hymn,   10
      Might leave their portals,
      And at my feet learn
      The harping of mortals.

II

Where wings to rustle use,
    But this poor tarrier—   15
Searching my spirit's eaves—
    Find I for carrier.
Ah! bring them back to me
    Swiftly, sweet comer!
Swift, swift, and bring with you   20
    Song's Indian summer!
      Seraphim,
      Her to hymn,
      Might leave their portals;
      And at my feet learn   25
      The harping of mortals!

III

Whereso your angel is,
　My angel goeth;
I am left guardianless,
　Paradise knoweth! 30
I have no Heaven left
　To weep my wrongs to;
Heaven, when you went from us,
　Went with my songs too.
　　Seraphim, 35
　　Her to hymn,
　　Might leave their portals;
　　And at my feet learn
　　The harping of mortals!

IV

I have no angels left 40
　Now, Sweet, to pray to:
Where you have made your shrine
　They are away to.
They have struck Heaven's tent,
　And gone to cover you: 45
Whereso you keep your state
　Heaven is pitched over you!
　　Seraphim,
　　Her to hymn,
　　Might leave their portals; 50
　　And at my feet learn
　　The harping of mortals!

V

She that is Heaven's Queen
　Her title borrows,
For that she pitiful 55
　Beareth our sorrows.
So thou, *Regina mi,*
　Spes infirmorum;
With all our grieving crowned
　Mater dolorum! 60
　　Seraphim,
　　Her to hymn,
　　Might leave their portals;
　　And at my feet learn
　　The harping of mortals! 65

VI

Yet, envious coveter
 Of other's grieving!
This lonely longing yet
 'Scapeth your reaving.
Cruel! to take from a   70
 Sinner his Heaven!
Think you with contrite smiles
 To be forgiven?
  Seraphim,
  Her to hymn,   75
  Might leave their portals;
  And at my feet learn
  The harping of mortals!

VII

Penitent! give me back
 Angels, and Heaven;   80
Render your stolen self,
 And be forgiven!
How frontier Heaven from you?
 For my soul prays, Sweet,
Still to your face in Heaven,   85
 Heaven in your face, Sweet!
  Seraphim,
  Her to hymn,
  Might leave their portals;
  And at my feet learn   90
  The harping of mortals!

57 *Regina mi* my Queen. **58** *Spes infirmorum* hope of the weak. **60** *Mater dolorum* Mother of sorrows. **69** *reaving* stealing.

5 *Scala Jacobi Portaque Eburnea*

The title can be loosely translated as 'Jacob's Ladder and the Gates of Ebony'.

> Her soul from earth to Heaven lies,
> Like the ladder of the vision,
> > Whereon go
> > To and fro,
> In ascension and demission,   5
> Star-flecked feet of Paradise.
>
> Now she is drawn up from me
> All my angels, wet-eyed, tristful,
> > Gaze from great
> > Heaven's gate   10
> Like pent children, very wistful,
> That below a playmate see.
>
> Dream-dispensing face of hers!
> Ivory port which loosed upon me
> > Wings, I wist,   15
> > Whose amethyst
> Trepidations have forgone me,—
> Hesper's filmy traffickers.

18 *Hesper* Greek form for Latin *Vesper*, evening. This could also allude to the skipper butterfly which is known as Hesperides.

6 *Gilded Gold*

> Thou dost to rich attire a grace,
> To let it deck itself with thee,
> And teachest pomp strange cunning ways
> To be thought simplicity.
> But lilies, stolen from grassy mold,   5
> No more curlèd state unfold
> Translated to a vase of gold;
> In burning throne though they keep still
> Serenities unthawed and chill.
> Therefore, albeit thou'rt stately so,   10
> In statelier state thou us'dst to go.

*

Though jewels should phosphoric burn
Through those night-waters of thine hair,
A flower from its translucid urn
Poured silver flame more lunar-fair.   15
These futile trappings but recall
Degenerate worshippers who fall
In purfled kirtle and brocade
To 'parel the white Mother-Maid.
For, as her image stood arrayed   20
In vests of its self-substance wrought
To measure of the sculptor's thought—
Slurred by those added braveries;
So for thy spirit did devise
Its Maker seemly garniture,   25
Of its own essence parcel pure,—
From grave simplicities a dress,
And reticent demureness,
And love encinctured with reserve;
Which the woven vesture would subserve.   30
For outward robes in their ostents
Should show the soul's habiliments.
Therefore I say,—Thou'rt fair even so,
But better Fair I used to know.

The violet would thy dusk hair deck   35
With graces like thine own unsought.
Ah! but such place would daze and wreck
Its simple, lowly rustic thought.
For so advancèd, dear, to thee,
It would unlearn humility!   40
Yet do not, with an altered look,
In these weak numbers read rebuke;
Which are but jealous lest too much
God's master-piece thou shouldst retouch.
Where a sweetness is complete,   45
Add not sweets unto the sweet!
Or, as thou wilt, for others so
In unfamiliar richness go;
But keep for mine acquainted eyes
The fashions of thy Paradise.   50

18 *purfled* embroidered. 31 *ostents* derivation from 'ostentation', pretentious display.

7 *Her Portrait*

Oh, but the heavenly grammar did I hold
Of that high speech which angels' tongues turn gold!
So should her deathless beauty take no wrong,
Praised in her own great kindred's fit and cognate tongue.
Or if that language yet with us abode   5
Which Adam in the garden talked with God!
But our untempered speech descends—poor heirs!
Grimy and rough-cast still from Babel's bricklayers:
Curse on the brutish jargon we inherit,
Strong but to damn, not memorise, a spirit!   10
A cheek, a lip, a limb, a bosom, they
Move with light ease in speech of working-day;
And women we do use to praise even so.
But here the gates we burst and to the temple go.
Their praise were her dispraise; who dare, who dare,   15
Adulate the seraphim for their burning hair?
How, if with them I dared, here should I dare it?,
How praise the woman, who but know the spirit?
How praise the colour of her eyes, uncaught
While they were coloured with her varying thought?   20
How her mouth's shape, who only use to know
What tender shape her speech will fit it to?
Or her lips' redness, when their joinèd veil
Song's fervid hand has parted till it wore them pale?

If I would praise her soul (temerarious if!),   25
All must be mystery and hieroglyph.
Heaven, which not oft is prodigal of its more
To singers, in their song too great before;
By which the hierarch of large poesy is
Restrained to his one sacred benefice;   30
Only for her the salutary awe
Relaxes and stern canon of its law;
To her alone concedes pluralities,
In her alone to reconcile agrees
The Muses, the Graces, and the Charities;   35
To her, who can the trust so well conduct,
To her it gives the use, to us the usufruct.

What of the dear administress then may
I utter, though I spoke her own carved perfect way?

What of her daily gracious converse known,   40
Whose heavenly despotism must needs dethrone
And subjugate all sweetness but its own?
Deep in my heart subsides the infrequent word,
And there dies slowly throbbing like a wounded bird.
What of her silence, that outsweetens speech?   45
What of her thoughts, high marks for mine own thoughts to reach?
Yet (Chaucer's antique sentence so to turn),
Most gladly will she teach, and gladly learn;
And teaching her, by her enchanting art,
The master threefold learns for all he can impart.   50
Now all is said, and all being said,—aye me!
There yet remains unsaid the very She.
Nay, to conclude (so to conclude I dare),
If of her virtues you evade the snare,
Then for her faults you'll fall in love with her.   55

Alas, and I have spoken of her Muse—
Her Muse, that died with her auroral dews!
Learn, the wise cherubim from harps of gold
Seduce a trepidating music manifold!
But the superior seraphim do know   60
None other music but to flame and glow.
So she first lighted on our frosty earth,
A sad musician, of cherubic birth,
Playing to alien ears—which did not prize
The uncomprehended music of the skies—   65
The exiled airs of her far Paradise.
But soon from her own harpings taking fire,
In love and light her melodies expire.
Now Heaven affords her, for her silenced hymn,
A double portion of the seraphim.   70

At the rich odours from her heart that rise,
My soul remembers its lost Paradise,
And antenatal gales blow from Heaven's shores of spice;
I grow essential all, uncloaking me
From this encumbering virility,   75
And feel the primal sex of heaven and poetry:
And parting from her, in me linger on
Vague snatches of Uranian antiphon.

How to the petty prison could she shrink
Of femineity?—Nay, but I think   80

In a dear courtesy her spirit would
Woman assume, for grace of womanhood.
Or, votaress to the virgin Sanctitude
Of reticent withdrawals sweet, courted pale,
She took the cloistral flesh, the sexual veil,   85
Of her sad, aboriginal sisterhood;
The habit of cloistral flesh which founding Eve indued.

Thus do I know her: but for what men call
Beauty—the loveliness corporeal,
Its most just praise a thing unproper were   90
To singer or to listener, me or her.
She wears that body but as one indues
A robe, half careless, for it is the use;
Although her soul and it so fair agree,
We sure may, unattaint of heresy,   95
Conceit it might the soul's begetter be.
The immortal could we cease to contemplate,
The mortal part suggests its every trait.
God laid His fingers on the ivories
Of her pure members as on smoothèd keys,   100
And there out-breathed her spirit's harmonies.
I'll speak a little proudly:—I disdain
To count the beauty worth my wish or gain,
Which the dull daily fool can covet or obtain.
I do confess the fairness of the spoil,   105
But from such rivalry it takes a soil.
For her I'll proudlier speak:—how could it be
That I should praise the gilding of the psaltery?
'Tis not for her to hold that prize a prize,
Or praise much praise, though proudest in its wise,   110
To which even hopes of merely women rise.
Such strife would to the vanquished laurels yield,
Against *her* suffered to have lost a field.
Herself must with herself be sole compeer,
Unless the people of her distant sphere   115
Some gold migration send to melodise the year.
But first our hearts must burn in larger guise,
To reformate the uncharitable skies,
And so the deathless plumage to acclimatise:
Since this, their sole congener in our clime,   120
Droops her sad, ruffled thoughts for half the shivering time.

*

Yet I have felt what terrors may consort
In women's cheeks, the Graces' soft resort;
My hand hath shook at gentle hands' access,
And trembled at the waving of a tress;   125
My blood known panic fear, and fled dismayed,
Where ladies' eyes have set their ambuscade.
The rustle of a robe hath been to me
The very rattle of love's musketry;
Although my heart hath beat the loud advance,   130
I have recoiled before a challenging glance,
Proved gay alarms where warlike ribbons dance.
And from it all, this knowledge have I got,—
The whole that others have, is less than they have not;
All which makes other women noted fair,   135
Unnoted would remain and overshone in her.

How should I gauge what beauty is her dole,
Who cannot see her countenance for her soul;
As birds see not the casement for the sky?
And as 'tis check they prove its presence by,   140
I know not of her body till I find
My flight debarred the heaven of her mind.
Hers is the face whence all should copied be,
Did God make replicas of such as she;
Its presence felt by what it does abate,   145
Because the soul shines through tempered and mitigate:
Where—as a figure labouring at night
Beside the body of a splendid light—
Dark Time works hidden by its luminousness;
And every line he labours to impress   150
Turns added beauty, like the veins that run
Athwart a leaf which hangs against the sun.

There regent Melancholy wide controls;
There Earth-and-Heaven-Love play for aureoles;
There Sweetness out of Sadness breaks at fits,   155
Like bubbles on dark water, or as flits
A sudden silver fin through its deep infinites;
There amorous Thought has sucked pale Fancy's breath,
And Tenderness sits looking toward the lands of death;
There Feeling stills her breathing with her hand,   160
And Dream from Melancholy part wrests the wand;

And on this lady's heart, looked you so deep,
Poor Poetry has rocked himself to sleep:
Upon the heavy blossom of her lips
Hangs the bee Musing; nigh her lids eclipse   165
Each half-occulted star beneath that lies;
And in the contemplation of those eyes,
Passionless passion, wild tranquillities.

8 *Babel's bricklayers* The completion of the Tower of Babel, symbol of human pride and
ambition, was frustrated by the confusion of tongues which has since divided mankind
(Gen. 11:9). **37** *usufruct* right of enjoying the use and advantages of another's property
(*OED*). **47** *Chaucer's antique sentence* 'And gladly woulde he lerne and gladly teche' (*Canterbury Tales*, Prol., 308). **108** *psaltery* medieval stringed instrument.

Epilogue
To the Poet's Sitter

Wherein he excuseth himself for the manner of the Portrait

Thompson's note above refers to the previous poem.

Alas! now wilt thou chide, and say (I deem),
My figured descant hides the simple theme:
Or in another wise reproving, say
I ill observe thine own high reticent way.
Oh, pardon, that I testify of thee   5
What thou couldst never speak, nor others be!

Yet (for the book is not more innocent
Of what the gazer's eyes makes so intent),
She will but smile, perhaps, that I find my fair
Sufficing scope in such strait theme as her.   10
'Bird of the sun! the stars' wild honey-bee!
Is your gold browsing done so thoroughly?
Or sinks a singèd wing to narrow nest in me?'
(Thus she might say: for not this lowly vein
Out deprecates her deprecating strain.)   15
Oh, you mistake, dear lady, quite; nor know
Ether was strict as you, its loftiness as low!

The heavens do not advance their majesty
Over their marge; beyond his empery

The ensigns of the wind are not unfurled,   20
His reign is hooped by the pale o' the world.
'Tis not the continent, but the contained,
That pleasaunce makes or prison, loose or chained.
Too much alike or little captives me,
For all oppression is captivity.   25
What groweth to its height demands no higher;
The limit limits not, but the desire.
Give but my spirit its desirèd scope,—
A giant in a pismire, I not grope;
Deny it,—and an ant, with on my back   30
A firmament, the skiey vault will crack.
Our minds make their own termini, nor call
The issuing circumscriptions great or small;
So high constructing Nature lessens to us all;
Who optics gives accommodate to see   35
Your countenance large as looks the sun to be,
And distant greatness less than near humanity.

We, therefore, with a sure instinctive mind,
An equal spaciousness of bondage find
In confines far or near, of air or our own kind.   40
Our looks and longings, which affront the stars,
Most richly bruised against their golden bars,
Delighted captives of their flaming spears,
Find a restraint restraintless which appears
As that is, and so simply natural,   45
In you;—the fair detention freedom call,
And overscroll with fancies the loved prison wall.

Such sweet captivity, and only such,
In you, as in those golden bars, we touch!
Our gazes for sufficing limits know   50
The firmament above, your face below;
Our longings are contented with the skies,
Contented with the heaven, and your eyes.
My restless wings, that beat the whole world through,
Flag on the confines of the sun and you;   55
And find the human pale remoter of the two.

19 *empery* rule **28–31** omitted in *Works*. **32** *termini* Terminus was the Roman god who
gave special protection to the stones marking boundaries.

MISCELLANEOUS POEMS

To the Dead Cardinal of Westminster

ME, February 1892

Cardinal Manning died on 14 January 1892 and this obituary poem was written, at Meynell's request, for the next issue of *ME*. Meynell reprinted it later the same year in his *Memorials of Cardinal Manning*, published under his pseudonym William Oldcastle. Before its appearance in *Poems* Thompson made extensive deletions, the earlier version having even more explicit personal associations than the final text. These arose from a meeting between himself and the Cardinal that took place shortly before Manning's death. Despite the contrast between the Cardinal's self-imposed asceticism and his own enforced suffering and poverty, Thompson was also aware of a distinct affinity in their shared anger at the conditions of the London poor. (See *BHCC*, pp. 149–50.) The deletions and first versions are given in the endnotes, showing the overall improvement to the final text.

> I will not perturbate
> Thy Paradisal state
>   With praise
>   Of thy dead days;
>
> To the new-heavened say,—   5
> 'Spirit, thou wert fine clay'.
>   This do,
>   Thy praise who knew.
>
> Therefore my spirit clings
> Heaven's porter by the wings,   10
>   And holds
>   Its gated golds
>
> Apart, with thee to press
> A private business;—
>   Whence,   15
>   Deign me audience.
>
> Anchorite, who didst dwell
> With all the world for cell!
>   My soul
>   Round me doth roll   20

A sequestration bare.
Too far alike we were,
    Too far
  Dissimilar.

For its burning fruitage I   25
Do climb the tree o' the sky;
    Do prize
  Some human eyes.

You smelt the Heaven-blossoms,
And all the sweets embosoms   30
    The dear
  Uranian year.

Those Eyes my weak gaze shuns,
Which to the suns are Suns,
    Did   35
  Not affray your lid.

The carpet was let down
(With golden mouldings strown)
    For you
  Of the angels' blue.   40

But I, ex-Paradised,
The shoulder of your Christ
    Find high
  To lean thereby.

So flaps my helpless sail,   45
Bellying with neither gale,
    Of heaven
  Nor Orcus even.

Life is a coquetry
Of Death, which wearies me,   50
    Too sure
  Of the amour;

A tiring-room where I
Death's divers garments try,
    Till fit
  Some fashion sit.   55

It seemeth me too much
I do rehearse for such
    A mean
   And single scene.   60

The sandy glass hence bear—
Antique remembrancer;
    My veins
   Do spare its pains.

With secret sympathy   65
My thoughts repeat in me
    Infirm
   The turn o' the worm

Beneath my appointed sod;
The grave is in my blood;   70
    I shake
   To winds that take

Its grasses by the top;
The rains thereon that drop
    Perturb   75
   With drip acerb

My subtly answering soul;
The feet across its knoll
    Do jar
   Me from afar.   80

As sap foretastes the spring;
As Earth ere blossoming
    Thrills
   With far daffodils,

And feels her breast turn sweet   85
With the unconceivèd wheat;
    So doth
   My flesh foreloathe

The abhorrèd spring of Dis,
With seething presciences   90
    Affirm
   The preparate worm.

I have no thought that I,
When at the last I die,
    Shall reach   95
  To gain your speech.

But you, should that be so,
May very well, I know,
    May well
  To me in hell   100

With recognising eyes
Look from your Paradise—
    'God bless
  Thy hopelessness!'

Call, holy soul, O call   105
The hosts angelical,
    And say,—
  'See, far away

'Lies one I saw on earth;
One stricken from his birth   110
    With curse
  Of destinate verse.

'What place doth He ye serve
For such sad spirit reserve,—
    Given,   115
  In dark lieu of Heaven,

'The impitiable Daemon,
Beauty, to adore and dream on,
    To be
  Perpetually   120

'Hers, but she never his?
He reapeth miseries,
    Foreknows
  His wages woes;

'He lives detachèd days;   125
He serveth not for praise;
    For gold
  He is not sold;

'Deaf is he to world's tongue;
He scorneth for his song   130
        The loud
    Shouts of the crowd;

'He asketh not world's eyes;
Not to world's ears he cries;
        Saith,—"These   135
    Shut if ye please;"

'He measureth world's pleasure
World's ease as Saints might measure;
        For hire
    Just love entire   140

'He asks, not grudging pain;
And knows his asking vain,
        And cries—
    "Love! Love!" and dies;

'In guerdon of long duty,   145
Unowned by Love or Beauty;
        And goes—
    Tell, tell, who knows!

'Aliens from Heaven's worth,
Fine beasts who nose i' the earth,   150
        Do there
    Reward prepare.

'But are *his* great desires
Food but for nether fires?
        Ah me,   155
    A mystery!

'Can it be his alone,
To find when all is known,
        That what
    He solely sought   160

'Is lost, and thereto lost
All that its seeking cost?
        That he
    Must finally,

'Through sacrificial tears,   165
And anchoretic years,
    Tryst
With the sensualist?'

So ask; and if they tell
The secret terrible,   170
    Good friend,
I pray thee send

Some high gold embassage
To teach my unripe age.
    Tell!   175
Lest my feet walk hell.

Between 8–9 *ME*:
    I saw thee only once;
    Although thy gentle tones,
        Said soft,—
      'Come hither oft.'

17–20 *ME*:
    Your singer did not come
    Back to that stern bare home:
        He knew
      Himself and you.

Between 20–1 *ME*:
    I saw, as seers do,
    That you were even you;
        And—why,
      I too was I.

    Both in the world, not of it,
    I scorned, but you could move it:
        My wall
      Material,

21 *ME*: And inward, like yours bare. **25–6** *ME*: I, in weak wayfaring, / Do need the poet's spring, **29–32** This verse is an example of FT's use of convoluted grammar, where the *Uranian year* becomes the subject of the herb *embosoms*. **32** *Uranian year* year of blessing for those who lead a life such as the Cardinal's. In his notes TLC suggests a possible reference to the planet Uranus, which takes 83 years to revolve round the sun; Manning died aged 84 (TLC*Poems*, p. 384).

33–6 *ME*:
    You saw the tender eyes
    Which light the upper skies.
        With blood
      Filled on the Rood.

Between 44–5 *ME*:
> I on a lower plane
> Walk in acquainted pain;
> > And take
> > It for mistake,

45–8 *ME*:
> If any sweet surprise
> Of undreamed respite rise
> > And say—,
> > 'Be glad today!'

48 *Orcus* Hades, or hell. **89** *The abhorrèd spring of Dis* Lake Avernus, the mythical entrance to Hades, here given its alternative name of Dis. For an alternative reading see T L C *Poems*, p. 385. **100** *To me in hell* Here F T uses the term as other Catholic writers do on occasion, to refer to purgatory, the place of purifying punishment rather than of eternal damnation feared as the poet's final fate at the end of the poem. **102, 109** These two lines are oblique references to F T's meeting with the Cardinal, the only ones made in the revised text.

A Fallen Yew

ME, January 1892

The original buildings at Ushaw College surrounded an ancient yew tree and the name of the College was taken from it, 'yew' being combined with 'shaw', the Anglo-Saxon word for shade or enclosure. It remained a much loved feature of the College until it was blown down in a storm in September 1891, the event which inspired this poem. When he revised the text for *Poems* Thompson added stanzas 6, 7 (lines 16–21) and 24 (lines 70–2).

> It seemed corrival of the world's great prime,
> > Made to un-edge the scythe of Time,
> > > And last with stateliest rhyme.

> No tender Dryad ever did indue
> > That rigid chiton of rough yew,   5
> > > To fret her white flesh through:

> But some god like to those grim Asgard lords,
> > Who walk the fables of the hordes
> > > From Scandinavian fjords,

> Upheaved its stubborn birth, and raised unriven   10
> > Against the whirl-blast and the levin,
> > > Defiant arms to Heaven.

> When doom puffed out the stars, we might have said,
> > It would decline its heavy head,
> > > And see the world to bed.   15

For this firm yew did from the vassal leas,
   And rain and air, its tributaries,
      Its revenues increase,

And levy impost on the golden sun,
   Take the blind years as they might run,   20
      And no fate seek or shun.

But now our yew is strook, is fallen—yea
   Hacked like dull wood of every day
      To this and that, men say.

Never!—To Hades' shadowy shipyards gone,   25
   Dim barge of Dis, down Acheron
      It drops, or Lethe wan.

Stirred by its fall—poor destined bark of Dis!—
   Along my soul a bruit there is
      Of echoing images,   30

Reverberations of mortality:
   Spelt backward from its death to me
      Its life reads saddenedly.

Its breast was hollowed as the tooth of eld;
   And boys there creeping unbeheld,   35
      A laughing moment dwelled.

Yet they, within its very heart so crept,
   Reached not the heart that courage kept
      With winds and years beswept.

And in its boughs did close and kindly nest   40
   The birds, as they within its breast,
      By all its leaves caressed.

But bird nor child might touch by any art
   Each other's or the tree's hid heart,
      A whole God's breadth apart;   45

The breadth of God, the breadth of death and life!
   Even so, even so, in undreamed strife
      With pulseless Law, the wife,—

The sweetest wife on sweetest marriage-day,—
  Their souls at grapple in mid-way,   50
    Sweet to her sweet may say:

'I take you to my inmost heart, my true!'
  Ah, fool! but there is one heart you
    Shall never take him to!

The hold that falls not when the town is got,   55
  The heart's heart, whose immurèd plot
    Hath keys yourself keep not!

Its ports you cannot burst—you are withstood—
  For him that to your listening blood
    Sends precepts as he would.   60

Its gates are deaf to Love, high summoner;
  Yea, Love's great warrant runs not there:
    You are your prisoner.

Yourself are with yourself the sole consortress
  In that unleaguerable fortress;   65
    It knows you not for portress.

Its keys are at the cincture hung of God;
  Its gates are trepidant to His nod;
    By Him its floors are trod.

And if His feet shall rock those floors in wrath,   70
  Or blest aspersion sleek His path,
    Is only choice it hath.

Yea, in that ultimate heart's occult abode
  To lie as in an oubliette of God,
    Or as a bower untrod,   75

Built by a secret Lover for His spouse;—
  Sole choice is this your life allows,
    Sad tree, whose perishing boughs
      So few birds house!

4–6 Dryads were mythical female inhabitants of trees, whose tender flesh is here contrasted with the 'chiton', or tunic, of the yew tree's bark. 7 *Asgard* a dwelling of the Norse

gods. **11** *levin* lightning. **25–7** *Hades* hell; *Dis* the underworld; *Acheron* river of darkness in Hades; *Lethe* river of oblivion associated with Hades. **44** There is a significant difference in the *ME* text: 'Its or each other's isolate heart'. **67** *cincture* girdle. **68** *trepidant* vulnerable. **74** *oubliette* dungeon that could only be entered from above.

Dream-Tryst

ME, May 1888

The two poems that Thompson is known to have sent to Meynell while living on the London streets were 'The Passion of Mary' (see p. 217) and 'Dream-Tryst'. After the appearance of 'Dream-Tryst' in *ME* his uncle, Edward Healy Thompson, described it as 'erotic', provoking Thompson's comment that the poem was addressed 'to the memory of a child known but once when I was eleven years old' (*Life*, p. 14; see also *BHCC*, p. 80).

> The breaths of kissing night and day
> Were mingled in the eastern Heaven:
> Throbbing with unheard melody
> Shook Lyra all its star-chord seven:
> When dusk shrunk cold, and light trod shy,   5
> And dawn's grey eyes were troubled grey;
> And souls went palely up the sky,
> And mine to Lucidé.
>
> There was no change in her sweet eyes
> Since last I saw those sweet eyes shine;   10
> There was no change in her deep heart
> Since last that deep heart knocked at mine.
> Her eyes were clear, her eyes were Hope's,
> Wherein did ever come and go
> The sparkle of the fountain-drops   15
> From her sweet soul below.
>
> The chambers in the house of dreams
> Are fed with so divine an air,
> That Time's hoar wings grow young therein,
> And they who walk there are most fair.   20
> I joyed for me, I joyed for her,
> Who with the Past meet girt about:
> Where our last kiss still warms the air,
> Nor can her eyes go out.

4 *Lyra* constellation of stars known in the ancient world as the Lyre of Hermes, or Orpheus (gods of poetry and song), here identified by the seven chords of the lyre. **8** *Lucidé* The name of the child addressed in the poem was Lucy.

A Corymbus for Autumn

ME, March 1891
Corymbus from the Latin *corymb*, a cluster of flowers or fruit.

Hearken my chant, 'tis
As a Bacchante's,
A grape-spurt, a vine-splash, a tossed tress, flown vaunt 'tis!
Suffer my singing,
Gipsy of Seasons, ere thou go winging;　　　　　5
Ere Winter throws
His slaking snows
In thy feasting-flagon's impurpurate glows!
The sopped sun—toper as ever drank hard—
Stares foolish, hazed,　　　　　10
Rubicund, dazed,
Totty with thine October tankard.
Tanned maiden! with cheeks like apples russet,
And breast a brown agaric faint-flushing at tip,
And a mouth too red for the moon to buss it,　　　　　15
But her cheek unvow its vestalship;
Thy mists enclip
Her steel-clear circuit illuminous,
Until it crust
Rubiginous　　　　　20
With the glorious gules of a glowing rust.

Far other saw we, other indeed,
The crescent moon, in the May-days dead,
Fly up with its slender white wings spread
Out of its nest in the sea's waved mead!　　　　　25
How are the veins of thee, Autumn, laden?
Umbered juices,
And pulpèd oozes
Pappy out of the cherry-bruises,
Froth the veins of thee, wild, wild maiden!　　　　　30
With hair that musters
In globèd clusters
In tumbling clusters, like swarthy grapes,
Round thy brow and thine ears o'ershaden;
With the burning darkness of eyes like pansies,　　　　　35
Like velvet pansies
Wherethrough escapes
The splendent might of thy conflagrate fancies;

With robe gold-tawny not hiding the shapes
    Of the feet whereunto it falleth down,   40
  Thy naked feet unsandallèd;
With robe gold-tawny that does not veil
    Feet where the red
    Is meshed in the brown,
Like a rubied sun in a Venice-sail.   45

The wassailous heart of the Year is thine!
His Bacchic fingers disentwine
    His coronal
    At thy festival;
His revelling fingers disentwine   50
    Leaf, flower, and all,
    And let them fall
Blossom and all in thy wavering wine.
The Summer looks out from her brazen tower,
  Through the flashing bars of July,   55
Waiting thy ripened golden shower;
  Whereof there cometh, with sandals fleet,
    The North-west flying viewlessly,
  With a sword to sheer, and untameable feet,
    And the gorgon-head of the Winter shown   60
    To stiffen the gazing earth as stone.

In crystal Heaven's magic sphere
  Poised in the palm of thy fervid hand,
  Thou seest the enchanted shows appear
  That stain Favonian firmament;   65
Richer than ever the Occident
  Gave up to bygone Summer's wand.
Day's dying dragon lies drooping his crest,
Panting red pants into the West.
Or a butterfly sunset claps its wings   70
  With flitter alit on the swinging blossom,
The gusty blossom, that tosses and swings,
  Of the sea with its blown and ruffled bosom;
Its ruffled bosom wherethrough the wind sings
Till the crispèd petals are loosened and strown   75
    Overblown, on the sand;
    Shed, curling as dead
  Rose-leaves curl, on the feckèd strand.

*

Or higher, holier, saintlier when, as now,
All nature sacerdotal seems, and thou.   80
   The calm hour strikes on yon golden gong,
     In tones of floating and mellow light
     A spreading summons to even-song:
       See how there
       The cowlèd night   85
       Kneels on the Eastern sanctuary-stair.
What is this feel of incense everywhere?
   Clings it round folds of the blanch-amiced clouds,
Upwafted by the solemn thurifer,
        The mighty spirit unknown,   90
That swingeth the slow earth before the embannered Throne?
   Or is't the Season under all these shrouds
Of light, and sense, and silence, makes her known
       A presence everywhere,
       An inarticulate prayer,   95
A hand on the soothed tresses of the air?
       But there is one hour scant
Of this Titanian, primal liturgy;
As there is but one hour for me and thee,
   Autumn, for thee and thine hierophant,   100
       Of this grave ending chant.
       Round the earth still and stark
Heaven's death-lights kindle, yellow spark by spark,
Beneath the dreadful catafalque of the dark.

       And I had ended there: 105
But a great wind blew all the stars to flare,
And cried, 'I sweep the path before the moon!
Tarry ye now the coming of the moon,
       For she is coming soon';
Then died before the coming of the moon.   110
And she came forth upon the trepidant air,
       In vesture unimagined fair,
       Woven as woof of flag-lilies;
       And curdled as of flag-lilies
       The vapour at the feet of her,   115
And a haze about her tinged in fainter wise,
   As if she had trodden the stars in press,
   Till the gold wine spurted over her dress,
   Till the gold wine gushed out round her feet,

      Spouted over her stainèd wear 120
    And bubbled in golden froth at her feet,
      And hung like a whirlpool's mist round her.
    Still, mighty Season, do I see't,
    Thy sway is still majestical!
    Thou hold'st of God, by title sure, 125
Thine indefeasible investiture,
    And that right round thy locks are native to;
The heavens upon thy brow imperial,
    This huge terrene thy ball,
And o'er thy shoulders thrown wide air's depending pall. 130
    What if thine earth be blear and bleak of hue?
      Still, still the skies are sweet!
    Still, Season, still thou hast thy triumphs there!
      How have I, unaware,
Forgetful of my strain inaugural, 135
    Cleft the great rondure of thy reign complete,
Yielding thee half, who hast indeed the all?
    I will not think thy sovereignty begun
      But with the shepherd sun
      That washes in the sea the stars' golden fleeces, 140
      Or that with day it ceases,
    Who sets his burning lips to the salt brine,
      And purples it to wine;
    While I behold how ermined Artemis
      Ordainèd weed must wear, 145
      And toil thy business;
      Who witness am of her,
    Her too in autumn turned a vintager;
    And, laden with its lampèd clusters bright,
    The fiery-fruited vineyard of this night. 150

Between 3–4 *ME*:
    Fuming song spilt from the heart lift up
    Of the reeling Maenad, as swirled from a cup
      That dripping aslant is
    Nay, blood from a heart that a grape palpitant is!

14 *agaric* mushroom.

17–19 *ME*:
    Yea, whose overleaned face, like the reflex rose
    Of a hanging vapour, its own grain shows
      In the candid cool
      Of the lunar pool;

> Whose mists enclip
> That steel-clear rondure illuminous,

21 *gules* red. **60** *gorgon* one of three mythical females whose countenances could turn the beholder to stone. **65** *Favonian:* Favonius was a name for the west wind. **88** *blanch-amiced clouds* clouds formed in colour and shape like an amice, a white cloth worn over the shoulders as part of a priest's vestments. **89** *thurifer* altar-server who carries the thurible, or censer, for incense. **98** *Titanian* The Titans were gods often identified as giants. **100** *hierophant* an officiator at the sacred mysteries, mainly associated with Greek religious rituals. **104** *catafalque* coffin of an important person, raised on a stage during the funeral and sometimes surmounted by a canopy. **116** A comma has been substituted for a full stop, to aid sense. **130–1** A division as between stanzas occurs here in *Works* and subsequent editions but is not present in *Poems*. **134** *ME*: I gave thee half, but lo! thou hast the all. **144** *Artemis* Greek moon goddess.

The Hound of Heaven

ME, July 1890

In a late notebook Thompson wrote that the idea for 'The Hound of Heaven' first came to him during his years on the London streets: 'It was a very rudimentary conception with nothing like the scope it took to itself, but I felt it great in suggestion . . .' In the same note he also provides the best short summary of the poem as it came to be written: '. . . certainly, with all its shortcomings, the greatest of my Odes: and this because it embodies a world-wide experience in an individual form of that experience, the universal becoming incarnated in the personal' (unnumbered notebook, M; quoted *BHCC*, p. 140). The poem may have evolved out of another, of which only a single stanza survives in one of the tattered notebooks (NB 47) which he kept while living on the London streets.

> Then last God came to me
> And said: 'Thou art of everything bereft,
>   Save one thing only left:
> With this thou must of thine own free will part.'
> And I with smiles said: 'Lord, what may it be?'
>   Then answered He:
>   'My child, give Me thy heart.'
>   And I thereat
> Cried out with tears, 'O Lord, not that, not that!'

When Thompson sent 'The Hound of Heaven' to Meynell for publication in *ME* he forgot to sign it. The original MS (BC) bears a signature 'forged' by Meynell, there being no time to obtain Thompson's own (T. L. Connolly, *Francis Thompson: In His Paths*, Bruce, Milwaukee 1944, p. 11).

There are no drafts for the Ode extant but in an unnumbered notebook (EMH) an early draft for part of *Sister Songs* is written over lines which, though partly erased, can be identified with lines from 'The Hound of Heaven' (see also *SHSS*, p. 262). Thompson was often short of paper and there are many instances of this kind in the MSS and notebooks. In the EMH collection there is a sheet of notes by Everard Meynell: 'Alternative readings in the HH, given me at the time he copied out the poem for Mr Cotterell'. He adds: 'Any of them better than the text, I think'. The connection with Cotterell was during Thompson's later years and this note appears to date from *c.* 1905. These readings are included in the end-notes, as 'EM note'.

The poem was begun soon after Thompson had completed his long essay on Shelley, in the autumn of 1889. The most immediate influence can be traced to Shelley's 'Prometheus Unbound', and its title may have arisen from that poem's lines:

> Once the hungry hours were hounds
> Which chased the day like a bleeding deer.
>   (Act 4, 73–4)

There are summaries of the wide range of other influences in *BHCC*, pp. 135–9; *SHSS*, pp. 259–61; TLC*Poems*, pp. 350–71.

I fled Him, down the nights and down the days;
 I fled Him, down the arches of the years;
I fled Him, down the labyrinthine ways
 Of my own mind; and in the mist of tears
I hid from Him, and under running laughter.   5
  Up vistaed hopes I sped;
  And shot, precipitated
 Adown Titanic glooms of chasmed fears,
From those strong Feet that followed, followed after.
  But with unhurrying chase,   10
  And unperturbèd pace,
 Deliberate speed, majestic instancy,
  They beat—and a Voice beat
  More instant than the Feet—
'All things betray thee, who betrayest Me'.   15

  I pleaded, outlaw-wise,
By many a hearted casement, curtained red,
 Trellised with intertwining charities;
(For, though I knew His love Who followèd,
  Yet was I sore adread   20
Lest, having Him, I must have naught beside)
But, if one little casement parted wide,
 The gust of His approach would clash it to.
 Fear wist not to evade, as Love wist to pursue.
Across the margent of the world I fled,   25
 And troubled the gold gateways of the stars,
  Smiting for shelter on their clangèd bars;
  Fretted to dulcet jars

And silvern chatter the pale ports o' the moon.
I said to dawn: Be sudden—to eve: Be soon;   30
    With thy young skiey blossoms heap me over
      From this tremendous Lover!
Float thy vague veil about me, lest He see!
    I tempted all His servitors, but to find
My own betrayal in their constancy,   35
In faith to Him their fickleness to me,
    Their traitorous trueness, and their loyal deceit.
To all swift things for swiftness did I sue;
    Clung to the whistling mane of every wind.
      But whether they swept, smoothly fleet,   40
    The long savannahs of the blue;
        Or whether, Thunder-driven,
    They clanged his chariot 'thwart a heaven,
Plashy with flying lightnings round the spurn o'their feet:—
    Fear wist not to evade as Love wist to pursue.   45
      Still with unhurrying chase,
      And unperturbèd pace,
    Deliberate speed, majestic instancy,
      Came on the following Feet,
      And a Voice above their beat—   50
    'Naught shelters thee, who wilt not shelter Me.'

I sought no more that, after which I strayed,
    In face of man or maid;
But still within the little children's eyes
    Seems something, something that replies,   55
They at least are for me, surely for me!
I turned me to them very wistfully;
But just as their young eyes grew sudden fair
    With dawning answers there,
Their angel plucked them from me by the hair.   60
'Come then, ye other children, Nature's—share
With me' (said I) 'your delicate fellowship;
    Let me greet you lip to lip,
    Let me twine with you caresses,
      Wantoning   65
    With our Lady-Mother's vagrant tresses,
      Banqueting
    With her in her wind-walled palace,
    Underneath her azured dais,

Quaffing, as your taintless way is, 70
From a chalice
Lucent-weeping out of the dayspring.'
So it was done:
I in their delicate fellowship was one—
Drew the bolt of Nature's secrecies. 75
I knew all the swift importings
On the wilful face of skies
I knew how the clouds arise
Spumèd of the wild sea-snortings;
All that's born or dies 80
Rose and drooped with—made them shapers
Of mine own moods, or wailful or divine—
With them joyed and was bereaven.
I was heavy with the even,
When she lit her glimmering tapers 85
Round the day's dead sanctities.
I laughed in the morning's eyes.
I triumphed and I saddened with all weather,
Heaven and I wept together,
And its sweet tears were salt with mortal mine; 90
Against the red throb of its sunset-heart
I laid my own to beat,
And share commingling heat;
But not by that, by that, was eased my human smart.
In vain my tears were wet on Heaven's grey cheek. 95
For ah! we know not what each other says,
These things and I; in sound *I* speak—
Their sound is but their stir, they speak by silences.
Nature, poor stepdame, cannot slake my drouth;
Let her, if she would owe me, 100
Drop yon blue bosom-veil of sky, and show me
The breasts o' her tenderness:
Never did any milk of hers once bless
My thirsting mouth.
Nigh and nigh draws the chase, 105
With unperturbèd pace
Deliberate speed majestic instancy
And past those noisèd Feet
A voice comes yet more fleet—
'Lo! naught contents thee, who content'st not Me.' 110

*

Naked I wait Thy love's uplifted stroke!
My harness piece by piece Thou has hewn from me,
  And smitten me to my knee;
  I am defenceless utterly.
  I slept, methinks, and woke,   115
And, slowly gazing, find me stripped in sleep.
In the rash lustihead of my young powers,
 I shook the pillaring hours
And pulled my life upon me; grimed with smears,
I stand amid the dust o' the mounded years— 120
My mangled youth lies dead beneath the heap.
My days have crackled and gone up in smoke,
Have puffed and burst as sun-starts on a stream.
  Yea, faileth now even dream
The dreamer, and the lute the lutanist;   125
Even the linked fantasies, in whose blossomy twist
I swung the earth a trinket at my wrist,
Are yielding; cords of all too weak account
For earth with heavy griefs so overplussed.
  Ah! is Thy love indeed   130
A weed, albeit an amaranthine weed,
Suffering no flowers except its own to mount?
  Ah! must—
  Designer infinite!—
Ah! must Thou char the wood ere Thou canst limn with it? 135
My freshness spent its wavering shower i' the dust;
And now my heart is as a broken fount,
Wherein tear-drippings stagnate, spilt down ever
  From the dank thoughts that shiver
Upon the sighful branches of my mind.   140
  Such is; what is to be?
The pulp so bitter, how shall taste the rind?
I dimly guess what Time in mists confounds;
Yet ever and anon a trumpet sounds
From the hid battlements of Eternity,   145
Those shaken mists a space unsettle, then
Round the half-glimpsèd turrets slowly wash again;
  But not ere him who summoneth
  I first have seen, enwound
With glooming robes purpureal, cypress-crowned; 150
His name I know, and what his trumpet saith.
Whether man's heart or life it be which yields

Thee harvest, must Thy harvest fields
Be dunged with rotten death?
   Now of that long pursuit   155
   Comes on at hand the bruit;
That Voice is round me like a bursting sea:
   'And is thy earth so marred,
   Shattered in shard on shard?
Lo, all things fly thee, for thou fliest Me!   160

   'Strange, piteous, futile thing!
Wherefore should any set thee love apart?
Seeing none but I makes much of naught' (He said),
'And human love needs human meriting:
   How hast thou merited—   165
Of all man's clotted clay the dingiest clot?
   Alack, thou knowest not
How little worthy of any love thou art!
Whom wilt thou find to love ignoble thee,
   Save Me, save only Me?   170
All which I took from thee I did but take,
   Not for thy harms,
But just that thou might'st seek it in My arms.
   All which thy child's mistake
Fancies as lost, I have stored for thee at home: 175
   Rise, clasp My hand, and come.'

   Halts by me that footfall:
   Is my gloom, after all,
Shade of His hand, outstretched caressingly?
   'Ah, fondest, blindest, weakest,   180
   I am He Whom thou seekest!
Thou dravest love from thee, who dravest Me.'

8 *Titanic* The Titans were the giant offspring of the union of the Earth (Gaia) and Heaven (Uranus). They are used here to continue the cosmic imagery of the flight and the fear aroused by their awe-inspiring size. **17** *hearted casement* apparently the human lovers with whom the protagonist has sought refuge from his Pursuer. **31** *skiey blossoms* stars. **36–7** EM note: 'they would not take my truth to him untrue.' **42** EM note: 'Or whether, by thee thunder driven.' **72** *Lucent-weeping out of the dayspring* overflowing with the light of dawn. **96** EM note: 'For ah! we know not each what other says.' **98** *they speak by silences* one of Thompson's finest uses of oxymoron, the juxtaposition of opposites. The idea may have come from a passage in the *Enneads* of Plotinus: 'And nature, asked why it brings forth its works, might answer if it cared to listen and to speak: "it would have been more becoming to put no question but to learn in silence just as I myself am silent and make no habit of talking" ' (*The Enneads*, 3:8., trans. Stephen Mackenna, 2nd edn 1956). **102**

EM note has alternate her/the for this line. **117–19** Samson's great strength enabled him to pull down the pillars of the pagan temple where he was held captive (Judges 16:30). **Between 129–30** *ME*: I grazed / Too closely Thy blue window as I gazed, / Jutted a careless elbow through clear heaven / And gashed me with the splinters. See, I bleed! **131** *amaranthine* unfading. Many commentators have wrongly identified the 'weed' as opium. **154–5** In *Works* and later editions there is a break here between stanzas that does not occur in *Poems*. **156** *bruit* clamour. **182** *dravest* MS: drivest; *ME*: drovest.

A Judgment in Heaven

ME, October 1893

The spelling of 'Judgment' is as it appears in *Poems* and is therefore followed here. In a letter to Alice Meynell written in August 1892, Thompson referred to the Epilogue to 'A Judgment in Heaven' and the idea behind the poem as a whole: 'I do firmly think that none are lost who have not wilfully closed their eyes to the known light: that such as fall with constant striving, battling with their temperament; or through ill training, circumstances which shuts from them true light, etc.; that all these shall taste of God's justice, which for them is better than man's mercy' (*Letters*, p. 81). In the same letter he contrasts this lenient view (unusual at the time) with his own personal fear of hell, drawing attention to the lines on Cardinal Manning, 'which I do not care to read again'. He prefixed the poem 'A Judgment in Heaven' with the following 'Note': 'I have throughout this poem used an asterisk to indicate the caesura in the middle of the line, after the manner of the old Saxon section-point.' He was therefore familiar with the metre of Old English verse at a time when very few outside academic circles possessed such knowledge.

Athwart the sod which is treading for God * the poet paced with his
    splendid eyes;
Paradise-verdure he stately passes * to win to the Father of Paradise,
Through the conscious and palpitant grasses * of intertangled relu-
    cent dyes.

The angels a-play on its fields of Summer * (their wild wings rustled
    his guides' cymars)
Looked up from disport at the passing comer, * as they pelted
    each other with handfuls of stars;   5
And the warden-spirits with startled feet rose, * hand on sword, by
    their tethered cars.

With plumes night-tinctured englobed and cinctured, * of Saints, his
    guided steps held on
To where on the far crystàlline pale * of that transtellar Heaven there
    shone
The immutable crocean dawn * effusing from the Father's Throne.

Through the reverberant Eden-ways * the bruit of his great advent
  driven,   10
Back from the fulgent justle and press * with mighty echoing so was
  given,
As when the surly thunder smites * upon the clangèd gates of
  Heaven.

Over the bickering gonfalons, * far-ranged as for Tartarean wars,
Went a waver of ribbèd fire *—as night-seas on phosphoric bars
Like a flame-plumed fan shake slowly out * their ridgy reach of
  crumbling stars.   15

At length to where on His fretted Throne * sat in the heart of His
  aged dominions
The great Triune, and Mary nigh, * lit round with spears of their
  hauberked minions,
The poet drew, in the thunderous blue * involvèd dread of those
  mounted pinions.

As in a secret and tenebrous cloud * the watcher from the disquiet
  earth
At momentary intervals * beholds from its raggèd rifts break forth   20
The flash of a golden perturbation, * the travelling threat of a
  witchèd birth;

Till heavily parts a sinister chasm, * a grisly jaw, whose verges soon,
Slowly and ominously filled * by the on-coming plenilune
Supportlessly congest with fire, * and suddenly spit forth the
  moon:—

With beauty, not terror, through tangled error * of night-dipt
  plumes so burned their charge;   25
Swayed and parted the globing clusters * so,—disclosed from their
  kindling marge,
Roseal-chapleted, splendent-vestured, * the singer there where
  God's light lay large.

Hu, hu! a wonder! a wonder! see, * clasping the singer's glories clings
A dingy creature, even to laughter * cloaked and clad in patchwork
  things,
Shrinking close from the unused glows * of the seraphs' versicoloured wings.   30

A rhymer, rhyming a futile rhyme, * he had crept for convoy through
    Eden-ways
Into the shade of the poet's glory, * darkened under his prevalent
    rays,
Fearfully hoping a distant welcome * as a poor kinsman of his lays.

The angels laughed with a lovely scorning: *—'Who has done this
    sorry deed in
The garden of our Father God? * 'mid his blossoms to sow this weed
    in?   35
Never our fingers knew this stuff: * not so fashion the looms of
    Eden!'

The singer bowed his brow majestic, * searching that patchwork
    through and through,
Feeling God's lucent gazes traverse * his singing- stoling and spirit
    too:
The hallowed harpers were fain to frown * on the strange thing come
    'mid their sacred crew,
Only the singer that was earth * his fellow-earth and his own self
    knew.   40

But the poet rent off robe and wreath, * so as a sloughing serpent
    doth,
Laid them at the rhymer's feet, * shed down wreath and raiment
    both,
Stood in a dim and shamèd stole, * like the tattered wing of a musty
    moth.

'Thou gav'st the weed and wreath of song, * the weed and wreath are
    solely Thine,
And this dishonest vesture * is the only vesture that is mine;   45
The life *I* textured, Thou the song *—my* handicraft is not divine!'

He wrested o'er the rhymer's head * that garmenting which wrought
    him wrong;
A flickering tissue argentine * down dripped its shivering silvers
    long:—
'Better thou wov'st thy woof of life * than thou didst weave thy woof
    of song!'

Never a chief in Saintdom was, * but turned him from the Poet then; 50
Never an eye looked mild on him * 'mid all the angel myriads ten,
Save sinless Mary, and sinful Mary *—the Mary titled Magdalen.

'Turn yon robe,' spake Magdalen, * 'of torn bright song, and see and
    feel.'
They turned the raiment, saw and felt * what their turning did
    reveal—
All the inner surface piled * with bloodied hairs, like hairs of steel.   55

'Take, I pray, yon chaplet up, * thrown down ruddied from his head.'
They took the roseal chaplet up, * and they stood astonishèd:
Every leaf between their fingers, * as they bruised it, burst and bled.

'See his torn flesh through those rents, * see the punctures round his
    hair,
As if the chaplet-flowers had driven * deep roots in to nourish
    there—   60
Lord, who gav'st him robe and wreath, * *what* was this thou gav'st for
    wear?'

'Fetch forth the Paradisal garb!' * spake the Father, sweet and low;
Drew them both by the frightened hand * where Mary's throne made
    irised bow—
'Take, Princess Mary, of thy good grace, * two spirits greater than
    they know.'

Epilogue

    Virtue may unlock hell, or even
    A sin turn in the wards of Heaven,
    (As ethics of the text-book go),
    So little men their own deeds know,
    Or through the intricate *mêlée*   5
    Guess whitherward draws the battle-sway;
    So little, if they knew the deed,
    Discern what therefrom shall succeed.
    To wisest moralists 'tis but given
    To work rough border-law of Heaven,   10
    Within this narrow life of ours,
    These marches 'twixt delimitless Powers.
    Is it, if Heaven the future showed,
    Is it the all-severest mode
    To see ourselves with the eyes of God?   15
    God rather grant, at His assize,
    He see us not with our own eyes!
        *

Heaven, which man's generations draws
Nor deviates into replicas,
Must of as deep diversity   20
In judgment as creation be.
There is no expeditious road
To pack and label men for God,
And save them by the barrel-load.
Some may perchance, with strange surprise,   25
Have blundered into Paradise.
In vasty dusk of life abroad,
They fondly thought to err from God,
Nor knew the circle that they trod;
And wandering all the night about,   30
Found them at morn where they set out.
Death dawned; Heaven lay in prospect wide:—
Lo! they were standing by His side!

The rhymer a life uncomplex,
With just such cares as mortals vex,   35
So simply felt as all men feel,
Lived purely out to his soul's weal.
A double life the Poet lived,
And with a double burthen grieved;
The life of flesh and life of song   40
The pangs to both lives that belong;
Immortal knew and mortal pain,
Who in two worlds could lose and gain,
And found immortal fruits must be
Mortal through his mortality.   45
The life of flesh and life of song!
If one life worked the other wrong,
What expiating agony
May for him damned to poesy
Shut in that little sentence be—   50
What deep austerities of strife—
'He lived his life.' He lived *his* life!

---

1 *treading* perhaps used here as a noun in the sense of anything made by treading. 3 *relucent* gleaming. 4 *cymars* flowing robes worn by Eastern women. 8 *crystàlline pale* sea surrounding the Throne of God (Apoc. 4:6). 9 *crocean* saffron-coloured. 11 *fulgent* shining. 13 *bickering gonfalons* gleaming ensigns, or banners, often carried on a lance; *Tartarian wars* wars waged against the lower regions (of Hades, or Tartarus). 14–15 *nightseas . . . crumbling stars* The sea breaking on a sand bar at night gives off a phosphorous light which can appear like sparks, or stars, in the darkness. As a child, FT was fascinated

by this phenomenon while on holiday at Colwyn Bay (*Life*, p. 12). He first made use of the image in an early 'Epithalamium', where he added this explanatory note: 'I do not know whether the image is altogether clear to the ordinary reader, as it was in my own mind. Anyone, however, who has ever seen on a dark night a phosphorescent sea breaking in long billows of light on the viewless beach, while as the hidden pools or recessed waters of the strand are stirred by the onrush, they respond through the darkness in swarms of jewel-like flashes, will understand the image at once' ('Notebook of Early Poems'). **17** *hauberked* clad in mail armour. **19** *tenebrous* dark. **23** *plenilune* full moon. **27** *Roseal-chapleted* wearing a wreath of roses or, literally, a rose-coloured wreath. *OED* cites sixteenth- and seventeenth-century references for *roseal* as rose-coloured: see also FT 'The Making of Viola' **32** on p. 50: 'roseal hoverings'. **30** *versicoloured* variegated. **38** A comma has been substituted for a hyphen between singing and stoling to make sense of this line. **44** In *Works* the stanza is prefixed by 'The Poet addresses his Maker'. **47** In *Works* the stanza is prefixed by 'The Poet addresses the Rhymer'.

POEMS ON CHILDREN

Daisy

ME, March 1890

The poem was based on an incident that took place while Thompson was staying at the Priory at Storrington in Sussex during the summer of 1889. Daisy Stanford, the child who is its subject, was one of a number of local children who would accompany him on his walks. She recalled this incident of the raspberry-picking many years later when she wrote to Everard Meynell in a letter dated 17 October 1917: 'He helped me fill my basket and, child-like, any extra fine one I got I gave him to eat' (Letter at M, quoted in BHCC, p. 129). Although there is a distinct influence from Wordsworth's 'Lucy' poems, Thompson's concentration on the poet's personal response is very different from the objectivity of Wordsworth's treatment of childhood.

> Where the thistle lifts a purple crown
>   Six foot out of the turf,
> And the harebell shakes on the windy hill—
>   O the breath of the distant surf!—
>
> The hills look over on the South,   5
>   And southward dreams the sea;
> And, with the sea-breeze hand in hand,
>   Came innocence and she.
>
> Where 'mid the gorse the raspberry
>   Red for the gatherer springs,   10
> Two children did we stray and talk
>   Wise, idle, childish things.

She listened with big-lipped surprise,
   Breast-deep mid flower and spine:
Her skin was like a grape, whose veins   15
   Run snow instead of wine.

She knew not those sweet words she spake,
   Nor knew her own sweet way;
But there's never a bird, so sweet a song
   Thronged in whose throat that day!   20

Oh, there were flowers in Storrington
   On the turf and on the spray;
But the sweetest flower on Sussex hills
   Was the Daisy-flower that day!

Her beauty smoothed earth's furrowed face!   25
   She gave me tokens three:—
A look, a word of her winsome mouth,
   And a wild raspberry.

A berry red, a guileless look,
   A still word,—strings of sand!   30
And yet they made my wild, wild heart
   Fly down to her little hand.

For standing artless as the air,
   And candid as the skies,
She took the berries with her hand,   35
   And the love with her sweet eyes.

The fairest things have fleetest end:
   Their scent survives their close,
But the rose's scent is bitterness
   To him that loved the rose!   40

She looked a little wistfully,
   Then went her sunshine way:—
The sea's eye had a mist on it,
   And the leaves fell from the day.

She went her unremembering way,   45
   She went and left in me
The pang of all the partings gone,
   And partings yet to be.

She left me marvelling why my soul
    Was sad that she was glad;   50
At all the sadness in the sweet,
    The sweetness in the sad.

Still, still I seemed to see her, still
    Look up with soft replies,
And take the berries with her hand,   55
    And the love with her lovely eyes.

Nothing begins, and nothing ends,
    That is not paid with moan;
For we are born in others' pain,
    And perish in our own.   60

51–2 In his notes TLC refers to FT's essay 'Crashaw' (*Academy*, 20 November 1897) where he calls attention to the line in Crashaw's 'The Weeper': 'Sweetness so sad, sadness so sweet'. The frequent appearance of this oxymoron in literature has been traced back to Sappho's lines 'To Athis' (TLC*Poems*, p. 303). **Between 57–60** *ME*: And what she said, if others heard, / Was a simple speech as may be: / But they've not the ear within the ear:— / Have they, vanished Daisy? When WM printed the poem in an anthology, *The Child Set in the Midst* (1892), 57–8 appear as: Nothing begins and nothing ends, / I think, without some moan,

The Making of Viola

ME, May 1892

Referring to 'The Making of Viola' and 'A Judgment in Heaven', Thompson wrote in a late notebook that 'the spirit of such poems . . . is no mere medieval imitation, but the natural temper of my Catholic training in a simple provincial home' (unnumbered notebook at M, quoted in *Life*, p. 59). The comment can be said to apply more distinctly to this poem than the other. Viola was the second of the Meynells' daughters. In a letter to the poetess Katharine Tynan, dated 15 July 1892, Thompson describes the metre for this poem as originating with 'the Saxon and Early English poets'. He points out that although some attempts have been made to revive it, only Miss Tynan has succeeded, notably in her poem 'Poppies'. He then explains how the metre works, writing as one poet to another:

> The true law is, that you take a metre (the more received and definite the better), and then vary it by the omission of syllables, leaving the lines so treated to be *read* into the given length by pause, and dwelling on the syllables preceding or following the hiatus. The omission of syllables is the exception, not the system, of the metre; and the art of the poet is shown in skillfully varying the position and manner of the omissions. In this way the most delightful effects of loving, lingering, and delicate modulation, on the one hand; or airy, dance-like measures and emphasis on the other, may be compassed.

(*Letters*, p. 76)

I

The Father of Heaven
> Spin, daughter Mary, spin,
> Twirl your wheel with silver din;
> Spin, daughter Mary, spin,
>   Spin a tress for Viola.

Angels
> Spin, Queen Mary, a   5
> Brown tress for Viola.

II

The Father of Heaven
> Weave, hands angelical,
> Weave a woof of flesh to pall—
> Weave, hands angelical—
>   Flesh to pall our Viola.   10

Angels
> Weave, singing brothers, a
> Velvet flesh for Viola!

III

The Father of Heaven
> Scoop, young Jesus, for her eyes,
> Wood-browned pools of Paradise—
> Young Jesus, for the eyes,   15
>   For the eyes of Viola.

Angels
> Tint, Prince Jesus, a
> Duskèd eye for Viola!

IV

The Father of Heaven
> Cast a star therein to drown
> Like a torch in cavern brown,   20
> Sink a burning star to drown
>   Whelmed in eyes of Viola.

Angels
> Lave, Prince Jesus; a
> Star in eyes of Viola!

V

The Father of Heaven

         Breathe, Lord Paraclete,   25
         To a bubbled crystal meet—
         Breathe, Lord Paraclete—
            Crystal soul for Viola.

Angels

         Breathe, Regal Spirit, a
         Flashing soul for Viola!   30

VI

The Father of Heaven

         Child-angels, from your wings
         Fall the roseal hoverings,
         Child-angels, from your wings,
            On the cheeks of Viola.

Angels

         Linger, rosy reflex, a   35
         Quenchless stain, on Viola!

VII

All things being accomplished, saith the Father of Heaven:

         Bear her down, and bearing, sing,
         Bear her down on spyless wing,
         Bear her down, and bearing, sing,
            With a sound of viola.   40

Angels

         Music as her name is, a
         Sweet sound of Viola!

VIII

         Wheeling angels, past espial,
         Danced her down with sound of viol;
         Wheeling angels, past espial,   45
            Descanting on 'Viola'.

Angels

         Sing, in our footing, a
         Lovely lilt of 'Viola!'

IX

Baby smiled, mother wailed,
Earthward while the sweetling sailed;   50
Mother smiled, baby wailed,
    When to earth came Viola.

And her elders shall say:
So soon have we taught you a
Way to weep, poor Viola!

X

Smile, sweet baby, smile,   55
For you will have weeping-while;
Native in your Heaven is smile,—
    But your weeping, Viola?

Whence your smiles we know, but ah!
Whence your weeping, Viola?—   60
    Our first gift to you is a
    Gift of tears, my Viola!

32 *roseal* rose-coloured; see 'A Judgment in Heaven', 27.

To My Godchild

Francis M. W. M.

ME, June 1891

Francis, the last of the Meynell children, was born on 12 May 1891. When Thompson was asked to be the godfather he wrote this poem in grateful response.

This labouring, vast, Tellurian galleon,
Riding at anchor off the orient sun
Had broken its cable, and stood out to space
Down some frore Arctic of the aërial ways:
And now, back warping from the inclement main,   5
Its vaporous shroudage drenched with icy rain,
It swung into its azure roads again;
When, floated on the prosperous sun-gale, you
Lit, a white halcyon auspice, 'mid our frozen crew.
       *

To the Sun, stranger, surely you belong,   10
Giver of golden days and golden song;
Nor is it by an all-unhappy plan
You bear the name of me, his constant Magian.
Yet ah! from any other that it came,
Lest, fated to my fate you be, as to my name.   15
When at the first those tidings did they bring,
My heart turned troubled at the ominous thing:
Though well may such a title him endower,
For whom a poet's prayer implores a poet's power.
The Assisian, who kept plighted faith to three,   20
To Song, to Sanctitude, and Poverty,
(In two alone of whom most singers prove
A fatal faithfulness of during love!);
He the sweet Sales, of whom we scarcely ken
How God he could love more, he so loved men;   25
The crown and crowned of Laura and Italy;
And Fletcher's fellow—from these, and not from me,
Take you your name, and take your legacy!

Or, if a right successive you declare
When worms, for ivies, intertwine my hair,   30
Take but this Poesy that now followeth
My clayey hest with sullen servile breath,
Made then your happy freedman by testating death.
My song I do but hold for you in trust,
I ask you but to blossom from my dust.   35
When you have compassed all weak I began,
Diviner poet, and ah! diviner man;
The man at feud with the perduring child
In you before song's altar nobly reconciled;
From the wise heavens I half shall smile to see   40
How little a world, which owned you, needed me.
If, while you keep the vigils of the night,
For your wild tears make darkness all too bright,
Some lone orb through your lonely window peeps,
As it played lover over your sweet sleeps;   45
Think it a golden crevice in the sky,
Which I have pierced but to behold you by!

And when, immortal mortal, droops your head,
And you, the child of deathless song, are dead;
Then, as you search with unaccustomed glance   50

The ranks of Paradise for my countenance,
Turn not your tread along the Uranian sod
Among the bearded counsellors of God;
For if in Eden as on earth are we,
I sure shall keep a younger company: 55
Pass where beneath their rangèd gonfalons
The starry cohorts shake their shielded suns,
The dreadful mass of their enridgèd spears;
Pass where majestical the eternal peers,
The stately choice of the great Saintdom, meet— 60
A silvern segregation, globed complete
In sandalled shadow of the Triune feet;
Pass by where wait, young poet-wayfarer,
Your cousined clusters, emulous to share
With you the roseal lightnings burning 'mid their hair; 65
Pass the crystalline sea, the Lampads seven:—
Look for me in the nurseries of Heaven.

1 *Tellurian galleon* the world, from Tellus, the earth. **5** *back warping* drawn back as a vessel is 'warped', i.e. moved to a different position by drawing on a rope fixed to a bollard. **9** *halcyon* kingfisher, thought to make a floating nest which calmed the sea; *auspice* omen, particularly associated with the flight of birds. **13** *Magian* priest or prophet from the East. **20** *The Assisian* St Francis of Assisi. **24** *sweet Sales* St Francis of Sales, whose writings are filled with his love for mankind. **26** The line refers to Francisco Petrarch, the fourteenth-century Italian poet who celebrated his love for Laura in a series of famous sonnets. **27** *Fletcher's fellow* Francis Beaumont, the Elizabethan poet and dramatist. **30** *ivies* symbol of Dionysus, god of inspiration. **33** *testating* inheritance-granting. **52** *Uranian sod* from Uranus, or Heaven. **56** *gonfalons* banners with streamers attached to them. **61** *globed complete* surrounded by a globe (of crystal light). **64** *cousined clusters* groups of poets awaiting the arrival of another. **66** *crystalline sea* the sea of crystal surrounding the Throne of God (see 'A Judgment in Heaven', 8); *Lampads seven* the seven lamps burning before the heavenly Throne (Apoc. 4 : 5). See last lines of Coleridge's 'Ne Plus Ultra'. The Lampads Seven / That watched the Throne of Heaven. **67** This line is inscribed on FT's tomb in St Mary's Catholic Cemetery, Kensal Green.

The Poppy

To Monica

ME, August 1891

The incident that inspired this poem took place during a holiday Thompson shared with the Meynell family at Friston in Norfolk in the summer of 1891. He preserved the poppy in accordance with Monica Meynell's wish, pressed and sewn into a notebook where it still survives (unnumbered notebook, M). In his notes Connolly gives Monica's age at the time of the poem as 15 years (TLC-*Poems*, p. 303). His calculation is based on the first line of a poem, 'Retrospect', which Monica wrote on Thompson and which Meynell printed in *Eyes of Youth*,

p. 81: 'You loved the child of fifteen years'. The line must refer to a different occasion, for Monica was born on 24 March 1880, making her 11 years old at the time of the Friston holiday in 1891—a much more likely age for the incident.

Summer set lip to earth's bosom bare,
And left the flushed print in a poppy there:
Like a yawn of fire from the grass it came,
And the fanning wind puffed it to flapping flame.

With burnt mouth red like a lion's it drank   5
The blood of the sun as he slaughtered sank,
And dipped its cup in the purpurate shine
When the eastern conduits ran with wine.

Till it grew lethargied with fierce bliss
And hot as a swinked gipsy is   10
And drowsed in sleepy savageries,
With mouth wide a-pout for a sultry kiss.

A child and man paced side by side,
Treading the skirts of the eventide;
But between the clasp of his hand and hers   15
Lay, felt not, twenty withered years.

She turned, with the rout of her dusk South hair,
And saw the sleeping poppy there;
And snatched and snapped it in swift child's whim,
With—'Keep it, long as you live!'—to him.   20

And his smile, as nymphs from their laving meres,
Trembled up from a bath of tears;
And joy, like a mew sea-rocked apart,
Tossed on the wave of his troubled heart.

For *he* saw what she did not see,   25
That—as kindled by its own fervency—
The verge shrivelled inward smoulderingly:

And suddenly twixt his hand and hers
He knew the twenty withered years—
No flower, but twenty shrivelled years.   30

'Was never such thing until this hour,'
Low to his heart he said; 'the flower

Of sleep brings wakening to me,
And of oblivion memory.'

'Was never this thing to me,' he said,   35
'Though with bruisèd poppies my feet are red!'
And again to his own heart very low:
'O child! I love, for I love and know;

'But you, who love nor know at all
The diverse chambers in Love's guest-hall,   40
Where some rise early, few sit long:
In how differing accents hear the throng
His great Pentecostal tongue;

'Who know not love from amity,
Nor my reported self from me;   45
A fair fit gift is this, meseems,
You give—this withering flower of dreams.

'O frankly fickle, and fickly true,
Do you know what the days will do to you?
To your Love and you what the days will do,   50
O frankly fickle, and fickly true?

'You have loved me, Fair, three lives—or days:
'Twill pass with the passing of my face.
But where *I* go, your face goes too,
To watch lest I play false to you.   55

'I am but, my sweet, your foster-lover,
Knowing well when certain years are over
You vanish from me to another;
Yet I know, and love, like the foster-mother.

'So, frankly fickle, and fickly true!   60
For my brief life-while I take from you
This token, fair and fit, meseems,
For me—this withering flower of dreams.'

                    *   *   *   *   *

The sleep-flower sways in the wheat its head,   65
Heavy with dreams, as that with bread:
The goodly grain and the sun-flushed sleeper
The reaper reaps, and Time the reaper.

I hang 'mid men my needless head,
And my fruit is dreams, as theirs is bread: 70
The goodly men and the sun-hazed sleeper
Time shall reap, but after the reaper
The world shall glean of me, me the sleeper!

Love! love! your flower of withered dream
In leavèd rhyme lies safe, I deem,   75
Sheltered and shut in a nook of rhyme,
From the reaper man, and his reaper Time.

Love! *I* fall into the claws of Time:
But lasts within a leavèd rhyme
All that the world of me esteems—   80
My withered dreams, my withered dreams.

27 *verge* the edge of the poppy's petals.

To Monica Thought Dying

According to a note by Meynell in his own copy of *Selected Poems* (for which see
the headnote to 'Before Her Portrait in Youth' on p. 4) these lines were written
when Monica was suffering from pleurisy contracted at the funeral of Cardinal
Manning in January 1892. The poem was first published in *Poems*.

You, O the piteous you!
Who all the long night through
Anticipatedly
Disclose yourself to me
Already in the ways   5
Beyond our human comfortable days
How can you deem what Death
Impitiably saith
To me, who listening wake
For your poor sake?   10
When a grown woman dies
You know we think unceasingly
What things she said, how sweet, how wise;
And these do make our misery.
But you were (you to me   15
The dead anticipatedly!)
You—eleven years, was't not, or so?—

Were just a child, you know;
   And so you never said
Things sweet immeditatably and wise   20
To interdict from closure my wet eyes:
   But foolish things, my dead, my dead!
   Little and laughable,
   Your age that fitted well.
And was it such things all unmemorable,   25
   Was it such things could make
Me sob all night for your implacable sake?

   Yet, as you said to me,
In pretty make-believe of revelry,
   So the night long said Death   30
   With his magniloquent breath;
   (And that remembered laughter
Which in our daily uses followed after,
Was all untuned to pity and to awe):
   'A cup of chocolate,   35
   One farthing is the rate,
   You drink it through a straw.'

   How could I know, how know
Those laughing words when drenched with sobbing so?
Another voice than yours, than yours, he hath!   40
   My dear, was't worth his breath,
His mighty utterance?—yet he saith, and saith!
This dreadful Death to his own dreadfulness
   Doth dreadful wrong,
This dreadful childish babble on his tongue!   45
That iron tongue made to speak sentences,
And wisdom insupportably complete,
Why should it only say the long night through,
   In mimicry of you,—
   'A cup of chocolate,   50
   One farthing is the rate,
You drink it through a straw, a straw, a straw!'
   Oh, of all sentences,
   Piercingly incomplete!
Why did you teach that fatal mouth to draw,   55
   Child, impermissible awe
   From your old trivialness?

Why have you done me this
Most unsustainable wrong,
And into Death's control   60
Betrayed the secret places of my soul?
Teaching him that his lips,
Uttering their native earthquake and eclipse,
Could never so avail
To rend from neck to hem the ultimate veil   65
Of this most desolate
Spirit, and leave it stripped and desecrate,—
Nay, never so have wrung
From eyes and speech weakness unmanned, unmeet;
As when his terrible dotage to repeat   70
Its little lesson learneth at your feet;
As when he sits among
His sepulchres, to play
With broken toys your hand hath cast away,
With derelict trinkets of the darling young.   75
Why have you taught—that he might so complete
His awful panoply
From your cast playthings—why,
This dreadful childish babble to his tongue,
Dreadful and sweet?   80

20 *immeditatably* When FT was preparing the poem for publication there was some objection from the Meynells to this word on account of its obscurity. In a letter to WM dated 14 September 1893, he wrote: 'As for "immeditatably" it is in all respects the only right word for the line; as regards the exact shade of meaning and feeling, and as regards the rhythmical movement it gives to the line. So it must absolutely and without any question stand' (*Letter*, p. 107). FT coined the word from an obscure use of 'immediate' signifying clarity and directness. **35–7** Here and elsewhere in the poem FT recalls Monica's childhood make-believe 'shop' where she 'sold' chocolate to members of the family.

Sister Songs
An Offering to Two Sisters
(1895)

These 'twin' poems were completed as a gift to the Meynells for Christmas, 1890. The first is addressed to the younger of the two sisters, Madeleine, who was known in the family as Sylvia, and the second to Monica, who was probably Thompson's favourite of the Meynell girls. But despite the dedication the concluding 'Inscription' makes it clear that this was an offering more appropriate for the parents.

When he left the poems at the Meynells' home in Palace Court, Thompson added the following note: 'I leave with this on the mantelpiece (in an exercise book) the poem of which I spoke. If intensity of labour could make it good, good it would be. One way or the other, it will be an effectual test. I have taken the advantage of a theme on which I have never yet written ill; if from it I have failed to draw poetry, then I may as well take down my sign' (*Letters*, p. 56). Thompson was very unwilling to publish them when pressed to do so following the success of *Poems*. He was much more aware of his tendency to excess by then and, having agreed at first to a private printing, submitted the whole to rigorous revision. The proof sheets survive (at BC) to show how extensive this was. The privately-printed edition was circulated early in 1895 under the title 'Songs Wing to Wing', which Thompson subsequently changed to 'Sister Songs' for the publication later that year. It is worth noting here the exclamation by Oscar Wilde reported by Meynell: 'Why cannot I write poetry like this? I have wanted all my life to write poetry like this' (WM Note). Thompson's original idea for the title was 'Amphicypellon: wrought and upbrimmed for two sisters'. He gave the explanation in a letter to Meynell written soon after the gift was made:

> Now, many years ago, when Schliemann's things from Troy were first exhibited at South Kensington [i.e. the Victoria and Albert Museum] I remember seeing among them a drinking-cup labelled 'perhaps the amphicypellon of Homer'. It was a boat-shaped cup of plain gold, open at the top and with a crescentic aperture at either extremity of the rim, through which the wine could either be poured or drunk . . . In a certain sense, therefore, it was a double cup. And it had also two handles, one at each end of its boat-shaped sides, so that it was a two-handled cup. You will see at once why I have applied the name to my double poem.
>
> (*Letters*, pp. 61–2)

In the same letter he translates the word itself as 'a cup on either side' with a handle on each end 'which Hephaestus, in Homer, bears round to the gods when he acts as cup-bearer by way of joke'.

The present text, reprinted here from the separate publication of 1895, retains Thompson's divisions between the stanzas which, in *Works* and since, have been altered and reduced. The proofs as well as most of the manuscripts survive: several passages deleted in the proofs were later printed in the Boston College journal *Stylus* in 1934 and are included in the endnotes.

Preface

This poem, though new in the sense of being now for the first time printed, was written some four years ago, about the same date as the *Hound of Heaven* in my former volume. One image in the *Proem* was an unconscious plagiarism from the beautiful image in Mr Patmore's *St Valentine's Day*:

> 'O baby Spring,
> That flutter'st sudden 'neath the breast of Earth,
> A month before the birth!'

Finding I could not disengage it without injury to the passage in which it is embedded, I have preferred to leave it, with this acknowledgment to a Poet rich enough to lend to the poor.

Francis Thompson 1895

The Proem

Shrewd winds and shrill—were these the speech of May?
    A ragged, slag-grey sky—invested so,
    Mary's spoilt nursling! wert thou wont to go?
      Or *thou*, Sun-god and song-god, say
Could singer pipe one tiniest linnet-lay,   5
    While Song did turn away his face from song?
      Or who could be
    In spirit or in body hale for long,—
      Old Æsculap's best Master!—lacking thee?
        At length, then, thou art here!   10
        On the earth's lethèd ear
    Thy voice of light rings out exultant, strong;
Through dreams she stirs and murmurs at that summons dear:
    From its red leash my heart strains tamelessly,
For Spring leaps in the womb of the young year!   15
      Nay, was it not brought forth before,
        And we waited, to behold it,
        Till the sun's hand should unfold it,

What the year's young bosom bore?
Even so; it came, nor knew we that it came,   20
    In the sun's eclipse.
    Yet the birds have plighted vows,
And from the branches pipe each other's name;
    Yet the season all the boughs
      Has kindled to the finger-tips,—   25
Mark yonder, how the long laburnum drips
Its jocund spilth of fire, its honey of wild flame!
Yea, and myself put on swift quickening,
And answer to the presence of a sudden Spring.
From cloud-zoned pinnacles of the secret spirit   30
    Song falls precipitant in dizzying streams;
And, like a mountain-hold when war-shouts stir it,
The mind's recessèd fastness casts to light
Its gleaming multitudes, that from every height
    Unfurl the flaming of a thousand dreams.   35
Now therefore, thou who bring'st the year to birth,
    Who guid'st the bare and dabbled feet of May;
Sweet stem to that rose Christ, who from the earth
Suck'st our poor prayers, conveying them to Him;
    Be aidant, tender Lady, to my lay!   40
    Of thy two maidens somewhat must I say,
Ere shadowy twilight lashes, drooping, dim
      Day's dreamy eyes from us;
      Ere eve has struck and furled
The beamy-textured tent transpicuous,   45
    Of webbèd cœrule wrought and woven calms,
      Whence has paced forth the lambent-footed sun.
And Thou disclose my flower of song upcurled,
      Who from Thy fair irradiant palms
    Scatterest all love and loveliness as alms;   50
      Yea, Holy One,
Who coin'st Thyself to beauty for the world!

Then, Spring's little children, your lauds do ye upraise
To Sylvia, O Sylvia, her sweet, feat ways!
    Your lovesome labours lay away,   55
    And trick you out in holiday,
      For syllabling to Sylvia;
And all you birds on branches, lave your mouths with May,
    To bear with me this burthen,
      For singing to Sylvia.   60

Part the First

I

The leaves dance, the leaves sing,
The leaves dance in the breath of the Spring.
    I bid them dance,
      I bid them sing,
        For the limpid glance   5
          Of my ladyling;
For the gift to the Spring of a dewier spring,
For God's good grace of this ladyling!
I know in the lane, by the hedgerow track,
    The long, broad grasses underneath   10
Are warted with rain like a toad's knobbed back;
      But here May weareth a rainless wreath.
In the new-sucked milk of the sun's bosom
Is dabbled the mouth of the daisy-blossom;
        The smouldering rosebud chars through its sheath;   15
The lily stirs her snowy limbs,
      Ere she swims
Naked up through her cloven green,
Like the wave-born Lady of Love Hellene;
And the scattered snowdrop exquisite   20
        Twinkles and gleams
    As if the showers of the sunny beams
Were splashed from the earth in drops of light.
        Everything
        That is child of Spring   25
    Casts its bud or blossoming
Upon the stream of my delight.

Their voices, that scents are, now let them upraise
To Sylvia, O Sylvia, her sweet, feat ways!
    Their lovely mother them array,   30
    And prank them out in holiday,
      For syllabling to Sylvia;
And all the birds on branches lave their mouths with May,
    To bear with me this burthen,
      For singing to Sylvia.   35

II

While thus I stood in mazes bound
    Of vernal sorcery,

I heard a dainty dubious sound,
   As of goodly melody;
Which first was faint as if in swound,   40
   Then burst so suddenly
In warring concord all around,
   That, whence this thing might be,
      To see
The very marrow longed in me!   45
   It seemed of air, it seemed of ground,
     And never any witchery
   Drawn from pipe, or reed, or string,
   Made such dulcet ravishing.
   'Twas like no earthly instrument,   50
   Yet had something of them all
   In its rise, and in its fall;
As if in one sweet consort there were blent
   Those archetypes celestial
Which our endeavouring instruments recall.   55
   So heavenly flutes made murmurous plain
   To heavenly viols, that again
   —Aching with music—wailed back pain;
   Regals release their notes, which rise
   Welling, like tears from heart to eyes;   60
   And the harp thrills with thronging sighs.
   Horns in mellow flattering
     Parley with the cithern-string:—
   Hark!—the floating, long-drawn note
     Woos the throbbing cithern-string!   65

Their pretty, pretty prating those citherns sure upraise
For homage unto Sylvia, her sweet, feat ways:
   Those flutes do flute their vowelled lay,
Their lovely languid language say,
     For lisping to Sylvia;   70
Those viols' lissom bowings break the heart of May,
   And harps harp their burthen,
     For singing to Sylvia.

III

Now at that music and that mirth
Rose, as 'twere, veils from earth;   75
   And I spied
   How beside

Bud, bell, bloom, an elf
Stood, or was the flower itself;
    'Mid radiant air   80
    All the fair
Frequence swayed in irised wavers.
Some against the gleaming rims
    Their bosoms prest
    Of the kingcups, to the brims   85
Filled with sun, and their white limbs
Bathèd in those golden lavers;
Some on the brown, glowing breast
Of that Indian maid, the pansy,
(Through its tenuous veils confest   90
Of swathing light), in a quaint fancy
Tied her knot of yellow favours;
Others dared open draw
Snapdragon's dreadful jaw:
Some, just sprung from out the soil,   95
Sleeked and shook their rumpled fans
    Dropt with sheen
    Of moony green;
Others, not yet extricate,
On their hands leaned their weight,   100
And writhed them free with mickle toil,
Still folded in their veiny vans:
And all with an unsought accord
Sang together from the sward;
Whence had come, and from sprites   105
Yet unseen, those delights,
As of tempered musics blent,
Which had given me such content.
For haply our best instrument,
Pipe or cithern, stopped or strung,   110
Mimics but some spirit tongue.

Their amiable voices, I bid them upraise
To Sylvia, O Sylvia, her sweet, feat ways;
    Their lovesome labours laid away
    To linger out this holiday   115
        In syllabling to Sylvia;
While all the birds on branches lave their mouths with May,
    To bear with me this burthen,
        For singing to Sylvia.

IV

Next I saw, wonder-whist,   120
How from the atmosphere a mist,
So it seemed, slow uprist;
And, looking from those elfin swarms,
   I was 'ware
   How the air   125
Was all populous with forms
Of the Hours, floating down,
Like Nereids through a watery town.
Some, with languors of waved arms,
Fluctuous oared their flexile way;   130
Some were borne half resupine
On the aërial hyaline,
Their fluid limbs and rare array
Flickering on the wind, as quivers
Trailing weed in running rivers;   135
And others, in far prospect seen,
Newly loosed on this terrene,
Shot in piercing swiftness came,
With hair a-stream like pale and goblin flame.
As crystàlline ice in water,   140
Lay in air each faint daughter;
Inseparate (or but separate dim)
Circumfused wind from wind-like vest,
Wind-like vest from wind-like limb.
But outward from each lucid breast,   145
When some passion left its haunt,
Radiate surge of colour came,
Diffusing blush-wise, palpitant,
Dying all the filmy frame.
With some sweet tenderness they would   150
Turn to an amber-clear and glossy gold;
Or a fine sorrow, lovely to behold,
Would sweep them as the sun and wind's joined flood
   Sweeps a greening-sapphire sea;
   Or they would glow enamouredly   155
Illustrious sanguine, like a grape of blood;
    Or with mantling poetry
Curd to the tincture which the opal hath,
Like rainbows thawing in a moonbeam bath.
So paled they, flushed they, swam they, sang melodiously.   160
    *

Their chanting, soon fading, let them, too, upraise
For homage unto Sylvia, her sweet, feat ways;
    Weave with suave float their wavèd way,
    And colours take of holiday,
        For syllabling to Sylvia;   165
And all the birds on branches lave their mouths with May,
        To bear with me this burthen,
        For singing to Sylvia.

                                    V

        Then, through these translucencies,
        As grew my senses clearer clear,   170
        Did I see, and did I hear,
        How under an elm's canopy
        Wheeled a flight of Dryades
        Murmuring measured melody.
        Gyre in gyre their treading was,   175
        Wheeling with an adverse flight,
        In twi-circle o'er the grass,
        These to left, and those to right;
            All the band
        Linkèd by each other's hand;   180
        Decked in raiment stainèd as
        The blue-helmèd aconite.
        And they advance with flutter, with grace,
            To the dance
        Moving on with a dainty pace,   185
        As blossoms mince it on river swells.
        Over their heads their cymbals shine,
        Round each ankle gleams a twine
            Of twinkling bells—
        Tune twirled golden from their cells.   190
        Every step was a tinkling sound,
        As they glanced in their dancing-ground.
        Clouds in cluster with such a sailing
        Float o'er the light of the wasting moon,
        As the cloud of their gliding veiling   195
        Swung in the sway of the dancing-tune.
        There was the clash of their cymbals clanging,
        Ringing of swinging bells clinging their feet;
        And the clang on wing it seemed a-hanging,
        Hovering round their dancing so fleet.—   200
        I stirred, I rustled more than meet;

Whereat they broke to the left and right,
With eddying robes like aconite
   Blue of helm;
And I beheld to the foot o' the elm.   205

They have not tripped those dances, betrayed to my gaze,
To glad the heart of Sylvia, beholding of their maze;
   Through barky walls have slid away,
   And tricked them in their holiday
     For other than for Sylvia;   210
While all the birds on branches lave their mouths with May,
   And bear with me this burthen,
     For singing to Sylvia.

VI

Where its umbrage was enrooted,
   Sat white-suited,   215
Sat green-amiced, and bare-footed,
   Spring amid her minstrelsy;
There she sat amid her ladies,
   Where the shade is
Sheen as Enna mead ere Hades'   220
   Gloom fell thwart Persephone.
Dewy buds were interstrown
Through her tresses hanging down,
   And her feet
   Were most sweet,   225
Tinged like sea-stars, rosied brown.
A throng of children like to flowers were sown
About the grass beside, or clomb her knee:
I looked who were that favoured company.
   And one there stood   230
   Against the beamy flood
Of sinking day, which, pouring its abundance,
Sublimed the illuminous and volute redundance
Of locks that, half dissolving, floated round her face;
   As see I might   235
Far off a lily-cluster poised in sun
   Dispread its gracile curls of light.
I knew what chosen child was there in place!
I knew there might no brows be, save of one,
With such Hesperian fulgence compassèd,   240
Which in her moving seemed to wheel about her head.
   *

O Spring's little children, more loud your lauds upraise,
For this is even Sylvia, with her sweet, feat ways!
   Your lovesome labours lay away,
    And prank you out in holiday,   245
      For syllabling to Sylvia;
And all you birds on branches, lave your mouths with May,
   To bear with me this burthen
      For singing to Sylvia!

VII

Spring, goddess, is it thou, desirèd long?   250
And art thou girded round with this young train?—
If ever I did do thee ease in song,
Now of thy grace let me one meed obtain,
    And list thou to one plain.
      Oh, keep still in thy train   255
After the years when others therefrom fade,
   This tiny, well-belovèd maid!
To whom the gate of my heart's fortalice,
    With all which in it is,
And the shy self who doth therein immew him   260
'Gainst what loud leaguerers battailously woo him,
    I, bribèd traitor to him,
    Set open for one kiss.

Then suffer, Spring, thy children, that lauds they should upraise
To Sylvia, this Sylvia, her sweet, feat ways;   265
   Their lovely labours lay away,
    And trick them out in holiday,
      For syllabling to Sylvia;
And that all birds on branches lave their mouths with May,
   To bear with me this burthen,   270
    For singing to Sylvia.

VIII

   A kiss? for a child's kiss?
   Aye, goddess, even for this.
   Once, bright Sylviola! in days not far,
Once—in that nightmare-time which still doth haunt   275
My dreams, a grim, unbidden visitant—
    Forlorn, and faint, and stark,
I had endured through watches of the dark

The abashless inquisition of each star,
Yea, was the outcast mark 280
    Of all those heavenly passers' scrutiny;
    Stood bound and helplessly
For time to shoot his barbèd minutes at me;
Suffered the trampling hoof of every hour
    In night's slow-wheelèd car; 285
    Until the tardy dawn dragged me at length
    From under those dread wheels, and, bled of strength,
    I waited the inevitable last.
    Then there came past
A child; like thee, a spring-flower; but a flower 290
Fallen from the budded coronal of Spring,
And through the city-streets blown withering.
She passed,—O brave, sad, lovingest, tender thing!—
And of her own scant pittance did she give,
    That I might eat and live: 295
Then fled, a swift and trackless fugitive.
    Therefore I kissed in thee
The heart of Childhood, so divine for me;
    And her, through what sore ways,
    And what unchildish days, 300
Borne from me now, as then, a trackless fugitive.
    Therefore I kissed in thee
    Her, child! and innocency,
And spring, and all things that have gone from me,
    And that shall never be; 305
All vanished hopes, and all most hopeless bliss,
    Came with thee to my kiss.
And ah! so long myself had strayed afar
From child, and woman, and the boon earth's green,
And all wherewith life's face is fair beseen; 310
    Journeying its journey bare
Five suns, except of the all-kissing sun
    Unkissed of one;
    Almost I had forgot
    The healing harms, 315
And whitest witchery, a-lurk in that
Authentic cestus of two girdling arms:
    And I remembered not
  The subtle sanctities which dart
From childish lips' unvalued precious brush, 320

Nor how it makes the sudden lilies push
   Between the loosening fibres of the heart.
      Then, that thy little kiss
      Should be to me all this,
Let workaday wisdom blink sage lids thereat;   325
Which towers a flight three hedgerows high, poor bat!
   And straightway charts me out the empyreal air.
Its chart I wing not by, its canon of worth
Scorn not, nor reck though mine should breed it mirth:
And howso thou and I may be disjoint,   330
Yet still my falcon spirit makes her point
      Over the covert where
Thou, sweetest quarry, hast put in from her!

(Soul, hush these sad numbers, too sad to upraise
In hymning bright Sylvia, unlearn'd in such ways!   335
   Our mournful moods lay we away,
   And prank our thoughts in holiday,
      For syllabling to Sylvia;
When all the birds on branches lave their mouths with May,
   To bear with us this burthen,   340
      For singing to Sylvia!)

IX

Then thus Spring, bounteous lady, made reply:
'O lover of me and all my progeny,
      For grace to you   345
I take her ever to my retinue.
Over thy form, dear child, alas! my art
Cannot prevail; but mine immortalising
      Touch I lay upon thy heart.
      Thy soul's fair shape
In my unfading mantle's green I drape,   350
And thy white mind shall rest by my devising
   A Gideon-fleece amid life's dusty drouth.
If Even burst yon globèd yellow grape
(Which is the sun to mortals' sealèd sight)
      Against her stainèd mouth;   355
      Or if white-handed light
Draw thee yet dripping from the quiet pools,
      Still lucencies and cools,
Of sleep, which all night mirror constellate dreams;

Like to the sign which led the Israelite,   360
    Thy soul, through day or dark,
A visible brightness on the chosen ark
    Of thy sweet body and pure,
      Shall it assure,
With auspice large and tutelary gleams,   365
Appointed solemn courts, and covenanted streams.'

Cease, Spring's little children, now cease your lauds to raise
That dream is past, and Sylvia, with her sweet, feat ways.
    Our lovèd labour, laid away,
    Is smoothly ended; said our say,   370
      Our syllabling to Sylvia.
Make sweet, you birds on branches! make sweet your mouths with May!
    But borne is this burthen,
      Sung unto Sylvia.

Part the Second

And now, thou elder nursling of the nest;
    Ere all the intertangled west
      Be one magnificence
Of multitudinous blossoms that o'errun
The flaming brazen bowl o' the burnished sun   5
      Which they do flower from,
How shall I 'stablish *thy* memorial?
Nay, how or with what countenance shall I come
    To plead in my defence
    For loving thee at all?   10
I who can scarcely speak my fellows' speech,
Love their love, or mine own love to them teach;
A bastard barred from their inheritance,
    Who seem, in this dim shape's uneasy nook,
Some sun-flower's spirit which by luckless chance   15
Has mournfully its tenement mistook;
When it were better in its right abode,
Heartless and happy lackeying its god.
How com'st thou, little tender thing of white,
Whose very touch full scantly me beseems,   20
How com'st thou resting on my vaporous dreams,
    Kindling a wraith there of earth's vernal green?

Even so as I have seen,
In night's aërial sea with no wind blust'rous,
A ribbèd tract of cloudy malachite   25
    Curve a shored crescent wide;
And on its slope marge shelving to the night
   The stranded moon lay quivering like a lustrous
    Medusa newly washed up from the tide,
Lay in an oozy pool of its own deliquious light.   30

Yet hear how my excuses may prevail,
  Nor, tender white orb, be thou opposite!
Life and life's beauty only hold their revels
In the abysmal ocean's luminous levels.
There, like the phantasms of a poet pale,   35
    The exquisite marvels sail:
Clarified silver; green and azures frail
As if the colours sighed themselves away,
And blent in supersubtile interplay
  As if they swooned into each other's arms;   40
    Repured vermilion
    Like ear-tips 'gainst the sun;
And beings that, under night's swart pinion,
Make every wave upon the harbour-bars
    A beaten yolk of stars.   45
But where day's glance turns baffled from the deeps,
    Die out those lovely swarms;
And in the immense profound no creature glides or creeps.

Love and love's beauty only hold their revels
In life's familiar, penetrable levels: 50
    What of its ocean-floor?
    I dwell there evermore.
    From almost earliest youth
    I raised the lids o' the truth,
And forced her bend on me her shrinking sight;   55
Ever I knew me Beauty's eremite,
  In antre of this lowly body set,
    Girt with a thirsty solitude of soul.
     Natheless I not forget
How I have, even as the anchorite,   60
  I too, imperishing essences that console.
Under my ruined passions, fallen and sere,

The wild dreams stir like little radiant girls,
Whom in the moulted plumage of the year
    Their comrades sweet have buried to the curls.   65
Yet, though their dedicated amorist,
How often do I bid my visions hist,
    Deaf to them, pleading all their piteous fills;
Who weep, as weep the maidens of the mist
    Clinging the necks of the unheeding hills: 70
And their tears wash them lovelier than before,
That from grief's self our sad delight grows more.
Fair are the soul's uncrispèd calms, indeed,
    Endiapered with many a spiritual form
        Of blosmy-tinctured weed;   75
But scarce itself is conscious of the store
    Suckled by it, and only after storm
Casts up its loosened thoughts upon the shore.
    To this end my deeps are stirred;
    And I deem well why life unshared   80
Was ordainèd me of yore.
In pairing-time, we know, the bird
Kindles to its deepmost splendour,
    And the tender
    Voice is tenderest in its throat: 85
Were its love, for ever nigh it,
    Never by it,
    It might keep a vernal note,
The crocean and amethystine
    In their pristine   90
    Lustre linger on its coat.
Therefore must my song-bower lone be,
    That my tone be
    Fresh with dewy pain alway;
She, who scorns my dearest care ta'en,   95
    An uncertain
    Shadow of the sprite of May.
And is my song sweet, as they say?
'Tis sweet for one whose voice has no reply,
    Save silence's sad cry: 100
And are its plumes a burning bright array?
They burn for an unincarnated eye.
A bubble, charioteered by the inward breath
    Which, ardorous for its own invisible lure,

Urges me glittering to aërial death,   105
    I am rapt towards that bodiless paramour;
Blindly the uncomprehended tyranny
      Obeying of my heart's impetuous might.
          The earth and all its planetary kin,
Starry buds tangled in the whirling hair   110
That flames round the Phoebean wassailer,
      Speed no more ignorant, more predestined flight,
          Than I, *her* viewless tresses netted in.
As some most beautiful one, with lovely taunting,
Her eyes of guileless guile o'ercanopies,   115
         Does her hid visage bow,
And miserly your covetous gaze allow,
         By inchmeal, coy degrees,
         Saying—'Can you see me now?'
Yet from the mouth's reflex you guess the wanting   120
        Smile of the coming eyes
In all their upturned grievous witcheries,
        Before that sunbreak rise;
And each still hidden feature view within
Your mind, as eager scrutinies detail   125
The moon's young rondure through the shamefast veil
        Drawn to her gleaming chin:
         After this wise,
From the enticing smile of earth and skies
I dream my unknown Fair's refusèd gaze;   130
And guessingly her love's close traits devise
      Which she with subtle coquetries
Through little human glimpses slow displays,
        Cozening my mateless days
        By sick, intolerable delays.   135
And so I keep mine uncompanioned ways;
And so my touch, to golden poesies
Turning love's bread, is bought at hunger's price.
So,—in the inextinguishable wars
Which roll song's Orient on the sullen night   140
Whose ragged banners in their own despite
Take on the tinges of the hated light,—
So Sultan Phœbus has his Janizars.

But if mine unappeasèd cicatrices
        Might get them lawful ease;   145

Were any gentle passion hallowed me,
 Who must none other breath of passion feel
 Save such as winnows to the fledgèd heel
  The tremulous Paradisal plumages;
  The conscious sacramental trees   150
   Which ever be
   Shaken celestially,
Consentient with enamoured wings, might know my love for thee.

Yet is there more, whereat none guesseth, love!
 Upon the ending of my deadly night   155
(Whereof thou hast not the surmise, and slight
Is all that any mortal knows thereof),
 Thou wert to me that earnest of day's light,
When, like the back of a gold-mailèd saurian
 Heaving its slow length from Nilotic slime 160
The first long gleaming fissure runs Aurorian
 Athwart the yet dun firmament of prime.
Stretched on the margin of the cruel sea
  Whence they had rescued me,
 With faint and painful pulses was I lying; 165
   Not yet discerning well
If I had 'scaped, or were an icicle,
  Whose thawing is its dying.
Like one who sweats before a despot's gate,
Summoned by some presaging scroll of fate, 170
And knows not whether kiss or dagger wait;
And all so sickened is his countenance,
The courtiers buzz, 'Lo, doomed!' and look at him askance:
  At Fate's dread portal then
  Even so stood I, I ken,   175
Even so stood I, between a joy and fear,
And said to mine own heart, 'Now, if the end be here!'

  They say, Earth's beauty seems completest
   To them that on their death-beds rest;
 Gentle lady! she smiles sweetest   180
   Just ere she clasp us to her breast.
And I,—now *my* Earth's countenance grew bright,
Did she but smile me towards that nuptual-night?
But, whileas on such dubious bed I lay, 185
   One unforgotten day,

As a sick child waking sees
    Wide-eyed daisies
Gazing on it from its hand,
Slipped there for its dear amazes;
So between thy father's knees   190
    I saw *thee* stand,
    And through my hazes
Of pain and fear thine eyes' young wonder shone.
Then, as flies scatter from a carrion,
  Or rooks in spreading gyres like broken smoke   195
  Wheel, when some sound their quietude has broke,
Fled, at thy countenance all that doubting spawn:
    The heart which I had questioned spoke,
A cry impetuous from its depths was drawn,—
'I take the omen of this face of dawn!'   200
And with the omen to my heart cam'st thou.
    Even with a spray of tears
That one light draft was fixed there for the years.

    And now?—
The hours I tread ooze memories of thee, Sweet!   205
    Beneath my casual feet.
    With rainfall as the lea,
    The day is drenched with thee;
  In little exquisite surprises
Bubbling deliciousness of thee arises   210
    From sudden places,
  Under the common traces
Of my most lethargied and customed paces.

    As an Arab journeyeth
    Through a sand of Ayaman,   215
Lean Thirst, lolling its cracked tongue,
Lagging by his side along;
And a rusty-wingèd Death
    Grating its low flight before,
Casting ribbèd shadows o'er   220
The blank desert, blank and tan:
He lifts by hap toward where the morning's roots are
    His weary stare,—
  Sees, although they plashless mutes are,
    Set in a silver air   225

Fountains of gelid shoots are,
     Making the daylight fairest fair;
  Sees the palm and tamarind
Tangle the tresses of a phantom wind;—
A sight like innocence when one has sinned!   230
A green and maiden freshness smiling there,
     While with unblinking glare
The tawny-hided desert crouches watching her.

     'Tis a vision:
    Yet the greeneries Elysian   235
    He has known in tracts afar;
    Thus the enamouring fountains flow,
    Those the very palms that grow,
By rare-gummed Sava, or Herbalimar.—

    Such a watered dream has tarried   240
    Trembling on my desert arid;
     Even so
    Its lovely gleamings
     Seemings show
    Of things not seemings;   245
     And I gaze,
  Knowing that, beyond my ways,
     Verily
All these *are*, for these are she.
Eve no gentlier lays her cooling cheek   250
On the burning brow of the sick earth,
  Sick with death, and sick with birth,
Aeon to aeon, in secular fever twirled,
  Than thy shadow soothes this weak
  And distempered being of mine.   255
In all I work, my hand includeth thine;
    Thou rushest down in every stream
Whose passion frets my spirit's deepening gorge;
Unhood'st mine eyas-heart, and fliest my dream;
    Thou swing'st the hammers of my forge;   260
As the innocent moon, that nothing does but shine,
Moves all the labouring surges of the world.
  Pierce where thou wilt the springing thought in me,
And there thy pictured countenance lies enfurled,
  As in the cut fern lies the imaged tree.   265

This poor song that sings of thee,
This fragile song, is but a curled
Shell outgathered from thy sea,
And murmurous still of its nativity.
Princess of Smiles!   270
Sorceress of most unlawful-lawful wiles!
Cunning pit for gazers' senses,
Overstrewn with innocences!
Purities gleam white like statues
In the fair lakes of thine eyes,   275
And I watch the sparkles that use
There to rise,
Knowing these
Are bubbles from the calyces
Of the lovely thoughts that breathe   280
Paving, like water-flowers, thy spirit's floor beneath.

O thou most dear!
Who art thy sex's complex harmony
God-set more facilely;
To thee may love draw near   285
Without one blame or fear,
Unchidden save by his humility:
Thou Perseus' Shield! wherein I view secure
The mirrored Woman's fateful-fair allure!
Whom Heaven still leaves a twofold dignity,   290
As girlhood gentle, and as boyhood free;
With whom no most diaphanous webs enwind
The barèd limbs of the rebukeless mind.
Wild Dryad! all unconscious of thy tree,
With which indissolubly   295
The tyrannous time shall one day make thee whole;
Whose frank arms pass unfretted through its bole:
Who wear'st thy femineity
Light as entrailèd blossoms, that shalt find
It erelong silver shackles unto thee.   300
Thou whose young sex is yet within thy soul;—
As hoarded in the vine
Hang the gold skins of undelirious wine,
As air sleeps, till it toss its limbs in breeze:—
In whom the mystery which lures and sunders,   305
Grapples and thrusts apart; endears, estranges;

—The dragon to its own Hesperides—
   Is gated under slow-revolving changes,
Manifold doors of heavy-hingèd years.
     So once, ere Heaven's eyes were filled with wonders   310
       To see Laughter rise from Tears,
        Lay in beauty not yet mighty,
         Conchèd in translucencies,
        The antenatal Aphrodite,
Caved magically under magic seas;   315
Caved dreamlessly beneath the dreamful seas.

     'Whose sex is in thy soul!'
       What think we of thy soul?
     Which has no parts, and cannot grow,
      Unfurled not from an embryo;   320
Born of full stature, lineal to control;
   And yet a pigmy's yoke must undergo.
Yet must keep pace and tarry, patient, kind,
With its unwilling scholar, the dull, tardy mind;
Must be obsequious to the body's powers,   325
Whose low hands mete its paths, set ope and close its ways;
     Must do obeisance to the days,
And wait the little pleasure of the hours;
      Yea, ripe for kingship, yet must be
Captive in statuted minority!   330
So is all power fulfilled, as soul in thee.
So still the ruler by the ruled takes rule,
And wisdom weaves itself i' the loom o' the fool.
The splendent sun no splendour can display,
Till on gross things he dash his broken ray,   335
From cloud and tree and flower re-tossed in prismy spray.
Did not obstruction's vessel hem it in,
Force were not force, would spill itself in vain;
We know the Titan by his champèd chain.
Stay is heat's cradle, it is rocked therein,   340
And by check's hand is burnished into light;
If hate were none, would love burn lowlier bright?
God's Fair were guessed scarce but for opposite sin;
Yea, and His Mercy, I do think it well,
Is flashed back from the brazen gates of Hell.   345
     The heavens decree
All power fulfill itself as soul in thee.

For supreme Spirit subject was to clay,
    And Law from its own servants learned a law,
And Light besought a lamp unto its way,   350
      And Awe was reined in awe,
    At one small house of Nazareth;
      And Golgotha
Saw Breath to breathlessness resign its breath,
And Life do homage for its crown to death.   355

So is all power, as soul in thee increased!
    But, knowing this, in knowledge's despite
    I fret against the law severe that stains
      Thy spirit with eclipse;
  When—as a nymph's carven head sweet water drips   360
    For others oozing so the cool delight
    Which cannot steep her stiffened mouth of stone—
Thy nescient lips repeat maternal strains.
      Memnonian lips!
Smitten with singing from thy mother's east,   365
    And murmurous with music not their own:
    Nay, the lips flexile, while the mind alone
      A passionless statue stands.
      Oh, pardon, innocent one!
      Pardon at thine unconscious hands!   370
'Murmurous with music not their own,' I say?
And in that saying how do I missay,
    When from the common sands
Of poorest common speech of common day
Thine accents sift the golden musics out!   375
    And ah, we poets, I misdoubt,
    Are little more than thou!
We speak a lesson taught we know not how,
    And what it is that from us flows
The hearer better than the utterer knows.   380

    Thou canst foreshape thy word;
    The poet is not lord
    Of the next syllable may come
    With the returning pendulum;
    And what he plans to-day in song,   385
Tomorrow sings it in another tongue.
    Where the last leaf fell from his bough,

He knows not if a leaf shall grow,
Where he sows he doth not reap,
He reapeth where he did not sow;   390
He sleeps, and dreams forsake his sleep
To meet him on his waking way.
Vision will mate him not by law and vow:
    Disguised in life's most hodden-grey,
By the most beaten road of everyday   395
She waits him, unsuspected and unknown.
    The hardest pang whereon
He lays his mutinous head may be a Jacob's stone.
In the most iron crag his foot can tread
    A Dream may strew her bed,   400
    And suddenly his limbs entwine,
And draw him down through rock as sea-nymphs might
    through brine.
But, unlike those feigned temptress-ladies who
In guerdon of a night the lover slew,
When the embrace has failed, the rapture fled,   405
Not he, not he, the wild sweet witch is dead!
    And, though he cherisheth
The babe most strangely born from out her death,
Some tender trick of her it hath, maybe,—
    It is not she!   410

Yet, even as the air is rumorous of fray
  Before the first shafts of the sun's onslaught
    From gloom's black harness splinter,
    And Summer move on Winter
With the trumpet of the March, and the pennon of the May; 415
    As gesture outstrips thought;
So, haply, toyer with ethereal strings!
Are thy blind repetitions of high things
The murmurous gnats whose aimless hoverings
    Reveal song's summer in the air;   420
The outstretched hand, which cannot thought declare,
    Yet is thought's harbinger.
These strains the way for thine own strains prepare;
We feel the music moist upon this breeze,
And hope the congregating poesies.   425
    Sundered yet by thee from us
    Wait, with wild eyes luminous,

All thy wingèd things that are to be;
They flit against thee, Gate of Ivory!
They clamour on the portress Destiny,—   430
'Set her wide, so we may issue through!
Our vans are quick for that they have to do!'
            Suffer still your young desire;
Your plumes but bicker at the tips with fire,
Tarry their kindling; they will beat the higher.   435
And thou, bright girl, not long shalt thou repeat
Idly the music from thy mother caught;
            Not vainly has she wrought,
Not vainly from the cloudward-jetting turret
Of her aërial mind, for thy weak feet,   440
Let down the silken ladder of her thought.
    She bare thee with a double pain,
        Of the body and the spirit;
    Thou thy fleshly weeds hast ta'en,
            Thy diviner weeds inherit!   445
The precious streams which through thy young lips roll
Shall leave their lovely delta in thy soul:
    Where sprites of so essential kind
            Set their paces,
    Surely they shall leave behind   450
            The green traces
    Of their sportance in the mind,
    And thou shalt, ere we well may know it,
        Turn that daintiness, a poet,—
            Elfin-ring   455
    Where sweet fancies foot and sing.
        So it may be, so it *shall* be,—
        Oh, take the prophecy from me!
What if the old fastidious sculptor, Time,
        This crescent marvel of his hands   460
        Carveth all too painfully,
And I who prophesy shall never see?
What if the niche of its predestined rhyme,
        Its aching niche, too long expectant stands?
        Yet shall he after sore delays   465
        On some exultant day of days
        The white enshrouding childhood raise
From thy fair spirit, finished for our gaze;
        While we (but 'mongst that happy 'we'

       The prophet cannot be!)   470
While we behold with no astonishments,
With that serene fulfilment of delight
         Wherewith we view the sight
      When the stars pitch the golden tents
Of their high campment on the plains of night.   475
Why should amazement be our satellite?
        What wonder in such things?
If angels have hereditary wings,
     If not by Salic law is handed down
           The poet's crown,   480
      To thee, born in the purple of the throne,
        The laurel must belong:
        Thou, in thy mother's right
Descendant of Castalian-chrismed kings—
        O Princess of the Blood of Song!   485

Peace; too impetuously have I been winging
    Toward vaporous heights which beckon and beguile.
      I sink back, saddened to my inmost mind;
Even as I list a-dream that mother singing
    The poesy of sweet tone, and sadden, while   490
       Her voice is cast in troubled wake behind
       The keel of her keen spirit. Thou art enshrined
In a too primal innocence for this eye—
Intent on such untempered radiancy—
Not to be pained; my clay can scarce endure   495
Ungrieved the effluence near of essences so pure.
      Therefore, little, tender maiden,
      Never be thou overshaden
      With a mind whose canopy
      Would shut out the sky from thee;   500
Whose tangled branches intercept Heaven's light:
      I will not feed my unpastured heart
      On thee, green pleasaunce as thou art,
To lessen by one flower thy happy daisies white.
The water-rat is earth-hued like the runlet   505
      Whereon he swims; and how in me should lurk
Thoughts apt to neighbour thine, thou creature sunlit?
      If through long fret and irk
Thine eyes within their browed recesses were
Worn caves where thought lay couchant in its lair;   510

Wert thou a spark among dank leaves, ah, ruth!
With age in all thy veins, while all thy heart was youth;
   Our contact might run smooth.
But life's Eoan dews still moist thy ringèd hair;
    Dian's chill finger-tips   515
Thaw if at night they happen on thy lips;
The flying fringes of the sun's cloak frush
The fragile leaves which on those warm lips blush;
    And joy only lurks retirèd
    In the dim gloaming of thine irid.   520
Then since my love drags this poor shadow, me,
And one without the other may not be,
    From both I guard thee free.
    It still is much, yes, it is much,
Only—my dream!—to love my love of thee;   525
    And it is much, yes, it is much,
In hands which thou hast touched to feel thy touch,
In voices which have mingled with thine own
    To hear a double tone.
As anguish, for supreme expression prest,   530
   Borrows its saddest tongue from jest,
   Thou hast of absence so create
   A presence more importunate;
   And thy voice pleads its sweetest suit
    When it is mute.   535
   I thank the once accursèd star
    Which did me teach
To make of Silence my familiar,
Who hath the rich reversion of thy speech,
Since the most charming sounds thy thoughts can wear,   540
Cast off, fall to that pale attendant's share;
    And thank the gift which made my mind
A shadow-world, wherethrough the shadows wind
Of all the loved and lovely of my kind.

    Like a maiden Saxon, folden,   545
    As she flits, in moon-drenched mist;
    Whose curls streaming flaxen-golden,
    By the misted moonbeams kist,
    Dispread their filmy floating silk
    Like honey steeped in milk: 550
    So, vague goldenness remote,

Through my thoughts I watch thee float.
When the snake summer casts her blazoned skin
We find it at the turn of autumn's path,
And think it summer that rewinded hath,   555
        Joying therein;
And this enamouring slough of thee, mine elf,
        I take it for thyself;
Content. Content? Yea, title it content.
The very loves that belt thee must prevent   560
My love, I know, with their legitimacy:
As the metallic vapours, that are swept
Athwart the sun, in his light intercept
        The very hues
Which *their* conflagrant elements effuse.   565
        But, my love, my heart, my fair,
        That only I should see thee rare,
Or tent to the hid core thy rarity,—
        This were a mournfulness more piercing far
        Than that those other loves my own must bar,   570
Or thine for others leave thee none for me.

        But on a day whereof I think,
        One shall dip his hand to drink
        In that still water of thy soul,
        And its imaged tremors race   575
        Over thy joy-troubled face,
        As the intervolved reflections roll
        From a shaken fountain's brink,
        With swift light wrinkling its alcove.
        From the hovering wing of Love   580
The warm stain shall flit roseal on thy cheek.
        Then, sweet blushet! whenas he,
The destined paramount of thy universe,
    Who has no worlds to sigh for, ruling thee,
    Ascends his vermeil throne of empery,   585
        One grace alone I seek.
Oh! may this treasure-galleon of my verse,
Fraught with its golden passion, oared with cadent rhyme,
Set with a towering press of fantasies,
        Drop safely down the time,   590
    Leaving mine islèd self behind it far
Soon to be sunken in the abysm of seas,

(As down the years the splendour voyages
  From some long ruined and night-submergèd star),
And in thy subject sovereign's havening heart   595
Anchor the freightage of its virgin ore;
    Adding its wasteful more
To his own overflowing treasury.
So through his river mine shall reach thy sea,
      Bearing its confluent part;   600
      In his pulse mine shall thrill;
And the quick heart shall quicken from the heart that's still.

Ah! help, my Dæmon that hast served me well!
  Not at this last, oh do not me disgrace!
  I faint, I sicken, darkens all my sight,   605
  As, poised upon this unprevisioned height,
    I lift into its place
The utmost aery traceried pinnacle.
So; it is builded, the high tenement,
    —God grant—to mine intent!   610
Most like a palace of the Occident,
    Up-thrusting, toppling maze on maze,
      Its mounded blaze,
And washèd by the sunset's rosy waves,
Whose sea drinks rarer hue from those rare walls it laves. 615
      Yet wail, my spirits, wail!
So few therein to enter shall prevail!
Scarce fewer could win way, if their desire
A dragon baulked, with involuted spire,
And writhen snout spattered with yeasty fire.   620
For at the elfin portal hangs a horn
    Which none can wind aright
    Save the appointed knight
Whose lids the fay-wings brushed when he was born.
      All others stray forlorn,   625
Or glimpsing, through the blazoned windows scrolled,
Receding labyrinths lessening tortuously
    In half obscurity;
With mystic images, inhuman, cold,
      That flameless torches hold.   630
      But who can wind that horn of might
(The horn of dead Heliades) aright,—
      Straight
Open for him shall roll the conscious gate;

And light leap up from all the torches there, 635
And life leap up in every torchbearer,
And the stone faces kindle in the glow,
And into the blank eyes the irids grow,
And through the dawning irids ambushed meanings show.
    Illumined this wise on, 640
He threads securely the far intricacies,
  With brede from Heaven's wrought vesture over-strewn;
Swift Tellus' purfled tunic, girt upon
With the blown chlamys of her fluttering seas;
    And the freaked kirtle of the pearlèd moon; 645
Until he gain the structure's core, where stands—
    A toil of magic hands—
The unbodied spirit of the sorcerer,
      Most strangely rare,
  As is a vision remembered in the noon; 650
Unbodied, yet to mortal seeing clear,
Like sighs exhaled in eager atmosphere.
From human haps and mutabilities
It rests exempt, beneath the edifice
    To which itself gave rise; 655
Sustaining centre to the bubble of stone
Which, breathed from it, exists by it alone.
Yea, ere Saturnian earth her child consumes,
    And I lie down with outworn ossuaries,
Ere death's grim tongue anticipates the tomb's 660
    Siste viator, in this storied urn
      My living heart is laid to throb and burn,
  Till end be ended, and till ceasing cease.

And thou by whom this strain hath parentage;
  Wantoner between the yet untreacherous claws 665
  Of newly-whelped existence! ere he pause,
What gift to thee can yield the archimage?
  For coming seasons' frets
  What aids, what amulets,
  What softenings, or what brightenings? 670
As Thunder writhes the lash of his long lightnings
  About the growling heads of the brute main
  Foaming at mouth, until it wallow again
  In the scooped oozes of its bed of pain;
So all the gnashing jaws, the leaping heads 675
Of hungry menaces, and of ravening dreads,

    Of pangs
Twitch-lipped, with quivering nostrils and immitigate fangs,
 I scourge beneath the torment of my charms
That their relentless nature fear to work thee harms.   680
And as yon Apollonian harp-player,
   Yon wandering psalterist of the sky,
With flickering strings which scatter melody,
The silver-stolèd damsels of the sea,
   Or lake, or fount, or stream,   685
 Enchants from their ancestral heaven of waters
To Naiad it through the unfrothing air;
  My song enchants so out of undulous dream
 The glimmering shapes of its dim-tressèd daughters,
And missions each to be thy minister.   690
   Saying; 'O ye,
The organ-stops of being's harmony;
The blushes on existence's pale face,
  Lending it sudden grace;
Without whom we should but guess Heaven's worth 695
By blank negations of this sordid earth,
  (So haply to the blind may light
Be but gloom's undetermined opposite;)
Ye who are thus as the refracting air
Whereby we see Heaven's sun before it rise   700
Above the dull line of our mortal skies;
As breathing on the strainèd ear that sighs
From comrades viewless unto strainèd eyes,
Soothing our terrors in the lampless night;
Ye who can make this world where all is deeming, 705
What world ye list, being arbiters of seeming;
Attend upon her ways, benignant powers!
Unroll ye life a carpet for her feet,
And cast ye down before them blossomy hours,
Until her going shall be clogged with sweet!   710
All dear emotions whose new-bathèd hair
Still streaming from the soul, in love's warm air
Smokes with a mist of tender fantasies;
   All these,
And all the heart's wild growths which, swiftly bright, 715
Spring up the crimson agarics of a night,
No pain in withering, yet a joy arisen;
And all thin shapes more exquisitely rare,
   More subtly fair,

Than these weak ministering words have spell to prison   720
Within the magic circle of this rhyme;
And all the fays who in our creedless clime
            Have sadly ceased
Bearing to other children childhood's proper feast;
Whose robes are fluent crystal, crocus-hued,   725
    Whose wings are wind a-fire, whose mantles wrought
        From spray that falling rainbows shake.
        These, ye familiars to my wizard thought,
        Make things of journal custom unto her;
            With lucent feet imbrued,   730
        If young Day tread, a glorious vintager,
The wine-press of the purple-foamèd east;
Or round the nodding sun, flush-faced and sunken,
            His wild bacchantes drunken
Reel, with rent woofs a-flaunt, their westering rout.'   735
—But lo! at length the day is lingered out,
At length my Ariel lays his viol by;
We sing no more to thee, child, he and I;
        The day is lingered out:
            In slow wreaths folden   740
    .   Around yon censer, spherèd, golden,
        Vague Vesper's fumes aspire;
        And glimmering to eclipse
        The long laburnum drips
Its honey of wild flame, its jocund spilth of fire.   745

Now pass your ways, fair bird, and pass your ways,
        If you will;
    I have you through the days!
    And flit or hold you still,
    And perch you where you list   750
        On what wrist,—
    You are mine through the times!
I have caught you fast for ever in a tangle of sweet rhymes.
    And in your young maiden morn,
        You may scorn   755
    But you must be
    Bound and sociate unto me;
With this thread from out the tomb my dead hand shall tether thee!

Go, sister-songs, to that sweet sister-pair
For whom I have your frail limbs fashionèd,   760
   And framèd feateously;—
For whom I have your frail limbs fashionèd
With how great shamefastness and how great dread,
Knowing you frail, but not if you be fair,
   Though framèd feateously;   765
   Go unto them from me.
Go from my shadow to their sunshine sight,
   Made for all sights' delight;
Go like twin swans that oar the surgy storms
To bate with pennoned snows in candent air: 770
   Nigh with abasèd head,
Yourselves linked sisterly, that sister-pair,
   And go in presence there;
Saying—'Your young eyes cannot see our forms,
Nor read the yearning of our looks aright;   775
But time shall trail the veilings from our hair,
And cleanse your seeing with his euphrasy,
(Yea, even your bright seeing make more bright,
   Which is all sights' delight),
And ye shall know us for what things we be.   780

'Whilom, within a poet's calyxed heart,
A dewy love we trembled all apart;
   Whence it took rise
   Beneath your radiant eyes,
Which misted it to music. We must long,   785
A floating haze of silver subtile song,
   Await love-laden
   Above each maiden
The appointed hour that o'er the hearts of you—
   As vapours in dew   790
   Unweave, whence they were wove,—
Shall turn our loosening musics back to love.'

Inscription

When the last stir of bubbling melodies
Broke as my chants sank underneath the wave
Of dulcitude, but sank again to rise
Where man's embaying mind those waters lave,

(For music hath its Oceanides 5
Flexuously floating through their parent seas,
　　And such are these),
I saw a vision—or may it be
The effluence of a dear desired reality?
　　I saw two spirits high,— 10
Two spirits, dim within the silver smoke
　　Which is for ever woke
By snowing lights of fountained Poesy.
Two shapes they were, familiar as love;
　　They were those souls, whereof 15
One twines from finest gracious daily things,
Strong, constant, noticeless, as are heart-strings,
The golden cage wherein this song-bird sings;
And the other's sun gives hue to all my flowers,
Which else pale flowers of Tartarus would grow, 20
Where ghosts watch ghosts of blooms in ghostly bowers;—
　　For we do know
The hidden player by his harmonies,
And by my thoughts I know what still hands thrill the keys.

And to these twain—as from the mind's abysses 25
All thoughts draw toward the awakening heart's sweet kisses,
With proffer of their wreathen fantasies,—
　　Even so to these
I saw how many brought their garlands fair,
Whether of song, or simple love, they were,— 30
Of simple love, that makes best garlands fair.
But one I marked who lingered still behind,
As for such souls no seemly gift had he:
　　He was not of their strain,
Nor worthy of so bright beings to entertain, 35
Nor fit compeer for such high company.
Yet was he, surely, born to them in mind,
Their youngest nursling of the spirit's kind.
　　Last stole this one,
With timid glance, of watching eyes adread, 40
And dropped his frightened flower when all were gone;
And where the frail flower fell, it witherèd.
But yet methought those high souls smiled thereon;
As when a child, upstraining at your knees
Some fond and fancied nothings, says, 'I give you these!' 45

PROEM

3 *Mary's spoilt nursling* May, the month traditionally dedicated to the Blessed Virgin. **6** *Song* the sun, source of poetic inspiration. **9** *Æsculap* Æsculapius, god of medicine. **27** *spilth* overflow. **38** *Sweet stem to that rose Christ* traditional emblem for the Blessed Virgin. **45** *beamy-textured tent* the sky;–*transpicuous* transparent, lucid. **46** *coerule* blue, colour of the sky and associated with calm. **54** *feat* neat.

PART THE FIRST

19 *Lady of Love Hellene* Aphrodite, the Greek goddess of love, who was born from the sea. **79** semi-colon added. **82** *Frequence* as in musical beat, so many per minute. **127** *Hours* nymphs associated with the seasons. **128** *Nereids* sea nymphs. **132** *aërial hyaline* crystal-clear air. **175** *Gyre* gyration. **216** *amiced* from amice, vestment worn over a priest's shoulders. **220–1** *Enna mead . . . Persephone* the meadow at Enna, scene of Pluto's abduction of Persephone to the underworld. **237** *gracile* slender. **240** *Hesperian fulgence* light of the setting sun. **258** *fortalice* small fortress. **274–296** This passage contains FT's only description of his encounter with the street girl, whose tarnished innocence he compares and contrasts with the unspoiled freshness of the child he is addressing. **312–13** *Five suns . . . Unkissed of one* could refer to the period of five years since the death of his mother in 1880. **317** *cestus* girdle. **341** Lines follow here which were deleted in the proofs and published in *Stylus* (see headnote), and which describe an idol, or figurine, which had taken Madeleine Meynell's youthful fancy. FT was obviously captivated by her liking for what must have been a hideously crude version of a child's doll. Accordingly, he describes it in outlandish and often invented words (*lurdane* heavy, dull).

> But out, alack, unhappy me!
> For I have a rival,
> A rival from the ancestral East.
> Never such a rival
> Heard I that a human
> Heart for its trial
> Was sent by the spawning East
> Out of her crew!
> Never did such a rival
> Teach a lover sighing,
> Never such a suitor
> Man yet knew!
> A wooden Burmese idol,
> In passing favour help;
> To whom the dusky knees have kneeled,
> (Abominable rival!
> I am glad he has lost his bell.)
> A wry-mouthed idol,
> A lurdane Burmese idol,
> Most grisly and gruesome,
> Most hideous of hue.
> Ah, had the gods but made me,
> But made me, but made me,
> A wooden Burmese idol,
> Most hideous and rueful,
> Most dreadful to view!
> Then small lips would sue me,
> And small hands coy me,
> And small mouths call me 'Beautiful'—

> Sweet little toyers!
> Sweet wooers to woo!
> *O lurdane Burmese idol! no voice can you upraise*
> *To Sylvia, O Sylvia her feat, sweet ways!*
> *Within your veins no holiday*
> *Pricks you on, this vernal day,*
> *To syllable to Sylvia:*
> *Though all the birds on branches lave their mouths with May,*
> *You will not bear this burthen,*
> *For singing to Sylvia!*

352 *Gideon-fleece* This refers to the Old Testament story of the fleece on which alone, at Gideon's prayer, God caused dew to appear (Judges 6 : 36–8). Thompson would have been familiar with the image as an emblem of virginal purity often applied to the Blessed Virgin. **360** *the sign* the luminous cloud that overhung the Ark of the Covenant carried by the Israelites on their journey through the Wilderness (Exodus 13:21). **365.** *auspice* omen. **366** *solemn courts, and covenanted streams* resting places of refreshment for the Ark in the Wilderness. The image is applied to the future course of the child's life. After 379 the following remaining lines were deleted in the proofs and published in *Stylus*. In the last line *strook* is an anachronistic version of struck.

> *I bid all my children companion voices raise*
> *To Sylvia, their Sylvia, her sweet, feat ways;*
> *Their lovesome labours lay away,*
> *And trick them out in holiday*
> *For syllabling to Sylvia;*
> *While all my birds on branches lave their mouths with May*
> *And burthen bring of welcome,*
> *For singing to Sylvia.*

> But for that lurdane idol,
> To Burmah I doom him,
> Back to his land of chrysoberyl and jade,
>   Topaz and amber;
> Where swelter in Magoung
> The clusters swart, or on the mountained marble
>   Moil, or in aurate waters;
> Burman, Panthay, and Shan
> There may him round environ
> Brown faces glooming,
> With all their snaky silken swathe
> Of hues in zig-zag banded:
> That in Pegu
> Worship their monstrous god, enthronised, carven,
> Cowled Naga-Rajah;
> Or where Tartarian strook Pagan.

PART THE SECOND

18 *lackeying its god* The sunflower (cf. 15) always turns its head towards the sun. **20** *scantly* sparingly. **29** *Medusa* here, a kind of jellyfish. **30** *deliquious light* cf. Crashaw, 'Glorious Epiphanie', **114** 'a long deliquiunt'. **43–5** minute creatures that cause the sea to become phosphorescent in the dark. **56** *eremite* hermit. **57** *antre* cave, here an image for the body as dwelling-place for the hermit-poet dedicated to solitude in pursuit of beauty. **69** *maidens of the mist* clouds. **89** *crocean* saffron-coloured. **102** As in *Works*, a full stop has been added here to make sense. **111** *Phoebean wassailer* the sun. A wassailer is a reveller and Phoebus is another name for Apollo, the sun god. **118** *inchmeal* gradual degrees. *OED* cites sixteenth-century references. **134** *Cozening* deceiving. **137–8** refers to Midas, who in the fable was granted his request to turn all he touched into gold; but when this included his food he had to pray for the gift to be removed. **143** *Sultan Phoebus* the sun;– *Janizars* bodyguards of the Sultan. **144** *cicatrices* scars. **148** *winnows to the fledgèd heel* wing-beats of the winged feet of Hermes, a god associated with poetry. **159** *gold-mailèd saurian* crocodile. **160** *Nilotic slime* mud of the Nile. **161** *Aurorian* like morning light, from Aurora, goddess of dawn. **215** *Ayaman* word invented to convey Eastern flavour. **226** *gelid* cool. **228** *tamarind* tropical tree whose roots are used to make a cooling drink. **239** *Sava, Herbalimar* invented words as in **215**. **259** *eyas* young falcon or hawk. **279** *calyces* outer coverings of a flower. **288–9** *Perseus' Shield . . . mirrored Woman* The Gorgon Medusa's glance turned all who approached her to stone, but when it was reflected back to her in the brilliance of Perseus' shield, he remained unharmed. **294** *Wild Dryad* a nymph constrained to live inside a tree. **307** *Hesperides* the mythical land where the Golden Apples were guarded by a dragon. **314** *antenatal Aphrodite* Aphrodite, Greek goddess of love, was born from the sea. **321** *lineal* in line, destined. **339** *the Titan* Prometheus, one of the giant-sized Titans, was chained to a rock. **364** *Memnonian lips* The 'column of Memnon' at Thebes was damaged by an earthquake in 27 BC, after which it was said to produce a musical sound when touched by the sunrise—interpreted as King Memnon's greeting to his mother. **398** *Jacob's stone* the stone on which Jacob rested his head to dream of the ladder joining heaven and earth (Genesis 27 : 11–12). **404** *guerdon* reward. **429** *Gate of Ivory* the mythical Gate of Sleep where dreams enter the human world from the world beyond. **432** As in *Works*, an exclamation mark and closing inverted commas are added. **479** *Salic law* law that denied female right of inheritance. **484** *Castalian-chrismed kings* from Castalia, a fountain on Mount Parnassus, the home of the Muses dedicated to poetry. Hence poets are the 'Kings' anointed by its waters. **514** *Eoan* from Eos, a dawn goddess. **515** *Dian's chill finger-tips* moonbeams. Diana was the moon goddess. **517** *frush* strike. **520** *irid* iris, part of the eye. **527** As in *Works*, a comma is added to aid sense. **581** *roseal* from Crashaw (see 'A Judgment in Heaven', note to 27). **588** As in *Works*, a comma is added to aid sense. **603** *Daemon* spirit of poetic inspiration. **613** *Works* has 'moulded' for 'mounded'. **626** As in *Works*, a comma is added at end to aid sense. **632** *Heliades* the three daughters of Helios, the sun, who on the death of their brother were turned into poplar trees on the bank of a stream and whose continuing tears became amber as they dropped into the water. **642** *brede* braid. **643** *Tellus* the earth; *purfled* embroidered. **644** *chlamys* a cloak. **645** *freaked* flecked. **658** *Saturnian earth* harvest-time. Saturn was the god of seed-time and harvest. **661** *Siste viator* 'Stop, traveller.' Words often inscribed on a tombstone. The 'storied urn' is this poem. **667** *archimage* magician or wizard. **678** *immitigate* derivation from immitigable, 'that cannot be softened' (*OED*). **681** *Apollonian harp-player* the sun, from Apollo, the sun god. **687** *Naiad* water-nymph. **715** As in *Works*, a comma is added to aid sense. **716** *agarics* mushrooms. **730** *imbrued* stained. **741** *yon censer* the sun. **742** *Vesper's fumes* evening clouds. **744–5** In the MS and the proofs these lines are expanded to:

> The long laburnum drips
> Its stalactites of flame, its icicles of fire.
> Oh, that this verse were strong as its desire
> I had built a thing might scorn at fortune's spurns,
>> Until doom overturns
>> The broken stellèd urns
> While lapsing through the Heaven the spilled splendour burns.

761 *feateously* derivation from featly, adroitly. **777** *euphrasy* eyebright (a plant).

INSCRIPTION

5 *Oceanides* sea-nymphs. **14, 17** As in *Works*, commas are added to aid sense.

New Poems (1897)

Although this second collection of poems draws on a number already published, the title is fully justified by the much greater number composed for it and by the rigorous revisions to which the earlier work was subjected. The effort it involved is clear from a letter Thompson wrote to Alice Meynell after submitting the manuscript in May 1896.

> The whole book I look back to as a bad dream, so unexampled in my previous experience was the labour I bestowed on it. Indeed during the last six months, over and above the rewriting upon rewriting of the poems which were ready to hand, I must have written about thirty new poems, long and short; for there were not above twenty or so when I began on the book. I hardly wrote more than thirty in the whole five years preceding my first book; so that was an unprecedented strain for me.
>
> (*Letters*, p. 156)

Dedication

To Coventry Patmore

Lo, my book thinks to look Time's leaguer down,
Under the banner of your spread renown!
Or if these levies of impuissant rhyme
Fall to the overthrow of assaulting Time,
Yet this one page shall fend oblivious shame,
Armed with your crested and prevailing Name.

Note: This dedication was written while the dear friend and great Poet to whom it was addressed yet lived. It is left as he saw it—the last verses of mine that were ever to pass under his eyes. F.T.

1 *leaguer* siege.

SIGHT AND INSIGHT

> Wisdom is easily seen by them that love her, and is found by them
> that seek her. To think therefore upon her is perfect understanding.
>
> (Wisdom 6 : 13, 16)

Thompson wrote a preface for *New Poems* which he cancelled before publication
but which survives in the original manuscript. He was right to leave the poems to
speak for themselves, but his observations on the 'Sight and Insight' group are of
value as they contradict the critics who, from the first, have tried to include him
with the mystical writers and poets. His earlier title for the group was 'Poems
Partly Mystical', to which his words here refer: 'The first section exhibits mysticism in a limited and varying degree. I felt my instrument yet too imperfect to
profane by it the higher ranges. Much is transcendental rather than truly mystic.'
His later title is far more closely related to the underlying theme, where the 'sight'
of the poet of the natural and human world unites in these poems with the
'insight' of the poet who aspires to a world beyond. The group contains the twelve
poems that Thompson regarded as the most important of the whole collection. In
Works, Meynell added two further poems: 'Carmen Genesis' and 'Ad Castitatem:
de Profundis'. In the present edition they appear with poems first published in
Works, on pp. 310–16.

The Mistress of Vision

When Thompson described the *Sight and Insight* poems in the discarded Preface
quoted above, he drew special attention to the first one: 'The opening poem is a
fantasy with no more than an allusive tinge of psychic significance.' His words
should be kept in mind for there are many interpretations of the theme as a mystical experience, identifying the Lady of the Rose Garden with the Blessed Virgin
as Queen of Poetry. Others see it as a product of the period, recalling Swinburne
or Beardsley's 'Mysterious Rose Garden'. It has been regarded as mere 'nonsense
verse' or as evoking a response to esoteric mystery akin to Coleridge's 'Kubla
Khan'. However the treatment is regarded, the main theme sets the direction for
the rest of the group in the conflict between the Lady as the poetic ideal and the
ideal of Christian asceticism. There is no reconciliation in the closing stanzas, giving the poem a depth of feeling which, from its imagery and self-conscious
refrain, it would otherwise seem to lack.

I

Secret was the garden;
Set i' the pathless awe
Where no star its breath can draw.
Life, that is its warden,
Sits behind the fosse of death. Mine eyes saw not, and I saw.   5

II

It was a mazeful wonder;
Thrice three times it was enwalled
With an emerald—
Sealèd so asunder.
All its birds in middle air hung a-dream, their music thralled.   10

III

The Lady of fair weeping,
At the garden's core,
Sang a song of sweet and sore
And the after-sleeping;
In the land of Luthany, and the tracts of Elenore.   15

IV

With sweet-panged singing,
Sang she through a dream-night's day;
That the bowers might stay,
Birds bate their winging,
Nor the wall of emerald float in wreathèd haze away.   20

V

The lily kept its gleaming,
In her tears (divine conservers!)
Washèd with sad art;
And the flowers of dreaming
Palèd not their fervours,   25
For her blood flowed through their nervures;
And the roses were most red, for she dipt them in her heart.

VI

There was never moon,
Save the white sufficing woman:
Light most heavenly-human—   30
Like the unseen form of sound,
Sensed invisibly in tune,—
With a sun-derivèd stole
Did inaureole
All her lovely body round;   35
Lovelily her lucid body with that light was inter-strewn.

VII

The sun which lit that garden wholly,
Low and vibrant visible,
Tempered glory woke;
And it seemèd solely   40
Like a silver thurible
Solemnly swung, slowly,
Fuming clouds of golden fire, for a cloud of incense-smoke.

VIII

But woe's me, and woe's me,
For the secrets of her eyes!   45
In my visions fearfully
They are ever shown to be
As fringèd pools, whereof each lies
Pallid-dark beneath the skies
Of a night that is   50
But one blear necropolis.
And her eyes a little tremble, in the wind of her own sighs.

IX

Many changes rise on
Their phantasmal mysteries.
They grow to an horizon   55
Where earth and heaven meet;
And like a wing that dies on
The vague twilight-verges,
Many a sinking dream doth fleet
Lessening down their secrecies.   60
And, as dusk with day converges,
Their orbs are troublously
Over-gloomed and over-glowed with hope and fear of things to be.

X

There is a peak on Himalay,
And on the peak undeluged snow,   65
And on the snow not eagles stray;
There if your strong feet could go,—
Looking over tow'rd Cathay
From the never-deluged snow—
Farthest ken might not survey   70
Where the peoples underground dwell whom antique fables know.

XI

East, ah, east of Himalay,
Dwell the nations underground;
Hiding from the shock of Day,
For the sun's uprising-sound: 75
Dare not issue from the ground
At the tumults of the Day,
So fearfully the sun doth sound
Clanging up beyond Cathay;
For the great earthquaking sunrise rolling up beyond Cathay.   80

XII

Lend me, O lend me
The terrors of that sound,
That its music may attend me,
Wrap my chant in thunders round;
While I tell the ancient secrets in that Lady's singing found.   85

XIII

On Ararat there grew a vine,
When Asia from her bathing rose;
Our first sailor made a twine
Thereof for his prefiguring brows.
Canst divine   90
Where, upon our dusty earth, of that vine a cluster grows?

XIV

On Golgotha there grew a thorn
Round the long-prefigured Brows.
Mourn, O mourn!
For the vine have we the spine? Is this all the Heaven allows?   95

XV

On Calvary was shook a spear;
Press the point into thy heart—
Joy and fear!
All the spines upon the thorn into curling tendrils start.

XVI

O dismay!   100
I, a wingless mortal, sporting
With the tresses of the sun?

I, that dare my hand to lay
On the thunder in its snorting?
Ere begun,   105
Falls my singed song down the sky, even the old Icarian way.

XVII

From the fall precipitant
These dim snatches of her chant
Only have remainèd mine;—
That from spear and thorn alone   110
May be grown
For the front of saint or singer any divinising twine.

XVIII

Her song said that no springing
Paradise but evermore
Hangeth on a singing   115
That has chords of weeping,
And that sings the after-sleeping
To souls which wake too sore.
'But woe the singer, woe!' she said; 'beyond the dead his singing-lore,
All its art of sweet and sore,   120
He learns, in Elenore!'

XIX

Where is the land of Luthany,
Where is the tract of Elenore?
I am bound therefor.

XX

'Pierce thy heart to find the key;   125
With thee take
Only what none else would keep;
Learn to dream when thou dost wake,
Learn to wake when thou dost sleep.
Learn to water joy with tears,   130
Learn from fears to conquer fears;
To hope, for thou dar'st not despair,
Exult, for that thou dar'st not grieve;
Plough thou the rock until it bear;
Know, for thou else couldst not believe;   135
Lose, that the lost thou may'st receive;
Die, for none other way canst live.

When earth and heaven lay down their veil,
And that apocalypse turns thee pale;
When thy seeing blindeth thee   140
To what thy fellow-mortals see;
When their sight to thee is sightless;
Their living, death; their light, most lightless;
Search no more—
Pass the gates of Luthany, tread the region Elenore.'   145

XXI

Where is the land of Luthany,
And where the region Elenore?
I do faint therefor.
'When to the new eyes of thee
All things by immortal power,   150
Near or far,
Hiddenly
To each other linkèd are,
That thou canst not stir a flower
Without troubling of a star;   155
When thy song is shield and mirror
To the fair snake-curlèd Pain,
Where thou dar'st affront her terror
That on her thou may'st attain
Perséan conquest; seek no more,   160
O seek no more!
Pass the gates of Luthany, tread the region Elenore.'

XXII

So sang she, so wept she,
Through a dream-night's day;
And with her magic singing kept she—   165
Mystical in music—
That garden of enchanting
In visionary May;
Swayless for my spirit's haunting,
Thrice-threefold walled with emerald from our mortal mornings grey. 170

XXIII

And as a necromancer
Raises from the rose-ash
The ghost of the rose;
My heart so made answer

To her voice's silver plash,—   175
Stirred in reddening flash,
And from out its mortal ruins the purpureal phantom blows.

XXIV

Her tears made dulcet fretting,
Her voice had no word,
More than thunder or the bird.   180
Yet, unforgetting,
The ravished soul her meanings knew. Mine ears heard not and I heard.

XXV

When she shall unwind
All those wiles she wound about me,
Tears shall break from out me,   185
That I cannot find
Music in the holy poets to my wistful want, I doubt me!

15 *Luthany, Elenore* invented places, suggestive of the mysterious world inhabited by the Lady as the source of poetic inspiration. 33 *stole* long strip of cloth worn over the shoulders as part of a priest's vestments. 34 *inaureole* surround with light. 41 *thurible* censer. 51 *necropolis* cemetery. 86 *Ararat* mountain in Eastern Turkey where Noah's Ark is said to have come to rest after the Flood. 106 *Icarian way* Icarus attached wings to himself that enabled him to fly but, according to the myth, he flew too near the sun so that the wax holding the wings together melted and he fell to his death. 160 *Perséan conquest* Perseus could approach the Gorgon Medusa when his shield protected him from the direct gaze that turned others to stone: so the poet confronts pain without fear when protected by his dedicated Muse. 187 *holy poets* FT uses the term here and elsewhere to describe those poets who, following Wordsworth, set out to celebrate the 'return to nature'. From these he can expect no lasting inspiration as 'the poet of the return to God'. (See Introduction, and also 'Victorian Ode', 18, p. 260, and 'Nineteenth Century', 24, p. 272.)

Contemplation

This morning saw I, fled the shower,
The earth reclining in a lull of power:
The heavens, pursuing not their path,
Lay stretched out naked after bath,
Or so it seemed; field, water, tree, were still,   5
Nor was there any purpose on the calm-browed hill.

The hill, which sometimes visibly is
Wrought with unresting energies,

Looked idly; from the musing wood,
And every rock, a life renewed 10
Exhaled like an unconscious thought
When poets, dreaming unperplexed,
Dream that they dream of nought.
Nature one hour appears a thing unsexed,
Or to such serene balance brought 15
That her twin natures cease their sweet alarms,
And sleep in one another's arms.
The sun with resting pulses seems to brood,
And slacken its command upon my unurged blood.

The river has not any care 20
Its passionless water to the sea to bear;
The leaves have brown content;
The wall to me has freshness like a scent,
And takes half animate the air,
Making one life with its green moss and stain; 25
And life with all things seems too perfect blent
For anything of life to be aware.
The very shades on hill, and tree, and plain,
Where they have fallen doze, and where they doze remain.

No hill can idler be than I; 30
No stone its inter-particled vibration
Investeth with a stiller lie;
No heaven with a more urgent rest betrays
The eyes that on it gaze.
We are too near akin that thou shouldst cheat 35
Me, Nature, with thy fair deceit.
In poets floating like a water-flower
Upon the bosom of the glassy hour,
In skies that no man sees to move,
Lurk untumultuous vortices of power, 40
For joy too native, and for agitation
Too instant, too entire for sense thereof,
Motion like gnats when autumn suns are low,
Perpetual as the prisoned feet of love
On the heart's floors with painèd pace that go. 45
From stones and poets you may know,
Nothing so active is, as that which least seems so.

*

For he, that conduit running wine of song,
Then to himself does most belong,
When he his mortal house unbars   50
To the importunate and thronging feet
That round our corporeal walls unheeded beat;
Till, all containing, he exalt
His stature to the stars, or stars
Narrow their heaven to his fleshly vault: 55
When, like a city under ocean,
To human things he grows a desolation,
And is made a habitation
For the fluctuous universe
To lave with unimpeded motion.   60
He scarcely frets the atmosphere
With breathing, and his body shares
The immobility of rocks;
His heart's a drop-well of tranquillity;
His mind more still is than the limbs of fear,   65
And yet its unperturbed velocity
The spirit of the simoom mocks.
He round the solemn centre of his soul
Wheels like a dervish, while his being is
Streamed with the set of the world's harmonies,   70
In the long draft of whatsoever sphere
He lists the sweet and clear
Clangour of his high orbit on to roll,
So gracious is his heavenly grace;
And the bold stars does hear,   75
Every one in his airy soar,
For evermore
Shout to each other from the peaks of space,
As thwart ravines of azure shouts the mountaineer.

31 *inter-particled vibration* an example of FT's use of scientific theory to enhance poetic meaning. According to a note by TLC this is a reference to the science of atoms which teaches that all inorganic matter is composed of minute particles held together in a tension similar to that governing the planetary system (TLC*Poems*, p. 443). 32 *lie* state of stability represented by the stone. 67 *simoom* sand wind of the desert. 72 *lists* chooses.

By Reason of Thy Law

The title is taken from Psalm 129, known as the 'De Profundis', (v. 4): 'For with thee there is merciful forgiveness: and by reason of thy law, I have waited for thee, O Lord.' From the title Thompson shows that he is determined to abide within the 'law' of his religious background: but the theme and imagery of the poem indicate how often he finds it at variance with his poetic instincts.

> Here I make oath—
> Although the heart that knows its bitterness
> Hear loath,
> And credit less—
> That he who kens to meet Pain's kisses fierce 5
> Which hiss against his tears,
> Dread, loss, nor love frustrate,
> Nor all iniquity of the froward years
> Shall his inurèd wing make idly bate,
> Nor of the appointed quarry his staunch sight 10
> To lose observance quite;
> Seal from half-sad and all-elate
> Sagacious eyes
> Ultimate Paradise;
> Nor shake his certitude of haughty fate. 15
>
> Pacing the burning shares of many dooms,
> I with stern tread do the clear-witting stars
> To judgment cite,
> If I have borne aright
> The proving of their pure-willed ordeal. 20
> From food of all delight
> The heavenly Falconer my heart debars,
> And tames with fearful glooms
> The haggard to His call;
> Yet sometimes comes a hand, sometimes a voice withal, 25
> And she sits meek now, and expects the light.
>
> In this Avernian sky,
> This sultry and incumbent canopy
> Of dull and doomed regret;
> Where on the unseen verges yet, O yet, 30
> At intervals,
> Trembles, and falls,
> Faint lightning of remembered transient sweet—

Ah, far too sweet
But to be sweet a little, a little sweet, and fleet;   35
Leaving this pallid trace,
This loitering and most fitful light a space,
Still some sad space,
For Grief to see her own poor face:—
Here where I keep my stand   40
With all o'er-anguished feet,
And no live comfort near on any hand;
Lo, I proclaim the unavoided term,
When this morass of tears, then drained and firm,
Shall be a land—   45
Unshaken I affirm—
Where seven-quired psalterings meet;
And all the gods move with calm hand in hand,
And eyes that know not trouble and the worm.

5–15 Using imagery from falconry the poet determines to confront the effects of pain in the same way as the overworked falcon still seeks its prey, which for the poet is the goal beyond pain, 'ultimate paradise'. **24** *haggard* wild hawk that is caught and tamed. **27** *Avernian sky* Lake Avernus, in Campania in Italy, was known as the 'birdless lake' on account of the poisonous vapour said to kill any birds that flew over it. **47** *seven-quired psalterings* music of the seven quires of angels.

The Dread of Height

If ye were blind, ye should have no sin: but now ye say:
We sin: your sin remaineth.

(John 9 : 41)

Not the Circean wine
Most perilous is for pain:
Grapes of the heavens' star-loaden vine,
Whereto the lofty-placed
Thoughts of fair souls attain,   5
Tempt with a more retributive delight,
And do disrelish all life's sober taste.
'Tis to have drunk too well
The drink that is divine,
Maketh the kind earth waste,   10
And breath intolerable.

*

Ah me!
How shall my mouth content it with mortality?
Lo, secret music, sweetest music,
From distances of distance drifting its lone flight,   15
Down the arcane where Night would perish in night,
Like a god's loosened locks slips undulously:
Music that is too grievous of the height
For safe and low delight,
Too infinite,   20
For bounded hearts which yet would girth the sea!

So let it be,
Though sweet be great, and though my heart be small:
So let it be,
O music, music, though you wake in me   25
No joy, no joy at all;
Although you only wake
Uttermost sadness, measure of delight,
Which else I could not credit to the height,
Did I not know,   30
That ill is statured to its opposite;
Did I not know,
And even of sadness so,
Of utter sadness make,
Of extreme sad a rod to mete   35
The incredible excess of unsensed sweet,
And mystic wall of strange felicity.
So let it be,
Though sweet be great, and though my heart be small,
And bitter meat   40
The food of gods for men to eat;
Yea, John ate daintier, and did tread
Less ways of heat,
Than whom to their wind-carpeted
High banquet-hall,   45
And golden love-feasts, the fair stars entreat.

But ah withal,
Some hold, some stay,
O difficult Joy, I pray,
Some arms of thine,   50
Not only, only arms of mine!

Lest like a weary girl I fall
From clasping love so high,
And lacking thus thine arms, then may
Most hapless I   55
Turn utterly to love of basest rate;
For low they fall whose fall is from the sky.
Yea, who shall me secure
But I of height grown desperate
Surcease my wing, and my lost fate   60
Be dashed from pure
To broken writhings in the shameful slime:
Lower than man, for I dreamed higher,
Thrust down, by how much I aspire,
And damned with drink of immortality?   65
For such things be,
Yea, and the lowest reach of reeky Hell
Is but made possible
By foreta'en breath of Heaven's austerest clime.

These tidings from the vast to bring   70
Needeth not doctor nor divine,
Too well, too well
My flesh doth know the heart-perturbing thing;
That dread theology alone
Is mine,   75
Most native and my own;
And ever with victorious toil
When I have made
Of the deific peaks dim escalade,
My soul with anguish and recoil   80
Doth like a city in an earthquake rock,
As at my feet the abyss is cloven then,
With deeper menace than for other men,
Of my potential cousinship with mire;
That all my conquered skies do grow a hollow mock,   85
My fearful powers retire,
No longer strong,
Reversing the shook banners of their song.

Ah, for a heart less native to high Heaven,
A hooded eye, for jesses and restraint,   90
Or for a will accipitrine to pursue!

The veil of tutelar flesh to simple livers given,
Or those brave-fledging fervours of the Saint,
Whose heavenly falcon-craft doth never taint,
Nor they in sickest time their ample virtue mew.   95

1 *Circean wine* In the *Odyssey*, Circe was a sorceress whose drugged wine turned Odysseus and his companions into swine. **42** *John ate daintier* St John the Baptist, while living in the desert, ate only locusts and wild honey (Mark 1 : 6; Matt. 3 : 4). **89–95** The imagery from falconry strengthens the connection with the preceding poem. The poet sighs for the restraining 'jesses' (straps) of the hawk tied to the falconer's wrist; or for a will which like that of the hawk seeks only that which it is bidden to pursue. **95** *mew* confine.

Orient Ode

In July 1895 Thompson wrote to Coventry Patmore that this ode 'was written soon after Easter, and was suggested by passages in the liturgies of Holy Saturday' (*Letters*, p. 128). He copied the passages into the notebook containing the first draft of the poem. They are given in the endnotes.

Lo, in the sanctuaried East,
Day, a dedicated priest
In all his robes pontifical exprest,
Lifteth slowly, lifteth sweetly,
From out its Orient tabernacle drawn,   5
Yon orbèd sacrament confest,
Which sprinkles benediction through the dawn.
And when the grave procession's ceased,
The earth with due illustrious rite
Blessed,—ere the frail fingers featly   10
Of twilight, violet-cassocked acolyte,
His sacerdotal stoles unvest—
Sets, for high close of the mysterious feast,
The sun in august exposition meetly
Within the flaming monstrance of the West.   15

O salutaris hostia,
Quae coeli pandis ostium!
Through breachèd darkness' rampart, a
Divine assaulter, art thou come!
God whom none may live and mark!   20
Borne within thy radiant ark,
While the Earth, a joyous David,
Dances before thee from the dawn to dark.

The moon, O leave, pale ruined Eve;
Behold her fair and greater daughter   25
Offers to thee her fruitful water,
Which at thy first white *Ave* shall conceive!
Thy gazes do on simple her
Desirable allures confer;
What happy comelinesses rise   30
Beneath thy beautifying eyes!
Who was, indeed, at first a maid
Such as, with sighs, misgives she is not fair,
And secret views herself afraid,
Till flatteries sweet provoke the charms they swear: 35
Yea, thy gazes, blissful lover,
Make the beauties they discover!
What dainty guiles and treacheries caught
From artful prompting of love's artless thought
Her lowly loveliness teach her to adorn,   40
When thy plumes shiver against the conscious gates of morn!

And so the love which is thy dower,
Earth, though her first-frightened breast
Against the exigent boon protest,
(For she, poor maid, of her own power   45
Has nothing in herself, not even love,
But an unwitting void thereof,)
Gives back to thee in sanctities of flower;
And holy odours do her bosom invest,
That sweeter grows for being prest: 50
Though dear recoil, the tremorous nurse of joy,
From thine embrace still startles coy,
Till Phosphor lead, at thy returning hour,
The laughing captive from the wishing West.

Nor the majestic heavens less   55
Thy formidable sweets approve,
Thy dreads and thy delights confess,
That do draw, and that remove.
Thou as a lion roar'st, O sun,
Upon thy satellites' vexèd heels;   60
Before thy terrible hunt thy planets run;
Each in his frighted orbit wheels,
Each flies through inassuageable chase,

Since the hunt o' the world begun,
The puissant approaches of thy face,   65
And yet thy radiant leash he feels.
Since the hunt o' the world begun,
Lashed with terror, leashed with longing,
The mighty course is ever run;
Pricked with terror, leashed with longing,   70
Thy rein they love, and thy rebuke they shun.
Since the hunt o' the world began,
With love that trembleth, fear that loveth,
Thou join'st the woman to the man;
And Life with Death   75
In obscure nuptuals moveth,
Commingling alien, yet affinèd breath.

Thou art the incarnated Light
Whose Sire is aboriginal, and beyond
Death and resurgence of our day and night;   80
From him is thy vicegerent wand
With double potence of the black and white.
Giver of Love, and Beauty, and Desire,
The terror, and the loveliness, and purging,
The deathfulness and lifefulness of fire!   85
Samson's riddling meanings merging
In thy twofold sceptre meet:
Out of thy minatory might,
Burning Lion, burning Lion,
Comes the honey of all sweet,   90
And out of thee, the eater, comes forth meat.
And though, by thine alternate breath,
Every kiss thou dost inspire
Echoeth
Back from the windy vaultages of death;   95
Yet thy clear warranty above
Augurs the wings of death too must
Occult reverberations stir of love
Crescent and life incredible;
That even the kisses of the just   100
Go down not unresurgent to the dust.
Yea, not a kiss which I have given,
But shall triumph upon my lips in heaven,
Or cling a shameful fungus there in hell.
                      *

Know'st thou me not, O sun? Yea, well   105
Thou know'st the ancient miracle,
The children know'st of Zeus and May;
And still thou teachest them, O splendent Brother,
To incarnate, the antique way,
The truth which is their heritage from their Sire   110
In sweet disguise of flesh from their sweet Mother.
My fingers thou hast taught to con
Thy flame-chorded psalterion,
Till I can translate into mortal wire—
Till I can translate passing well—   115
The heavenly harping harmony,
Melodious sealed, inaudible,
Which makes the dulcet psalter of the world's desire.
Thou whisperest in the Moon's white ear,
And she does whisper into mine,—   120
By night together, I and she—
With her virgin voice divine,
The things I cannot half so sweetly tell
As she can sweetly speak, I sweetly hear.

By her, the Woman, does the Earth live, O Lord,   125
Yet she for Earth, and both in thee.
Light out of Light!
Resplendent and prevailing Word
Of the Unheard!
Not unto thee, great Image, not to thee   130
Did the wise heathen bend an idle knee;
And in an age of faith grown frore
If I too shall adore,
Be it accounted unto me
A bright sciential idolatry!   135
God has given thee visible thunders
To utter thine apocalypse of wonders;
And what want I of prophecy,
That at the sounding from thy station
Of thy flagrant trumpet, see   140
The seals that melt, the open revelation?
Or who a God-persuading angel needs,
That only heeds
The rhetoric of thy burning deeds?
Which but to sing, if it may be,   145

In worship-warranting moiety,
So I would win
In such a song as hath within
A smouldering core of mystery,
Brimmèd with nimbler meanings up   150
Than hasty Gideons in their hands may sup;—
Lo, my suit pleads
That thou, Isaian coal of fire,
Touch from yon altar my poor mouth's desire,
And the relucent song take for thy sacred meeds.   155

To thine own shape
Thou round'st the chrysolite of the grape,
Blind'st thy gold lightnings in his veins;
Thou storest the white garners of the rains.
Destroyer and preserver, thou   160
Who medicinest sickness, and to health
Art the unthankèd marrow of its wealth;
To those apparent sovereignties we bow
And bright appurtenances of thy brow!
Thy proper blood dost thou not give,   165
That Earth, the gusty Maenad, drink and dance?
Art thou not life of them that live?
Yea, in glad twinkling advent, thou dost dwell
Within our body as a tabernacle!
Thou bittest with thine ordinance   170
The jaws of Time, and thou dost mete
The unsustainable treading of his feet.
Thou to thy spousal universe
Art Husband, she thy Wife and Church;
Who in most dusk and vidual curch,   175
Her Lord being hence,
Keeps her cold sorrows by thy hearse.
The heavens renew their innocence
And morning state
But by thy sacrament communicate;   180
Their weeping night the symbol of our prayers,
Our darkened search,
And sinful vigil desolate.
Yea, biune in imploring dumb,
Essential Heavens and corporal Earth await,   185
The Spirit and the Bride say: Come!

Lo, of thy Magians I the least
Haste with my gold, my incenses and myrrhs,
To thy desired epiphany, from the spiced
Regions and odorous of Song's traded East.   190
Thou, for the life of all that live
The victim daily born and sacrificed;
To whom the pinion of this longing verse
Beats but with fire which first thyself did give.
To thee, O Sun—or is't perchance, to Christ?   195

Ay, if men say that on all high heaven's face
The saintly signs I trace
Which round my stolèd altars hold their solemn place,
Amen, amen! For oh, how could it be,—
When I with wingèd feet had run   200
Through all the windy earth about,
Quested its secret of the sun,
And heard what thing the stars together shout,—
I should not heed thereout
Consenting counsel won:—   205
'By this, O Singer, know we if thou see.
When men shall say to thee: Lo! Christ is here,
When men shall say to thee: Lo, Christ is there,
Believe them: yea, and this—then art thou seer,
When all thy crying clear   210
Is but: Lo here! lo there!—ah me, lo everywhere!'

The passages from the liturgy of Holy Saturday referred to in the headnote were copied by FT from the Latin text in use before the liturgical changes following the Second Vatican Council. They are given here in the authorised translation, also dating from before the changes.

O God, who hast bestowed on the faithful the fire of thy brightness by thy Son, who is the cornerstone, sanctify this new fire produced from a flint that it may be profitable to us: and grant that by this Paschal festival we may be so inflamed with heavenly desires, that with pure minds we may be able to arrive at the festival of perpetual light.

O Lord God Almighty, Father, unfailing light, who art the author of all lights, bless this light that is blessed and sanctified by thee, who hast enlightened the whole world; that we may be inflamed with the light and enlightened by the fire of thy brightness: and as thou didst give light to Moses when he went out of Egypt, so illumine our hearts and senses, that we may deserve to arrive at light and life everlasting.

(Introductory Collects for the Blessing of the New Fire)

O truly blessed night, which alone deserved to know the time and hour in which Christ rose again from the grave! This is the night of which it is written: and the night shall be enlightened as the day; and the night is my light in my enjoyments.

(From the Blessing of the Paschal Candle)

Therefore in this sacred night, receive, O holy Father, the evening sacrifice of this incense . . .

> (From the prayer as five grains of incense are placed in the Candle)

O truly blessed night, which despoiled the Egyptians and enriched the Hebrews! A night in which heavenly things are united with those of earth, and things divine to those which are human. We beseech thee therefore, O Lord, that this candle, consecrated in honour of thy name, may continue to burn to dissipate the darkness of this night. And being accepted as a sweet savour, may be mixed with the heavenly lights. May the morning star find its flame alive.

> (From the prayer as the lights are lit)

1–15 The main source for the imagery is the service of Benediction. The priest, in his vestments and accompanied by acolytes, or altar servers, removes the Blessed Sacrament from the tabernacle where it is reserved and, to the accompaniment of specific Latin hymns, places it in a monstrance in order to bestow on the congregation the blessing of Christ himself. **16–17** The first of the hymns, *O salutaris hostia*, begins with the lines: O saving Victim, opening wide / The gate of heaven to man below! **21–3** When the Ark of the Covenant was brought to its true resting place in Jerusalem, King David danced before it in an ecstasy of joy (2 Samuel 6 : 14). **25** *greater daughter* the earth (FT's own note for this line). **53** *Phosphor* the morning star. **59–77** From the imagery of these lines FT's studies of ancient mythologies appear to have included the Inca sun worship, known more widely in recent years since Peter Shaffer's play *The Royal Hunt of the Sun*. **86–91** In the Biblical story Samson in his great strength killed a lion with his bare hands and later discovered a swarm of bees in the mouth of the carcass. He then devised a riddle based on the occurrence: 'Out of the eater came forth meat and out of the strong came forth sweetness' (Judges 14). **105–11** The lines refer to the birth of Mercury (or Hermes in Greek mythology), the god of poetry, from the union of Zeus and Maia, the most beautiful of the seven Pleiades, who were destined to become stars. **132** *frore* frozen. **135** *sciential* scientific. **151** *hasty Gideons* those followers of Gideon who did not pause to drink water in their cupped hands but, beast-like, lapped the water direct from the stream (Judges 7 : 6). **153** *Isaian coal of fire* At the start of his career the lips of the prophet Isaiah were cleansed during a vision when an angel touched them with a coal of fire (Isaiah 6:6–7). **155** *meeds* rewards. **166** *Maenad* female follower of the god Dionysus who took part in the bacchic ecstasy generated by his worship. **171** *mete* allot. **175** *vidual curch* headcovering worn by a widow. **184** *biune* two in one.

New Year's Chimes

What is the song the stars sing?
    (And a million songs are as song of one.)
This is the song the stars sing:
    Sweeter song's none.

One to set, and many to sing,   5
    (And a million songs are as song of one,)
One to stand, and many to cling,
The many things, and the one Thing,
    The one that runs not, the many that run.

The ever new weaveth the ever old   10
   (And a million songs are as song of one.)
Ever telling the never told;
The silver saith, and the said is gold,
    And done ever the never done.

The chase that's chased is the Lord o' the chase   15
   (And a million songs are as song of one,)
And the pursued cries on the race;
    And the hounds in leash are the hounds that run.

Hidden stars by the shown stars' sheen;
   (And a million suns are but as one;)   20
Colours unseen by the colours seen,
And sounds unheard heard sounds between,
    And a night is in the light of the sun.

An ambuscade of light in night,
   (And a million secrets are but as one,)   25
And a night is dark in the sun's light,
    And a world in the world man looks upon.

Hidden stars by the shown stars' wings,
   (And a million cycles are but as one,)   30
And a world with unapparent strings
Knits the simulant world of things;
    Behold, and vision thereof is none.

The world above is the world below
   (And a million worlds are but as one,)   35
And the One in all; as the sun's strength so
Strives in all strength, glows in all glow
    Of the earth that wits not, and man thereon.

Braced in its own fourfold embrace
   (And a million strengths are as strength of one,) 40
And round it all God's arms of grace,
The world, so as the Vision says,
    Doth with great lightning-tramples run.

And thunder bruiteth into thunder,
   (And a million sounds are as sounds of one,)   45
From stellate peak to peak is tossed a voice of wonder,
And the height stoops down to the depths thereunder,
    And sun leans forth to his brother-sun.

And the more ample years unfold
   (With a million songs as song of one,) 50
A little new of the ever old,
A little told of the never told,
   Added act of the never done.

Loud the descant, and low the theme,
   (A million songs are as song of one;) 55
And the dream of the world is dream in dream,
But the one Is is, or nought could seem;
   And the song runs round to the song begun.

This is the song the stars sing,
   (Tonèd all in time;) 60
Tintinnabulous, tuned to ring
A multitudinous-single thing,
   Rung all in rhyme.

From the Night of Forebeing

An Ode after Easter

The ode was written soon after Easter 1894 and the theme is drawn from the ceremonies of the Easter Vigil. When Thompson sent it to the Meynells towards the end of April he commented: 'My fear is that thought in it has strangled the poetic impulse.' But, he added, he was not the best judge (*Letters*, p. 117). Its first title was 'Lux in Tenebris', taken from the second of the two quotations at the head of the poem. For their particular sources see the endnotes.

   In the chaos of preordination, and night of our forebeings.
                             (Sir Thomas Browne)

   Et lux in tenebris erat, et tenebrae eam non comprehenderunt.
                             (St John)

Cast wide the folding doorways of the East,
For now is light increased!
And the wind-besomed chambers of the air,
See they be garnished fair;
And look the ways exhale some precious odours, 5
And set ye all about wild-breathing spice,
Most fit for Paradise.
Now is no time for sober gravity,
Season enough has Nature to be wise;

But now discinct, with raiment glittering free,   10
Shake she the ringing rafters of the skies
With festal footing and bold joyance sweet,
And let the earth be drunken and carouse!
For lo, into her house
Spring is come home with her world-wandering feet,   15
And all things are made young with young desires;
And all for her is light increased
In yellow stars and yellow daffodils,
And East to West, and West to East,
Fling answering welcome-fires,   20
By dawn and day-fall on the jocund hills.
And ye, winged minstrels of her fair meinie,
Being newly coated in glad livery,
Upon her steps attend,
And round her treading dance and without end   25
Reel your shrill lutany.
What popular breath her coming does out-tell
The garrulous leaves among!
What little noises stir and pass
From blade to blade along the voluble grass!   30
O Nature, never-done
Ungaped-at Pentecostal miracle,
We hear thee, each man in his proper tongue!
Break, elemental children, break ye loose
From the strict frosty rule   35
Of grey-beard Winter's school.
Vault, O young winds, vault in your tricksome courses
Upon the snowy steeds that reinless use
In coerule pampas of the heaven to run;
Foaled of the white sea-horses,   40
Washed in the lambent waters of the sun.
Let even the slug-abed snail upon the thorn
Put forth a conscious horn!
Mine elemental co-mates, joy each one;
And ah, my foster-brethren, seem not sad—   45
No, seem not sad,
That my strange heart and I should be so little glad.
Suffer me at your leafy feast
To sit apart, a somewhat alien guest,
And watch your mirth,   50
Unsharing in the liberal laugh of earth;

Yet with a sympathy,
Begot of wholly sad and half-sweet memory—
The little sweetness making grief complete;
Faint wind of wings from hours that distant beat, 55
When I, I too,
Was once, O wild companions, as are you,
Ran with such wilful feet.
Wraith of a recent day and dead,
Risen wanly overhead, 60
Frail, strengthless as a noon-belated moon,
Or as the glazing eyes of watery heaven,
When the sick night sinks into deathly swoon.

A higher and a solemn voice
I heard through your gay-hearted noise; 65
A solemn meaning and a stiller voice
Sounds to me from far days when I too shall rejoice,
Nor more be with your jollity at strife.
O prophecy
Of things that are, and are not, and shall be! 70
The great-vanned Angel March
Hath trumpeted
His clangorous 'Sleep no more' to all the dead—
Beat his strong vans o'er earth, and air, and sea.
And they have heard; 75
Hark to the *Jubilate* of the bird
For them that found the dying way to life!
And they have heard,
And quicken to the great precursive word;
Green spray showers lightly down the cascade of the larch; 80
The graves are riven,
And the Sun comes with power amid the clouds of heaven!
Before his way
Went forth the trumpet of the March;
Before his way, before his way 85
Dances the pennon of the May!
O earth, unchilded, widowed earth, so long
Lifting in patient pine and ivy-tree
Mournful belief and steadfast prophecy,
Behold how all things are made true! 90
Behold your bridegroom cometh in to you,
Exceeding glad and strong.

Raise up your eyes, O raise your eyes abroad!
No more shall you sit sole and vidual,
Searching, in servile pall,   95
Upon the hieratic night the star-sealed sense of all:
Rejoice, O barren, and look forth abroad!
Your children gathered back to your embrace
See with a mother's face.
Look up, O mortals, and the portent heed;   100
In very deed,
Washed with new fire to their irradiant birth,
Reintegrated are the heavens and earth!
From sky to sod,
The world's unfolded blossom smells of God.   105

O imagery
Of that which was the first, and is the last!
For as the dark, profound nativity,
God saw the end should be,
When the world's infant horoscope He cast.   110
Unshackled from the bright Phoebean awe,
In leaf, flower, mould, and tree,
Resolved into dividual liberty,
Most strengthless, unparticipant, inane,
Or suffered the ill peace of lethargy,   115
Lo, the Earth eased of rule:
Unsummered, granted to her own worst smart
The dear wish of the fool—
Disintegration, merely which man's heart
For freedom understands,   120
Amid the frog-like errors from the damp
And quaking swamp
Of the low popular levels spawned in all the lands.
But thou, O Earth, dost much disdain
The bondage of thy waste and futile reign,   125
And sweetly to the great compulsion draw
Of God's alone true-manumitting law,
And Freedom, only which the wise intend,
To work thine innate end.
Over thy vacant counterfeit of death   130
Broods with soft urgent breath
Love, that is child of Beauty and of Awe:
To intercleavage of sharp warring pain,

As of contending chaos come again,
Thou wak'st, O Earth,   135
And work'st from change to change and birth to birth
Creation old as hope, and new as sight;
For meed of toil not vain,
Hearing once more the primal fiat toll:—
'Let there be light!'   140

And there is light!
Light flagrant, manifest;
Light to the zenith, light from pole to pole;
Light from the East that waxeth to the West,
And with its puissant goings-forth   145
Encroaches on the South and on the North;
And with its great approaches does prevail
Upon the sullen fastness of the height,
And summoning its levied power
Crescent and confident through the crescent hour,   150
Goes down with laughters on the subject vale.
Light flagrant, manifest;
Light to the sentient closeness of the breast,
Light to the secret chambers of the brain!
And thou up-floatest, warm, and newly-bathed,   155
Earth, through delicious air,
And with thine own apparent beauties swathed,
Wringing the waters from thine arborous hair;
That all men's hearts, which do behold and see,
Grow weak with their exceeding much desire,   160
And turn to thee on fire,
Enamoured with their utter wish of thee,
Anadyomene!
What vine-outquickening life all creatures sup,
Feel, for the air within its sapphire cup   165
How it does leap, and twinkle headily!
Feel, for Earth's bosom pants, and heaves her scarfing sea;
And round and round in bacchanal rout reel the swift
        spheres intemperably.

My little-worlded self! the shadows pass
In this thy sister-world, as in a glass,   170
Of all the processions that revolve in thee:
Not only of cyclic Man

Thou here discern'st the plan,
Not only of cyclic Man, but the cyclic Me.
Not solely of Mortality's great years   175
The reflex just appears,
But thine own bosom's year, still circling round
In ample and in ampler gyre
Toward the far completion, wherewith crowned,
Love unconsumed shall chant in his own furnace-fire.   180
How many trampled and deciduous joys
Enrich thy soul for joys deciduous still,
Before the distance shall fulfill
Cyclic unrest with solemn equipoise!
Happiness is the shadow of things past,   185
Which fools still take for that which is to be!
And not all foolishly:
For all the past, read true, is prophecy,
And all the firsts are hauntings of some Last,
And all the springs are flash-lights of one Spring.   190
Then leaf, and flower, and falless fruit
Shall hang together on the unyellowing bough;
And silence shall be Music mute
For her surchargèd heart. Hush thou!
These things are far too sure that thou should'st dream   195
Thereof, lest they appear as things that seem.

Shade within shade! for deeper in the glass
Now other imaged meanings pass;
And as the man, the poet there is read.
Winter with me, alack!   200
Winter on every hand I find:
Soul, brain, and pulses dead;
The mind no further by the warm sense fed,
The soul weak-stirring in the arid mind,
More tearless-weak to flash itself abroad   205
Than the earth's life beneath the frost-scorched sod.
My lips have drought and crack,
By laving music long unvisited.
Beneath the austere and macerating rime
Draws back constricted in its icy urns   210
The genial flame of Earth, and there
With torment and with tension does prepare
The lush disclosures of the vernal time.

All joys draw inward to their icy urns,
Tormented by constraining rime, 215
And there
With undelight and throe prepare
The bounteous efflux of the vernal time.
Nor less beneath compulsive Law
Rebukèd draw 220
The numbèd musics back upon my heart;
Whose yet-triumphant course I know
And prevalent pulses forth shall start,
Like cataracts that with thunderous hoof charge the
      disbanding snow.
All power is bound 225
In quickening refusal so;
And silence is the lair of sound;
In act its impulse to deliver,
With fluctuance and quiver
The endeavouring thew grows rigid; 230
Strong
From its retracted coil strikes the resilient song.

Giver of spring,
And song, and every young new thing!
Thou only seest in me, so stripped and bare, 235
The lyric secret waiting to be born,
The patient term allowed
Before it stretch and flutteringly unfold
Its rumpled webs of amethyst-freaked, diaphanous gold.
And what hard task abstracts me from delight, 240
Filling with hopeless hope and dear despair
The still-born day and parchèd fields of night,
That my old way of song, no longer fair,
For lack of serene care,
Is grown a stony and a weed-choked plot, 245
Thou only know'st aright,
Thou only know'st, for I know not.
How many songs must die that this may live!
And shall this most rash hope and fugitive,
Fulfilled with beauty and with might 250
In days whose feet are rumorous on the air
Make me forget to grieve
For songs which might have been, nor ever were?

Stern the denial, the travail slow,
The struggling wall will scantly grow: 255
And though with that dread rite of sacrifice
Ordained for during edifice,
How long, how long ago!
Into that wall which will not thrive
I build myself alive,   260
Ah, who shall tell me will the wall uprise?
Thou wilt not tell me, who dost only know!
Yet still in mind I keep,
He which observes the wind shall hardly sow,
He which regards the clouds shall hardly reap.   265
Thine ancient way! I give,
Nor wit if I receive;
Risk all, who all would gain: and blindly. Be it so.

'And blindly,' said I?—No!
That saying I unsay: the wings   270
Hear I not in praevenient winnowings
Of coming songs, that lift my hair and stir it?
What winds with music wet do the sweet storm foreshow!
Utter stagnation
Is the solstitial slumber of the spirit,   275
The blear and blank stagnation of all life:
But these sharp questionings mean strife, and strife
Is the negation of negation.
The thing from which I turn my troubled look,
Fearing the gods' rebuke;   280
That perturbation putting glory on,
As is the golden vortex in the West
Over the foundered sun;
That—but low breathe it lest the Nemesis
Unchild me, vaunting this—   285
Is bliss, the hid, hugged, swaddled bliss!
O youngling Joy carest!
That on my first-mothered breast
Pliest the strange wonder of thine infant lip,
What this aghast surprise of keenest panging,   290
Wherefrom I blench, and cry thy soft mouth rest?
Ah hold, withhold, and let the sweet mouth slip!
So, with such pain, recoils the woolly dam,
Unused, affrighted, from her yeanling lamb:

I, one with her in cruel fellowship, 295
Marvel what unmaternal thing I am.

Nature, enough! within thy glass
Too many and too stern the shadows pass.
In this delighted season, flaming
For thy resurrection-feast, 300
Ah, more I think the long ensepulture cold,
Than stony winter rolled
From the unsealed mouth of the holy East;
The snowdrop's saintly stoles less heed
Than the snow-cloistered penance of the seed. 305
'Tis the weak flesh reclaiming
Against the ordinance
Which yet for just the accepting spirit scans.
Earth waits, and patient heaven,
Self-bonded God doth wait 310
Thrice-promulgated bans
Of his fair nuptual-date.
And power is man's,
With that great word of 'wait',
To still the sea of tears, 315
And shake the iron heart of Fate.
In that one word is strong
An else, alas, much-mortal song;
With sight to pass the frontier of all spheres,
And voice which does my sight such wrong. 320

Not without fortitude I wait
The dark majestical ensuit
Of destiny, nor peevish rate
Calm-knowledged Fate.
I, that no part have in the time's bragged way 325
And its loud bruit;
I, in this house so rifted, marred,
So ill to live in, hard to leave;
I, so star-weary, over-warred,
That have no joy in this your day— 330
Rather foul fume englutting, that of day
Confounds all ray—
But only stand aside and grieve;
I yet have sight beyond the smoke,

And kiss the gods' feet, though they wreak 335
Upon me stroke and again stroke;
And this my seeing is not weak.
The Woman I behold, whose vision seek
All eyes and know not; t'ward whom climb
The steps o' the world, and beats all wing of rhyme, 340
And knows not; 'twixt the sun and moon
Her inexpressible front enstarred
Tempers the wrangling spheres to tune;
Their divergent harmonies
Concluded in the concord of her eyes, 345
And vestal dances of her glad regard.
I see, which fretteth with surmise
Much heads grown unsagacious-grey,
The slow aim of wise-hearted Time,
Which folded cycles within cycles cloak: 350
We pass, we pass, we pass; this does not pass away,
But holds the furrowing earth still harnessed to its yoke.
The stars still write their golden purposes
On heaven's high palimpsest, and no man sees,
Nor any therein Daniel; I do hear 355
From the revolving year
A voice which cries:
'All dies;
Lo, how all dies! O seer,
And all things too arise: 360
All dies, and all is born;
But each resurgent morn, behold, more near the Perfect Morn.'

Firm is the man, and set beyond the cast
Of Fortune's game, and the iniquitous hour,
Whose falcon soul sits fast, 365
And not tends her high sagacious tour
Or ere the quarry sighted; who looks past
To slow much sweet from little instant sour,
And in the first does always see the last.

PREFIXED QUOTATIONS

1 From Sir Thomas Browne, *Hydriotaphia, Urn Burial,* Ch. 5, par. 17: Pious spirits, who passe their days in raptures of futurity, made little more of this world than the world that was before it, while they lay obscure in the chaos of preordination and night of our forebeings.

2 And the light shineth in darkness and the darkness did not comprehend it. (John 1:5)

10 *discinct* ungirdled, **22** *meinie* retinue **71** *vanned* winged. **94** *vidual* like a widow. **96** *hieratic* from hieroglyphic writing, hard to understand. **111** *Phoebean* from Phoebus, the sun. **158** *arborous hair* Trees are the earth's 'hair'. **163** *Anadyomene* another name for Aphrodite, goddess of love, alluding to her birth from the sea. **211** *falless* fallness in *Works*. **217** *throe* birth-pang. **230–1** In *Works* these line are compressed into one. Subsequent line numbers therefore follow the *New Poems* text. **254–62** cf. 'John Henry Newman' (p. 226), with significant variation in last two lines. **264, 265** *which* in *Works*: that. **271** *praevenient* coming before, heralded; *winnowings* wing-beats. **275** *solstitial slumber* winter solstice, when the sun is at its lowest. **284** *Nemesis* one of the goddesses of Fate, associated with punishment of human pride. **294** *yeanling* newborn. **310–12** The three days Christ passed in the tomb are likened to the threefold reading of the marriage bans, followed by his resurrection as the 'nuptual date' between supernatural and natural life. **354** *palimpsest* parchment from which earlier writing has been erased. **355** *nor any therein Daniel* compressed meaning: no-one can follow the prophet Daniel in his interpretation of a divine message (Daniel 5). **364–9** cf. falcon imagery in 'By Reason of Thy Law' and 'The Dread of Height' and its application to the poet's condition. It is recorded that these lines were quoted in the House of Commons by Captain J. H. F. McEwen MP on 4 October 1938 'as an expression of England's hope in that dark hour' (TLC, *Francis Thompson: In His Paths*, Bruce, Milwaukee 1944, p. 75).

Any Saint

ME, January 1894

Thompson used the same metre here as in 'To the Dead Cardinal of Westminster' and this poem was written during the summer of 1893, when he was revising the 'Dead Cardinal' for *Poems*. The theme can be said to arise from that of the earlier poem. There, the poet's own human weakness was the barrier between himself and sanctity as displayed by the Cardinal. Here, such weakness becomes the means for seeking and finding God within his creation.

> His shoulder did I hold
> Too high that I, o'erbold
>   Weak one,
>   Should lean thereon.
>
> But He a little hath   5
> Declined His stately path,
>   And my
>   Feet set more high;
>
> That the slack arm may reach
> His shoulder, and faint speech   10
>   Stir
>   His unwithering hair.

And bolder now and bolder
I lean upon that shoulder,
    So dear   15
   He is and near:

And with His aureole
The tresses of my soul
    Are blent
   In wished content.   20

Yea, this too gentle Lover
Hath flattering words to move her
    To pride
   By His sweet side.

Ah, Love! somewhat let be!   25
Lest my humility
    Grow weak
   When thou dost speak!

Rebate thy tender suit,
Lest to herself impute   30
    Some worth
   Thy bride of earth!

A maid too easily
Conceits herself to be
    Those things   35
   Her lover sings;

And being straitly wooed,
Believes herself the Good
    And Fair
   He seeks in her.   40

Turn something of Thy look,
And fear me with rebuke,
    That I
   May timorously

Take tremors in Thy arms,   45
And with contrivèd charms
    Allure
   A love unsure.

Not to me, not to me,
Builded so flawfully,   50
    O God,
  Thy humbling laud!

Not to this man, but Man,—
Universe in a span;
    Point   55
  Of the spheres conjoint;

In whom eternally
Thou, Light, dost focus Thee!—
    Didst pave
  The way o'the wave.   60

Rivet with stars the Heaven,
For causeways to Thy driven
    Car
  In its coming far

Unto him, only him!   65
In Thy deific whim
    Didst bound
  Thy works' great round

In this small ring of flesh;
The sky's gold-knotted mesh   70
    Thy wrist
  Did only twist

To take him in that net,—
Man! swinging-wicket set
    Between   75
  The Unseen and Seen,

Lo, God's two worlds immense,
Of spirit and of sense,
    Wed
  In this narrow bed;   80

Yea, and the midge's hymn
Answers the seraphim
    Athwart
  Thy body's court!

Great arm-fellow of God!   85
To the ancestral clod
   Kin,
  And to cherubin;

Bread predilectedly
O' the worm and Deity!   90
   Hark,
  O God's clay-sealed Ark,

To praise that fits thee, clear
To the ear within the ear,
   But dense   95
  To clay-sealed sense.

All the Omnific made
When in a word He said,
   (Mystery!)
  He uttered *thee*;   100

Thee His great utterance bore,
O secret metaphor
   Of what
  Thou dream'st no jot!

Cosmic metonymy!   105
Weak world–unshuttering key!
   One
  Seal of Solomon!

Trope that itself not scans
Its huge significance,   110
   Which tries
  Cherubic eyes.

Primer where the angels all
God's grammar spell in small,
   Nor spell   115
  The highest too well.

Point for the great descants
Of starry disputants;
   Equation
  Of creation.   120

Thou meaning, could'st thou see,
Of all which dafteth thee;
    So plain,
  It mocks thy pain;

Stone of the Law indeed,   125
Thine own self couldst thou read;
    Thy bliss
  Within thee is.

Compost of Heaven and mire,
Slow foot and swift desire!   130
    Lo,
  To have Yes, choose No;

Gird, and thou shalt unbind;
Seek not, and thou shalt find;
    To eat,   135
  Deny thy meat;

And thou shalt be fulfilled
With all sweet things unwilled:
    So best
  God loves to jest.   140

With children small—a freak
Of heavenly hide-and-seek
    Fit
  For thy wayward wit,

Who art thyself a thing   145
Of whim and wavering;
    Free
  When His wings pen thee;

Sole fully blest, to feel
God whistle thee at heel;   150
    Drunk up
  As a dew-drop,

When He bends down, sun-wise,
Intemperable eyes;
    Most proud,   155
  When utterly bowed,

To feel thyself and be
His dear nonentity—
   Caught
  Beyond human thought   160

In the thunder-spout of Him
Until thy being dim,
   And be
  Dead deathlessly.

Stoop, stoop; for thou dost fear   165
The nettle's wrathful spear,
   So slight
  Art thou of might!

Rise; for Heaven hath no frown
When thou to thee pluck'st down,   170
   Strong clod!
  The neck of God.

1–4 cf. 'To the Dead Cardinal', 41–4. **55–6** *ME*: 'Laud / Thou Thine antipode!' **85–8** *ME*: 'Empyreal five-foot-odd / Great armfellow of God! / Mud-kin / Of cherubin!' **91–2** *ME*: 'Man / Who recite thee can?' **93–6** Not in *ME*. **97** *Omnific* all-creating. **105** *metonymy* 'substituting the name of an attribute for that of the object meant' (*OED*). **108** *Seal of Solomon* According to TLC: 'It is mentioned in the apocrypha of the Rabins, as a ring worn by Solomon in which there was a chased stone bearing the name of God. Through the instrumentality of this seal, Solomon learned everything he desired to know and had power to confine beneath the earth, the evil spirits called Jenn' (TLC*Poems*, p. 474). **109** *Trope* use of a word in a different sense to its accepted meaning. **116** *highest ME*: best. **117** *descants* discourses. **119–20** *ME*: 'Strong / Pinion for their song'.

Between 120–1 *ME*:
     They their high numbering
     In these to product bring,
       Equation
      Of creation.

     And having cast the amount
     Of all the sphery count
       The sum
      Right Man doth come.

     Keystone to the strange dome
     Of God's far-builded Home,
       Which stands
      Not made with hands.

122 *dafteth* puzzles. **123–4** *ME*: The chant / Is in thy heart. **125** *Stone of the Law* The Law of God first inscribed on stone tablets finds its true meaning when inscribed on the human heart (cf. Romans 11 : 15). **126–8** *ME*: Which thyself canst not read: / Wouldst win / What hast within. **131–2** *ME*: Hail / To thee, winged snail. **133–48** four verses not in *ME*. For their theme of Christian asceticism and its underlying paradox, cf. 'The Mistress of Vision', 125–45. **152** *ME*: Like one dewdrop.

Assumpta Maria

'Thou need'st not sing new songs, but say the old.'
(Cowley)

ME, December 1893

When Thompson sent this poem to Alice Meynell in the autumn of 1893, he wrote:

> I send some verses—I don't know what they are like. They are almost entirely taken, some from the Office of the Assumption, some from the Canticle, a few images from the heathen mythology. Some very beautiful images are from a hymn of St Nerses the Armenian, flabbily rendered in *Carmina Mariana*. You will perceive, therefore, the reason of the motto from Cowley . . . They are almost absurdly easy to defend. I have made sure of careful deference to orthodoxy.
>
> (*Letters*, pp. 108–9)

Thompson's source from the hymn of St Nerses is given in the endnotes. His study of ancient religions and their symbolism, kept largely to himself, gives rise to his defence of the poem's 'orthodoxy' despite its use of 'heathen mythology'. He may have said more, for the letter has been mutilated by cutting and pasting. His underlying anxiety appears to have been well founded, for when Meynell reprinted the poem in *Works* he omitted stanzas 5, 6, 7 and 10. Consequently, they have not appeared in any subsequent editions until now.

> *Mortals, that behold a Woman,*
>   *Rising 'twixt the Moon and Sun;*
> *Who am I the heavens assume? an*
>   *All am I, and I am one.*

Multitudinous ascend I,   5
    Dreadful as a battle arrayed,
For I bear you whither tend I;
    Ye are I: be undismayed!
I, the Ark that for the graven
    Tables of the Law was made;   10
Man's own heart was one, one Heaven,
    Both within my womb were laid.
        For there Anteros with Eros
            Heaven with man conjoinèd was,—
        Twin-stone of the Law, *Ischyros*,   15
            Agios Athanatos.

I, the flesh-girt Paradises
  Gardenered by the Adam new,
Daintied o'er with sweet devices
  Which He loveth, for He grew.   20
I the boundless strict savannah
  Which God's leaping feet go through;
I, the heaven whence the Manna,
  Weary Israel, slid on you!
    He the Anteros and Eros,   25
      I the body, He the Cross;
    He upbeareth me, *Ischyros*,
      Agios Athanatos!

I am Daniel's mystic Mountain,
  Whence the mighty stone was rolled;   30
I am the four rivers' fountain,
  Watering Paradise of old;
Cloud down-raining the Just One am,
  Danae of the Shower of Gold;
I the Hostel of the Sun am;   35
    He the Lamb, and I the Fold.
    He the Anteros and Eros,
      I the body, He the Cross;
    He is fast to me, *Ischyros*,
      Agios Athanatos!   40

I, the presence-hall where Angels
  Do enwheel their placèd King—
Even my thoughts which, without change else,
  Cyclic burn and cyclic sing.
To the hollow of Heaven transplanted,   45
  I a breathing Eden spring,
Where with venom all outpanted
  Lies the slimed Curse shrivelling.
    For the brazen Serpent clear on
      That old fangèd knowledge shone;   50
    I to Wisdom rise, *Ischyron*,
      Agion Athanaton!

See in highest heaven pavilioned
  Now the maiden Heaven rest,
The many-breasted sky out-millioned   55

By the splendours of her vest.
Lo, the Ark this holy tide is
   The un-handmade Temple's guest,
And the dark Egyptian bride is
   Whitely to the Spouse-Heart prest!   60
     He the Anteros and Eros,
       Nail me to Thee, sweetest Cross!
     He is fast to me, *Ischyros*,
      Agios Athanatos!

'Tell me, tell me, O Belovèd,   65
   Where Thou dost in mid-day feed!
For my wanderings are reprovèd,
   And my heart is salt with need.'
'Thine own self not spellest God in,
   Nor the lisping papyrus reed?   70
Follow where the flocks have trodden,
   Follow where the shepherds lead.'
     He, the Anteros and Eros,
      Mounts me in Aegyptic car,
     Twin-yoked; leading me, *Ischyros*,   75
      Trembling to the untempted Far.

'Make me chainlets, silvern, golden,
   I that sow shall surely reap;
While as yet my spouse is holden
   Like a Lion in mountained sleep.'   80
'Make her chainlets, silvern, golden,
   She hath sown and she shall reap;
Look up to the mountain olden,
   Whence help comes with lioned leap.'
     By what gushed the bitter Spear on,   85
      Pain, which sundered, maketh one;
     Crucified to Him, *Ischyron*,
      Agion Athanaton!

Then commanded and spoke to me
   He who framed all things that be;   90
And my Maker entered through me,
   In my tent His rest took He.
Lo! He standeth, Spouse and Brother;
   I to Him, and He to me,

Who upraised me where my mother   95
    Fell, beneath the apple-tree.
        Risen, 'twixt Anteros and Eros,
            Blood and Water, Moon and Sun,
        He upbears me, He *Ischyros*,
            I bear Him, the *Athanaton!*   100

Where is laid the Lord arisen?
    In the light we walk in gloom;
Though the sun has burst his prison,
    We know not his biding-room.
Tell us where the Lord sojourneth,   105
    For we find an empty tomb.
'Whence He sprung, there He returneth,
    Mystic Sun,—the Virgin's Womb.'
        Hidden Sun, His beams so near us,
            Cloud empillared as He was   110
        From of old, there He, *Ischyros*,
            Waits our search, *Athanatos.*

Who will give Him me for brother,
    Counted of my family,
Sucking the sweet breasts of my Mother?—   115
    I His flesh, and mine is He;
To my Bread myself the bread is,
    And my Wine doth drink me: see,
His left hand beneath my head is,
    His right hand embraceth me!   120
        Sweetest Anteros and Eros,
            Lo, her arms He leans across;
        Dead that we die not, stopped to rear us,
            Thanatos Athanatos.

Who is She, in candid vesture,   125
    Rushing up from out the brine?
Treading with resilient gesture
    Air, and with that Cup divine?
She in us and we in her are,
    Beating Godward: all that pine,   130
Lo, a wonder and a terror!
    The Sun hath blushed the Sea to Wine!
        He the Anteros and Eros,

She the Bride and Spirit; for
   Now the days of promise near us,   135
   And the Sea shall be no more.

Open wide thy gates, O Virgin,
   That the King may enter thee!
At all gates the clangours gurge in,
   God's paludament lightens, see!   140
Camp of Angels! Well we even
   Of this thing may doubtful be,—
If thou art assumed to Heaven,
   Or is Heaven assumed to thee!
      Consummatum. Christ the promised,   145
         Thy maiden realm is won, O Strong!
      Since to such sweet Kingdom comest,
         Remember me, poor Thief of Song!

Cadent fails the stars along:—
   Mortals, that behold a woman   150
   Rising 'twixt the Moon and Sun;
   Who am I the heavens assume? an
   All am I, and I am one.

Title literally 'Mary Assumed'. The feast of the Assumption on which the poem is based celebrates the taking up of the Blessed Virgin into heaven at her death with no separation of her soul from her body. **Motto** from Abraham Cowley's ode 'On the Death of Crashaw'. Thompson's reference to the 'flabbily rendered lines of St Nerses' is to 'Titles of Our Lady' which he copied into a current notebook (NB2):

        Hostel where the sun finds resting
        Dwelling of the Fire of Glory;
        Moses' bush which flames consumed not;
        Daniel's great Stone-bearing Mountain;
        Solomon's fair Hill of Incense.
        Gideon in the fleece beheld thee,
        David saw the rain descending.
        Noah's Ark, the true, the liking;
        Spikenard of the Spirit's Sweetness
        Fountain whence the four streams issue;
        Censer of the sweetest incense
        Where the fourfold spices mingle!

In another notebook (NB BC11) FT began making his own translation, which though incomplete, justifies his criticism:

        I am the mystic mount of Daniel
           Wherefrom of old the weighty rock was thrown
        The fountain whence the four great rivers fell,
           Which watered Eden in past days unknown
        I am the cloud which did the just rain down

> I am the dance of the golden shower;
> And I the inn whereto the sun has flown,
> He is the lamb, and I myself the bower.

1–2, 6 lines derived from the *Song of Songs*, which FT refers to as the Canticle, often applied to the Blessed Virgin: 'Who is she that cometh forth as the morning rising fair as the moon, bright as the sun, terrible as an army set in array' (Song 6:9). **9–10** *Ark . . . Tables of the Law* The Tablets of the Law signified God's presence among the Israelites, giving the Ark which contained them its special consecration. The Blessed Virgin is compared with this Ark as she carried Christ, who brought the New Law, in her womb. **13** *Anteros* divine love; *Eros* human love. **15–16** *Ischyros, Agios, Athanatos* the Strong One, the Holy One, the Immortal One. These Greek words survive from the earliest Christian liturgies and are used in the Good Friday ceremonies. **29** *Daniel's mystic Mountain* the mountain of King Nebuchadnezzar's dream (cf. Daniel 11:31–45). **31** *four rivers' fountain* Traditionally, the Garden of Eden was watered by four rivers flowing from a central fountain. **34** *Danae of the Shower of Gold* Danae, daughter of Acrisius King of Argos, conceived her son Perseus when the god Zeus visited her in the form of a shower of gold. **40** In the earlier *ME* text a stanza appears here which FT deleted from his revised text:

> I, the burning bush of Moses,
>   Afire with God, yet unconsumed;
> Gladder Vine in me that grows is,
>   Than rash Semele enwombed.
> Arethusa fount through roses
>   Springs in me, that sank engloomed
> From the source of Eve; and closes,
>   With the primal laugh relumed.
>   Flows 'twixt Eros and Anteros,
>   Blood immingled from the Cross;
>   Lovely-lighted, rosy-clear as
>   Ever wine of Cana was!

'Rash Semele' refers to Semele as the mortal beloved by Zeus who became the mother of Dionysus, god of wine and song. 'Arethusa' was the nymph who, pursued by Alpheus, was changed into a fountain whose waters ran for some distance underground. **46–8** *breathing Eden . . . slimed Curse* The Blessed Virgin is often identified as the 'New Eve', her womb as the restored Eden where God again dwells with man and where the wiles of the serpent give way before the true Wisdom that is Christ. **53–88** Three stanzas omitted from *Works* and since. **57–8** *un-handmade Temple's guest* The Ark of the Covenant is here a type, or figure, for the Blessed Virgin, and the Temple a type for the Godhead. She is his guest and, as a virgin, untouched by human hands. **59** *dark Egyptian bride* cf. Song 1:4. The imagery in 59–84 is based on that of the *Song of Songs* where the union of the Lover and the Bride traditionally represents the union of divine and human life—and so in turn, the union of Christ with his Mother in heaven. **74** *Aegyptic car* Egyptian chariot of the sun god. **85–6** The meaning here is condensed but the lines refer to the spear that pierced Christ's side, from which flowed water and blood. **98** *Blood and Water, Moon and Sun* contrasting pairs of images signifying the union of God and Man in Christ. Blood and Sun represent his divinity, Water and Moon his humanity. The symbolism has been taken over from ancient pagan rites, drawing together earth and heaven, matter and spirit. **110** *Cloud empillared* Christ's divinity is concealed as, in the Old Testament, the presence of God was concealed in the pillar of cloud (Exodus 13:21–2). **113–24** stanza added to *ME* text for *New Poems* but deleted from *Works*. The Mass here becomes part of the theme of incarnation. **128** *Cup divine* Christ's human nature. **132** *The Sun* Christ, who has transformed human nature by sharing in it. **135–6** cf. Apoc. 21:1: 'And I saw a new heaven and a new earth. For the first heaven and the first earth was gone, and the sea is now no more.' **137–8** from the Office of the Assumption. 'Lift up your gates, O ye princes, and be ye lifted up, O eternal gates: and the King of Glory shall enter in' (Psalms 23 : 9). **139** *gurge* normally a noun, whirlpool. **140** *paludament* cloak worn by Roman generals. **145** *Consummatum* 'It is consummated', as spoken by Christ on the cross (John 19 : 30).

The After Woman

In the manuscript for *New Poems* this poem is the second of two, with the common title 'The New Woman'. It was published with the title as given above, but the first poem remained unpublished and so is included in the present edition with the manuscript poems under its subtitle as in the manuscript, 'The New Which Is the Old', pp. 417–21. In the manuscript both poems are accompanied by extracts from the Liturgy: this one is prefixed by quotations from the Office of the Assumption and the Easter Vigil which do not appear with the poem as printed in *New Poems*. It is possible that they were intended as a linking theme between these poems and the preceding 'Assumpta Maria', to which they apply more directly. But as there is no way of knowing this with any certainty the extracts are given here as they appear in the manuscript. Translations will be found in the endnotes.

In omnibus requiem quaésivi, et in haereditate Domine morabor.
Tunc praecepit, et dixit mihi Creator omnium: et qui creavit me, requievit in tabernaculo meo.
Virgo prudentissima, quo progrederis, quasi aurora valde rutilans?
Filia Sion, tota formosa et suavis es, pulcra ut luna, electa ut sol.
Vidi speciosam sicut columbam, ascendentem desuper rivos aquarum; ejus inaestimabilis odor erat nimis in vestimentis ejus:
Et sicut dies verni circumdabant eam flores rosarum, et lilia convallium. Equitatui meo in curribus Pharaonis assimilavi te, amica mea.

(From Matins of the Assumption)

Deus, . . . Novum hunc ignum sanctifica: et concede nobis, ita per haec festa paschalia coelestibus desideriis inflammari, ut ad perpetuae claritatis, puris mentibus, valeamus festa pertingere.
Et sicut illuminasti Moysem exuntem de Aegypto, ita illumines corda et sensus nostros: ut ad vitam et lucem aeternam pervenire mereamur.

(From the Blessing of the Candle and the New Fire, Holy Saturday)

[A continuing passage from the same ceremony has been crossed out.]
At the end of the poem Thompson has copied the following passage from the same Holy Saturday liturgy of the Blessing of the New Fire:

In hujus igitur Noctis gratia, suscipe, sancte Pater, incensi hujus sac-
rificium vespertinum . . .
Cereus hic in honorem tui Nominis consecratus, ad Noctis hujus
caliginem destruendam, indeficiens perseveret. Et in odorem suavi-
tatis acceptus, supernis luminaribus misceatur. Flammas ejus
Lucifer matutinus inveniat.

Daughter of the ancient Eve,
We know the gifts ye gave—and give.
Who knows the gifts which *you* shall give,
Daughter of the newer Eve?
You, if my soul be augur, you   5
Shall—O what shall you not, Sweet, do?
The celestial traitress play,
And all mankind to bliss betray;
With sacrosanct cajoleries
And starry treachery of your eyes,   10
Tempt us back to Paradise!
Make heavenly trespass;—ay, press in
Where faint the fledge-foot seraphin,
Blest Fool! Be ensign of our wars,
And shame us all to warriors!   15
Unbanner your bright locks,—advance
Girl, their gilded puissance,
I' the mystic vaward, and draw on
After the lovely gonfalon
Us to out-folly the excess   20
Of your sweet foolhardiness;
To adventure like intense
Assault against Omnipotence!

Give me song, as She is, new,
Earth should turn in time thereto!   25
New, and new, and thrice so new,
All old sweets, New Sweet, meant you!
Fair, I had a dream of thee,
When my young heart beat prophecy,
And in apparition elate   30
Thy little breasts knew waxèd great,
Sister of the Canticle,
And thee for God grown marriageable.
How my desire desired your day,

That, wheeled in rumour on its way, 35
Shook me thus with presentience! Then
Eden's lopped tree shall shoot again:
For who Christ's eyes shall miss, with those
Eyes for evident nuncios?
O who be tardy to His call 40
In your accents augural?
Who shall not feel the Heavens hid
Impend, at tremble of your lid,
And divine advent shine avowed
Under that dim and lucid cloud; 45
Yea, 'fore the silver apocalypse
Fail, at the unsealing of your lips?
When to love *you* is (O Christ's Spouse!)
To love the beauty of His house;
Then come the Isaian days; the old 50
Shall dream; and our young men behold
Vision—yea, the vision of Thabor mount,
Which none to other shall recount,
Because in all men's hearts shall be
The seeing and the prophecy. 55
For ended is the Mystery Play,
When Christ is life, and you the way;
When Egypt's spoils are Israel's right,
And Day fulfils the married arms of Night.
But here my lips are still. 60
Until
You and the hour shall be revealed,
This song is sung and sung not, and its words are sealed.

TRANSLATIONS OF PRELIMINARY TEXTS

In all these I sought rest, and I shall abide in the inheritance of the Lord. Then the creator of all things commanded, and said to me: and he that made me, rested in my tabernacle.

(Eccles. 24 : 11–12)

Most prudent virgin, where do you go, shining brightly like the dawn? Daughter of Sion you are all beauty and sweetness, as beautiful as the moon, chosen like the sun. I have seen her lovely as a dove ascending above the streams of water; the scent of her clothes is beyond price. And like the days of spring rose blossoms and lilies of the vale surround her. O my beloved I have likened you to my horsemen, among the chariots of Pharaoh.

(From Matins of the Assumption)

O God . . . Bless this fire and grant that through this paschal feast we may be so inflamed with heavenly desires that we may with pure minds reach the feast of everlasting brilliance. And as you enlightened Moses as he came out of Egypt, so may you enlighten our hearts and senses that we may deserve to come to the eternal life and light.

(From the Blessing of the Candle and the New Fire, Holy Saturday)

TRANSLATION OF CONCLUDING TEXT

Therefore in the grace of this Night, receive, holy Father, the evening sacrifice of this incense. May this candle, consecrated to the honouring of your name, to remove the darkness of this Night, continue without failing. And being received as a sweet scent, let it be mingled with the heavenly lights. May Lucifer, the Morning Star, still find its flames burning.

4 *newer Eve* the Blessed Virgin. The woman of the pagan past is contrasted with the contemporary woman who has her as model. 18 *vaward* vanguard. 19 *gonfalon* banner with streamers attached. 31–2 cf. Song 8:8. 39 *evident nuncios* distinct messengers. 50 *Isaian days* days prophesied by Isaiah when the old shall see visions and the young dream dreams. 56–9 The Mystery Plays did not baulk at incorporating pagan elements within their Christian context. 58–9 *Egypt's spoils . . . Night* Worship of the fertility goddess Ashtaroth is embraced and purified by the Christian ideal as 'Day fulfils the married arms of Night'. 60–3 The time is not yet ready for such a vision to be revealed.

Grace of the Way

'My brother!' spake she to the sun;
　The kindred kisses of the stars
Were hers; her feet were set upon
　The moon. If slumber solved the bars

Of sense, or sense transpicuous grown   5
　Fulfillèd seeing unto sight,
I know not; nor if 'twas my own
　Ingathered self that made her night.

The windy trammel of her dress,
　Her blown locks, took my soul in mesh;   10
God's breath they spake, with visibleness
　That stirred the raiment of her flesh:

And sensible, as her blown locks were,
　Beyond the precincts of her form
I felt the woman flow from her—   15
　A calm of intempestuous storm.

I failed against the affluent tide;
    Out of this abject earth of me
I was translated and enskied
    Into the heavenly-regioned She.   20

Now of that vision I bereaven
    This knowledge keep, that may not dim:—
Short arm needs man to reach to Heaven,
    So ready is Heaven to stoop to him.

Which sets, to measure of man's feet,   25
    No alien Tree for trysting-place;
And who can read, may read the sweet
    Direction in his Lady's face.

And pass and pass the daily crowd,
    Unwares, occulted Paradise;   30
Love the lost plot cries silver-loud,
    Nor any know the tongue he cries.

The light is in the darkness, and
    The darkness doth not comprehend:
God hath no haste; and God's sons stand   35
    Yet a Day, tarrying for the end.

Dishonoured Rahab still hath hid,
    Yea still, within her house of shame,
The messengers by Jesus bid
    Forerun the coming of His Name.   40

The Word was flesh, and crucified,
    From the beginning, and blasphemed:
Its profaned raiment men divide,
    Damned by what, reverenced, had redeemed.

Thy Lady, was thy heart not blind,   45
    One hour gave to thy witless trust
The key thou go'st about to find;
    And thou hast dropped it in the dust.

Of her, the Way's one mortal grace,
    Own, save thy seeing be all forgot,   50
That truly, God was in this place,
    And thou, unblessèd, knew it not.

But some have eyes, and will not see;
   And some would see, and have not eyes;
And fail the tryst, yet find the Tree,   55
   And take the lesson for the prize.

16 *intempestuous* According to *OED* 'an erroneous form or perhaps a misprint for intempestious: untimely . . . inopportune'. **17** *affluent* flowing. **26** *alien Tree* the tree in Paradise from which Eve took the apple. **30** *occulted* secret, hidden. **31** *the lost plot* Paradise. **33–4** cf. John 1 : 5. **37** *Dishonoured Rahab* the harlot who hid the spies sent by Joshua to Jericho (Joshua 2). **53–6** There are some who only go so far in responding to God's grace, who mistake natural love, *the lesson*, for its supernatural fulfilment, *the prize*.

Retrospect

Alas, and I have sung
Much song of matters vain,
And a heaven-sweetened tongue
Turned to unprofiting strain
Of vacant things, which though   5
Even so they be, and throughly so,
It is no boot at all for thee to know,
But babble and false pain.

What profit if the sun
Put forth his radiant thews,   10
And on his circuit run,
Even after my device, to this and to that use;
And the true Orient, Christ,
Make not His cloud of thee?
I have sung vanity,   15
And nothing well devised.

And though the cry of stars
Give tongue before his way
Goldenly as I say,
And each from wide Saturnus to hot Mars   20
He calleth by its name,
Lest that its bright feet stray;
And thou have lore of all,
But to thine own Sun's call
Thy path disorbed hast never wit to tame;   25
It profits not withal,
And my rede is but lame.

*

Only that, 'mid vain vaunt
Of wisdom ignorant,
A little kiss upon the feet of Love   30
My hasty verse has stayed
Sometimes a space to plant;
It has not wholly strayed,
Not wholly missed near sweet, fanning proud plumes above.

Therefore I do repent   35
That with religion vain,
And misconceivèd pain,
I have my music bent
To waste on bootless things its skiey-gendered rain:
Yet shall a wiser day   40
Fulfil more heavenly way,
And with approvèd music clear this slip.
I trust in God most sweet;
Meantime the silent lip,
Meantime the climbing feet.   45

10 *thews* muscles. 27 *rede* teaching.

A NARROW VESSEL

*Being a Little Dramatic Sequence on the Aspect of Primitive
Girl-nature towards a Love beyond Its Capacities*

When Thompson sent the manuscript of *New Poems* to the Meynells he insisted
that this section should follow the 'Sight and Insight' poems: 'I have put a whole
section of the lightest poems I ever wrote after the first terribly trying section, to
soothe the critics' gums. If they are decent to the measure of their slight aim, that
is all I care for; they aimed little as poetry. That they are true to girl-nature I have a
woman's certificate, beside the fact that I studied them—with one exception—
from an actual original' (*Letters*, p. 150; 'Love Declared' is the exception, as the
headnote to that poem makes clear).

For the sequence as a whole, the 'Narrow Vessel' is the young girl's heart in
danger of being cracked or even broken by love of an order beyond her limited
comprehension. Later, Thompson elaborated the idea in a lengthy exposition of
the poems as allegories of the love between God and the soul (cf. *Life*, pp. 230–2).
He cites the 'Epilogue' as indicative of the general theme but it is too slender a
poem to carry the weight of his claim for the rest. During most of the four years
Thompson was at Pantasaph he lodged with the Brien family and the sequence is

addressed to the oldest daughter, Maggie. The relationship it describes lasted only for the first few months, but on both sides there appear to have been times when it could have gone further and when it may have caused pain.

A Girl's Sin
1 In Her Eyes

Cross child! red, and frowning so?
   'I, the day just over,
Gave a lock of hair to—no!
   How *dare* you say, my lover?'

He asked you?—Let me understand;   5
   Come, child, let me sound it!
'Of course, he *would* have asked it, and—
   And so—somehow—he found it.

'He told it out with great loud eyes—
   Men have such little wit!   10
His sin I ever will chastise
   Because I gave him it.

'Shameless in me the gift, alas!
   In him his open bliss:
But for the privilege he has   15
   A thousand he shall miss!

'His eyes, where once I dreadless laughed,
   Call up a burning blot:
I hate him, for his shameful craft
   That asked by asking not!'   20

Luckless boy! and all for hair
   He never asked, you said?
'Not just—but then he gazed—I swear
   He gazed it from my head!

'His silence on my cheek like breath   25
   I felt in subtle way;
More sweet than aught another saith
   Was what he did not say.

'He'll think me vanquished, for this lapse,
   Who should be above him;   30
Perhaps he'll think me light; perhaps—
   Perhaps he'll think I—love him!

'Are his eyes conscious and elate,
   I hate him that I blush;
Or are they innocent, still I hate—   35
   They mean a thing's to hush.

'Before he nought amiss could do,
   Now all things show amiss;
'Twas all my fault, I know that true,
   But all my fault was his.   40

'I hate him for his mute distress,
   'Tis insult he should care!
Because my heart's all humbleness,
   All pride is in my air.

'With him, each favour that I do   45
   Is bold suit's hallowing text;
Each gift a bastion levelled, to
   The next one and the next.

'Each wish whose grant may him befall
   Is clogged by those withstood;   50
He trembles, hoping one means all,
   And I, lest perhaps it should.

'Behind me piecemeal gifts I cast,
   My fleeing self to save;
And that's the thing must go at last,   55
   For that's the thing he'd have.

'My lock the enforcèd steel did grate
   To cut; its root-thrills came
Down to my bosom. It might sate
   His lust for my poor shame!   60

'His sifted dainty this should be
   For a score ambrosial years!
But his too much humility
   Alarums me with fears.

'My gracious grace a breach he counts   65
    For graceless escalade;
And, though he's silent ere he mounts,
    My watch is not betrayed.

'My heart hides from my soul he's sweet:
    Ah dread, if he divine!   70
One touch, I might fall at his feet,
    And he might rise from mine.

'To hear him praise my eyes' brown gleams
    Was native, safe delight;
But now it usurpation seems,   75
    Because I've given him right.

'Before I'd have him not remove,
    Now would not have him near;
With sacrifice I called on Love,
    And the apparition's Fear.'   80

Foolish to give it!—' 'Twas my whim,
    When he might parted be,
To think that I should stay by him
    In a little piece of me.

'He always said my hair was soft—   85
    What touches he will steal!
Each touch and look (and he'll look oft)
    I almost thought I'd feel.

'And then, when first he saw the hair,
    To think his dear amazement!   90
As if he wished from skies a star,
    And found it in his casement.

'He'd kiss the lock—and I had toyed
    With dreamed delight of this:
But ah, in proof, delight was void—   95
    I could not *see* his kiss!'

So, fond one, half this agony
    Were spared, which my hand hushes,
Could you have played, Sweet, the sweet spy,
    And blushed not for your blushes.   100

61 *sifted dainty* refined delight, referring to the lock of hair. **99–100** The poet comments here: Could you have been more perceptive and less self-conscious.

A Girl's Sin
2 In His Eyes

Can I forget her cruelty
Who, brown miracle, gave you me?
Or with unmoisted eye think on
The proud surrender overgone,
(Lowlihead in haughty dress),   5
Of the tender tyranness?
And ere thou for my joy was given,
How rough the road to that blest heaven!
With what pangs I fore-expiated
Thy cold outlawry from her head;   10
How was I trampled and brought low,
Because her virgin neck was so;
How thralled beneath the jealous state
She stood at point to abdicate;
How sacrificed, before to me   15
She sacrificed her pride and thee;
How did she, struggling to abase
Herself to do me strange, sweet grace,
Enforce unwitting me to share
Her throes and abjectness with her;   20
Thence heightening that hour when her lover
Her grace, with trembling, should discover,
And in adoring trouble be
Humbled at her humility!
And with what pitilessness was I   25
After slain, to pacify
The uneasy *manes* of her shame,
Her haunting blushes!—Mine the blame:
What fair injustice did I rue
For what I—did not tempt her to?   30
Nor aught the judging maid might win
Me to assoil from *her* sweet sin.
But nought were extreme punishment
For that beyond-divine content,
When my with-thee-first-giddied eyes   35
Stooped ere their due on Paradise!
O hour of consternating bliss
When I heavened me in thy kiss;
Thy softness (daring overmuch!)

Profanèd with my licensed touch;   40
Worshipped, with tears, on happy knee,
Her doubt, her trust, her shyness free,
Her timorous audacity!

27 *manes* ghosts. 31–2 There is nothing her self-criticism can get me to pardon her for.

Love Declared

This is clearly the exception from the rest of the 'Narrow Vessel' poems that Thompson noted in the letter quoted above, at the start of the sequence. The experience described here could not have formed part of his relationship with Maggie Brien as recorded in the poems or in the letter. There is a draft of 'Love Declared' with the manuscript of 'A Dead Astronomer' (p. 194) and a portion of the essay on Shelley. This indicates a date for composition in the summer of 1889, when he was working on the essay, and the poem therefore almost certainly concerns his recent memories of his relationship with the street girl. Referring again to the letter quoted at the start of the sequence, the poem is in fact also recalling 'an original' model, but not the one of the rest of the poems. By making the distinction, Thompson probably hoped that the personal element here would be discounted.

I looked, she drooped, and neither spake, and cold,
We stood, how unlike all forecasted thought
Of that desirèd minute! Then I leaned
Doubting; whereat she lifted—oh, brave eyes
Unfrighted:—forward like a wind-blown flame   5
Came bosom and mouth to mine!
                              That falling kiss
Touching long-laid expectance, all went up
Suddenly into passion; yea, the night
Caught, blazed, and wrapt us round in vibrant fire.   10

Time's beating wing subsided, and the winds
Caught up their breathing, and the world's great pulse
Stayed in mid-throb, and the wild train of life
Reeled by, and left us stranded on a hush.
This moment is a statue unto Love   15
Carved from a fair white silence.
                              Lo, he stands
Within us—are we not one now, one, one roof,
His roof, and the partition of weak flesh
Gone down before him, and no more, for ever?—   20

Stands like a bird new-lit, and as he lit,
Poised in our quiet being; only, only
Within our shaken hearts the air of passion,
Cleft by his sudden coming, eddies still
And whirs round his enchanted movelessness.   25

A film of trance between two stirrings! Lo,
It bursts; yet dream's snapped links cling round the limbs
Of waking: like a running evening stream
Which no man hears, or sees, or knows to run,
(Glazed with dim quiet), save that there the moon   30
Is shattered to a creamy flicker of flame,
Our eyes' sweet trouble were hid, save that the love
Trembles a little on their impassioned calms.

The Way of a Maid

The lover whose soul shaken is
In some decuman billow of bliss,
Who feels his gradual-wading feet
Sink in some sudden hollow of sweet,
And 'mid love's usèd converse comes   5
Sharp on a mood which all joy sums—
An instant's fine compendium of
The liberal-leavèd writ of love;
His abashed pulses beating thick
At the exigent joy and quick,   10
Is dumbed by aiming utterance great
Up to the miracle of his fate.
The wise girl, such Icarian fall
Saved by her confidence that she's small,—
As what no kindred word will fit   15
Is uttered best by opposite,
Love in the tongue of hate exprest,
And deepest anguish in a jest,—
Feeling the infinite must be
Best said by triviality,   20
Speaks, where expression bates its wings,
Just happy, alien, little things;
What of all words is in excess
Implies in a sweet nothingness,

With dailiest babble shows her sense   25
That full speech were full impotence;
And while she feels the heavens lie bare,
She only talks about her hair.

2 *decuman* especially large (*OED*). 13 *Icarian fall* see 'Mistress of Vision', note to 106.

Beginning of the End

She was aweary of the hovering
Of Love's incessant and tumultuous wing;
Her lover's tokens she would answer not—
'Twere well she should be strange to him somewhat:
A pretty babe, this Love,—but fie on it,   5
That would not suffer her lay it down a whit!
Appointed tryst defiantly she balked,
And with her lightest comrade lightly walked,
Who scared the chidden Love to hide apart,
And peep from some unnoticed corner of her heart.   10
She thought not of her lover, deem it not
(There yonder, in the hollow, that's *his* cot),
But she forgot not that he was forgot.
She saw him at his gate, yet stilled her tongue—
So weak she felt her, that she would feel strong,   15
And she must punish him for doing him wrong:
Passed, unoblivious of oblivion still;
And if she turned upon the brow o' the hill,
It was so openly, so lightly done,
You saw she thought he was not thought upon.   20
He through the gate went back in bitterness;
She that night woke and stirred, with no distress,
Glad of her doing,—sedulous to be glad,
Lest perhaps her foolish heart suspect that it was sad.

Penelope

Penelope was the wife of Ulysses and, during his long absence at the Trojan war, was besieged by suitors. She succeeded in outwitting them by obtaining their agreement that she must complete a woven robe for her father-in-law before declaring which of them she would accept. Each night she undid the work done the previous day, so postponing any such choice.

Love, like a wind, shook wide your blosmy eyes,
You trembled, and your breath came sobbing-wise
    For that you loved me.

You were so kind, so sweet, none could withhold
To adore, but that you were so strange, so cold;   5
    For that you loved me.

Like to a box of spikenard did you break
Your heart about my feet. What words you spake!
    For that you loved me.

Life fell to dust without me; so you tried   10
All carefullest ways to drive me from your side,
    For that you loved me.

You gave yourself as children give, that weep
And snatch back, with—'I meant you not to keep!'
    For that you loved me.   15

I am no woman, girl, nor ever knew
That love could teach all ways that hate could do
    To her that loved me.

Have less of love, or less of woman in
Your love, or loss may even from this begin—   20
    That you so love me.

For, wild Penelope, the web you wove
You still unweave, unloving all your love;
    Is this to love me,

Or what rights have I that scorn could deny?   25
Even of your love, alas, poor Love must die,
    If so you love me!

---

1 *blosmy* blossomy substituted in *Works*, but does not scan.

The End of It

She did not love to love; but hated him
For making her to love, and so her whim
From passion taught misprision to begin;
And all this sin
Was because love to cast out had no skill   5
Self, which was regent still.
Her own self-will made void her own self's will.

3 *misprision* an offence. **5–6** love had no skill to cast out self.

Epilogue

The third verse of the poem as published in *New Poems* has been omitted in *Works* and other editions.

If I have studied here in part
A tale as old as maiden's heart,
    'Tis that I do see herein
    Shadow of more piteous sin.

She, that but giving part, not whole,   5
Took even the part back, is the Soul:
    And that so disdainèd Lover—
    Best unthought, since Love is over.

Love to invite, desire, and fear,
And Love's exactions cost too dear   10
    Count for Love's possession,—ah,
    Thy way, *misera Anima!*

To give the pledge, and yet be pined
That a pledge should have force to bind,
    This, O Soul, too often still   15
    Is the recreance of thy will!

Out of Love's arms to make fond chain,
And, because struggle bringeth pain,
    Hate Love for Love's sweet constraint,
    Is the way of Souls that faint.   20

Such a Soul, for saddest end,
  Finds Love the foe in Love the friend;
    And—ah, grief incredible!—
  Treads the way of Heaven, to Hell.

9–11 Love, once invited, brings desire and fear, and love's exactions are too dear for love to bear. 12 *misera Anima* O sad soul. 16 *recreance* from recreant: craven, cowardly (*OED*)

MISCELLANEOUS ODES

Ode to the Setting Sun

ME, September 1889

Thompson recorded the composition of this, his first major poem, in three separate notebook entries: ' "Ode to the Setting Sun", begun in the field of the Cross at sunset—finished ascending and descending Jacob's Ladder (mid or late noon?).' (NB BC27; also in NB3 and NB 23A) The Field of the Cross formed part of the grounds of the Priory at Storrington and Jacob's Ladder was the local name for a steep approach to the downs frequently taken by Thompson. The revisions of the text for *New Poems* are particularly significant for his poetic development during the intervening years.

Prelude

The wailful sweetness of the violin
  Floats down the hushèd waters of the wind,
The heart-strings of the throbbing harp begin
  To long in aching music. Spirit-pined,

In wafts that poignant sweetness drifts, until   5
  The wounded soul ooze sadness. The red sun,
A bubble of fire, drops slowly toward the hill,
  While one bird prattles that the day is done.

O setting Sun, that as in reverent days
  Sinkest in music to thy smoothèd sleep,   10
Discrowned of homage, though yet crowned with rays,
  Hymned not at harvest more, though reapers reap;

For thee this music wakes not. O deceived,
  If thou hear in these thoughtless harmonies
A pious phantom of adorings reaved,   15
  And echo of fair ancient flatteries!

Yet, in this field where the Cross planted reigns,
    I know not what strange passion bows my head
To thee, whose great command upon my veins
    Proves thee a god for me not dead, not dead!   20

For worship it is too incredulous,
    For doubt—oh, too believing-passionate!
What wild divinity makes my heart thus
    A fount of most baptismal tears?—thy straight

Long beam lies steady on the Cross. Ah me!   25
    What secret would thy radiant finger show?
Of thy bright mastership is this the key?
    Is *this* thy secret then? And is it woe?

Fling from thine ear the burning curls, and hark
    A song thou hast not heard in Northern day;   30
For Rome too daring, and for Greece too dark,
    Sweet with wild wings that pass, that pass away!

Ode

Alpha and Omega, sadness and mirth,
    The springing music, and its wasting breath—
The fairest things in life are Death and Birth,
    And of these two the fairer thing is Death.
Mystical twins of Time inseparable,   5
    The younger hath the holier array,
        And hath the awfuller sway:
    It is the falling star that trails the light,
    It is the breaking wave that hath the might,
The passing shower that rainbows maniple.   10
    Is it not so, O thou down-stricken Day,
That draw'st thy splendours round thee in thy fall?
High was thine Eastern pomp inaugural;
But thou dost set in statelier pageantry,
    Lauded with tumults of a firmament: 15
Thy visible music-blasts make deaf the sky,
    Thy cymbals clang to fire the Occident,
Thou dost thy dying so triumphally:
I *see* the crimson blaring of thy shawms!
        Why do those lucent palms   20
Strew thy feet's failing thicklier than their might,

Who dost but hood thy glorious eyes with night,
And vex the heels of all the yesterdays?
      Lo! this loud, lackeying praise
Will stay behind to greet the usurping moon,   25
    When they have cloud-barred over thee the West.
Oh, shake the bright dust from thy parting shoon!
    The earth not paeans thee, nor serves thy hest,
Be godded not by Heaven! avert thy face,
      And leave to blank disgrace   30
The oblivious world! unsceptre thee of state and place!

Ha! but bethink thee what thou gazedst on,
  Ere yet the snake Decay had venomed tooth;
The name thou bar'st in those vast seasons gone—
      Candid Hyperion,   35
  Clad in the light of thine immortal youth!
      Ere Dionysus bled thy vines,
Or Artemis drave her clamours through the wood,
    Thou saw'st how once against Olympus' height
        The brawny Titans stood,   40
And shook the gods' world 'bout their ears, and how
Enceladus (whom Etna cumbers now)
  Shouldered me Pelion with its swinging pines,
The river unrecked, that did its broken flood
Spurt on his back: before the mountainous shock   45
      The rankèd gods dislock,
Scared to their skies; wide o'er rout-trampled night
Flew spurned the pebbled stars: those splendours then
    Had tempested on earth, star upon star
    Mounded in ruin, if a longer war   50
Had quaked Olympus and cold-fearing men.
    Then did the ample marge
      And circuit of thy targe
    Sullenly redden all the vaward fight,
      Above the blusterous clash   55
      Wheeled thy swung falchion's flash,
    And hewed their forces into splintered flight.

Yet ere Olympus thou wast, and a god!
    Though we deny thy nod,
We cannot spoil thee of thy divinity.   60
    What know we elder than thee?

When thou didst, bursting from the great void's husk,
Leap like a lion on the throat o' the dusk;
  When the angles rose-chapleted
    Sang each to other,   65
   The vaulted blaze overhead
   Of their vast pinions spread,
    Hailing thee brother;
How chaos rolled back from the wonder,
And the First Morn knelt down to thy visage of thunder! 70
   Thou didst draw to thy side
    Thy young Auroral bride,
   And lift her veil of night and mystery;
    Tellus with baby hands
    Shook off her swaddling-bands,   75
   And from the unswathèd vapours laughed to thee.

Thou twi-form deity, nurse at once and sire!
 Thou genitor that all things nourishest!
 The earth was suckled at thy shining breast,
And in her veins is quick thy milky fire.   80
Who scarfed her with the morning? and who set
Upon her brow the day-fall's carcanet?
  Who queened her front with the enrondured moon?
   Who dug night's jewels from their vaulty mine
   To dower her, past an eastern wizard's dreams, 85
When hovering on him through his haschish-swoon,
  All the rained gems of the old Tartarian line
Shiver in lustrous throbbings of tinged flame?
   Whereof a moiety in the Paolis' seams
   Statelily builded their Venetian name.   90
   Thou hast enwoofèd her
   An empress of the air.
And all her births are propertied by thee:
   Her teeming centuries
   Drew being from thine eyes: 95
Thou fatt'st the marrow of all quality.

Who lit the furnace of the mammoth's heart?
 Who shagged him like Pilatus' ribbèd flanks?
  Who raised the columned ranks
Of that old pre-diluvian forestry,   100
Which like a continent torn oppressed the sea,

When the ancient heavens did in rains depart,
  While the high-dancèd whirls
Of the tossed scud made hiss thy drenchèd curls?
    Thou rear'dst the enormous brood;   105
    Who hast with life imbued
The lion maned in tawny majesty,
    The tiger velvet-barred,
    The stealthy-stepping pard
And the lithe panther's flexuous symmetry.   110

How came the entombèd tree a light-bearer,
     Though sunk in lightless lair?
      Friend of the forgers of earth,
    Mate of the earthquake and thunders volcanic,
    Clasped in the arms of the forces Titanic   115
     Which rock like a cradle the girth
      Of the ether-hung world;
     Swart son of the swarthy mine,
     When flame on the breath of his nostrils feeds
      How is his countenance half-divine,   120
      Like thee in thy sanguine weeds?
    Thou gavest him his light,
    Though sepultured in night
Beneath the dead bones of a perished world;
    Over his prostrate form   125
    Though cold, and heat, and storm,
The mountainous wrack of a creation hurled.

    Who made the splendid rose
    Saturate with purple glows;
Cupped to the marge with beauty; a perfume-press   130
    Whence the wind vintages
Gushes of warmèd fragrance richer far
    Than all the flavorous ooze of Cyprus' vats?
Lo, in yon gale which waves her green cymar,
    With dusky cheeks burnt red   135
    She sways her heavy head,
Drunk with the must of her own odorousness;
    While in a moted trouble the vexed gnats
Maze, and vibrate, and tease the noontide hush.
    Who girt dissolvèd lightnings in the grape?   140
Summered the opal with an Irised flush?

Is it not thou that dost the tulip drape,
　　And huest the daffodilly,
　　Yet who hast snowed the lily,
And her frail sister, whom the waters name,　　　　　145
　　Dost vestal-vesture 'mid the blaze of June,
　　Cold as the new-sprung girlhood of the moon
Ere Autumn's kiss sultry her cheek with flame?
　　　　Thou sway'st thy sceptred beam
　　　　O'er all delight and dream,　　　　　150
　　Beauty is beautiful but in thy glance:
　　　　And like a jocund maid
　　　　In garland-flowers arrayed,
Before thy ark Earth keeps her sacred dance.

And now, O shaken from thine antique throne,　　　155
　　And sunken from thy coerule empery,
Now that the red glare of thy fall is blown
In smoke and flame about the windy sky,
Where are the wailing voices that should meet
　　From hill, stream, grove, and all of mortal shape　　160
Who tread thy gifts, in vineyards as stray feet
　　Pulp the globed weight of juiced Iberia's grape?
　　　　Where is the threne o' the sea?
　　　　And why not dirges thee
The wind, that sings to himself as he makes stride　　165
　　Lonely and terrible on the Andéan height?
　　　　Where is the Naiad 'mid her sworded sedge?
　　The Nymph wan-glimmering by her wan fount's verge?
The Dryad at timid gaze by the wood-side?
　　　　The Oread jutting light　　　　　170
　　On one up-strainèd sole from the rock-ledge?
　　　　The Nereid tip-toe on the scud o' the surge,
With whistling tresses dank athwart her face,
And all her figure poised in lithe Circean grace?
　　　　Why withers their lament?　　　　　175
　　　　Their tresses tear-besprent,
　　Have they sighed hence with trailing garment-hem?
　　　　O sweet, O sad, O fair!
　　　　I catch your flying hair,
Draw your eyes down to me, and dream on them!　　180
　　　　　　*

A space, and they fleet from me. Must ye fade—
O old, essential candours, ye who made
    The earth a living and a radiant thing—
        And leave her corpse in our strained, cheated arms?
        Lo ever thus, when Song with chorded charms   185
Draws from dull death his lost Eurydice,
    Lo ever thus, even at consummating,
    Even in the swooning minute that claims her his,
    Even as he trembles to the impassioned kiss
    Of reincarnate Beauty, his control   190
    Clasps the cold body, and foregoes the soul!
      Whatso looks lovelily
Is but the rainbow on life's weeping rain.
Why have we longings of immortal pain,
And all we long for mortal? Woe is me,   195
And all our chants but chaplet some decay,
As mine this vanishing—nay, vanished Day.
The low sky-line dusks to a leaden hue,
    No rift disturbs the heavy shade and chill,
Save one, where the charred firmament lets through   200
    The scorching dazzle of Heaven; 'gainst which the hill
      Out-flattened sombrely,
Stands black as life against eternity.
      Against eternity?
      A rifting light in me   205
Burns through the leaden broodings of the mind:
    O blessèd Sun, thy state
    Uprisen or derogate
Dafts me no more with doubt; I seek and find.

    If with exultant tread   210
      Thou foot the Eastern sea,
      Or like a golden bee
    Sting the West to angry red,
    Thou dost image, thou dost follow
      That King-Maker of Creation,   215
    Who, ere Hellas hailed Apollo,
      Gave thee, angel-god, thy station;
Thou art of Him a type memorial.
    Like Him thou hang'st in dreadful pomp of blood
      Upon thy Western rood;   220
    And His stained brow did veil like thine to night,

Yet lift once more Its light,
And, risen again departed from our ball,
But when It set on earth arose in Heaven.
Thus hath He unto death His beauty given: 225
And so of all which form inheriteth
    The fall doth pass the rise in worth;
For birth hath in itself the germ of death,
   But death hath in itself the germ of birth.
It is the falling acorn buds the tree,   230
The falling rain that bears the greenery,
   The fern-plants moulder when the ferns arise.
  For there is nothing lives but something dies,
And there is nothing dies but something lives.
    Till skies be fugitives,   235
Till Time, the hidden root of change, updries,
Are Birth and Death inseparable on earth;
For they are twain yet one, and Death is Birth.

After-Strain

Now with wan ray that other sun of Song
  Sets in the bleakening waters of my soul:
One step, and lo! the Cross stands gaunt and long
  'Twixt me and yet bright skies, a presaged dole.

Even so, O Cross! thine is the victory.   5
  Thy roots are fast within our fairest fields;
Brightness may emanate in Heaven from thee,
  Here thy dread symbol only shadow yields.

Of reapèd joys thou art the heavy sheaf
  Which must be lifted, though the reaper groan;   10
Yea, we may cry till Heaven's great ear be deaf,
  But we must bear thee, and must bear alone.

Vain were a Simon; of the Antipodes
  Our night not borrows the superfluous day.
Yet woe to him that from his burden flees!   15
  Crushed in the fall of what he cast away.

Therefore, O tender Lady, Queen Mary,
  Thou gentleness that dost enmoss and drape
The Cross's rigorous austerity,
  Wipe thou the blood from wounds that needs must gape.20

'Lo, though suns rise and set, but crosses stay,
    I leave thee ever,' saith she, 'light of cheer.'
'Tis so: yon sky still thinks upon the Day;
    And showers aërial blossoms on his bier.

Yon cloud with wrinkled fire is edgèd sharp;   25
    And once more welling through the air, ah me!
How the sweet viol plains him to the harp,
    Whose pangèd sobbings throng tumultuously.

Oh, this Medusa-pleasure with her stings!
    This essence of all suffering, which is joy!   30
I am not thankless for the spell it brings,
    Though tears must be told down for the charmed toy.

No; while soul, sky, and music bleed together,
    Let me give thanks even for those griefs in me,
The restless windward stirrings of whose feather   35
    Prove them the brood of immortality.

My soul is quitted of death-neighbouring swoon,
    Who shall not slake her immitigable scars
Until she hear 'My sister!' from the moon,
    And take the kindred kisses of the stars.   40

PRELUDE

When FT revised the original text he virtually rewrote the Prelude. The change
in his poetic outlook, with self-doubt in place of the earlier expectations, is clear
when the revised text is compared with this in *ME*:

The wailful sweetness of the violin
    Floats down the hushèd waters of the wind,
The passionate strings of the throbbed harp begin
    To long in aching music: spirit-pined,

In wafts that poignant sweetness drifts, until
    The wounded soul ooze sadness. The red sun,
A bubble of fire, drops slowly towards the hill
    While one bird twitters that the day is done.

Behind, a leaden-purple shadow lies,
    And shadowed on that shadow rests the hill;
Above, a greening-yellow tincture dies
    Where two long reefs of kindled primrose thrill;

Stretches of carmined flame hang yet more high,
    As the wine-god had spilt his burning wine
Upon the drenchèd woofing of the sky;
    Beneath in semi-circled line on line

Descends the gradual landscape, greyly green;
   This windmill stands up black amid the cool;
Nature and I scarce breathe; far down is seen
   The ghostly shining of a shadowed pool.

O setting Sun, that as in reverent days
   Sinkest in music to thy smoothèd sleep,
Discrowned of homage, though yet crowned with rays,
   Hymned not at harvest more, though reapers reap;

Methinks that pomp whereof thou art not shorn
   Should strike a pæaned singing out of me;
For Song is the true deathless babe that's born
   When fire embraces the soul's Semele.

ODE

1 *Alpha and Omega* First and Last (cf. Apoc. 1:8). 10 *maniple* verb invented from maniple, piece of cloth worn over the arm as part of a priest's vestments. Its probable origin was as a handkerchief to wipe sweat from the face, so becoming a sign for present sorrows leading to future joys in heaven. Here it becomes a sign of hope similar to that of the rainbow. 18 *ME*: And peeling ardours flush to ardorous dye. 34 *bar'st ME*: barest. 35 *Hyperion* the sun god. 37 *Dionysus* god of wine, also of poetic inspiration. 38 *Artemis* another name for Diana, goddess of the hunt. 39–45 According to TLC, FT has confused the struggle of the Titans against the gods with that of the Giants: 'It was during the latter struggle that the Giants piled Mt. Ossa upon Mt. Pelion in an attempt to reach the heavens. In this same struggle, Athene threw the island of Sicily containing Mt. Etna upon the Giant Enceladus as he fled from the conflict. According to another version all the Giants were finally buried alive under Mt. Etna' (TLC*Poems*, p. 377). 42 *cumbers ME*: throttles. 43 *Shouldered ME*: shoulders. 44 *ME*: And cataracts, while Peneus' broken flood 46 *ME*: Their rent host reels, while from the strand of night 48 *those splendours then ME*: Heaven's cressets then 51 *and cold-fearing men ME*: and beshuddered men 53 *targe* shield. 54 *vaward* vanguard; *ME*: Flame in the torrent clangours of that fight; 56 *falchion* curved sword. 72 *Auroral bride* creation's first morning, from Aurora, the dawn goddess 74 *Tellus* the Earth. 82 *carcanet*: coronet. 86 *hovering on him ME*: reeling flashing 87 *old Tartarian line* the Mongol emperors, famed for their wealth 89–90 A portion of the Mongol wealth was helped to bring back by Marco Polo and his uncles the Paoli, who invested it in the salt mines that helped to bring fame and wealth to Venice. 96 *fatt'st ME*: fattest. 98 *Pilatus' ribbèd flanks* Mount Pilatus in Switzerland is so named for the legend that Pontius Pilate drowned himself in a lake near its summit. In shape it is said to resemble a mammoth, with the trees on its lower slopes likened to the animal's ribs. **Between 98–9 *ME*:**

>   O vivifying Sun,
> Did not thy fervours to his blood impart
>   The hum of that impulse,
> Shake the lashed arteries of the mastodon,
>   Beat ope the sluices of his troubled veins,
> And turge [control?] the bondless heavings of his pulse?

100–1 the forests dating from before the Flood, having been submerged beneath the sea. 111–27 These lines refer to coal and coal mining.

Between 112–13 *ME*:

>   Hearing for ever from his lair
> The spasm and nightmare of hell's labouring breast
>   Heaving in thick unrest?

120 *How is ME*: Who made.

Between 121–2 *ME*:

> When flame on the breath of his nostrils feeds?
> How hot is his pulse of desire!
> How is he, groom to the eager fire?
>> And the smoke ebon-curled,
> Smoke, his dark daughter, how doth she aspire?

133 *Cyprus' vats* Cyprus was famed in the ancient world for its luxury and fine wine. **134** *cymar* robe worn by Eastern women. **137** *must* new wine. **150–4** *ME* (punctuation added to first line):

> O'er all Earth's broad loins' teem;
> She sweats thee through her pores to verdurous spilth:
>> Thou art light in her light,
>> Thou art might in her might,
> Fruitfulness in her fruit, and foison in her tilth.

154 The line recalls King David's sacred dance before the Ark of the Covenant (2 Kings 6:14). **163** *threne* lament. **167** *Naiad*: water nymph. **169** *Dryad* tree nymph. **170** *Oread* mountain nymph. **172** *Nereid* sea nymph. **174** *figure ME*: body; *Circean grace* Circe was a daughter of the sun god. **186** *Eurydice* wife of Orpheus, god of music and poetry. On their wedding night she was killed by a serpent and so lay dead in his arms. **209** *Dafts* confuses. **216** *Hellas* Greece; *Apollo* the sun god. **226** *form ME*: that form. **Between 229–30** *ME*:

> So, when thy course is done,
> Thy pale-robed spirit through the vault star-sown
> Doth mount unto its throne.

235 *ME*: Till rot the centuries,

AFTER-STRAIN **13–16** *ME*:

> No Cyrenaean shall give a passing ease
>> To the galled shoulder of our aching heart;
> Yet woe the heart that from its burden flees!
> Crushed 'neath the fall of what it flung apart.

A Captain of Song

(On a Portrait of Coventry Patmore by J. S. Sargent, R. A.)

The Athenaeum, 5 December 1896

Coventry Patmore died in November 1896 and Thompson's ode followed the obituary notice in *The Athenaeum*. According to a note added there by him but not included in *New Poems* it was written the previous year: 'As the meaning of this poem cannot be appreciated without the knowledge that it was written to a living man and bears reference to spiritual experience and not to death, the reader has now to take note of the date, the summer of 1895.'

> Look on him. This is he whose works ye know;
> Ye have adored, thanked, loved him,—no, not him!
> But that of him which proud portentous woe

To its own grim
Presentment was not potent to subdue,   5
Not all the reek of Erebus to dim.
This, and not him, ye knew.
Look on him now. Love, worship if ye can,
The very man.
Ye may not. He has trod the ways afar,   10
The fatal ways of parting and farewell,
Where all the paths of painèd greatness are;
Where round and always round
The abhorrèd words resound,
The words accursed of comfortable men,—   15
'For ever'; and infinite glooms intolerable
With spacious replication give again,
And hollow jar,
The words abhorred of comfortable men.
You the stern pities of the gods debar   20
To drink where he has drunk
The moonless mere of sighs,
And pace the places infamous to tell,
Where God wipes not the tears from any eyes,
Where-through the ways of dreadful greatness are.   25
He knows the perilous rout
That all those ways about
Sink into doom, and sinking, still are sunk.
And if his sole and solemn term thereout
He has attained, to love ye shall not dare   30
One who has journeyed there;
Ye shall mark well
The mighty cruelties which arm and mar
That countenance of control,
With minatory warnings of a soul   35
That hath to its own selfhood been most fell,
And is not weak to spare:
And lo, that hair
Is blanchèd with the travel-heats of hell.

If any be   40
That shall with rites of reverent piety
Approach this strong
Sad soul of sovereign Song,
Nor fail and falter with the intimidate throng;
If such there be,   45

These, these are only they
Have trod the self-same way;
The never-twice-revolving portals heard
Behind them clang infernal, and that word
Abhorrèd sighed of kind mortality,   50
As he—
Ah, even as he!

6 *Erebus* Hell, or Hades. **49–50** *that word . . . mortality* begged for death from kind mortality.

Against Urania

Thompson here addresses Urania according to the Renaissance usage, when the Muse of Astronomy was also associated with poetic inspiration. She is addressed in this manner by Milton in *Paradise Lost* (Bk 7, 1–20).

Lo I, Song's most true lover plain me sore
That worse than other women she can deceive,
For she being goddess, I have given her more
Than mortal ladies from their lovers receive:
And first of her embrace   5
She was not coy, and gracious were her ways,
That I forgot all virgins to adore;
Nor did I greatly grieve
To bear through arid days
The pretty foil of her divine delays;   10
And one by one to cast
Life, love, and health,
Content, and wealth,
Before her, thinking ever on her praise,
Until at last   15
Nought had I left she would be gracious for.
Now of her cozening I complain me sore,
Seeing her uses,
That still, more constantly she is pursued,
And straitlier wooed,   20
Her only-adorèd favour more refuses,
And leaves me to implore
Remembered boon in bitterness of blood.

From mortal woman thou may'st know full well,
O poet, that dost deem the fair and tall   25

Urania of her ways not mutable,
What things shall thee befall
When thou art toilèd in her sweet, wild spell.
Do they strow for thy feet
A little tender favour and deceit   30
Over the sudden mouth of hidden hell?—
As more intolerable
Her pit, as her first kiss is heavenlier-sweet.
Are they, the more thou sigh,
Still the more watchful-cruel to deny?—   35
Know this, that in her service thou shalt learn
How harder than the heart of woman is
The immortal cruelty
Of the high goddesses.
True is his witness who doth witness this,   40
Whose gaze too early fell—
Nor thence shall turn,
Nor in those fires shall cease to weep and burn—
Upon her ruinous eyes and ineludible.

1 *plain* complain.

An Anthem of Earth

ME, November 1894

When Thompson sent this poem to Alice Meynell he noted that it 'was written
only as an exercise in blank verse', the subject matter being based largely on his
prose writings. As poetry, it was very much an experiment: 'It is my first serious
attempt to handle that form, and it is not likely that I have succeeded all at once;
especially as I have not confined myself to the strict limits of the metre, but have
laid my hands at one clash among all the licenses with which the Elizabethans
build up their harmonies' (*Letters*, p. 120). After its appearance in *New Poems* he
wrote in more detail on its blank verse form to the critic William Archer: 'It is
from the later Shakespeare. Unlike most critics, I have always considered Shakespeare's late blank verse to be his greatest and most characteristic . . . I
deliberately took it as model; thinking that my life long study would enable me to
do what critics have pronounced impossible, what even Coleridge confessed he
had tried to do and failed—i.e. catch the rhythm of Shakespeare's verse' (*Letters*,
p. 192). The ideas behind many passages in the poem had earlier formed the subject matter for an essay, 'A Threnody of Birth', which was only published long
after Thompson's death, in *The Real Robert Louis Stevenson and Other Critical
Essays by Francis Thompson* (ed. T. L. Connolly, University Publishers, New York
1959).

Præmion

Immeasurable Earth!
Through the loud vast and populacy of Heaven,
Tempested with gold schools of ponderous orbs,
That cleav'st with deep-revolving harmonies
Passage perpetual, and behind thee draw'st   5
A furrow sweet, a cometary wake
Of trailing music! What large effluence,
Not sole the cloudy sighing of thy seas,
Nor thy blue-coifing air, encases thee
From prying of the stars, and the broad shafts   10
Of thrusting sunlight tempers? For, dropped near
From my removèd tour in the serene
Of utmost contemplation, I scent lives.
This is the efflux of thy rocks and fields,
And wind-cuffed forestage, and the souls of men,   15
And aura of all treaders over thee;
A sentient exhalation, wherein close
The odorous lives of many-throated flowers,
And each thing's mettle effused; that so thou wear'st
Even like a breather on a frosty morn,   20
Thy proper suspiration. For I know,
Albeit, with custom-dulled perceivingness,
Nestled against thy breast, my sense not take
The breathings of thy nostrils, there's no tree,
No grain of dust, nor no cold-seeming stone,   25
But wears a fume of its circumfluous self.
Thine own life, and the lives of all that live,
The issue of thy loins,
Is this thy gaberdine,
Wherein thou walkest through thy large demesne   30
And sphery pleasances,—
Amazing the unstalèd eyes of Heaven,
And us that still a precious seeing have
Behind this dim and mortal jelly.
                        Ah!   35
If not in all too late and frozen a day
I come in rearward of the throat of song,
Unto the deaf sense of the agèd year
Singing with doom upon me; yet give heed!
One poet with sick pinion, that still feels   40
Breath through the Orient gateways closing fast,
Fast closing t'ward the undelighted night!

Anthem

In nescientness, in nescientness,
Mother, we put these fleshly lendings on
Thou yield'st to thy poor children; took thy gift
Of life, which must, in all the after-days,
Be craved again with tears,—   5
With fresh and still-petitionary tears.
Being once bound thine almsmen for that gift,
We are bound to beggary, nor our own can call
The journal dole of customary life,
But after suit obsequious for't to thee.   10
Indeed this flesh, O Mother,
A beggar's gown, a client's badging,
We find, which from thy hands we simply took,
Nought dreaming of the after penury,
In nescientness.   15

In a little joy, in a little joy,
We wear awhile thy sore insignia,
Not know thy heel o' the neck. O Mother! Mother!
Then what use knew I of thy solemn robes,
But as a child, to play with them? I bade thee   20
Leave thy great husbandries, thy grave designs,
Thy tedious state which irked my ignorant years,
Thy winter-watches, suckling of the grain,
Severe premeditation taciturn
Upon the brooded Summer, thy chill cares,   25
And all thy ministries majestical,
To sport with me, thy darling. Thought I not
Thou set'st thy seasons forth processional
To pamper me with pageant,—thou thyself
My fellow-gamester, appanage of mine arms?   30
Then what wild Dionysia I, young Bacchanal,
Danced in thy lap! Ah for thy gravity!
Then, O Earth, thou rang'st beneath me,
Rocked to Eastward, rocked to Westward,
Even with the shifted   35
Poise and footing of my thought!
I brake through thy doors of sunset,
Ran before the hooves of sunrise,
Shook thy matron tresses down in fancies
Wild and wilful   40

As a poet's hand could twine them;
Caught in my fantasy's crystal chalice
The Bow, as its cataract of colours
Plashed to thee downward;
Then when thy circuit swung to nightward,   45
Night the abhorrèd, night was a new dawning,
Celestial dawning
Over the ultimate marges of the soul;
Dusk grew turbulent with fire before me,
And like a windy arras waved with dreams.   50
Sleep I took not for my bedfellow,
Who could waken
To a revel, an inexhaustible
Wassail of orgiac imageries;
Then while I wore thy sore insignia   55
In a little joy, O Earth, in a little joy;
Loving thy beauty in all creatures born of thee,
Children, and the sweet-essenced body of woman;
Feeling not yet upon my neck thy foot,
But breathing warm of thee as infants breathe   60
New from their mother's morning bosom. So I,
Risen from thee, restless winnower of the heaven,
Most Hermes-like, did keep
My vital and resilient path, and felt
The play of wings about my fledgèd heel—   65
Sure on the verges of precipitous dream,
Swift in its springing
From jut to jut of inaccessible fancies,
In a little joy.

In a little thought, in a little thought,   70
We stand and eye thee in a grave dismay,
With sad and doubtful questioning, when first
Thou speak'st to us as men: like sons who hear
Newly their mother's history, unthought
Before, and say—'She is not as we dreamed: 75
Ah me! we are beguiled!' What art thou, then,
That art not our conceiving? Art thou not
Too old for thy young children? Or perchance,
Keep'st thou a youth perpetual-burnishable
Beyond thy sons decrepit? It is long   80
Since Time was first a fledgling;

Yet thou may'st be but as a pendant bulla
Against his stripling bosom swung. Alack!
For that we seem indeed
To have slipped the world's great leaping-time, and come   85
Upon thy pinched and dozing days: these weeds,
These corporal leavings, thou not cast'st us new,
Fresh from thy craftship, like the lilies' coats,
But foist'st us off
With hasty tarnished piecings negligent,   90
Snippets and waste
From old ancestral wearings,
That have seen sorrier usage; remainder-flesh
After our father's surfeits; nay with chinks,
Some of us, that if speech may have free leave   95
Our souls go out at elbows. We are sad
With more than our sires' heaviness, and with
More than their weakness weak; we shall not be
Mighty with all their mightiness, nor shall not
Rejoice with all their joy. Ay, Mother! Mother!   100
What is this Man, thy darling kissed and cuffed,
Thou lustingly engender'st,
To sweat, and make his brag, and rot,
Crowned with all honour and all shamefulness?
From nightly towers   105
He dogs the secret footsteps of the heavens,
Sifts in his hands the stars, weighs them as gold-dust,
And yet is he successive unto nothing
But patrimony of a little mould,
And entail of four planks. Thou hast made his mouth   110
Avid of all dominion and all mightiness,
All sorrow, all delight, all topless grandeurs,
All beauty, and all starry majesties,
And dim transtellar things;—even that it may,
Filled in the ending with a puff of dust,   115
Confess—'It is enough.' The world left empty
What that poor mouthful crams. His heart is builded
For pride, for potency, infinity,
All heights, all deeps, and all immensities,
Arrased with purple like the house of kings,—   120
To stall the grey-rat, and the carrion-worm
Statelily lodge. Mother of mysteries!
Sayer of dark sayings in a thousand tongues,

Who bringest forth no saying yet so dark
As we ourselves, thy darkest! We the young,   125
In a little thought, in a little thought,
At last confront thee, and ourselves in thee,
And wake disgarmented of glory: as one
On a mount standing, and against him stands,
On the mount adverse, crowned with westering rays,   130
The golden sun, and they two brotherly
Gaze each on each;
He faring down
To the dull vale, his Godhead peels from him
Till he can scarcely spurn the pebble—   135
For nothingness of new-found mortality—
That mutinies against his gallèd foot.
Littly he sets him to the daily way,
With all around the valleys growing grave,
And known things changed and strange; but he holds on,   140
Though all the land of light be widowèd,
In a little thought.

In a little strength, in a little strength,
We affront thy unveiled face intolerable,
Which yet we do sustain.   145
Though I the Orient never more shall feel
Break like a clash of cymbals, and my heart
Clash through my shaken body like a gong;
Nor ever more with spurted feet shall tread
I' the winepresses of song; nought's truly lost   150
That moulds to sprout forth gain: now I have on me
The high Phœbean priesthood, and that craves
An unrash utterance; not with flaunted hem
May the Muse enter in behind the veil,
Nor, though we hold the sacred dances good,   155
Shall the holy Virgins mænadize: ruled lips
Befit a votaress Muse.
Thence with no mutable, nor no gelid love,
I keep, O Earth, thy worship,
Though life slow, and the sobering Genius change   160
To a lamp his gusty torch. What though no more
Athwart its roseal glow
Thy face look forth triumphal? Thou put'st on
Strange sanctities of pathos; like this knoll

Made derelict of day,   165
Couchant and shadowèd
Under dim Vesper's overloosened hair:
This, where embossèd with the half-blown seed
The solemn purple thistle stands in grass
Grey as an exhalation, when the bank   170
Holds mist for water in the nights of Fall.
Not to the boy, although his eyes be pure
As the prime snowdrop is,
Ere the rash Phœbus break her cloister
Of sanctimonious snow;   175
Or Winter fasting sole on Himalay
Since those dove-nuncioed days
When Asia rose from bathing;
Not to such eyes,
Uneuphrasied with tears, the hierarchical   180
Vision lies unoccult, rank under rank
Through all create down-wheeling, from the Throne
Even to the basis of the pregnant ooze.
This is the enchantment, this the exaltation,
The all-compensating wonder,   185
Giving to common things wild kindred
With the gold-tesserate floors of Jove;
Linking such heights and such humilities
Hand in hand in ordinal dances,
That I do think my tread,   190
Stirring the blossoms in the meadow-grass,
Flickers the unwithering stars.
This to the shunless fardel of the world
Nerves my uncurbèd back; that I endure,
The monstrous Temple's moveless caryatid,   195
With wide eyes calm upon the whole of things,
In a little strength.

In a little sight, in a little sight,
We learn from what in thee is credible
The incredible, with bloody clutch and feet   200
Clinging the painful juts of jaggèd faith.
Science, old noser in its prideful straw,
That with anatomising scalpel tents
Its three-inch of thy skin, and brags—'All's bare',
The eyeless worm, that boring works the soil,   205

Making it capable for the crops of God;
Against its own dull will
Ministers poppies to our troublous thought,
A Balaam come to prophecy,—parables,
Nor of its parable itself is ware,   210
Grossly unwotting; all things has expounded
Reflux and influx, counts the sepulchre
The seminary of being, and extinction
The Ceres of existence: it discovers
Life in putridity, vigour in decay;   215
Dissolution even, and disintegration,
Which in our dull thoughts symbolise disorder,
Finds in God's thoughts irrefragable order,
And admirable the manner of our corruption
As of our health. It grafts upon the cypress   220
The tree of Life—Death dies on his own dart
Promising to our ashes perpetuity,
And to our perishable elements
Their proper imperishability; extracting
Medicaments from out mortality   225
Against too mortal cogitation; till
Even of the *caput mortuum* we do thus
Make a *memento vivere*. To such uses
I put the blinding knowledge of the fool,
Who in no order seeth ordinance;   230
Nor thrust my arm in nature shoulder-high,
And cry—'There's nought beyond!' How should I so,
That cannot with these arms engirdle
All which I am; that am a foreigner
In mine own region? Who the chart shall draw   235
Of the strange courts and vaulty labyrinths,
The spacious tenements and wide pleasances,
Innumerable corridors far-withdrawn,
Where I wander darkling, of myself?
Darkling I wander, nor I dare explore   240
The long arcane of those dim catacombs,
Where the rat memory does its burrows make,
Close-seal them as I may, and my stolen tread
Starts populace, a *gens lucifuga*;
That too strait seems my mind my mind to hold,   245
And I myself incontinent of me.
Then go I, my foul-venting ignorance

With scabby sapience plastered, aye forsooth!
Clap my wise foot-rule to the walls o' the world,
And vow—*A goodly house, but something ancient,*   250
And I can find no Master? Rather, nay,
By baffled seeing, something I divine
Which baffles, and a seeing set beyond;
And so with strenuous gazes sounding down,
Like to the day-long porer on a stream,   255
Whose last look is his deepest, I beside
This slow perpetual Time stand patiently,
In a little sight.

In a little dust, in a little dust,
Earth, thou reclaim'st us, who do all our lives   260
Find of thee but Egyptian villeinage.
Thou dost this body, this enhavocked realm,
Subject to ancient and ancestral shadows;
Descended passions sway it; it is distraught
With ghostly usurpation, dinned and fretted   265
With the still-tyrannous dead; a haunted tenement,
Peopled from barrows and outworn ossuaries.
Thou giv'st us life not half so willingly
As thou undost thy giving; thou that teem'st
The stealthy terror of the sinuous pard,   270
The lion maned with curlèd puissance,
The serpent, and all fair strong beasts of ravin;
Thyself most fair and potent beast of ravin;
And thy great eaters thou, the greatest, eat'st.
Thou hast devoured mammoth and mastodon   275
And many a floating bank of fangs,
The scaly scourges of thy primal brine,
And the tower-crested plesiosaure.
Thou fill'st thy mouth with nations, gorgest slow
On purple aeons of kings; man's hulking towers   280
Are carcase for thee, and to modern sun
Disglutt'st their splintered bones.
Rabble of Pharaohs and Arsacidæ
Keep their cold house within thee; thou hast sucked down
How many Ninevehs and Hecatompyloi,   285
And perished cities whose great phantasmata
O'er brow the silent citizens of Dis:—
Hast not thy fill?

Tarry awhile, lean Earth, for thou shalt drink,
Even till thy dull throat sicken,   290
The draught thou grow'st most fat on; hear'st thou not
The world's knives bickering in their sheaths? O patience!
Much offal of a foul world comes thy way,
And man's superfluous cloud shall soon be laid
In a little blood.   295

In a little peace, in a little peace,
Thou dost rebate thy rigid purposes
Of imposed being, and relenting, mend'st
Too much, with nought. The westering Phœbus' horse
Paws i' the lucent dust as when he shocked   300
The East with rising; O how may I trace
In this decline that morning when we did
Sport 'twixt the claws of newly-whelped existence,
Which had not yet learned rending? We did then
Divinely stand, not knowing yet against us   305
Sentence had passed of life, nor commutation
Petitioning into death. What's he that of
The Free State argues? Tellus! bid him stoop,
Even where the low *hic jacet* answers him;
Thus low, O Man! there's freedom's seignory,   310
Tellus' most reverend sole free commonweal,
And model deeply-policied: there none
Stands on precedence, nor ambitiously
Woos the impartial worm, whose favours kiss
With liberal largesse all; there each is free   315
To be e'en what he must, which here did strive
So much to be he could not; there all do
Their uses just, with no flown questioning.
To be took by the hand of equal earth
They doff her livery, slip to the worm,   320
Which lacqueys them, their suits of maintenance,
And that soiled workaday apparel cast,
Put on condition: Death's ungentle buffet
Alone makes ceremonial manumission;
So are the heavenly statutes set, and those   325
Uranian tables of the primal Law.
In a little peace, in a little peace,
Like fierce beasts that a common thirst makes brothers,
We draw together to one hid dark lake;

In a little peace, in a little peace,   330
We drain with all our burthens of dishonour
Into the cleansing sands o' the thirsty grave.
The fiery pomps, brave exhalations,
And all the glistering shows o' the teeming world,
Which the sight aches at, we unwinking see   335
Through the smoked glass of Death; Death wherewith's fined
The muddy wine of life; that earth doth purge
Of her plethora of man; Death, that doth flush
The cumbered gutters of humanity;
Nothing of nothing king, with front uncrowned,   340
Whose hand holds crownets; playmate swart o' the strong;
Tenebrous moon that flux and refluence draws
Of the high-tided man; skull-housèd asp
That stings the heel of kings; true Fount of Youth,
Where he that dips is deathless; being's drone-pipe;   345
Whose nostril turns to blight the shrivelled stars,
And thicks the lusty breathing of the sun;
Pontifical Death, that doth the crevasse bridge
To the steep and trifid God; one mortal birth
That broker is of immortality.   350
Under the dreadful brother uterine,
This kinsman feared, Tellus, behold me come,
Thy son stern-nursed; who mortal-motherlike
To turn thy weanlings' mouth averse, embitter'st
Thine over-childed breast. Now, mortal son-like,   355
I thou hast suckled, Mother, I at last
Shall sustenant be to thee. Here I untrammel,
Here I pluck loose the body's cementing,
And break the tomb of life; here I shake off
The bur o' the world, man's congregation shun,   360
And to the antique order of the dead
I take the tongueless vows: my cell is set
Here in thy bosom; my little trouble is ended
In a little peace.

PROEMION

6 *cometary* movement like that of a comet. 16 *aura* emanation, or diffused atmosphere
(*OED*) 26 *fume* exhalation; *circumfluous* flowing round.

ANTHEM

1 *nescientness* from nescient, unaware, unknown. 30 *appanage* accompaniment. 31 *Dionysia* Greek festivals in honour of Dionysus, god of wine; *Bacchanal* follower of Bacchus,
an epithet for Dionysus, later adopting a separate existence identified with riotous

feasting. **63** *Hermes-like* Hermes was the god of poetry. **65** *fledgèd heel* Hermes had wings on his heels. **82** *bulla* an amulet that could be worn round the neck. **110** *entail of four planks* a coffin, entail being an estate bequeathed to certain members of a family. **152** *Phœbean priesthood* sun-worshippers. **156** *mænadize* dance like a Mænad, a priestess of Bacchus. **177** *dove-nuncioed days* time after the Flood when the dove was sent from the Ark in search of dry land; from nuncio, an envoy or messenger (Gen. 8:8–12). **178** *Asia rose from bathing* The continent of Asia was said to have taken its form on rising from the receding Flood. **180** *Uneuphrasied* from the plant Euphrasia, whose healing properties for the eyes are here applied to the healing of the inner spiritual vision. **181** *unoccult* revealed, clear. **193** *fardel* burden. **195** *caryatid* carved female figure which functions as a column in classical architecture. **203** *tents* probes **213** *seminary* here, meaning seedbed. **214** *Ceres* goddess of the harvest. **218** Science finds, through God, indisputable order, even in dissolution and disintegration, **227** *caput mortuum* the dead. **228** *memento vivere* words suggested by the phrase *memento mori*, 'remember thou must die', here becoming a 'reminder of life'. **244** *gens lucifuga* a race who avoids the light. **261** *Egyptian* TLC suggests that Egyptian may here denote extreme fear of bodily corruption (TLC *Poems*, p. 510). Alternatively it could refer to the bondage of the Israelites in Egypt. *villeinage* tenure of land in return for menial service. **267.** *barrows* pagan burial mounds; *ossuaries* charnel houses. **269** *teem'st* bring forth **270** *pard* leopard. **282** *Disglutt'st* spit out (?). **283** *Arsacidæ* Parthian kings. **285** *Ninevehs* Nineveh was the capital of ancient Assyria: *Hecatompyloi* Hecatompylus was a Parthian city. **287** *Dis* the Underworld. **308** *Tellus* the Roman earth goddess. **310** *seignory* estate, condition. **321** *maintenance* livery **326** *Uranian tables* heav- enly tablets (of the Law, as given to Moses). **345** *drone-pipe* base pipe of a bagpipe that only gives out a continuous background droning note. **348** *Pontifical* from *pontifex*, which can mean both priest and bridge builder. **349** *trifid God* the Holy Trinity. **351** *brother uterine* Death, as twin brother to Life.

MISCELLANEOUS POEMS

'Ex Ore Infantium'

ME, May 1893

In a letter written soon after his arrival at Pantasaph in December 1892, Thompson noted that he had 'spent Xmas eve writing verses—a poor thing but mine own' (*Letters*, p. 92). The verses were the rough draft for this poem, later completed and published in *ME* under the title 'Little Jesus', which was also the title used in *Works*. But in *New Poems* Thompson entitled it as above—'out of the mouth of babes'. There was a tradition at the Friary that he composed the poem in the chapel, near the Christmas crib.

> Little Jesus, wast Thou shy
> Once, and just as small as I?
> And what did it feel like to be
> Out of Heaven, and just like me?
> Didst Thou sometimes think of *there*,   5

And ask where all the angels were?
I should think that I would cry
For my house all made of sky;
I would look about the air,
And wonder where my angels were;   10
And at waking 'twould distress me—
Not an angel there to dress me!
Hadst Thou ever any toys,
Like us little girls and boys?
And didst Thou play in Heaven with all   15
The angels that were not too tall,
With stars for marbles? Did the things
Play *Can you see me?* through their wings?
And did Thy Mother let Thee spoil
Thy robes, with playing on *our* soil?   20
How nice to have them always new
In Heaven, because 'twas quite clean blue!

Didst Thou kneel at night to pray,
And didst Thou join Thy hands this way?
And did they tire sometimes, being young,   25
And make the prayer seem very long?
And dost Thou like it best, that we
Should join our hands to pray to Thee?
I used to think, before I knew,
The prayer not said unless we do.   30
And did Thy Mother at the night
Kiss Thee, and fold the clothes in right?
And didst Thou feel quite good in bed,
Kissed, and sweet, and Thy prayers said?

Thou canst not have forgotten all   35
That it feels like to be small:
And Thou know'st I cannot pray
To Thee in my father's way—
When Thou wast so little, say,
Couldst Thou talk Thy Father's way?—   40
So, a little Child, come down
And hear a child's tongue like Thy own;
Take me by the hand and walk,
And listen to my baby-talk.
To Thy Father show my prayer   45

(He will look, Thou art so fair,)
And say: 'O Father, I Thy Son,
Bring the prayer of a little one.'

And He will smile, that children's tongue
Has not changed since Thou wast young!

A Question

O bird with heart of wassail,
   That toss the Bacchic branch,
And slip your shaken music,
   An elfin avalanche;

Come tell me, O tell me,   5
   My poet of the blue!
What's *your* thought of me, Sweet?—
   Here's *my* thought of you.

A small thing, a wee thing,
   A brown fleck of nought;   10
With winging and singing
   That who could have thought?

A small thing, a wee thing,
   A brown amaze withal,
That fly a pitch more azure   15
   Because you're so small.

Bird, I'm a small thing—
   My angel descries;
With winging and singing
   That who could surmise?   20

Ah, small things, ah, wee things,
   Are the poets all,
Whose tour's the more azure
   Because they're so small.

The angels hang watching   25
   The tiny men-things:—
'The dear speck of flesh, see,
   With such daring wings!

'Come, tell us, O tell us,
   Thou strange mortality!   30
What's *thy* thought of us, Dear?—
   Here's *our* thought of thee.'

'Alack! you tall angels,
   I can't think so high!
I can't think what it feels like   35
   Not to be I.'

Come tell me, O tell me,
   My poet of the blue!
What's *your* thought of me, Sweet?—
   Here's *my* thought of you.   40

Field-Flower

A Phantasy

God took a fit of Paradise-wind,
   A slip of coerule weather,
A thought as simple as Himself,
   And ravelled them together.
Unto His eyes He held it there,   5
To teach it gazing debonair
   With memory of what, perdie,
A God's young innocences were.
His fingers pushed it through the sod—
It came up redolent of God,   10
Garrulous of the eyes of God
   To all the breezes near it;
Musical of the mouth of God
   To all had ears to hear it;
Mystical with the mirth of God,   15
   That glow-like did ensphere it.
  And—'Babble! babble! babble!' said;
   'I'll tell the whole world one day!'
There was no blossom half as glad,
   Since sun of Christ's first Sunday.   20

A poet took a flaw of pain,
   A hap of skiey pleasure,

A thought had in his cradle lain,
   And mingled them in measure.
That chrism he laid upon his eyes,   25
And lips, and heart, for euphrasies,
   That he might see, feel, sing, perdie,
The simple things that are the wise.
Beside the flower he held his ways,
And leaned him to it gaze for gaze—   30
He took its meaning, gaze for gaze,
   As baby looks on baby;
Its meaning passed into his gaze
   Native as meaning may be;
He rose with all his shining gaze   35
   As children's eyes at play be.
     And—'Babble! babble! babble!' said;
      'I'll tell the whole world one day!'
    There was no poet half so glad,
     Since man grew God that Sunday.

7 *perdie* assuredly. 14 *ears* eyes in NP; assumed to be the typesetter's slip. 26 *euphrasies* the plant eyebright, providing a herbal treatment for bad eyes.

The Cloud's Swan Song

There is a parable in the pathless cloud,
There's prophecy in heaven,—they did not lie,
The Chaldee shepherds; sealèd from the proud,
To cheer the weighted heart that mates the seeing eye.

A lonely man, oppressed with lonely ills,   5
And all the glory fallen from my song,
Here do I walk among the windy hills,
The wind and I keep one monotoning tongue.

Like grey clouds one by one my songs upsoar
Over my soul's cold peaks; and one by one   10
They loose their little rain, and are no more;
And whether well or ill, to tell me there is none.

For 'tis an alien tongue, of alien things,
From all men's care, how miserably apart!
Even my friends say: 'Of what is this he sings?'   15
And barren is my song, and barren is my heart.

For who can work, unwitting his work's worth?
Better, meseems, to know the work for naught,
Turn my sick course back to the kindly earth,
And leave to ampler plumes the jetting tops of thought.   20

And visitations, that do often use,
Remote, unhappy, inauspicious sense
Of doom, and poets widowed of their muse,
And what dark 'gan, dark ended, in me did commence.

I thought of spirit wronged by mortal ills,   25
And my flesh rotting on my fate's dull stake;
And how self-scornèd they the bounty fills
Of others, and the bread, even of their dearest take.

I thought of Keats, that died in perfect time,
In predecease of his just-sickening song;   30
Of him that set, wrapt in his radiant rhyme,
Sunlike in sea. Life longer had been life too long.

But I, exanimate of quick Poesy,—
O then, no more but even a soulless corse!
Nay, my Delight dies not; 'tis I should be   35
Her dead, a stringless harp on which she had no force.

Of my wild lot I thought; from place to place,
Apollo's song-bowed Scythian, I go on;
Making in all my home, with pliant ways,
But, provident of change, putting forth root in none.   40

Now, with starved brain, sick body, patience galled
With fardels even to wincing; from fair sky
Fell sudden little rain, scarce to be called
A shower, which of the instant was gone wholly by.

What cloud thus died I saw not; heaven was fair.   45
Methinks my angel plucked my locks: I bowed
My spirit, shamed; and looking in the air:—
'Even so,' I said, 'even so, my brother the good Cloud?'

It was a pilgrim of the fields of air,
Its home was allwheres the wind left it rest,   50
And in a little forth again did fare,
And in all places was a stranger and a guest.

It harked all breaths of heaven, and did obey
With sweet peace their uncomprehended wills;
It knew the eyes of stars which made no stay,   55
And with the thunder walked upon the lonely hills.

And from the subject earth it seemed to scorn,
It drew the sustenance whereby it grew
Perfect in bosom for the married Morn,
And of his life and light full as a maid kissed new.   60

Its also darkness of the face withdrawn,
And the long waiting for the little light,
So long in life so little. Like a fawn
It fled with tempest breathing hard at heel of flight.

And having known full East, did not disdain   65
To sit in shadow and oblivious cold,
Save what all loss doth of its loss retain,
And who hath held hath somewhat that he still must hold.

Right poet! Who thy rightness to approve,
Having all liberty, didst keep all measure,   70
And with a firmament for ranging, move
But at the heavens' uncomprehended pleasure.

With amplitude unchecked, how sweetly thou
Didst wear the ancient custom of the skies,
And yoke of used prescription; and thence how   75
Find gay variety no license could devise!

As we the quested beauties better wit
Of the one grove our own than forests great,
Restraint, by the delighted search of it,
Turns to right scope. For lovely moving intricate   80

Is put to fair devising in the curb
Of ordered limit; and all-changeful Hermes
Is Terminus as well. Yet we perturb
Our souls for latitude, whose strength in bound and term is.

How far am I from heavenly liberty,   85
That play at policy with change and fate,
Who should my soul from foreign broils keep free,
In the fast-guarded frontiers of its single state!

Could I face firm the Is, and with To-Be
Trust Heaven; to Heaven commit the deed, and do;   90
In power contained, calm in infirmity,
And fit myself to change with virtue ever new;

Thou hadst not shamed me, cousin of the sky,
Thou wandering kinsman, that didst sweetly live
Unnoted, and unnoted sweetly die,   95
Weeping more gracious song than any I can weave;

Which these gross-tissued words do sorely wrong.
Thou hast taught me on powerlessness a power;
To make song wait on life, not life on song;
To hold sweet not too sweet, and bread for bread though sour; 100

By law to wander, to be strictly free.
With tears ascended from the heart's sad sea,
Ah, such a silver song to Death could I
Sing, Pain would list, forgetting Pain to be,
And Death would tarry marvelling, and forget to die!   105

3 *Chaldee shepherds* The Chaldeans were said to be the first astronomers (TLC*Poems*,
p. 549). **27–8** How like I am to those who rely on others' support and scorn themselves
for doing so. **31–2** *him that set . . . Sunlike in sea* Shelley, who died by drowning. **42**
fardels burdens. **77** *wit* know. **82–3** *Hermes, Terminus* Hermes was the god of poetry,
Terminus the god who protected boundaries.

To the Sinking Sun

How graciously thou wear'st the yoke
    Of use that does not fail!
The grasses, like an anchored smoke,
    Ride in the bending gale;
This knoll is snowed with blosmy manna,   5
    And fire-dropped as a seraph's mail.

Here every eve thou stretchest out
    Untarnishable wing,
And marvellously bring'st about
    Newly an olden thing;   10
Nor ever through like-ordered heaven
    Moves largely thy grave progressing.

Here every eve thou goest down
    Behind the self-same hill,
Not ever twice alike go'st down   15
    Behind the self-same hill;
Nor like-ways in one flame-sopped flower
    Possessed with glory past its will.

Not twice alike! I am not blind,
    My sight is live to see;   20
And yet I do complain of thy
    Weary variety.
O sun! I ask thee less or more,
    Change not at all, or utterly!

O give me unprevisioned new,   25
    Or give to change reprieve!
For new in me is olden too,
    That I for sameness grieve.
O flowers! O grasses! be but once
    The grass and flower of yester-eve!   30

Wonder and sadness are the lot
    Of change: thou yield'st mine eyes
Grief of vicissitude, but not
    Its penetrant surprise.
Immutability mutable   35
    Burthens my spirit and the skies.

O altered joy, all joyed of yore,
    Plodding in unconned ways!
O grief grieved out, and yet once more
    A dull, new, staled amaze!   40
I dream, and all was dreamed before,
    Or dream I so? The dreamer says.

11 *Nor* and (archaic).

Grief's Harmonics

At evening, when the lank and rigid trees,
To the mere forms of their sweet day-selves drying,
On heaven's blank leaf seem pressed and flattenèd;
Or rather, to my sombre thoughts replying,
Of plumes funereal the thin effigies;   5
That hour when all old dead things seem most dead,
And their death instant most and most undying,
That the flesh aches at them; there stirred in me
The babe of an unborn calamity,
Ere its due time to be deliverèd.   10
Dead sorrow and sorrow unborn so blent their pain,
That which more present was were hardly said,
But both more *now* than any Now can be.
My soul like sackcloth did her body rend,
And thus with Heaven contend:—   15
'Let pass the chalice of this coming dread,
Or that fore-drained O bid me not re-drain!'
So have I asked, who know my asking vain,
Woe against woe in antiphon set over,
That grief's soul transmigrates, and lives again,   20
And in new pang old pang's incarnated.

Memorat Memoria

The title can be translated as 'Remembered Memory'. On the fly-leaf of his own
   copy of *New Poems* Meynell wrote under the title:

This was written, I think, less in autobiography than in an imitative Swinburn-
ian mood. At the time of its composition he was often quoting Swinburne's
'Triumph of Time', some lines of which he left in his own writing:

I shall never be friends again with roses;
   I shall loathe sweet tunes, where a note grows strong
Relents and recoils, and climbs and closes,
   As a wave of the sea turned back by song.
There are sounds where the soul's delight takes fire,
   Face to face with its own desire;
A delight that rebels, a desire that reposes;
   I shall hate sweet music my whole life long.

('The Triumph of Time', 353–60; Meynell's copy of *New Poems* is in M.)
   If he was right, the poem must have been written before Thompson left Lon-

don for Wales, or Meynell would not have referred to his 'often quoting' Swinburne: no quotations appear in the letters. Meynell could have been uneasy at the distinct connection between the poem and Thompson's memories of the street girl, but admitting the influence from Swinburne need not affect the different message here or its intensity of feeling. Unlike other poems addressed to her, the theme reveals a conflict of emotions in the remembered relationship.

Come you living or dead to me, out of the silt of the Past,
With the sweet of the piteous first, and the shame of the shameful last?
Come with your dear and dreadful face through the passes of Sleep,
The terrible mask, and the face it masked—the face you did not keep?
You are neither two nor one—would you were one or two,   5
For your awful self is embalmed in the fragrant self I knew:
And Above may ken, and Beneath may ken, what I mean by these
        words of whirl,
But by my sleep that sleepeth not,—O Shadow of a Girl!—
Naught here but I and my dreams shall know the secret of this thing:—
For ever the songs I sing are sad with the songs I never sing,   10
Sad are sung songs, but how much more sad the songs we dare not
        sing!

Ah, the ill that we do in tenderness, and the hateful horror of love!
It has sent more souls to the unslaked Pit than it ever will draw above.
I damned you, girl, with my pity, who had better by far been thwart,
And drave you hard on the track to hell, because I was gentle of heart. 15
I shall have no comfort now in scent, no ease in dew, for this;
I shall be afraid of daffodils, and rose-buds are amiss;
You have made a thing of innocence as shameful as a sin,
I shall never feel a girl's soft arms without horror of the skin.
My child! what was it that I sowed, that I so ill should reap?   20
You have done this to me. And I, what I to you?—It lies with Sleep.

18–21 In his note quoted above, WM included a draft for the last four lines but without an MS source:

> A girl's kiss through my soul strikes echoes of ominous sin;
> I shall never feel a girl's soft arms without horror of the skin;
> At the breath of her hair, as a phantom, mine shall creep;
> You have done this to me—and I to you? it lies with sleep.

July Fugitive

Can you tell me where has hid her
    Pretty Maid July?
I would swear one day ago
    She passed by,
I would swear that I do know   5
    The blue bliss of her eye:
'Tarry, maid, maid,' I bid her;
    But she hastened by.
Do you know where she has hid her,
    Maid July?   10

Yet in truth it needs must be
    The flight of her is old;
Yet in truth it needs must be,
    For her nest, the earth, is cold.
No more in the poolèd Even   15
    Wade her rosy feet,
Dawn-flakes no more plash from them
    To poppies 'mid the wheat.
She has muddied the day's oozes
    With her petulant feet;   20
Scared the clouds that floated
    As sea-birds they were,
Slow on the coerule
    Lulls of the air,
Lulled on the luminous   25
    Levels of air:
She has chidden in a pet
    All her stars from her;
Now they wander loose and sigh
    Through the turbid blue,   30
Now they wander, weep, and cry—
    Yea, and I too—
'Where are you, sweet July,
    Where are you?'

Who hath beheld her footprints,   35
    Or the pathway she goes?
Tell me, wind, tell me, wheat,
    Which of you knows?
Sleeps she swathed in the flushed Arctic
    Night of the rose?   40

Or lie her limbs like Alp-glow
    On the lily's snows?
Gales, that are all-visitant,
    Find the runaway;
And for him who findeth her 45
    (I do charge you say)
I will throw largesse of broom
    Of this summer's mintage,
I will broach a honey-bag
    Of the bee's best vintage. 50
Breezes, wheat, flowers sweet,
    None of them knows!
How then shall we lure her back
    From the way she goes?
For it were a shameful thing, 55
    Saw we not this comer
Ere Autumn camp upon the fields
    Red with rout of Summer.

When the bird quits the cage,
    We set the cage outside, 60
With seed and with water,
    And the door wide,
Haply we may win it so
    Back to abide.
Hang her cage of earth out 65
    O'er Heaven's sunward wall,
Its four gates open, winds in watch
    By reinèd cars at all;
Relume in hanging hedgerows
    The rain-quenched blossom, 70
And roses sob their tears out
    On the gale's warm heaving bosom;
Shake the lilies till their scent
    Over-drip their rims;
That our runaway may see 75
    We do know her whims:
Sleek the tumbled waters out
    For her travelled limbs;
Strew and smoothe blue night thereon,
    There will—O not doubt her!— 80
The lovely sleepy lady lie,
    With all her stars about her!

To a Snowflake

ME, February 1891

The poem first appeared in *ME* under the title 'A Hymn to Snow'. There were 92
lines, from which Thompson extracted the last 22 for *New Poems*. The lines he
deleted are very inferior poetry to the poem as it stands here.

What heart could have thought you?—
Past our devisal
(O filigree petal!)
Fashioned so purely,
Fragilely, surely,   5
From what Paradisal
Imagineless metal,
Too costly for cost?
Who hammered you, wrought you,
From argentine vapour?—   10
'God was my shaper.
Passing surmisal,
He hammered, He wrought me,
From curled silver vapour,
To lust of His mind:—   15
Thou could'st not have thought me!
So purely, so palely,
Tinily, surely,
Mightily, frailly,
Insculped and embossed,   20
With His hammer of wind,
And His graver of frost.

14 *curled silver vapour* In an early essay on Crashaw, FT discusses the poet's use of 'curled
drops' as 'the characteristic trait of snowflakes' that he has found recorded nowhere else (cf.
ME, May 1889). 20 *Insculped* an invented word from 'sculpture' that could suggest familiarity with Hopkins (see Introduction, p. xxvii).

Nocturn

I walk, I only,
Not I only wake;
Nothing is, this sweet night,
But doth couch and wake
For its love's sake;   5
Everything, this sweet night,

Couches with its mate.
For whom but for the stealthy-visitant sun
Is the naked moon
Tremulous and elate?   10
The heaven hath the earth
Its own and all apart;
The hushèd pool holdeth
A star to its heart.
You may think the rose sleepeth,   15
But though she folded is,
The wind doubts her sleeping;
Not all the rose sleeps,
But smiles in her sweet heart
For crafty bliss.   20
The wind lieth with the rose,
And when he stirs, she stirs in her repose:
The wind hath the rose,
And the rose her kiss.
Ah, mouth of me!   25
Is it then that this
Seemeth much to thee?—
I wander only.
The rose hath her kiss.

A May Burden

NOTE The first two stanzas are from a French original—I have forgotten
what. F.T.

Through meadow-ways as I did tread,
The corn grew in great lustihead,
And hey! the beeches burgeonèd.
  By Goddès fay, by Goddès fay!
It is the month, the jolly month,   5
It is the jolly month of May.

God ripe the wines and corn, I say,
And wenches for the marriage-day,
And boys to teach love's comely play.
  By Goddès fay, by Goddès fay!   10
It is the month, the jolly month,
It is the jolly month of May.

As I went down by lane and lea,
The daisies reddened so, pardie!
'Blushets!' I said, 'I well do see,   15
    By Goddès fay, by Goddès fay!
The thing ye think of in this month,
Heigho! this jolly month of May.'

As down I went by rye and oats,
The blossoms smelt of kisses; throats   20
Of birds turned kisses into notes;
    By Goddès fay, by Goddès fay!
The kiss it is a growing flower,
I trow, this jolly month of May!

God send a mouth to every kiss,   25
Seeing the blossom of this bliss
By gathering doth grow, certes!
    By Goddès fay, by Goddès fay!
Thy brow-garland pushed all aslant
Tells—but I tell not, wanton May!

A Dead Astronomer

(Father Perry, S.J.)

ME, April 1890

Stephen Perry was a Jesuit who was also a noted astronomer. He died on board ship in December 1889 after completing his observations of an eclipse of the sun near French Guiana. Soon after the publication of the poem in *ME* Thompson wrote to his friend Canon John Carroll: 'The lines on Father Perry have taken hold of *Merry England* readers as nothing else of mine has done . . . [Whereas] I meant the thing merely for a pretty, graceful turned fancy; what the Elizabethans would have called an excellent conceit' (*Letters*, pp. 39–40).

Starry amorist, starward gone,
Thou art—what thou didst gaze upon!
Passed through thy golden garden's bars,
Thou seest the Gardener of the Stars.

She, about whose moonèd brows   5
Seven stars make seven glows,
Seven lights for seven woes;
She, like thine own Galaxy,

All lustres in one purity:—
What said'st thou, Astronomer,   10
When thou didst discover *her*?
When thy hand its tube let fall,
Thou found'st the fairest Star of all!

7 *seven woes* the seven sorrows of the Blessed Virgin, here forming part of the mystic significance of the number seven in a cosmic context.

'Chose Vue'

A Metrical Caprice

In his Notes TLC suggests that the title may be taken from a volume of essays by
Victor Hugo, *Choses Vues* (TLC*Poems*, p. 553).

Up she rose, fair daughter—well she was graced
As a cloud her going, stept from her chair,
As a summer-soft cloud, in her going paced,
Down dropped her riband-band, and all her waving hair
Shook like loosened music cadent to her waist;—   5
Lapsing like music, wavery as water,
    Slid to her waist.

'Whereto Art Thou Come?'

The title is from Christ's words to Judas at the betrayal on the Mount of Olives
(Matt. 25: 47–50).

'Friend, whereto art thou come?' Thus Verity;
Of each that to the world's sad Olivet
Comes with no multitude, but alone by night,
Lit with the one torch of his lifted soul,
Seeking her that he may lay hands on her;   5
Thus: and waits answer from the mouth of deed.
Truth is a maid, whom men woo diversely;
This, as spouse; that, as a light-o'-love,
To know, and having known, to make his brag.
But woe to him that takes the immortal kiss,   10
And not estates her in his housing life,
Mother of all his seed! So he betrays,

Not Truth, the unbetrayable, but himself:
And with his kiss's rated traitor-craft,
The Haceldama of a plot of days   15
He buys, to consummate his Judasry
Therein with Judas' guerdon of despair.

Heaven and Hell

'Tis said there were no thought of hell,
    Save hell were taught; that there should be
A Heaven for all's self-credible.
    Not so the thing appears to me.
'Tis Heaven that lies beyond our sights,   5
    And hell too possible that proves;
For all can feel the God that smites,
    But ah, how few the God that loves!

To a Child

ME, August 1892

According to a note by TLC, when Meynell was asked which of his children
Thompson was addressing in this poem he answered: 'I think it was Monica'
(TLC*Poems*, p. 542).

Whenas my life shall time with funeral tread
The heavy death-drum of the beaten hours,
Following, sole mourner, mine own manhood dead,
Poor forgot corse, where not a maid strows flowers;
When I you love am no more I you love,   5
But go with unsubservient feet, behold
Your dear face through changed eyes, all grim change prove;—
A new man, mockèd with misname of old;
When shamed Love keep his ruined lodging, elf!
When, ceremented in mouldering memory,   10
Myself is hearsèd underneath myself,
And I am but the monument of me:—
    O to that tomb be tender then, which bears
    Only the name of him it sepulchres!

This revised text in *New Poems* differs widely from the poem in *ME*, below:
        Whenas to you the tollèd tongue of Time
        Which threats me from the tower of Eternity,

Awaited spousals with your youth shall chime,
    The long affiance, childhood, laggèd by;
When he you love shall be not he you love,
    Shall go with feet that serve him not, behold
Your dear face through changed eyes, all grim change prove,—
A new man, whom our scoffing speech calls old;
    When shamed love keeps his ruined lodgement, elf!
When, ceremented in pale memory,
    Myself is hearsèd underneath myself,
And I am but the sepulchre of me;
    Oh! to that worn tomb will you grant some tears,
    For sake of the dead him whose name it bears.

Hermes

Hermes was the herald, or messenger, of the gods and patron of eloquence as well as the inventor of the lyre. He was the son of Zeus and the mortal Maia, so uniting in himself the divine and natural attributes of human nature.

Soothsay. Behold, with rod twy-serpented,
Hermes the prophet, twining in one power
The woman with the man. Upon his head
The cloudy cap, wherewith he hath in dower
The cloud's own virtue—change and counterchange,   5
To show in light, and to withdraw in pall,
As mortal eyes best bear. His lineage strange
From Zeus, Truth's sire, and maiden May—the all-
Illusive Nature. His fledged feet declare
That 'tis the nether self transdeified,   10
And the thrice-furnaced passions, which do bear
The poet Olympusward. In him allied
    Both parents clasp; and from the womb of Nature
    Stern Truth takes flesh in shows of lovely feature.

1 *rod twy-serpented* Hermes carried a caduceus, or magic wand, surmounted by two wings and entwined with two serpents, that could induce sleep. 3 *The woman with the man* Following a well-established tradition, FT equates the woman with the life of nature and the man with divine life. 4 *cloudy cap* the distinctive headdress worn by Hermes. 9 *fledged feet* Hermes is depicted with wings either on his heels or on his sandals.

House of Bondage

Two Sonnets

1

When I perceive Love's heavenly reaping still
Regard perforce the clouds' vicissitude,
That the fixed spirit loves not when it will,
But craves its seasons of the flawful blood;
When I perceive that the high poet doth   5
Oft voiceless stray beneath the uninfluent stars,
That even Urania of her kiss is loath,
And Song's brave wings fret on their sensual bars;
When I perceive the fullest-sailèd sprite
Lag at most need upon the lethèd seas,   10
The provident captainship oft voided quite,
And lamèd lie deep-draughted argosies;
   I scorn myself, that put forth such strange toys
   The wit of man to purposes of boys.

2

The spirit's ark, sealed with a little clay,
Was old ere Memphis grew a memory;
The hand pontifical to break away
That seal what shall surrender? Not the sea
Which did englut great Egypt and his war,   5
Nor all the desert-drownèd sepulchres.
Love's feet are stained with clay and travel-sore,
And dusty are Song's lucent wing and hairs.
O Love, that must do courtesy to decay,
Eat hasty bread standing with loins up-girt,   10
How shall this stead thy feet for their sore way?
Ah, Song, what brief embraces balm thy hurt!
   Had Jacob's toil full guerdon, casting his
   Twice-seven heaped years to burn in Rachel's kiss?

1 'The Ark of the Egyptian temple was sealed with clay, which the Pontiff-King broke when he entered the inner shrine to offer worship' (FT note). 11 *stead* aid. 13–14 TLC notes a minor error here: 'Rachel was given to Jacob after he had worked seven years and a week, but upon receiving her, he worked on and completed a second term of seven years' (cf. Gen. 21: 18–30; TLC*Poems*, p. 544).

The Heart

Two Sonnets

(To my Critic, who had objected to the phrase—'the heart's burning floors.')

According to TLC the 'critic' was Alice Meynell. The phrase may relate to an early version of 'Contemplation' (p. 103):

> ... The prisoned feet of love
> On the heart's floors with painèd pace that go.
>
> (TLC *Poems*, p. 544)

The second sonnet was incuded in *Selected Poems* (1908) under the title 'Correlated Greatness'.

I

The heart you hold too small and local thing,
Such spacious terms of edifice to bear.
And yet, since Poesy first shook her wing,
The mighty Love has been impalaced there;
That has she given him as his wide demesne,   5
And for his sceptre ample empery;
Against its door to knock has Beauty been
Content; it has its purple canopy,
A dais for the sovereign lady spread
Of many a lover, who the heaven would think   10
Too low an awning for her sacred head.
The world, from star to sea, cast down its brink—
    Yet shall that chasm, till He Who these did build
    An awful Curtius make Him, yawn unfilled.

2

O nothing, in this corporal earth of man,
That to the immanent heaven of his high soul
Responds with colour and with shadow, can
Lack correlated greatness. If the scroll
Where thoughts lie fast in spell of hieroglyph   5
Be mighty through its mighty habitants;
If God be in His Name; grave potence if
The sounds unbind of hieratic chants;
All's vast that vastness means. Nay, I affirm
Nature is whole in her least things exprest,   10
Nor know we with what scope God builds the worm.
Our towns are copied fragments from our breast;

> And all man's Babylons strive but to impart
> The grandeurs of his Babylonian heart.

1 8 Comma added. 14 *Curtius* a part of the Roman Forum which had been a chasm that could only be filled by the sacrifice of a Roman citizen. Curtius volunteered to die.

2 5 *hieroglyph* writing hard to understand, symbolic, from the ancient Egyptian writing. 8 *hieratic* priestly.

A Sunset

Thompson regarded this translation, from Victor Hugo's *Les Feuilles d'Automne*, the 35th poem, 'Soleils couchants', and the following one, from Hugo's 'Ce qu'on entend sur la montagne', as more important than later critics have done. In a letter to his publisher on the proposed contents of *New Poems* he wrote: 'I regret that I cannot consent to the omission of the translations . . . I said at Pantasaph that I would keep these, whatever I left out. They were held over from my first book and I will not hold them over again. I regard the 'Heard on the Mountain' as a feat in diction and metre . . .' (*Letters*, pp. 185–6).

> I love the evenings, passionless and fair, I love the evens,
> Whether old manor-fronts their ray with golden fulgence leavens,
>   In numerous leafage bosomed close;
> Whether the mist in reefs of fire extend its reaches sheer,
> Or a hundred sunbeams splinter in an azure atmosphere   5
>   On cloudy archipelagos.
>
> Oh gaze ye on the firmament! A hundred clouds in motion,
> Up-piled in the immense sublime beneath the winds' commotion,
>   Their unimagined shapes accord:
> Under their waves at intervals flames a pale levin through,   10
> As if some giant of the air amid the vapours drew
>   A sudden elemental sword.
>
> The sun at bay with splendid thrusts still keeps the sullen fold;
> And momently at distance sets, as a cupola of gold,
>   The thatched roof of a cot a-glance;   15
> Or on the blurred horizons joins his battle with the haze;
> Or pools the glooming fields about with inter-isolate blaze,
>   Great moveless meres of radiance.
>
> Then mark ye how there hangs athwart the firmament's swept track
> Yonder a mighty crocodile with vast irradiant back,   20

A triple row of pointed teeth?
Under its burnished belly slips a ray of eventide,
The flickerings of a hundred glowing clouds its tenebrous side
    With scales of golden mail ensheathe.

Then mounts a palace, then the air vibrates—the vision flees.   25
Confounded to its base, the fearful cloudy edifice
    Ruins immense in mounded wrack:
Afar the fragments strew the sky, and each envermeiled cone
Hangeth, peak downward, overhead, like mountains overthrown
    When the earthquake heaves its hugy back.   30

These vapours with their leaden, golden, iron, bronzèd glows,
Where the hurricane, the waterspout, thunder, and hell repose,
    Muttering hoarse dreams of destined harms,
'Tis God who hangs their multitude amid the skiey deep,
As a warrior that suspendeth from the roof-tree of his keep   35
    His dreadful and resounding arms!

All vanishes! The sun, from topmost heaven precipitated,
Like to a globe of iron which is tossed back fiery red
    Into the furnace stirred to fume,
Shocking the cloudy surges, plashed from its impetuous ire,   40
Even to the zenith spattereth in a flecking scud of ire
    The vaporous and inflamèd spume.

O contemplate the heavens! Whenas the vein-drawn day dies pale,
In every season, every place, gaze through their every veil,
    With love that has not speech for need;   45
Beneath their solemn beauty is a mystery infinite:
If winter hue them like a pall; or if the summer night
    Fantasy them with starry brede.

10 *levin* lightning. **48** *brede* braid.

Heard on the Mountain

This translation is from Victor Hugo's *Les Feuilles d'Automne*, the fifth poem, 'Ce qu'on entend sur la montagne'. Thompson added the following note: 'The metre of the second of these two translations is an experiment. The splendid fourteen-syllable metre of Chapman I have treated after the manner of Drydenian rhyming heroics; with the occasional triplet, and even the occasional Alexandrine,

represented by a line of eight accents—a treatment which can well extend, I
believe, the majestic resource of the metre.'

Have you sometimes, calm, silent, let your tread aspirant rise
Up to the mountain's summit, in the presence of the skies?
Was't on the borders of the south? or on the Bretagne coast?
And at the basis of the mount had you the Ocean tossed?
And there, leaned o'er the wave and o'er the immeasurableness,   5
Calm, silent, have you hearkened what it says? Lo, what it says!
One day at least, whereon my thought, enlicensèd to muse,
Had dropped its wing above the beachèd margent of the ooze,
And, plunging from the mountain height into the immensity,
Beheld upon one side the land, on the other side the sea.   10
I harkened, comprehended,—never, as from those abysses,
No, never issued from my mouth, nor moved an ear, such voice as
      this is!

A sound it was, at outset, vast, immeasurable, confused,
Vaguer than is the wind among the tufted trees effused,
Full of magnificent accords, suave murmurs, sweet as is   15
The evensong, and mighty as the shock of panoplies
When the hoarse *mêlée* in its arms the closing squadrons grips,
And pants, in furious breathings, from the clarions' brazen lips.
Unutterable the harmony, unsearchable its deep,
Whose fluid undulations round the world a girdle keep,   20
And through the vasty heavens, which by its surges are washed young,
Its infinite volitions roll, enlarging as they throng,
Even to the profound arcane, whose ultimate chasms sombre
Its shattered flood englut with time, with space and form and number.
Like to another atmosphere with thin o'erflowing robe,   25
The hymn eternal covers all the inundated globe:
And the world, swathed about with this investuring symphony,
Even as it trepidates in the air, so trepidates in the harmony.

And pensive, I attended the ethereal lutany,
Lost within this containing voice as if within the sea.   30

Soon I distinguished, yet as tone which veils confuse and smother,
Amid this voice two voices, one commingled with the other,
Which did from off the land and seas even to the heavens aspire;
Chanting the universal chant in simultaneous quire.
And I distinguished them amid that deep and rumorous sound,   35
As who beholds two currents thwart amid the fluctuous profound.

*

The one was of the waters; a be-radiant hymnal speech!
That was the voice o' the surges, as they parleyed each with each.
The other, which arose from our abode terranean,
Was sorrowful; and that, alack! the murmur was of man;   40
And in this mighty quire, whose chantings day and night resound,
Every wave had its utterance, and every man his sound.

Now, the magnificent Ocean, as I said, unbannering
A voice of joy, a voice of peace did never stint to sing,
Most like in Sion's temples to a psaltery psaltering,   45
And to creation's beauty reared the great lauds of his song.
Upon the gale, upon the squall, his clamour borne along
Unpausingly arose to God in more triumphal swell;
And every one among his waves, that God alone can quell,
When the other of its song made end, into the singing pressed.   50
Like that majestic lion whereof Daniel was the guest,
At intervals the Ocean his tremendous murmur awed;
And I, t'ward where the sunset fires fell shaggily and broad,
Under his golden mane, methought, that I saw pass the hand of God.

Meanwhile, and side by side with that august fanfaronnade,   55
The other voice, like the sudden scream of a destrier affrayed,
Like an infernal door that grates ajar its rusty throat,
Like to a bow of iron that gnarls upon an iron rote,
Grinded; and tears, and shriekings, the anathema, the lewd taunt,
Refusal of viaticum, refusal of the font,   60
And clamour, and malediction, and dread blasphemy, among
That hurtling crowd of rumour from the diverse human tongue,
Went by as who beholdeth, when the valleys thick t'ward night,
The long drifts of the birds of dusk pass, blackening flight on flight.
What was this sound whose thousand echoes vibrated unsleeping? 65
Alas! the sound was earth's and man's, for earth and man were weeping.

Brothers! of these two voices, strange and unimaginably,
Unceasingly regenerated, dying unceasingly,
Harkenèd of the Eternal throughout His Eternity,
The one voice uttereth: NATURE! and the other voice:
      HUMANITY!   70

Then I alit in reverie; for my ministering sprite
Alack! had never yet deployed a pinion of an ampler flight,
Nor ever had my shadow endured so large a day to burn:
And long I rested dreaming, contemplating turn by turn
Now that abyss obscure which lurked beneath the water's roll,   75

And now that other untemptable abyss which opened in my soul.
And I made question of me, to what issues are we here,
Whither should tend the thwarting threads of all this ravelled gear;
What doth the soul; to be or live if better worth it is;
And why the Lord, Who, only, reads within that book of His,   80
In fatal hymeneals hath eternally entwined
The vintage-chant of nature with the dirging cry of humankind?

43 *unbannering* invented word, probably from Hugo's *épandait*, a poetic word for scatter or spread (cf. TLC *Poems*, pp. 392–3). **55** *fanfaronnade* ostentatious display. **56** *destrier* from dester, a war-horse. **58** *rote* musical instrument, similar to a hurdy-gurdy. **60** *viaticum* last rites of confession before death; *font* baptism. **78** *thwarting* opposing, going crosswise.

ULTIMA

According to Alice Meynell ('Some Memories of Francis Thompson', *DR*, January 1908) the poems in this sequence were intended at first as a sequel to 'Love in Dian's Lap'. This would account for the change in *Works*, where two of the *Ultima* poems, 'Beneath a Photograph' and 'After Her Going', are removed and added to that earlier sequence. They are restored here to their original position.

Love's Almsman Plaineth His Fare

O you, love's mendicancy who never tried,
    How little of your almsman me you know!
Your little languid hand in mine you slide,
    Like to a child says—'Kiss me and let me go!'
And night for this is fretted with my tears,   5
    While I:—'How soon this heavenly neck doth tire
Bending to me from its transtellar spheres!'
    Ah, heart all kneaded out of honey and fire!
Who bound thee to a body nothing worth,
    And shamed thee much with an unlovely soul,   10
That the most strainedest charity of earth
    Distasteth soon to render back the whole
Of thine inflamèd sweets and gentilesse!
    Whereat, like an unpastured Titan, thou
Gnaw'st on thyself for famine's bitterness,   15

And leap'st against thy chain. Sweet Lady, how
Little a linking of the hand to you!
    Though I should touch yours careless for a year,
Not one blue vein would be divinelier blue
    Upon your fragile temple, to unsphere   20
The seraphim for kisses! Not one curve
    Of your sad mouth would droop more sad and sweet.
But little food love's beggars needs must serve,
    That eye your plenteous graces from the street.
A hand-clasp I must feed on for a night,   25
    A noon, although the untasted feast you lay,
To mock me, of your beauty. That you might
    Be lover for one space, and make essay
What 'tis to pass unsuppered to your couch,
    Keep fast from love all day; and so be taught   30
The famine which these craving lines avouch!
    Ah! miser of good things that cost thee naught,
How know'st thou poor men's hunger?—Misery!
When I go doleless and unfed by thee!

A Holocaust

*'No man ever attained supreme knowledge, unless his heart had been
torn up by the roots.'*

When I presage the time shall come—yea, now
    Perchance is come when you shall fail from me,
Because the mighty spirit, to whom you vow
    Faith of kin genius unrebukably,
Scourges my sloth, and from your side dismissed   5
      Henceforth this sad and most, most lonely soul
Must, marching fatally through pain and mist,
    The God-bid levy of its powers enrol;
When I presage that none shall hear the voice
    From the great Mount that clangs my ordained advance,   10
That sullen envy bade the churlish choice
    Yourself shall say, and turn your altered glance;
O God! Thou knowest if this heart of flesh
    Quivers like broken entrails, when the wheel
Rolleth some dog in middle street, or fresh   15
    Fruit when ye tear it bleeding from the peel;

If my soul cries the uncomprehended cry
   When the red agony oozed on Olivet!
Yet not for this, a caitiff, falter I,
   Beloved whom I must lose, nor thence regret   20
The doubly-vouched and twin allegiance owed
   To you in Heaven, and Heaven in you, Lady.
How could you hope, loose dealer with my God,
   That I should keep you for my fealty?
For still 'tis thus:—because I am so true,   25
My Fair, to Heaven, I am so true to you!

Beneath a Photograph

Phoebus, who taught me art divine,
Here tried his hand where I did mine;
And his white fingers in this face
Set my Fair's sigh-suggesting grace.
O sweetness past profaning guess,   5
Grievous with its own exquisiteness!
Vesper-like face, its shadows bright
With meanings of sequestered light;
Drooped with shamefast sanctities
She purely fears eyes cannot miss,   10
Yet would blush to know she *is*.
Ah, who can view with passionless glance
This tear-compelling countenance!
He has cozened it to tell
Almost its own miracle.   15
Yet I, all-viewing though he be,
Methinks saw further here than he;
And, Master gay! I swear I drew
Something the better of the two!

After Her Going

For this poem Meynell noted in his copy of *Selected Poems*: 'To AM [Alice Meynell] after the close of a visit to the poet at Pantasaph'. The visit was probably the one made at Easter 1894. For Meynell's copy of *Selected Poems* see the head-note to 'Memorat Memoria', p. 188.

The after-even! Ah, did I walk,
   Indeed, in her or even?
For nothing of me or around
   But absent She did leaven,
Felt in my body as its soul,   5
   And in my soul its heaven.

'Ah me! My very flesh turns soul,
   Essenced,' I sighed, 'with bliss!'
And the blackbird held his lutany,
   All fragrant-through with bliss;   10
And all things stilled were as a maid
   Sweet with a single kiss.

For grief of perfect fairness, eve
   Could nothing do but smile;
The time was far too perfect fair,   15
   Being but for a while;
And ah, in me, too happy grief
   Blinded herself with smile!

The sunset at its radiant heart
   Had somewhat unconfest: 20
The bird was loath of speech, its song
   Half-refluent on its breast,
And made melodious toyings with
   A note or two at best.

And she was gone, my sole, my Fair,   25
   Ah, sole my Fair, was gone!
Methinks, throughout the world 'twere right
   I had been sad alone;
And yet, such sweet in all things' heart,
   And such sweet in my own!

My Lady the Tyranness

Me since your fair ambition bows
Feodary to those gracious brows,
Is nothing mine will not confess
Your sovran sweet rapaciousness?
Though use to the white yoke innures,   5
Half-petulant is
Your loving rebel for somewhat his,
Not yours, my love, not yours!

Behold my skies, which make with me
One passionate tranquillity!   10
Wrap thyself in them as a robe,
She shares them not; their azures probe,
No countering wings thy flight endures.
Nay, they do stole
Me like an aura of her soul.   15
I yield them, love, for yours!

But mine these hills and fields, which put
Not on the sanctity of her foot.
Far off, my dear, far off the sweet
Grave *pianissimo* of your feet!   20
My earth, perchance, your sway abjures?—
Your absence broods
O'er all, a subtler presence. Woods,
Fields, hills, all yours, all yours!

Nay then, I said, I have my thought,   25
Which never woman's reaching raught;
Being strong beyond a woman's might,
And high beyond a woman's height,
Shaped to my shape in all contours.—
I looked, and knew   30
No thought but you were garden to.
All yours, my love, all yours!

Meseemeth still I have my life;
All-clement Her its resolute strife
Evades; contained, relinquishing   35
Her mitigating eyes; a thing
Which the whole girth of God secures.

Ah, fool, pause! pause!
I had no life, until it was
All yours, my love, all yours!   40

Yet, stern possession! I have my death,
Sole yielding up of my sole breath;
Which all within myself I die,
All in myself must cry the cry
Which the deaf body's wall immures.—   45
Thought fashioneth
My death without her.—Ah, even death
All yours, my love, all yours!

Death, then be hers. I have my heaven,
For which no arm of hers has striven;   50
Which solitary I must choose,
And solitary win or lose.—
Ah, but not heaven my own endures!
I must perforce
Taste you, my stream, in God your source,—   55
So steep my heaven in yours.

At last I said—I have my God,
Who doth desire me, though a clod,
And from His liberal Heaven shall He
Bar in mine arms His privacy.   60
Himself for mine Himself assures.—
None shall deny
God to be mine, but He and I
All yours, my love, all yours!

I have no fear at all lest I   65
Without her draw felicity.
God for His Heaven will not forego
Her whom I found such heaven below,
And she will train Him to her lures.
Nought, lady, I love   70
In you but more is loved above;
What made me, makes Him yours.

'I, thy sought own, am I forgot?'
Ha, thou?—thou liest, I seek thee not.
Why what, thou painted parrot, Fame,   75

What have I taught thee but her name?
Hear, thou slave Fame, while Time endures,
I give her thee;
Page her triumphal name!—Lady,
Take her, the thrall is yours.   80

Unto This Last

A boy's young fancy taketh love
Most simply, with the rind thereof;
A boy's young fancy tasteth more
The rind, than the deific core.
Ah, Sweet! to cast away the slips   5
Of unessential rind, and lips
Fix on the immortal core, is well;
But heard'st thou ever any tell
Of such a fool would take for food
Aspect and scent, however good,   10
Of sweetest core Love's orchards grow?
Should such a phantast please him so,
Love where Love's reverent self denies
Love to feed, but with his eyes,
All the savour, all the touch,   15
Another's—was there ever such?
Such were fool, if fool there be;
Such fool was I, and was for thee!

But if the touch and savour too
Of this fruit—say, Sweet, of you—   20
You unto another give
For sacrosanct prerogative,
Yet even scent and aspect were
Some elected Second's share;
And one, gone mad, should rest content   25
With memory of show and scent;
Would not thyself vow, if there sigh
Such a fool—say, Sweet, as I—
Treble frenzy it must be
Still to love, and to love thee?   30

Yet had I torn (man knoweth not,
Nor scarce the unweeping angels wot

Of such dread task the lightest part)
Her fingers from about my heart,
Heart, did we not think that she 35
Had surceased her tyranny?
Heart, we bounded, and were free!
O sacrilegious freedom!—Till
She came, and taught my apostate will
The winnowed sweet mirth cannot guess 40
And tear-fined peace of hopelessness;
Looked, spake, simply touched, and went.
Now old pain is fresh content,
Proved content is unproved pain.
Pangs fore-tempted, which in vain 45
I, faithless have denied, now bud
To untempted fragrance and the mood
Of contrite heavenliness; all days
Joy afrights me in my ways;
Extremities of old delight 50
Afflict me with new exquisite
Virgin piercings of surprise,—
Stung by those wild brown bees, her eyes!

Ultimum

Now in these last spent drops, slow, slower shed,
Love dies, Love dies, Love dies—ah, Love is dead!
Sad Love in life, sore Love in agony,
Pale Love in death; while all his offspring songs,
Like children, versed not in death's chilly wrongs, 5
About him flit, frighted to see him lie
So still, who did not know that Love could die.
One lifts his wing, where dulls the vermeil all
Like clotting blood, and shrinks to find it cold,
And when she sees its lapse and nerveless fall 10
Clasps her fans, while her sobs ooze through the webbèd gold.
Thereat all weep together, and their tears
Make lights like shivered moonlight on long waters.
Have peace, O piteous daughters!
He shall not wake more through the mortal years, 15
Nor comfort come to my soul widowèd,
Nor breath to your wild wings; for Love is dead!

I slew, that moan for him: he lifted me
Above myself, and that I might not be
Less than myself, need was that he should die;   20
Since Love that first did wing, now clogged me from the sky.
Yet lofty Love being dead thus passeth base—
There is a soul of nobleness which stays,
The spectre of the rose: be comforted,
Songs, for the dust that dims his sacred head!   25
The days draw on too dark for Song or Love;
O peace, my songs, nor stir ye any wing!
For lo, the thunder hushing all the grove,
And did Love live, not even Love could sing.

And, Lady, thus I dare to say,   30
Not all with you is passed away!
For your love taught me this:—'tis Love's true praise
To be, not staff, but writ of worthy days;
And that high worth in love unfortunate
Should still remain it learned in love elate.   35
Beyond your star, still, still the stars are bright;
Beyond your highness, still I follow height;
Sole I go forth, yet still to my sad view,
Beyond your trueness, Lady, Truth stands true.
This wisdom sings my song with last firm breath,   40
Caught from the twisted lore of Love and Death,
The strange inwoven harmony that wakes
From Pallas' straying locks twined with her ægis-snakes.
'On him the unpetitioned heavens descend,
Who heaven on earth proposes not for end;   45
The perilous and celestial excess
Taking with peace, lacking with thankfulness.
Bliss in extreme befits thee not, until
Thou'rt not extreme in bliss; be equal still:
Sweets to be granted think thyself unmeet   50
Till thou have learned to hold sweet not too sweet.'
This thing not far is he from wise in art
Who teacheth; nor who doth, from wise in heart.

32–5 Omitted in *Works*, probably on account of their obscurity. It is possible that 'writ' is a misprint for 'scrip', in which case the staff could be symbolic of a commodity soon finished whereas scrip – a wallet for food carried by the medieval pilgrim – could represent a reserve supply. It seems also that commas are required after 'worth' in 34 and 'remain' in 35.

Envoy

Go, songs, for ended is our brief, sweet play;
   Go, children of swift joy and tardy sorrow:
And some are sung, and that was yesterday,
   And some unsung, and that may be tomorrow.

Go forth; and if it be o'er stony way,   5
   Old joy can lend what newer grief must borrow:
And it was sweet, and that was yesterday,
   And sweet is sweet, though purchasèd with sorrow.

Go, songs, and come not back from your far way:
   And if men ask you why ye smile and sorrow,   10
Tell them ye grieve, for your hearts know Today,
   Tell them ye smile, for your eyes know Tomorrow.

PART TWO

POEMS PUBLISHED ELSEWHERE

Poems Published during Thompson's Lifetime

The Passion of Mary
Verses in Passiontide

ME, April 1888; reprinted in *Eyes of Youth* (1910) and in *Works*

According to Everard Meynell, it was a 'tradition' in the Thompson family that Francis began this poem soon after hearing a sermon in his church at Ashton-under-Lyne on the feast of Our Lady of Sorrows, 1885 (*Life*, p. 46; the feast falls on 15 September). He may have completed it while on the London streets, although no drafts appear for it in the surviving notebooks from those years. But it was one of the poems he sent to Wilfrid Meynell, who chose it to print in the Easter issue of *ME* in order to trace the poet. (See Biographical Summary, p. xxxvi.)

> O Lady Mary, thy bright crown
>   Is no mere crown of majesty;
> For with the reflex of His own
>   Resplendent thorns Christ circled thee.
>
> The red rose of this Passion-tide   5
>   Doth take a deeper hue from thee,
> In the five wounds of Jesus dyed,
>   And in thy bleeding thoughts, Mary!
>
> The soldier struck a triple stroke
>   That smote thy Jesus on the tree: 10
> He broke the Heart of Hearts, and broke
>   The Saint's and Mother's hearts in thee.
>
> Thy son went up the angels' ways,
>   His passion ended; but, ah me!
> *Thou* found'st the road of further days   15
>   A longer way of Calvary:
>
> On the hard cross of hope deferred
>   Thou hung'st in loving agony,
> Until the mortal-dreaded word
>   Which chills *our* mirth, spake mirth to thee.   20

The angel Death from this cold tomb
    Of life did roll the stone away;
And He thou barest in thy womb
    Caught thee at last into the day,
Before the living throne of Whom   25
    The Lights of Heaven burning pray.

L'Envoy

O Thou who dwellest in the day!
    Behold I pace amidst the gloom:
Darkness is ever round my way
    With little space for sunbeam-room.   30

Yet Christian sadness is divine
    Even as thy patient sadness was:
The salt tears in our life's dark wine
    Fell in it from the saving cross.

Bitter the bread of our repast;   35
    Yet doth a sweet the bitter leaven:
Our sorrow is the shadow cast
    Around it by the light of Heaven.

O light in Light, shine down from Heaven!

Not Even in Dream

ME, December 1888; reprinted in *Works*

It seems most likely that this sonnet was written soon after Thompson accepted the Meynells' hospitality and therefore refers to his recent parting from the street girl.

This love is crueller than the other love;
We had the dreams for tryst, we other pair:
But here there is no *we*; not anywhere
Returning breaths of sighs can I feel move.
No wings, even of the stuff which fancy wove,   5
Perturb sleep's air with a responsive flight
When mine sweep into dreams: my soul in fright
Circles, as round its widowed nest a dove.
         *

One shadow but usurps another's place,
And though this shadow more enthralling is,   10
Alas, it hath no lips at all to kiss!
I have not even that former poignant bliss,
That haunting sweetness, that forlorn, sad trace,
The phantom memory of a vanished kiss!

4 *can I feel move* *Works*: about me move.

Non Pax: Expectatio

ME, July 1889; reprinted in *Works*

The title can be translated as 'No Peace: Expectation'. From the date of publication in *ME* the sonnet appears to have been written under the stress of withdrawal
symptoms from opium, during Thompson's earlier months at Storrington.

Hush! 'tis the gap between two lightnings. Room
Is none for peace in this thou callest peace,
This breathing-while wherein the breathings cease.
The pulses sicken, hearkening through the gloom.
Afar the thunders of a coming doom   5
Ramp on the cowering winds: lo! at the dread,
Thy heart's tomb yawns and renders up its dead,—
The hopes 'gainst hope embalmèd in its womb.

Canst thou endure, if the pent flood o'erflows?—
Who is estated heir to constancy?   10
Behold, I hardly know if I outlast
The minute underneath whose heel I lie;
Yet I endure, have stayed the minute passed,
Perchance, may stay the next. Who knows, who knows?

Song of the Hours

ME, January 1890; reprinted in *Works*

The poem is based on ideas and images from Shelley's 'Prometheus Unbound'
and was composed during Thompson's earlier months at Storrington while he was
writing an extended essay on Shelley.

    At H there is a revised copy of the *ME* text, indicating that he intended to
reprint it in either *Poems* or *New Poems*. It was not, however, reprinted until it
appeared in *Works*, where it follows Thompson's revisions. As this represents his

final text it is reproduced here, with the earlier variants in the endnotes. But in *Works* six lines are omitted from the revised text which are now restored (93–6, 125–6; see endnotes).

SCENE: *Before the Palace of the Sun, into which a god has just passed as the guest of Hyperion.* TIME: *Dawn. The Hours of Night and Day advance on each other as the gates close.*

MORNING HOURS   In curbed expanses our wheeling dances
           Meet from the left and right;
      Under this vaporous awning
           Tarrying awhile in our flight,
      Waiting the day's advances,   5
           We, the children of light,
      Clasp you on verge of the dawning,
           Sisters of Even and Night!

CHORUS   We who lash from the way of the sun
           With the whip of the winds the thronging clouds,   10
      Who puff out the lights of the stars, or run
           To scare dreams back to their shrouds,
      Or tiar the temples of Heaven
           With a crystalline gleam of showers;

EVENING HOURS   While to flit with the soft moth, Even,   15
           Round the lamp of the day is ours;

NIGHT HOURS   And ours with her crescent argentine,
           To make Night's forehead fair,
      To wheel up her throne of the earth, and twine
           The daffodils in her hair;   20

ALL   We, moulted as plumes are,
           From the wings whereon Time is borne;

MORNING HOURS   We, buds who in blossoming foretell
           The date when our leaves shall be torn;

NIGHT HOURS   We, knowing our dooms are to plunge with the
                gloom's car,   25
      Down the steep ruin of morn;

ALL   We hail thee, Immortal!
      We robes of Life, mouldering while worn.

NIGHT HOURS   Sea-birds, winging o'er sea calm-strewn
       To the lure of the beacon-stars, are we,   30
   O'er the foamy wake of the white-sailed moon,
       Which to men is the Galaxy.

MORNING HOURS   Our eyes, through our pinions folden
       By the filtered flame are teased
   As we bow when the sun makes golden   35
       Earthquake in the East.

EVENING HOURS   And *we* shake on the sky a dusted fire
       From the ripened sunset's anther,
   While the flecked main, drowsing in gorged desire,
       Purrs like an outstretched panther.   40

MORNING HOURS   O'er the dead moon-maid
       We draw softly the day's white pall;
   And our children the Moments we see as
       In drops of the dew they fall,
   Or on light plumes laid they shoot the cascade   45
       Of colours some Heaven's bow call;

ALL   And we sing, Guest, to thee, as
       Thou pacest the crystal-paved hall!

We, while the sun with his hid chain swings
       The incense out of the blossomy earth   50
Who dare the lark with our passionate wings,
       And its mirth with our masterless mirth;
   Or—when that flying laughter
       Has sunk and died away
   Which beat against Heaven's rafter—   55
       Who vex the clear eyes of day,
Who weave for the sky in the loom of the cloud
       A mantle of waving rain,
We, whose hair is jewelled with joys, or bowed
       Under veilings of misty pain;   60
We hymn thee at leaving
       Who strew thy feet's coming, O Guest!
We, the linked cincture which girdles
       Mortality's feverous breast,
Who heave in its heaving, who grieve in its grieving,   65

Are restless in its unrest;
Our beings unstirred else
[Line missing in FT's revised text. See endnotes.]
We see the wind, like a light, swift leopard
 Leap on the flocks of the cloud that flee,   70
As we follow the feet of the radiant shepherd
 Whose bright sheep drink of the sea.
When that drunken Titan the Thunder
 Stumbles through staggered Heaven,
And spills on the scorched earth under   75
 The fiery wine of the levin,
With our mystic measure of rhythmic motion
 We charm him in snorting sleep,
While round him the sun enchants from ocean
 The walls of a cloudy keep.   80
 Beneath the deep umbers
Of night as we watch and hark,
 The dim-wingèd dreams which feed on
The blossoms of day we mark,
As in murmurous numbers they swarm to the slumbers 85
 That cell the hive of the dark;
And life shakes, a reed on
Our tide, in the death-wind stark.

Time, Eternity's fountain, whose waters
 Fall back thither from whence they rose,   90
Deweth with us, its showery daughters,
 The Life that is green in its flows.
  And some a dragoned Trouble
  May spit from its writhen jaw,
And some our babble and bubble   95
  From the urn a joy may draw;
But whether in grief or mirth we shower,
 We make not the thing we breed,
For what may come of the passing Hour
 Is what was hid in the seed.   100
  And now as wakes,
 Like Love in its first blind guesses,
  Or a snake just stirring its coils,
   Sweet tune into half-caresses,
Before the sun shakes the clinging flakes   105
  Of gloom from his spouting tresses,
 Let winds have toils

To catch at our fluttering dresses!

Winter, that numbeth the throstle and stilled wren,
   Has keen frost-edges our plumes to pare,   110
Till we break, with the Summer's laughing children,
   Over the fields of air.
      While the winds in their tricksome courses
     The snowy steeds vault upon
   That are foaled of the white sea-horses   115
    And washed in the streams of the sun.
Thaw, O thaw the enchanted throbbings
   Curdled at Music's heart;
Tread she her grapes till from their englobings
   The melodies spurt and smart!   120
     We fleet as a rain,
    Nor yearn for the being men own,
   With whom is naught beginneth
    Or endeth without some moan;
    Their life they gain in others' pain   125
     And lose it in their own;
  We soar to our zenith
   And are panglessly overblown.

Yet, if the roots of the truth were bare,
   Our transience is only a mortal seeming;   130
Fond men, we are fixed in a still despair,
   And we fleet but in your dreaming.
      We are columns in Time's hall, mortals,
       Wherethrough Life hurrieth;
     You pass in at birth's wide portals,   135
     And out at the postern of death.
As you chase down the vista your dream or your love
   The swift pillars race you by,
And you think it is we who move, who move,—
   It is you who die, who die!   140
    O firmament, even
     You pass, by whose fixture man voweth;
   God breathes you forth as a bubble
    And shall suck you back into His mouth!
   Through earth, sea, and heaven a doom shall be driven, 145
   And, sown in the furrows it plougheth,
    As fire bursts from stubble
     Shall spring the new wonders none troweth.

*

The bowed East lifteth the dripping sun,
   A golden cup, to the lips of Night,   150
Over whose cheek in flushes run
   The heats of the liquid light.

MORNING HOURS   To our very pinions' ridge
   We tremble expectantly;—
Is it ready, the burnished bridge   155
   We must cast for our King o'er the sea?
And who will kneel with sunbeam-slips
   To dry the flowers' sweet eyes?
Who touch with fire her finger-tips
   For the lamp of the grape, as she flies?   160

ALL   List, list to the prances, his chariot advances,
   It comes in a dust of light!
From under our brightening awning
   We wheel in a diverse flight:
Yet the hands we unclasp, as our dances   165
   Sweep off to the left and right,
Are but loosed on the verge of the dawning
   To join on the verge of the night.

38 *anther* pollen.

Between 48–9 *ME*:
        Lord of the vintage of lips,
          We soothe with a rapture's trinket,
       And chasten with thwarting whips:
    For a sigh deep as Dis's we sell thee Ulysses,
       Then some beckoning Hour by him trips,
         And away when none think it
       With your heart in his hand he slips.

68 Missing line in MS, added in *Works* from *ME*: Were it not for the bosom they pressed. **69–72** *ME*:
        When day goes forth as a victor of Ind does
         We chain to his chariot his dusky thrall,
    And our dyed robes gleam through the western windows
       As we light up his feasting-hall.

76 *levin* lightning. **93–6** deleted in *Works*. **109–16** *ME*:
        Rich-haired Music's golden harmonies
         Wave in cadence to her feet,
      Floating out of her dulcet charm an ease
        Smoothes our gliding feet.
         The silver clash of our pinions.
           As they flash to their felt expanse,
        Tells the sky that the minions
          Of change are speeding the dance.

125–6 deleted in *Works*.

Daphne

ME, May 1890; reprinted in *Works*

Daphne, daughter of the river god Penneus, was pursued by Apollo, the sun god and god also of poetry. As he was about to overtake her, her prayer for deliverance was answered when she was turned into a laurel tree. Thereafter the laurel became the tree most favoured by the god and, consequently, associated with poets and poetry. Thompson uses the myth as an allegory of a poet whose calling demands the sacrifice of natural love.

The river-god's daughter,—the sun-god sought her,
    Sleeping with never a zephyr by her.
Under the noon he made his prey sure,
Woofed in weeds of a woven azure,
    As down he shot in a whistle of fire.   5

Slid off, fair daughter! her vesturing water;
    Like a cloud from the scourge of the winds fled she:
With the breath in her hair of the keen Apollo,
And fleet the beat of the feet that follow,
    She throes in his arms to a laurel-tree.   10

Risen out of birth's waters the soul distraught errs,
    Nor whom nor whither she flieth knows she:
With the breath in her hair of the keen Apollo,
And fleet the beat of the feet that follow,
    She throes in his arms to a poet, woe's me!   15

You plucked the boughed verse the poet bears—
    It shudders and bleeds as it snaps from the tree.
A love-banning love, did the god but know it,
Which barks the man about with the poet,
    And muffles his heart of mortality!   20

Yet I translate—ward of song's gate!—
    Perchance all ill this mystery.
We both are struck with the self-same quarrel;
We grasp the maiden, and clasp the laurel!—
    Do we weep or laugh more, *Phœbe mi?*   25

'His own green lays, unwithering bays,
    Gird Keats' unwithering brow,' say ye?
O fools, that is only the empty crown!
The sacred head has laid it down
    With Hob, Dick, Marian, and Margery.   30

10 *throes* agonises.

To-day

ME, August 1890; not reprinted

'Widower of yesterday! why stand aloof?
    Know me thy child, and know me too thy bride;
    Thou must beget thy issue from my side.
The loom thou wroughtest, joy thee in the woof!
The plate thou gravedst, now behold the proof;   5
      All days but print afresh the yester-trace,
      Save each impression grows more poor and base:
Take me, who shalt take worse to thy life's roof.'

Then spat I out the ashes of my youth;—
'Thou liest a lie embittered with a truth!   10
    But one part in to-morrow's blood thou hast:
From many morrows and one higher me
The days shall be bred out to purity,
      And build on the drained marshes of the past.'

John Henry Newman

Weekly Register, 16 August 1890; reprinted in *SHSS* and *BHCC*

In this obituary poem on the occasion of Cardinal Newman's death, Thompson uses the term 'high church' in the original sense common among the English Catholic families surviving from the penal days. To them, the 'high' church denoted the new 'ultramontane' movement introduced from Europe during the nineteenth century. The phrase therefore gives the lines a significance which accounts for their omission from later collections, representing a view of Newman which has only been recognised in much more recent years.

When our high Church's builders planned
To re-erect within the land
    The ruined edifice,
    What was the building's price?

Stern was the toil, the profit slow,   5
The struggling wall could scantly grow.
    What way to expedite?—
    Men had of old a rite!

Into the walls that would not thrive
He gave him to be built alive,   10
    A human sacrifice.
    And lo! the walls uprise.

The Sere of the Leaf

ME, January 1891; reprinted in *Works*

Thompson addressed this poem to the Irish poet Katharine Tynan, a close friend
of the Meynell family. Like them, Thompson admired her work, although he had
not met her when the poem was written 'at the end of 1890', after she had visited
the Meynells the previous year (*Life*, p. 302). When reprinted in *Works* the sixth
and twelfth stanzas were deleted.

> Winter wore a flapping wind, and his beard, disentwined,
>   Blew cloudy in the face of the Fall,
> When a poet-soul flew South, with a singing in her mouth,
>   O'er the azure Irish parting-wall.
> There stood one beneath a tree whose matted greenery   5
>   Was fruited with the song of birds;
> By the melancholy water drooped the slender sedge its daughter,
>   Whose silence was a sadness passing words:
>   He held him very still,
>   And he heard the running rill,   10
> And the soul-voice singing blither than the birds.
>
> All Summer the sunbeams drew the curtains from the dreams
>   Of the rose-fay, while the sweet South wind
> Lapped the silken swathings close round her virginal repose
>   When the night swathed folding slumbers round her mind.   15
> *Now* the elf of the flower had sickened in her bower,
>   And fainted in a thrill of scent;
> But her lover of the South, with a moan upon his mouth,
>   Caught her spirit to his arms as it went:
>   Then the storms of West and North   20
>   Sent a gusty vaward forth,
> Sent a skirring desolation, and he went.
>
> And a troop of roving gales rent the lily's silver veils,
>   And tore her from her trembling leaves;
> And the autumn's smitten face flushed to a red disgrace,   25
>   And she grieved as a captive grieves.
> Once the gold-barred cage of skies with the sunset's moulted dyes
>   Was splendorously littered at the even;
>   Beauty-fraught o'er shining sea once the sun's argosy
>   To rich wreck on the Western reefs was driven;   30
>   *Now* the sun, in Indian pall,
>   Treads the russet-amber fall
> From the ruined trees of Heaven.

Too soon fails the light, and the swart boar, night,
 Gores to death the bleeding day;   35
And the dusk has no more a calm at its core,
 But is turbid with obscene array.
For the cloud a thing of ill, dilating baleful o'er the hill,
 Spreads a bulk like a huge Afreet
Drifting in gigantic sloth, or a murky behemoth,   40
 For the moon to set her silver feet;
  For the moon's white paces,
  And its nostril for her traces,
 As she urges it with wild witch-feet.

And the stars, forlornly fair, shiver keenly through the air, 45
 All an-aching till their watch be ceased;
And the hours like maimed flies lag on, ere night hatch her golden
  dragon
 In the mould of the upheaved East.
'As the cadent languor lingers after Music droops her fingers
 Beauty still falls dying, dying through the days;   50
But ah!' said he who stood in that autumn solitude,
 'Singing-soul, thou art 'lated with thy lays!
  All things that on this globe err
  Fleet into dark October,
When day and night encounter, the nights war down the days. 55

'Lo, how, his morion burnished round with the sun,
 Day lit about with lances flashed to fight!
His burning onset came an inextinguishable flame
 On the rocked ranks of the night.
See, the battle ebbs out West, with a riot of tossing crest 60
 And banner streaming rent, a panic-heap;
The stricken day drops dead on a field running red,
 While his golden crown rolls down the heavenly steep.
  Why with thy solicitings
  Tease the summer's lethèd strings,   65
Fretting Beauty's ear as she dies into sleep?

'For the song in thy mouth is all of the South,
 Though Winter wax in strength more and more,
And at eve with breath of malice the stained windows of day's palace
 Pile in shatters on the Western floor.'   70
But the song sank down his soul like a Naiad through her pool,

He could not bid the visitant depart;
For he felt the melody make tune like a bee
 In the red rose of his heart:
  Like a Naiad in her pool   75
  It lay within his soul,
Like a bee in the red rose of his heart.

She sang of the shrill East fled and bitterness surceased:—
 'O the blue South wind is musical!
And the garden's drenched with scent, and my soul hath its content, 80
 This eve or any eve at all.'
On his form the blushing shames of her ruby-plumaged flames
 Flickered hotly, like a quivering crimson snow:
'And hast thou thy content? Were some rain of it besprent
 On the soil where I am drifted to and fro!   85
  My soul, blown o'er the ways
  Of these arid latter days,
Would blossom like a rose of Jericho.

'I know not equipoise, only purgatorial joys,
 Griefs singing to the soul's instrument,   90
And forgetfulness which yet knoweth that it doth forget;
 But content—what is content?
For a harp of singeing wire, and a goblet dripping fire,
 And desires that hunt down Beauty through the Heaven
With unslackenable bounds, as the deep-mouthed thunder-hounds   95
 Bay at heel the fleeing levin,—
  The chaliced lucencies
  From pure holy-wells of eyes,
And the bliss unbarbed with pain I have given.

'Is—O framed to suffer joys!—*thine* the sweet without alloys 100
 Of the many, who art numbered with the few?
And thy flashing breath of song, does it do *thy* lips no wrong,
 Nor sear them as the heats spill through?
When the welling musics rise, like tears from heart to eyes,
 Is there not a pang dissolved in them for thee?   105
Does not Song, like the Queen of radiant Love, Hellene,
 Float up dripping from a bitter sea?
  No tunèd metal known
   Unless stricken yields a tone
Be it silver, or sad iron like to me.   110

     *

'Yet the rhymes still roll from the bell-tower of thy soul,
    Though no tongued griefs give them vent;
If they ring to me no gladness, if *my* joy be sceptred sadness,
    I am glad, yet, for *thy* content.
Not always does the lost, 'twixt the fires of heat and frost,   115
    Envy those whom the healing lustres bless;
But may sometimes in the pain of a yearning past attain
    Thank the angels for their happiness;
      'Twixt the fire and fiery ice,
      Looking up to Paradise   120
    Thank the angels for their happiness.

'Thy sunlight spirit strains through thy muse's painted panes
    In radiant shapes on my dark wall;
But most boughs verse may fold in its dusted emerald mould
    Were moisted dank with sorrow first of all.   125
Better lowly, satiate days, though they see not their own face
    In the hyaline of any metred stream,
Than the sweetest melodies were ever wet in Music's eyes,
    Her tear is still a tear, if it gleam;
      And her frail wraiths as they rise,   130
      Evanescing clarities,
    Sigh into silence and the drift of dream.

'The heart, a censered fire whence fuming chants aspire,
    Is fed with oozèd gums of precious pain;
And unrest swings denser, denser, the fragrance from that censer,   135
    With the heart-strings for its quivering chain.
Yet 'tis vain to scale the turret of the cloud-uplifted spirit,
    And bar the immortal in, the mortal out;
For sometime unaware comes footfall up the stair,
    And a soft knock under which no bolts are stout,   140
      And lo, there pleadeth sore
      The heart's voice at the door,
  'I am your child, you may not shut me out!'

'The breath of poetry in the mind's autumnal tree
    Shakes down the saddened thoughts in singing showers,   145
But fallen from their stem, what part have we in them?
    "Nay," pine the trees, "they were, but are not ours."
Not for the mind's delight these serèd leaves alight,
    But, loosened by the breezes, fall they must.

What ill if they decay? Yet some a little way   150
    May flit before deserted by the gust,
May touch some spirit's hair, may cling one moment there,—
    She turns; they tremble down. Drift o'er them, dust!'

4 *Irish parting-wall* FT note: 'Miss Katharine Tynan's visit to London, 1889.' 21 *vaward* advance-guard. 34–5 *swart boar . . . day* In Irish mythology a great boar dominates the heavens and each evening roots out the day with its snout. 39 *Afreet* mythical monster. 40 *behemoth* probably a hippopotamus (Job 40: 10). 56 *morion* helmet. 65 *lethèd* fading. 56–66. omitted in *Works*. 96 *levin* lightning. 106 *Queen of radiant Love, Hellene* the goddess Aphrodite. 122–32 omitted in *Works*. 127 *hyaline* crystal clear. 152 two lines in *Works*.

Lines for a Drawing of Our Lady of the Night

Ushaw Magazine, March 1891; reprinted in *Works*

There is an early draft in an unnumbered notebook in EMH. As the notebook contains drafts for several London street poems, this one was probably also composed while Thompson was living on the streets.

    This, could I paint my inward sight,
    This were Our Lady of the Night.

    She bears on her front's lucency
    The starlight of her purity.

    For as the white rays of that star   5
    The union of all colours are,

    She sums all virtues that may be
    In her sweet light of purity.

    The mantle which she holds on high
    Is the great mantle of the sky.   10

    Think, O sick toiler, when the night
    Comes on thee, sad and infinite,

    Think, sometimes, 'tis our own Lady
    Spreads her blue mantle over thee,

    And folds the earth, a wearied thing,   15
    Beneath its gentle shadowing;

    Then rest a little, and in sleep
    Forget to weep, forget to weep.

The Road's Rede

ME, August 1891; not reprinted

No author's name is given in *ME* but a fair copy of the poem with a few minor variants appears in NB BC16. In *ME* it is prefixed by the following quotation: "There is one of Nature's spiritual ditties that has not yet been set to words or human music: 'The Invitation to the Road': an air continually sounding in the ears of gipsies, and to whose inspiration our nomadic fathers journeyed all their days."R. L. Stevenson. Presumably this gave Thompson the idea of composing lines based on the gipsies' way of life. The title can be loosely rendered as 'The Lesson of the Road'.

O you who stand on yon heather-knoll
    As a tanned breast round and brown,
Why look you so? Why halt you so?
    I rede you hasten down.

Take you me for a mistress meet.   5
    'Groom of the road and rhyme!
I have a tune to teach your feet,
    As they beat in rhythm and time;

Your treading treadeth poems out,
    Although I be no talker;   10
Trees and dreams wave over me
    For the lusty walker;

My white dust wreathing, rising, seething,
    Swathing round his knees,
Is a cloud of climbing vision,   15
    Clinging fantasies;

My white folds, writhing up hills
    Are coils to lap about him,
And drag him down the distances
    That tempt, and twit, and flout him.   20

I taunt with 'ho!' the torrent's fume,
    With 'ha!' the wroth stream's surge,
Like a cataract's spurt I leap across
    Over from verge to verge.

I worm me into the close counsels   25
    Of the wild wood's hid heart,
Shrinking to a noteless path
    To play my traitorous part;

And when I am well quit of him,
   I loosen back to road,   30
A-gad through all the haunts of men
   To prate his ways abroad.

I cleave the haughty head o' the hill,
   Though helmed in triple rock;
I curb the grim wild of its will,   35
   Its silence laugh to mock.

Poplars like tall feather-grass
   In light ranks by me lean;
The larch rolls down, in leap on leap,
   Its cataract of green.   40

I lead your feet by waving wheat,
   And treasuries of broom;
The pines bear up, stark, straight, and sad,
   Their superincumbent gloom:

The pines, stern, sad Atlantes, groan   45
   With their firmament of gloom;
But I run out, swift, white, and glad,
   From the shade of their solemn doom.

Then take you me for your mistress meet,
   'Groom of the road and rhyme!   50
I have a tune to teach your feet,
   As they beat in rhythm and time.

And I will teach your blood to run
   In wanton wreaths as I;
While I fling a white laugh back beneath   55
   To the laugh of the sun on high.

And cry ha! ha! to the jolly sun,
   To the losel clouds ho! Ho!
For they loll and doze on the thirsting sky,
While lusty and hot stride you and I   60
   O'er the sweating earth below.

45 *Atlantes* sculpted male figures serving as pillars. 58 *losel* profligate.

Laus Legis

ME, September 1891; not reprinted

The title means: 'In praise of the Law', that is, the natural Law of God governing the universe. *Vox Quaerentis* is the Voice of the Enquirer; *Vox Legis*, the Voice of the Law.

VOX QUAERENTIS When the great floodgates God first sundered
     Of Himself on desolation,
   And round reverberate Heaven there thundered
     The growl of an unleashed Creation,
   What voice could cry to discord: 'Be   5
     Thou rampart round security?'

VOX LEGIS   I bade the frowning terror be
   Citadelled o'er security;
   Yea, at my stamp she cowers, and lies
   The warden-hound of Paradise.   10

VOX QUAERENTIS Leviathan earth, with back upstood from
     Chaos, shook its woody fells;
   Belching a conflagrant flood from
     Its Aetnean spiracles;
   And where then was there found a hand   15
   That could draw it to the land?

VOX LEGIS   I, with the finger of my hand,
   Plucked it to the heaven-strand;
   And with a twist I bound it there
   Of adamantean gossamer.   20

VOX QUAERENTIS Whose the hand that strews the manna
     For the mailèd birds of God,
   When congregating pennons fan a
     Flicker from the flame-grassed sod,
   With tinkling justle, and the clangours   25
   Intersweeping of sweet angers?

VOX LEGIS   I cast the paradisal grain
   In a sudden rainbow-rain;
   'Mid the clangour, clangour, clangour,
   Of their wings in argent anger.   30

VOX QUAERENTIS   Threating occidental rampires
        When the stellar hordes alight,
    Kindling their innumerous camp-fires
        On the champain of the night;
    What tactic ranks their rangèd wars?   35
    Who is Captain of the stars?

VOX LEGIS   My nod their linked battalia wait,
    Their wheeling ranks intrinsicate;
    Until this rotten earth become
    An apple 'twixt the jaws of doom.   40

VOX QUAERENTIS   Who hath seen the broods of lightnings
        Seething in their caverned cloud,
    And endured their dreadful brightenings
        With lids unblenched, with front unbowed?
    Whose countenance the strong thunders mutes,   45
    When they tear Heaven up by the roots?

VOX LEGIS   With moveless gaze enchant I these,
    And interspheral harmonies;
    I bid the levins' stroke and pause,
    Or twitch the sting from their hot jaws.   50

VOX QUAERENTIS   When Eve's blown vestures half uncover
        The lucence of her moonèd breast;
    And a red vortex gurges over
        The foundered sun in the tossed West,
    Who to the heavens' high-seas restores   55
    And sets it round with silver oars?

VOX LEGIS   I bid its banks of vibrant rays
    Beat to bright froth heaven's water-ways;
    Unmooring from Phosphorian shores
    The long flash of those silver oars.   60

VOX QUAERENTIS   When the lady lily, slipping
        Her green garment, stands up slight,
    With her white limbs newly dripping
        From the laving of the light;
    What hand can gird her safely pure,   65
    From her funeral mold renew her?

VOX LEGIS   I engird her safely pure,
                From sepulchral mold renew her;
                Till the dead stars that night enwombs
                Burst the lids o' their golden tombs.   70

VOX QUAERENTIS Who hath piped to every bird
                   Pipings of so diverse noise?
                Given each its little unknown word?
                   Perfumed with tone its diverse voice?
                Who steers the throngs of note on note   75
                That shake its multitudinous throat?

VOX LEGIS   I teach their passionate souls, small, strong
                To break and curdle into song;
                Allay or perturbate all notes
                That swarm within their populous throats.   80

VOX QUAERENTIS Who graved grief's face, a signet-ring for
                   God's own signet-hand to wear?
                Made smooth joy a mirroring for
                   Grief to see her own self fair?
                The fount of tears so near to rise,   85
                Their spray perturbs the calm-mered eyes?

VOX LEGIS   Through me, through me, doth joyance prove
                The way to grief, and grief to love;
                Yea, sadness sitteth, by my arts,
                A portress at the gate of hearts.   90

VOX QUAERENTIS Who is he of dread dominion,
                   That, upon the peal of doom,
                Weighs two firmaments of pinion,
                   Constellate of burning plume?
                Under his foot off-pushing into flight,   95
                The universe goes rocking down to night.

VOX LEGIS   That is I, oh, that is I!
                 By me what sprung, by me shall die:
                Back to God's stretched hand I fly,
                To perch there for eternity.   100
                The fates may gorge to their content,

To implacable desire,
On the shapes that drift asunder
Down the inundating thunder,—
Carrion hulks of continent,   105
Redly riven, and bleeding fire:
But I shadow with supernal
Wings of sway the fields eternal,
There my great empery feels not jars,
Though the sick heaven shall moult its stars.   110

14 *Aetnean spiracles* from Aetna, a volcanic mountain in Sicily, and spiracle, an orifice. **20** *adamantean* unbreakable. **31** *rampires* ramparts. **38** *intrinsicate* intricate. **49** *levins* lightning flashes. **53** *gurges* surges. **59** *Phosphorian* from Phosphorus, the morning star.

A Song of Youth and Age

ME, October, 1891; reprinted in *The Child Set in the Midst*, ed. Wilfrid Meynell, 1892

Watching a flight of fluttering laughters
    Dip their wings in her sparkling eyes,
How could I think her, how could I dream her
    A thing that dies!

'When you are older than you can number,   5
    Then do you die?' she said.
Seems the sum of our days so sumless,
    Little fair head?

The ills so many, the days are few;
    The ills they bring   10
That is the thing we cannot number,
    The only thing.

Thou who art whole in thine ignorance,
    Why should they make thee sick
With the damned drug knowledge? Nay, keep thou   15
    Thy happy arithmetic!

Work not the sum of the days, dear,
    It will make thee sad;
For in that cold sum we but subtract,
    And never, never add.   20

Thy sums make only the head ache,
   That sum makes the heart;
When it is done we say good-night,
   And lay life's slate apart.

When it is done we are very tired,   25
   And ready to say good-night:
And we sleep so sound, we never waken
   Till morning, mite;
Until we hear God saying,
   'Open your eyes, it's light.'   30

Yea, on this frozen Alp of life
   Is the hospice we call Death,
Whose trusty sickness seeketh us,
   Seeketh, and rescueth.

Ah! gladder lore thou art mistress in;   35
   Couched at thy feet
Enlighten my knowledge, teach me—dull knower—
   The Art to Know Not, sweet!

Alack and alack, I fear me
   There is not in all the schools   40
A teacher can teach us, once forgetting,
   Again its rules!

Life's rotten flooring her light feet shake not;
   Scarce can *I* think her a thing that dies,
Watching the wanton laughters   45
   Spray her sweet eyes.

A Broom-Branch at Twilight

ME, November 1891; not reprinted

Crocean from the marsh I win you,
And I hear the poems in you;
   I and they are wild for clasping,
But you will not yield them me.

You know, you that hive and show not,   5
What I ache to feel and know not —
   I, whose own heart speaks a hid tongue;
But you will say naught to me.

You know why the wind at even
Rends my heart as its is riven,   10
   And is sad, like me, at sadness;
But you will not teach this me.

And what hot heart splendently
Fumes to golden wrath the bee;
   Gold in your gold ear he sung it,   15
But you will not sing it me.

You know why your loveliness
Burthens me with strange distress
   Why I rest not that eve resteth;
But you will not hint it me.   20

You know why Beauty sits for ever,
Like the goddess of a river,
   With an urn of cold tear-oozes;
But you will not sigh it me.

Why Love hides his burning eyes   25
In Silence' dim hair, you surmise
   Silent at the heart of Silence;
But you will not whisper me.

And I hold you in my fingers;
And on songs for stateliest singers   30
   Does your golden frost lie heavy,
And you will not loose them me.

Evil timèd, evil timèd
Was my suit, and those unrhymèd
   Rhymes you fold some other poet   35
Sueless wins, withheld from me.

Marriage in Two Moods

ME, April 1892; reprinted in *Works*

Love that's loved from day to day
Loves itself into decay:
He that eats one daily fruit
Shrivels hunger at the root.
Daily pleasure grows a task;   5
Daily smiles become a mask.
Daily growth of unpruned strength
Expands to feebleness at length.
Daily increase thronging fast
Must devour itself at last.   10
Daily shining, even content
Would with itself grow discontent;
And the sun's life witnesseth
Daily dying is not death.
So love loved from day to day   15
Loves itself into decay.

Love to daily uses wed
Shall be sweetly perfected.
Life by repetitions grows
Unto its appointed close: 20
Day to day makes up the year;
All piles by repetition rise;
Shall not then Love's edifice?
Shall not Love, too, learn his writ,
Like Wisdom, by repeating it?   25
By the oft-repeated use
All perfections gain their thews;
And so, with daily uses wed,
Love, too, shall be perfected.

21 *Works:* Day to day fulfils one year. **Between 21–2** *Works:* Shall not Love by Love wax dear?

To a Traveller

From Victor Hugo

ME, September 1892; not reprinted

For Thompson's translations from Victor Hugo see the headnotes for 'A Sunset' and 'Heard on the Mountain' (pp. 201, 201). Like those poems, this one is from the group *Les Feuilles d'Automne*.

Friend, from such lengthy travel are you home,
Whence old betimes, and sages we become
    At quitting of the cot;
All surges have been subject to your eye,
Alack! and all the world is belted by   5
    The furrow of your boat.

The sun of twenty heavens has riped your life;
Where'er you wandered in your restless strife,
    Scattering and gathering too,
Like to the labouring hind that sows and reaps,   10
Each spot you passed a something gave, and keeps
    A something left of you.

Whiles that your friend, less wise and fortunate,
Under one same horizon did await
    The seasons as they come;   15
And like the tree which bides the green ensuit
Of leafy days beside his door, took root
    At threshold of his home!

And now, your heart laden with deep concerns,
Between your hands the fair heads of the bairns,   20
    Here sit and parley you,
And ask—ah! bitter questioning to bear!—
'Where is your sire? your son, your mother where?'
    Friend! they are travellers too!

If you will, when the moon is set to wane,   25
We two, there, where our elders long have lain
    Will mount the nighted steep.
And I will tell you, while your eyes look down,
On the dead town beside the sleeping town,
    Which has the better sleep!   30

Come; we two, mute and couched against the ground,
Will hear, while Paris her live tempest-sound
    Hushes the city thorough,
Those million dead, seed Calvary's sower sows,
Confusedly seethe within their tombs, as does   35
    The grain within the furrow!

How many joyous live, who should be keeping
For brother—or sister—shade eternal, weeping,
    Foiling the years' slow arts!
The dead soon die: we weep by epitaph.   40
Ah! in the grave they lapse to dust not half
    So swift as in our hearts!

Traveller! Traveller! Folly, our regrets!
Who knows how many dead each hour forgets,
    Though dear this, fair this was!   45
Who knows how sweetest sorrows are erased,
How many tombs upon the earth effaced
    By one day's growth of grass!

How the Singer's Singing Wailed for the Singer
A Dream Transcript

ME, November 1892; not reprinted

I

The poet sate
With inward desolation;
    His thoughts were throbbing,
Yet he could not write:
    He heard at gate   5
A voice of lamentation—
    A lonely sobbing
Burdened all the night.

'Why'—he let his fingers sink—
'Are tears immingled in my ink?   10
My pen leaves no words where it writ,
Because the tears ooze into it:

I write, and mar the page's white,
For tears may clot, but may not write.
Sink, sad weeping, sink!   15
For your tears disdain my ink.'

II

He dropped his pen;
He gave his thoughts in keeping
    To the skilled voice
Whose skill, nathless, was young: 20
    But ever then
That solitary weeping
    To its own noise
Turned all he would have sung.

'Why'—save to stint he had no choice—   25
'Have they put tears into my voice?
I hear not what my voice should say,
Because it sings the weeping-way:
I voice—no man shall dream what thing,
For tears may choke, but may not sing.   30
Cease, cease, mournful noise,
For your tears drench my voice!'

III

He passed—sick human!—
Under sickened stars
    Dismally where   35
The gate gloomed, like his fears:—
    Was't child, sprite, woman?
Quivering at the bars,
    All her dim hair
Dank, dank with night and tears.   40

Vested as in cinctured smoke,
Wherethrough her body's blanchness broke,
Like a slight white waterfall
Through its smoke investural:
And, too young for deep secrecies,   45
Did those waters of her eyes
By their perturbation show
What great wreck lay sunk below.

IV

'No demon black
Is she, to lure and damn!   50
   Weeping and clinging,
Who art thou, poor clinger?'
   She answered back,
Nor raised her head—'I am
   The Singer's Singing,   55
And I wail the Singer.

'I am the Singer's Singing, and I cry
Because I must go by, go by, go by!
   God gave him me, I had no other mate:
And I was little, and he nurtured me,   60
   Though therefore all men left him desolate;
And I was little, and he nurtured me,
   Though, having me, he had no other mate,
   And I was all too young for bride's estate,
And now the years fulfil themselves in me,   65
   And these my little breasts are waxing great;
I looked for bride-bed and maturity,
   And lo! I pass for ever from his gate;
   I, for whose sake he is made desolate!—

'I am the Singer's Singing, and I sigh   70
For ever barren, and most inconsolate,
With virgin bosom, and lips devirginate:
I am the Singer's Singing, and I cry
Because the call is on me, O misery!—
And I go hence, and I go by, go by!'   75

The morn dawned weeping-grey; and weeping-grey
He saw her mist into the weeping day,
And knew her tears had washed his name away.

Leonidas to the Three Hundred

(Compiled from the Latin Rhetoricians)

ME, January 1893; not reprinted

The event described in this sonnet took place in the year 480 BC when Leonidas King of Sparta (Laconia), with only three hundred men, defended the Pass of Thermopylae against the invading Persian army under Xerxes. He and his men died fighting as they held on for two days to cover the retreat of the Greek fleet.

Who shall adjudge this pass unfortified?
Three hundred Spartans are its muniment!
We shock the Persian with a front unrent,
Though, with a continent in arms allied,
The dreadful trample of his battailous pride   5
Shake the stars as is shook a swingèd lamp.
Though over against Heaven he set his camp,
We'll fight with gods in iron by our side!

In others be it cowardice to fly:
'Tis cowardice in a Laconian band   10
But to deliberate if they shall stand!
Fled are the Grecians? Have I no ally,
Left in Thermopylae, forsook, alone?—
Oh, joy! then Xerxes resteth all my own!

The Testament of Calvary

Ushaw Magazine, March 1893; not reprinted

Purpled in Thy royalty
On the throne of Calvary!
Framing of Thy testament
For Thy lovers' meek content,
What was Thine high legacy?   5
Bequeathed'st for Thy Church's wear
Thy blood-drenched robe to cling to her;
And the spear that piercèd Thee,
To the heart of sad Mary;
And to woman, for a glass   10
Of the fairness frail she has,
From Thy Golgotha a skull
To behold her beautiful:

And that desirèd, that abhorrèd,
Crown made vidual of Thy forehead   15
To our brows to get them ease.
'I to my belovèd, these
My Father gave Me, give again,—
Those stern, assigned seignories
To youthful gods which appertain;   20
The revenues that He has given
The young Apparent of His Heaven:
My princely appanage of Pain.'
We, meek lovers, are content
With Thy heavy testament,   25
Very humbly, though it be
Mystical deep legacy.

15 *made vidual* widowed. **23** *appanage* royal inheritance.

Desiderium Indesideratum

ME, June 1893; reprinted in *Works*
The title translates as 'Undesired Desire'.

O gain that lurk'st ungainèd in all gain!
O love we just fall short of in all love!
O height that in all heights art still above!
O beauty that dost leave all beauty pain!
Thou unpossessed that mak'st possession vain,   5
See these strained arms which fright the simple air,
And say what ultimate fairness holds thee, Fair!
They girdle Heaven, and girdle Heaven in vain;
They shut, and lo! but shut in their unrest.
Thereat a voice in me that voiceless was:—   10
'Whom seekest thou through the unmarged arcane,
And not discern'st to thine own bosom prest?'
I looked. My claspèd hands athwart my breast
Framed the august embraces of the Cross.

In Her Paths

ME, July 1893; reprinted in *Works*

In *Works* this poem is included in the 'Love in Dian's Lap' sequence. But the style and mood confirm the later date of composition, as indicated by the publication in *ME* while Thompson was at Pantasaph and when his relations with Alice Meynell, undoubtedly the subject here, had been influenced by his friendship with Coventry Patmore. The occasion appears to have been a visit from the Meynells in the spring of 1893 (see *BHCC*, p. 235).

And she has trod before me in these ways!
I think that she has left here heavenlier days;
And I should guess her passage, as the skies
    Of Holy Paradise
    Turn deeply holier,   5
And looking up with sudden new delight
One knows a seraph-wing has passed in flight.
The air is purer for her breathing, sure!
    And all the fields do wear
    The beauty fallen from her: 10
The winds do brush me with her robes' allure.
'Tis she has taught the heavens to look sweet,
    And they do but repeat
The heaven, heaven, heaven of her face!
The clouds have studied going from her grace: 15
The pools, whose marges had forgot the tread
Of Naiad disenchanted, fled,
    A second time must mourn,
    Bereaven and forlorn:
    The meads cry, 'She has trod us,   20
    Returned, authentic goddess!'
Ah, foolish pools and meads, you did not see
Essence of old essential-pure as she!
For this was even that lady, and none other,
My manhood dares call Love, my childhood Mother.   25

8–19 In *Works* these lines form a separate stanza. 20–1 omitted in *Works*. 25 *Works:* The man in me calls love, the child calls mother. The reason for the change appears to be WM's response to the line in connection with FT's feeling for Alice at this time.

Franciscus Christificatus

Franciscan Annals, October 1893; reprinted by P. D. R. Conway, 'The Capuchin Influence on the Life and Work of Francis Thompson', *Collecteana Franciscana*, 1955

The title can be rendered as 'Francis made [like to] Christ'. The theme recalls the impression on the saint's body of the stigmata, or five wounds of Christ.

Thief that has leaped Heaven's star-spiked wall!
Christ's exultant bacchanal!
Wine-smears on thy hand and foot
Of the vine that struck its root
Deep in virgin soil, and was   5
Trained against the rearèd Cross:
Nay, thy very side its stain
Hath, to make it redly plain
How in the wassail quaffed full part
That flown vintager, thy heart.   10
Christ in blood stamps Himself afresh
On thy Veronica-veil of flesh!

Lovers, looking with amaze on
Each other, would be that they gaze on;
So for man's love God would be   15
Man, and man for His love He:—
What God in Christ, man has in thee.
God gazed on man, and grew embodied,
Thou, on Him gazing, turn'st engodded!
But though He hold thy brow's spread tent   20
His little Heaven above Him bent,
The sceptring reed suffices *thee*,
Which smote Him into sovereignty.

Thou who thoughtest thee too low
For His priest, thou shalt not so   25
'Scape Him, and unpriested go!
In thy hand thou wouldst not hold Him,
In thy flesh thou shalt enfold Him;
Bread wouldst not change to Him—ah see!
How He doth change Himself to thee!   30

25 FT note: 'St Francis, as is well known, would never accept the priesthood.'

Elevaverunt Flumina

'St Monica'

ME, November 1893; reprinted in *Works* under the title 'St Monica'

The title translates as 'The waters have lifted up their voices', recalling Psalm 92 : 3: 'The floods have lifted up, O Lord, the floods have lifted up their voice.' The theme is based on the 'Stabat Mater', the great hymn to Our Lady of Sorrows. It is applied here to St Monica, as mother of the young Saint Augustine before his conversion from his dissolute way of life.

> At the Cross thy station keeping
> With the mournful Mother weeping,
> Thou unto the sinless Son
> Weepest for thy sinful one.
> Blood and water from His side   5
> Gush; in thee the streams divide:
> From thine eyes the one doth start,
> But the other from thy heart.
>
> Mary for thy sinner, see,
> To her Sinless mourns with thee: 10
> Could that Son the son not heed,
> For whom two such mothers plead?
> So thy child had baptism twice,
> And the whitest from thine eyes!
>
> The floods lift up, lift up their voice,   15
> With a many-watered noise!
> Down the centuries fall those sweet
> Sobbing waters to our feet,
> And our laden air still keeps
> Murmur of a Saint that weeps.   20
>
> Teach us but, to grace our prayers,
> Such divinity of tears,—
> Earth should be lustrate again
> With contrition of that rain,
> And celestial flood o'errise   25
> The high tops of Paradise!

'Lines on William Cardinal Massaia'

Franciscan Annals, February 1894; reprinted in *Collecteana Franciscana* (see headnote for 'Franciscus Christificatus')

The sonnet, translated from a sonnet by Pope Leo XIII, was composed for the publication of the Cardinal's history of his Ethiopian mission, which had been written at the Pope's instance. The Latin original appeared in the *Eco di Perugia*, 1894.

What overthrow of heavenly eloquence
Thou mak'st on the rude Ethiop's hard-won breast;
And leadest dusky sheep to Christ's sure pens!
Yet wouldst thou have thy deeds unstoried rest?
The travails for religion over-spent   5
'Tis comely to deliver to the crowd,
Thy feats for Christ of holy hardiment,
And stubborn battles joined, to speak aloud,
And solemn trophies 'neath His ensign won.
Speak; willing trust to the memorial page   10
The record high of deeds as highly done,
And let thy fame men's frequent mouths engage,
     And shake great hearts, and fire them to the war
     Where thou the vaward led'st so well before.

An Echo of Victor Hugo

Illustrated London News, 3 February 1894; reprinted in *Works*

As reprinted, the poem has been regarded as a translation from Hugo similar to 'A Sunset' and 'Heard on the Mountain'. But when it first appeared Thompson prefixed it with the following note: 'The first two stanzas are my own: the thoughts of the rest are from Victor Hugo, except for the sixth stanza, which is my own. The metre of the original is entirely departed from.'

Life's a veil the real has:
     All the shadows of our scene
Are but shows of things that pass
     On the other side the screen.

Time his glass sits nodding by;   5
     'Twixt its turn and turn a spawn
Of universes buzz and die,
     Like the ephemeris of the dawn.

Turn again the wasted glass!
  Kingly crown and warrior's crest   10
Are not worth the blade of grass
  God fashions for the swallow's nest.

Kings must lay gold circlets down
  In God's sepulchral ante-rooms,
The wear of Heaven's the thorny crown: 15
  He paves His temples with their tombs.

O our towered attitudes!
  O the lustres of our thrones!
What! old Time shall have his moods
  Like Caesars and Napoleons;   20

Have his towers and conquerors forth,
  Till he, weary of the toys,
Put back Rameses in the earth
  And break his Ninevehs and Troys.

Mystery of mysteries!   25
  Some few feet beneath the soil
The ancestral silences:
  On the surface such a coil!

---

5 A semi-colon has been added, as in *Works*. **9–12** To show how FT has created a distinct poem from Hugo's theme, the third verse can be compared here with the second in the original:

    Porte ailleurs ton regard sur Dieu seul arrêté.
    Rien ici-bas qui n'ait en soi sa vanité
      La gloire fuit à tire-d'aile;
    Couronnes, mitres d'or brillent, mais durent peu
    Elles ne valent pas le brin d'herbe que Dieu
      Fait pour le nid de l'hirondelle!

(Victor Hugo, *Œuvres Choisis*, Paris 1917, Vol. 5, pp. 70–1)

25–8 omitted in *Works*.

Cuckoo

(Verses for a Boy with Cuckoo for His Pet Name)

ME, July 1894; not reprinted

The verses were addressed to Everard Meynell, whose pet name was Cuckoo.

When the bud just parts a chink, and peers
To see if May be due;
And the earth rends off her mists and leaps,
Naked into the blue;

'Tis 'Cuckoo!' right, and 'Cuckoo!' left,   5
And 'Cuckoo!' distantly.
But there's one Cuckoo on the earth
That never was on tree.

O Lady Spring, your cuckoos sing,
But long as cuckoos do;   10
But I have a Cuckoo in my hand
That sings the round year through.

Oh, cuckoos here, and cuckoos there,
And cuckoos whole spring through;
But I have a Cuckoo in my hand,   15
That will not fly to-morrow.

The lark may troll at its wild bold will,
The linnet trill daintily;
But the cuckoo to one note is true,
And that's the bird for me.   20

The merle may have its raven black,
The finch gold bravery;
But the cuckoo has the woman's heart,
And that's the heart for me!

Oh, duskèd hair and gold are fair,   25
And fair finds open mart;
And you may love the woman's form,
But I the woman's heart.

My little boy, my own boy,
My winsome boy, my dear!   30
Thou bring'st the green into my breast
Ere the cuckoo to the year.

My Cuckoo-bird, my winsome bird,
My own bird to me!
Very sweet thou sing'st in my heart,   35
Past a Spring-fall on the tree.

Nest and sing there, nest and sing,
Embosom thee in me:
From out my heart's dim distances
The years shall list to thee.   40

21 *merle* blackbird.

Prose of Blessed Francis

By the Author of the Dies Iræ

Franciscan Annals, September 1894; *Weekly Register*, 8 September 1894, as 'Canticle of Blessed Francis'; reprinted in *Collecteana Franciscana* (see headnote for 'Franciscus Christificatus')

Thompson's translation of this medieval tribute to St Francis is prefixed by the note with the Latin text: 'Found in the National Library, Lisbon'. The note continues: 'The original Latin . . . has just been communicated to the Editor by the Archbishop of Glasgow. The document is a valuable one, and its authorship lends to the Prose a worth quite distinct from its intrinsic merits.' As in 'Franciscus Christificatus', the theme is based on the stigmata.

This the valiant conqueror,
Triumphal Francis, brake of yore
    The adversary of the Cross.
In his heart the Cross he bore,
Chief of spiritual war,   5
    Prime of heavenly lovers was.

Foresent by the King To-Be,
Prescient in counsel, presently
    That shall take the warlike field;
Armed by Him, that so might he   10
Close in battle dreadlessly
    Under safe celestial shield.
Chorus.—Tell us, Francis, why thou hast
        To the Cross been thus made fast?

*

For the Cross to contemplate   15
And my flesh to subjugate
   Was my still-assiduous care,
And the world to abdicate,
And the Cross to imitate
   In my life my Christ to bear.   20
Chorus.—Tell us, &.

Jesus' burning charities
Sucked my heart in most sweet wise,
   To my longings' added sum:
I, attent with upward eyes,   25
Jesus saw in seraph's guise
   Like a downward ardour come.
Chorus.—Say what didst thou do, O Francis
      After Jesus met thy glances?

Jesus sweet with whom I burned   30
From anear my gaze discerned,
   In seraphical aspéct;
That my face a fervour cast,
But the outward show was passed
   By the inward deep effect.   35

Six-fold wings His form en-net,
Five-fold wounds are on Him set,
All with dreadful blood He's wet,
   Thus He noted is with anguish:
Till that urging love beget   40
Nail-like pangs which me beset,
And my soul a change hath met—
   I grow He for Whom I languish.
Chorus.—What didst, Francis, tell us,
      Contemplating Christ wounded thus?   45

All my mind on fire I knew,
And my body sealed, till to
The refulgent form I grew
   Of the dear belovèd One.
Hands and feet were nailèd through,   50
Pierced my side; the copy true
On my flesh of Christ I drew,
   In the sort I gazed upon.

Chorus.—Francis, Cross-bearer, make known—
    Are thine impresses Christ's own?   55

Many an argument is there
For the form the Saviour bare.
Chorus.—Tell us, Francis, what it was
    That thou sawest on the Cross?

Living God's son I descried   60
Still for man's love crucified.
Chorus. Tell us, &.

Christ with nails infixèd torn,
On His head a crown of thorn.
Chorus.—There is more trust in Francis' truthful word   65
    Alone, than in the world's whole trustless herd.

We know the Cross's death Christ truly bare;
Have mercy on us, Kingly Vanquisher.—Alleluia.

To St Anthony of Padua

First published in Leopold de Chérance, *Saint Anthony of Padua*, trans. Fr Marianus, OFMCap. 1895; reprinted in *Capuchin Annual*, 1933; also in *Collecteana Franciscana* (see headnote for 'Franciscus Christificatus')

In Catholic tradition St Anthony is the saint who is invoked to find things that are lost.

Thou find'st, men say, the thing that's lost. Behold
This England, Anthony, which knows thee not;
For she hath lost
An antique pearl of price.
Her loss is old,   5
Wherefore she hath forgot
All but the lack which teacheth her its cost;
And quests with many a void device,
Indeed unwitting what.
And with religion vain,   10
All things she searcheth that are for her pain;
With veriest prayer
Importunes leading on all paths that err.
Yield, Anthony, her blind
Petition, after God's own mind   15

And those calm ways the unhasty heavens allot;—
The things she seeketh give her not to find,
Give her to find the thing she seeketh not.

A Chorus from Isaiah

ME, March 1895; not reprinted

The theme expands the prophecy of Christ's passion contained in Isaiah 63:1–7, drawing on a number of other Isaian references and returning at the end to the 'chorus' of the first stanza. It illustrates Thompson's familiarity with the Old Testament and the ease with which he could adapt it to his poetic purposes.

Who is He that cometh from Edom,
Cometh up with dyed raiment from Bosra,
And who hath forwritten His path?
And whence the red vintage His treading hath trodden,
This beautiful one in His wrath?   5

'I, in Whose mouth there is justice,
Whose arm is stretched forth unto surety,
For a strength unto those which are Mine.'
O whence is Thy raiment then red, like the raiment
Of them that tread wine?   10

'I have girded My raiment about Me,
And a vintage of kings and nations,
I have cast in the earth's shook vat.
And the must hath foamed up from the press of My wrath,
And the red sun hath leaped like a bacchanal,   15
Hath stumbled and sunk in his path,
And the heavens have reeled drunken thereat.

'Alone I have trodden out the winepress,
Of the Gentiles was none by My side;
And the wrath of My treading hath made terrible My feet,   20
And my garments are dyed.

'For the day of My wrath hath come to My heart,
And the year of My redemption begun:
I looked round about, and I found not a helper,
I sought, and was none.   25

'And I took to My help Mine own anger,
And Mine own arm hath lifted Me up.
My feet have gone over the nations in fury,
I have given them to drink a strong wine of My fury;
They have drunk, and are drunken, and vomit,⁣ 30
They have drunk, and are giddy, and fallen,
For the might of the fierceness of My cup.

'I thrust aside the heavens, and came down;
The mountains as withered scabs I broke;
I breathed, and the seas as a fume were loosened,⁣ 35
And went upwards like smoke.'

Who is He that cometh from Edom,
Cometh up with dyed raiment from Bosra,
And who shall stand forth in His path?
And who shall abide while He bruiseth His vintage?⁣ 40
He hath clothed His robe with the jets of His vintage,
Inassuageably fair in His wrath!

Hymn to St Anthony of Padua

(Si Quæris Miracula)

Franciscan Annals, August 1895; reprinted in *Collecteana Franciscana* (see headnote for 'Franciscus Christificatus')

Thompson's translation of the Latin verses by St Bonaventure is prefixed in the *Annals* by a note that they were recited each evening after Compline. The subtitle can be translated: if you are seeking miracles.

> Seekest thou for miracles?—
> Error, Death, Calamity,
> Leprosy and devils yield,
>   Sick have cure and saining;
>
> Giveth sea and shacklebolt;⁣ 5
> Members maimed, things derelict,
> Young and old have restore through him,
>   Asking and regaining.
>
> Peril, he thy peril is;
> He's thy law, Necessity!⁣ 10
> Witness, O thou Padua,
>   And all that seek, obtaining.

4 *saining* blessing. 5 *and* should be a or an.

Rejected Lovers

Catholic World, October 1895; not reprinted

POETA   I have loved women—they have paid my pains!
   I have loved nature—rather clasp the sea!
   I have loved children—look not there for gains:
    I have loved much, but I have not loved Thee.
   And yet when all these loves were loved and proved, 5
    None have loved me, but Thou, divine Unloved!

CHRISTUS Thou ask'st; I ask, and have not at thy hand.
   All ways are sought, and hast thou found no way?
   Ah child! And dost thou yet not understand,
    And in thine own, beholdest not My case? 10
   O little love! Does no man pity thee?
    Lo, it is writ, that none has pity on Me!

7 *and have not* and have not received anything.

Love and the Child

Catholic World, June 1896; reprinted in *Works*

The manuscript of this poem, with the title 'A Rebel', was included with the final texts for *New Poems* but was later withdrawn.

  'Why do you so clasp me
  And draw me to your knee?
  Forsooth you do but chafe me,
   I pray you let me be:
  I will be loved but now and then, 5
   When it liketh me!'
  So I heard a young child,
  A thwart child, a young child,
  Rebellious against love's arms,
   Make its peevish cry. 10
  To the tender God I turn:—
   'Pardon, Love most High!
  For I think those arms were even Thine,
   And that child even I.'

'A Sword-Fish for the Pope'

Franciscan Annals, September 1896; reprinted in *Collecteana Franciscana* (see headnote for 'Franciscus Christificatus')

Thompson's translation of the original Latin poem by Diego Vitrioli appeared in an anonymous article describing the presentation of a swordfish to Pope Leo XIII by the fishermen of Calabria.

> The mystic nets did Christ thy portion make,
> This sword-fish, therefore, Supreme Fisher, take;
> Near whirling Scylla caught by fisher's skill,
> Unto thy feet it comes with eager will.
> Nay, all the finny drove would gladly come   5
> Its comrades from the Pharos-crownèd foam.
> Our sword-fish, this old dweller of the flood,
> Alone shall be a Pontiff's tender food:
> What fish to brighter glory could aspire,
> Of which shall boast its trident-bearing Sire!   10
> Ye turbots, oysters, farewell, fellow-fish;
> The dainty sword-fish is a Pontiff's dish!

Victorian Ode

Privately printed, 1897; reprinted in *Works*, where it was entitled 'Ode for the Diamond Jubilee of Queen Victoria'

1897 was the year of Queen Victoria's Diamond Jubilee and a shortened text of this ode also appeared in the *Daily Chronicle*, 22 June, where the first 114 lines were deleted, probably on account of the length of the original.

> Night; and the street a corpse beneath the moon,
> Upon the threshold of the jubilant day
> That was to follow soon;
> Thickened with inundating dark
> 'Gainst which the drowning lamps kept struggle; pole   5
> And plank cast rigid shadows; 'twas a stark
> Thing waiting for its soul,
> The bones of the preluded pomp. I saw
> In the cloud-sullied moon a pale array,
> A lengthened apparition, slowly draw;   10
> And as it came,
> Brake all the street in phantom flame
> Of flag and flower and hanging, shadowy show
> Of the to-morrow's glories, as might suit

A pageant of the dead; and spectral bruit   15
I heard, where stood the dead to watch the dead,
The long Victorian line that passed with printless tread.

First went the holy poets, two on two,
And music, sown along the hardened ground,
Budded like frequence of glad daisies, where   20
Those sacred feet did fare;
Arcadian pipe, and psaltery, around,
And stringèd viol, sound
To make for them melodious due.
In the first twain of those great ranks of death   25
Went One, the impress recent on his hair
Where it was dinted by the Laureate wreath:
Who sang those goddesses with splendours bare
On Ida hill, before the Trojan boy;
And many a lovely lay,   30
Where Beauty did her beauties unarray
In conscious song. I saw young Love his plumes deploy,
And shake their shivering lustres, till the night
Was sprinkled and bedropt with starry play
Of versicoloured light,   35
To see that Poet pass who sang him well;
And I could hear his heart
Throb like the after-vibrance of a bell.

A Strength beside this Beauty, Browning went,
With shrewd looks and intent,   40
And meditating still some gnarlèd theme.
Then came, somewhat apart,
In a fastidious dream,
Arnold, with a half-discontented calm,
Binding up wounds, but pouring in no balm.   45
The fervid breathing of Elizabeth
Broke on Christina's gentle-taken breath.
Rossetti, whose heart stirred within his breast
Like lightning in a cloud, a spirit without rest,
Came on disranked: Song's hand was in his hair,   50
Lest Art should have withdrawn him from the band,
Save for her strong command;
And in his eyes high Sadness made its lair.
Last came a Shadow tall, with drooping lid,

Which yet not hid   55
The steel-like flashing of his armèd glance;
Alone he did advance,
And all the throngs gave room
For one that looked with such a captain's mien.
A scornful smile lay keen   60
On lips that, living, prophesied of doom;
His one hand held a lightning-bolt, the other
A cup of milk and honey blent with fire;
It seemed as in that quire
He had not, nor desired not, any brother.   65
A space his alien eye surveyed the pride
Of meditated pomp, as one that much
Disdained the sight, methought; then, at a touch,
He turned the heel, and sought with shadowy stride
His station in the dim,   70
Where the sole-thoughted Dante waited him.

What throngs illustrious next, of Art and Prose,
Too long to tell! but other music rose
When came the sabre's children: they who led
The iron-throated harmonies of war,   75
The march resounding of the armèd line,
And measured movement of battalia:
Accompanied their tread
No harps, no pipes of soft Arcadia,
But—borne to me afar—   80
The tramp of squadrons, and the bursting mine,
The shock of steel, the volleying rifle-crack,
And echoes out of ancient battles dead.
So Cawnpore unto Alma thundered back,
And Delhi's cannon roared to Gujerat: 85
Carnage through all those iron vents gave out
Her thousand-mouthèd shout.
As balefire answering balefire is unfurled,
From mountain-peaks, to tell the foe's approaches,
So ran that battle-clangour round the world,   90
From famous field to field
So that reverberated war was tossed;
And—in the distance lost—
Across the plains of France and hills of Spain
It swelled once more to birth,   95

And broke on me again,
The voice of England's glories girdling in the earth.

It caught like fire the main,
Where rending planks were heard, and broadsides pealed,
That shook were all the seas,   100
Which feared, and thought on Nelson. For with them
That struck the Russ, that brake the Mutineer,
And smote the stiff Sikh to his knee,—with these
Came them that kept our England's sea-swept hem,
And held afar from her the foreign fear.   105
After them came
They who pushed back the ocean of the Unknown,
And fenced some strand of knowledge for our own
Against the outgoing sea
Of ebbing mystery;   110
And on their banner 'Science' blazoned shone.
The rear were they that wore the statesman's fame,
From Melbourne, to
The arcane face of the much-wrinkled Jew.

Lo, in this day we keep the yesterdays,   115
And those great dead of the Victorian line.
They passed, they passed, but cannot pass away,
For England feels them in her blood like wine.
She was their mother, and she is their daughter,
This Lady of the water,   120
And from their loins she draws the greatness which they were.
And still their wisdom sways,
Their power lives in her.
Their thews it is, England, that lift thy sword,
They are the splendour, England, in thy song,   125
They sit unbidden at thy council-board,
Their fame doth compass all thy coasts from wrong,
And in thy sinews they are strong.
Their absence is a presence and a guest
In this day's feast;   130
This living feast is also of the dead,
And this, O England, is thine All Souls' Day.
And when thy cities flake the night with flames,
Thy proudest torches yet shall be their names.

*

O royal England! happy child   135
Of such a more than regal line;
Be it said
Fair right of jubilee is thine;
And surely thou art unbeguiled
If thou keep with mirth and play,   140
With dance, and jollity, and praise,
Such a To-day which sums such Yesterdays.
Pour to the joyous ones thy joy, thy oil
And wine to such as faint and toil.
And let thy vales make haste to be more green   145
Than any vales are seen
In less auspicious lands,
And let thy trees clap all their leafy hands,
And let thy flowers be gladder far of hue
Than flowers of other regions may;   150
Let the rose, with her fragrance sweetened through,
Flush as young maidens do,
With their own inward blissfulness at play.
And let thy sky twinkle an eagerer blue
Over our English isle   155
Than any otherwhere;
Till strangers shall behold, and own that she is fair.
Play up, play up, ye birds of minstrel June,
Play up your reel, play up your giddiest spring,
And trouble every tree with lusty tune,   160
Whereto our hearts shall dance
For overmuch pleasance,
And children's running make the earth to sing.
And ye soft winds, and ye white-fingered beams,
Aid ye to invest,   165
Our queenly England, in all circumstance
Of fair and feat adorning to be drest;
Kirtled in jocund green,
Which does befit a Queen,
And like our spirits cast forth lively gleams: 170
And let her robe be goodly garlanded
With store of florets white and florets red,
With store of florets white and florets gold,
A fair thing to behold;
Intrailed with the white blossom and the blue,   175
A seemly thing to view!

And thereunto,
Set over all a woof of lawny air,
From her head wavering to her sea-shod feet,
Which shall her lovely beauty well complete,   180
And grace her much to wear.

Lo, she is dressed, and lo, she cometh forth,
Our stately Lady of the North;
Lo, how she doth advance,
In her most sovereign eye regard of puissance,   185
And tiar'd with conquest her prevailing brow,
While nations to her bow.
Come hither, proud and ancient East,
Gather ye to this Lady of the North,
And sit down with her at her solemn feast,   190
Upon this culminant day of all her days;
For ye have heard the thunder of her goings-forth,
And wonder of her large imperial ways.
Let India send her turbans, and Japan
Her pictured vests from that remotest isle   195
Seated in the antechambers of the Sun:
And let her Western sisters for a while
Remit long envy and disunion,
And take in peace
Her hand behind the buckler of the seas,   200
'Gainst which their wrath has splintered; come, for she
Her hand ungauntlets in mild amity.

Victoria! Queen, whose name is victory,
Whose woman's nature sorteth best with peace,
Bid thou the cloud of war to cease   205
Which ever round thy wide-girt empery
Fumes, like to smoke about a burning brand,
Telling the energies which keep within
The light unquenched, as England's light shall be;
And let this day hear only peaceful din.   210
For, queenly woman, thou art more than woman;
Thy name the often-struck barbarian shuns:
Thou art the fear of England to her foemen,
The love of England to her sons.
And this thy glorious day is England's; who   215
Can separate the two?

She joys thy joys and weeps thy tears,
And she is one with all thy moods;
Thy story is the tale of England's years,
And big with all her ills, and all her stately goods. 220
Now unto thee
The plenitude of the glories thou didst sow
Is garnered up in prosperous memory;
And, for the perfect evening of thy day,
An untumultuous bliss, serenely gay, 225
Sweetened with silence of the after-glow.

Nor does the joyous shout
Which all our lips give out
Jar on that quietude; more than may do
A radiant childish crew, 230
With well-accordant discord fretting the soft hour,
Whose hair is yellowed by the sinking blaze
Over a low-mouthed sea. Exult, yet be not twirled,
England, by gusts of mere
Blind and insensate lightness; neither fear 235
The vastness of thy shadow on the world.
If in the East
Still strains against its leash the unglutted beast
Of War; if yet the cannon's lip be warm;
Thou, whom these portents warn but not alarm, 240
Feastest, but with thy hand upon the sword,
As fits a warrior race:
Not like the Saxon fools of olden days,
With the mead dripping from the hairy mouth,
While all the South 245
Filled with the shaven faces of the Norman horde.

---

18 *holy poets* poets of the later part of Victoria's reign. **26–7** *One . . . Laureate wreath* Tennyson, appointed Poet Laureate in 1850. **28–9** *goddesses . . . Trojan boy* the goddesses who met on Mount Ida before Paris, 'the Trojan boy', who was to judge which of them was the fairest. The reference is to Tennyson's poem 'Œnone'. **54–71** *a Shadow tall . . . waited him* extended tribute to Coventry Patmore. **84** *Cawnpore* the Indian city where there was a massacre of European residents during the Sepoy mutiny of 1857; *Alma* river in the Crimea where the Russians were defeated in 1854. **85** *Delhi* captured by the Sepoy mutineers in May 1857 and retaken by the British later that year; *Gujerat* scene of the decisive victory of the British over the Sikhs in 1849 leading to the annexation of the Punjab. **102** *the Russ . . . the Mutineer* the Russians and the Sepoys (cf. note to 84 above). **114** *much-wrinkled Jew* Disraeli. **197** *Western sisters* France and Spain. **237–9** In 1896 the aftermath of the war between Japan and China was giving rise to anxiety in England. **243** *Saxon fools* It is said that on the eve of the Battle of Hastings the Saxons spent the night in carousing.

To England

The Academy, 19 March 1898; not reprinted

Thompson shared Kipling's fears for England's future in the coming century—
which is his subject here rather than the cheap jingoism of Kipling's many
imitators.

England, that barest me, whose limbs are of thine earth!
Suckled'st me with thine air, milk of heroic worth!
What is this thing I hear? What is this thing they tell?
That save the sallow-visaged gold, thou lovest nothing well:
If thy first-born, Renown, cry: 'Mother, help, I bleed!'　　　5
Thou falterest thrifty saws of counsel, fear, and heed;
That thou has put from thee Honour, thy plumèd spouse,
To whom in armèd steel thou took'st the glancing vows;
Wisdom nor wrath can strip thy sword against the strong,
And what once stirred thy blood, now stirreth but thy tongue.　　　10
Only thou summonest heart when merchants cry to thee,
And plainly tell'st thy foes—they act uncivilly.
Say that the tale is false, a lie as deep as hell!
How is it not much more than false—impossible?

O England, O my mother, Lady of the Earth,　　　15
I thank thee for thy breasts, and thank thee for my birth!
The coward born of thee lacks courage to be cowed,
For thou art proud, and mak'st thy children to be proud.
And with thy great approach, whose steps are called Créci,
Poictiers, Azincour, Seringapatam, Delhi,　　　20
Trafalgar, Waterloo—each an heroic sound—
Thy halo has prevailed to the earth's utmost bound;
And as beneath the tread o' the sun red blossoms rise,
Whereso thy foot was set it printed victories.
All things thy hand has wrought to which thy hand was put;　　　25
In every clime and soil thy flag has stricken root,
The bannered stars behold thy flickering banners stand;
The leashes of the earth are gathered in thy hand.
Babylon did not know the regions thou dost tame,
Ears that were deaf to Rome are deafened with thy name.　　　30
Magnificent is thy state, and august is thy rule,
Thy hand is on the East, thou sett'st the West to school;
Thine awe is in their heart, thy law is in their soul,
All of thy ways found upright, equal thy control.
They whom her shaken locks have held in terror, they　　　35

Suck from the lioness's dugs the milk of sway.
They who their ancient kings adored with whitened lips,
They that were scourged with scorpions, thou dost correct with whips;
Therefore do all the seas groan scarrèd with thy ships,
The riches of the nations flow to thee like sand;   40
Thou givest them thy peace, their price is in thy hand.
Thy garners are made full, thy glories heaped and pressed,
Wherefore thou sayest to thy soul: 'Come, eat, and rest!'
Thy soul desireth peace, and may desire it well;
In shadow of thy peace all they that buy and sell,   45
The merchants of the four-nooked world their chaffer hold;
But what was won by iron, thou shalt not keep by gold.

If the world's wheels should slack, the heavens would part in war,
Sun march in battle against sun, star mounded upon star.
No less would be the ruin, if thou shouldst shirk thy fate,   50
Shouldst thou neglect, forget, the gods have made thee great.
O England, slothful, blind! too confident and high,
Who stoodest in thyself, and bad'st the world go by:
Saidst—'Go thy ways in peace, and leave my ways to me';
Know'st thou not no man's friend is all men's enemy?   55
One friend is thine in the East—what! dost thou count her cost?
Dost hesitate, falter? whilst thou falterest she is lost!
Count, if it please thee count, count what thy navies can,
Poised against Russia, France, Germany—and Japan!
O England, palterer, falterer! again I say to thee: 60
'Whoso is no man's friend is all men's enemy.'
Thou sayst: 'The nations hate me; how have I earned their hate?'
Thy sin is heavy, England; thou hast been too great,
The nations hate thee not for these or for those faults;
Nay, thou hast ruled the world, the world it is revolts.   65
Smitten on either cheek, from one to other hurled,
It is the world 'gainst England, England 'gainst the world.

On other marts than those where the hoarse trader yells,
There are things bought and sold which not the merchant sells.
The shares thereon are honour, and the investment blood,   70
And honour's shares must rise at length, though all the world with-
        stood.
A rich estate thou hold'st which thy forefathers got;
It is not thine to barter, thine to let it rot.
Thou guard'st it for thy sons, this regal-fair estate,

*

No jot of land or honour is thine to alienate: 75
Wilt thou, for present grant of despicable peace,
Mortgage the greatness, England, held in trust for these?
O keep thou chained the watch-dog War, 'tis well in truth:
But let it not grow old, sluggard, and gapped of tooth.
For in a cause approved and virile, we do hold   80
The gun's rough lips plead nobler than the voice of gold.
Our England, show 'tis false, thou stoop'st unto the vice
Of palsied years in persons and in peoples—avarice!
Yea, though if thou shouldst fall, it were such thunder-clap,
Have the heavens spatial silence to fill the after-gap?   85
Though over all the earth thy ruin would be hurled,
And desolate and unguided stand a motherless world;
Sooner than this, O fall with banner lifted high!
If mightily thou canst not live, take mighty ways to die;
If thou no more canst greatly live, choose—thou canst greatly die!   90

19–20 Crecy, Poitiers and Agincourt were three English victories in the Hundred Years
War; Seringapatam was the capital of Tipu Sultan of Mysore, captured by the young
Wellington in 1799; the recapture of Delhi was the turning point of the Sepoy Mutiny in
1857. **56** probably a reference to China.

Tom o' Bedlam's Song

The Dome, May 1898; not reprinted

Thompson prefixed the poem with the following note: 'Written round selected
verses—the third and fourth stanzas and the first five lines of the first stanza in the
following poem—from the well-known song in "Wit and Drollery".' The street
ballad as Thompson used it first appeared in the 1682 edition of *Wit and Drollery*.
He would also have known the version in the 1704 edition, both available to him in
the British Museum Library. In the later version the theme of the madman tormented by witches and hobgoblins is turned into a moral invective against the
rich, giving the poem a direction he would have appreciated. But the figure of the
madman haunting the lanes and alleys of London had appealed to the public
imagination since the later Middle Ages; Shakespeare was probably drawing on
this tradition for the 'mad Tom' of *King Lear*.

From the hag and hungry goblin
That into rags would rend ye,
All the spirits that stand
By the naked man,
In the book of moons, defend ye.   5
Beware of the black rider

Through blasted dreams borne nightly;
From Venus Queen
Saved may you bin,
And the dead that die unrightly.   10

With a wench of wanton beauties
I came unto this ailing:
Her breast was strewn
Like the half o' the moon
With a cloud of gliding veiling.   15
In her snow-beds to couch me
I had so white a yearning,
Like a moon-struck man
Her pale breast 'gan
To set my wits a-turning.   20

I know more than Apollo;
For oft, when he lies sleeping,
I behold the stars
At mortal wars,
And the round welkin weeping.   25
The moon's my constant mistress,
And the lovely owl my morrow;
The flaming drake
And the night-crow make
Me music, to my sorrow.   30

With a heart of furious fancies,
Whereof I am commander;
With a burning spear,
And a horse of air,
To the wilderness I wander: 35
With a knight of ghosts and shadows
I summoned am to tourney,
Ten leagues beyond
The wide world's end;
Methinks it is no journey!   40

The shadows plot against me,
And lie in ambush for me;
The stars conspire,
And a net of fire

Have set for my faring o'er me.   45
I ride by ways that are not,
   With a trumpet sounding to me
     From goblin lists
     And the maws of mist
   Are opened to undo me.   50

Hate, Terror, Lust, and Frenzy,
   Look in on me with faces;
     And monstrous haunch
     And toad-blown paunch
   Do show me loathed disgraces.   55
I hear on immanent cities
   The league-long watches armèd,
     Dead cities lost
     Ere the moon grew a ghost,
Phantasmal, viewless, charmèd.   60

With sights I, seeing, see not,
   The air is all a-bustle;
     Draughty with wings
     And seething things
   That without sound do rustle.   65
It is not light nor darkness
   In that place which is placeless:
     With horror of doom,
     Drift by like fume
   Faces that are most faceless.   70

As a burst and blood-blown insect
   Cleaves to the wall it dies on,
     The smearèd sun
     Doth clot upon
   A heaven without horizon.   75
I dare not but be dreadless,
   Because all things to dread are;
     With a trumpet blown
     Through the mists alone
From a land where the lists of the dead are.   80

27 *morrow* In some of the earliest versions of the poem this was 'marrow' meaning dear companion. 28 *drake* dragon. 31 *heart* 'host' in earliest versions. 45 *faring* journeying.

An Arab Love Song

The Dome, January 1899; reprinted in *Eyes of Youth*, 1910 and *Works*

These lines were influenced by Thompson's familiarity with Wilfrid Scawen Blunt's translations of Arab love poems. Blunt was a friend of the Meynells and Thompson had visited Blunt with them in October 1898. But the urgent personal emotion of the poem suggests that it was addressed, however privately, to Katie King.

> The hunchèd camels of the night
> Trouble the silver waters of the moon.
> The Lady of the Light with dewy shoon,
> The pearlèd Girl of Dawning, soon
> Through humid heaven will spring,   5
> Star-gathering:
> Now, while the dark about our loves is strewn,
> Light of my dark, blood of my heart, O come,
> And Night will catch her breath up, and be dumb!
>
> Leave thy father, leave thy mother,   10
> And thy brother;
> Leave the black tents of thy tribe apart,
> And come!
> Am not I thy father, I thy mother,
> And thy brother?   15
> And thou, what needest with thy tribe's black tents,
> Who hast the red pavilion of my heart?

1 In *Eyes of Youth* WM added a note: 'cloud-shapes often observed by travellers in the east'. TLC attributes the note to FT but it did not appear when the poem was first published in *The Dome* (TLC*Poems*, p. 395). 2–4 in *Eyes of Youth* and *Works*: Trouble the bright / And silver waters of the moon. / The Maiden of the Moon will soon / Through Heaven stray and sing, 13 omitted in *Eyes of Youth* and *Works*, 14–15 in *Eyes of Youth* and *Works*: Am not I thy father and thy brother, / And thy mother?

The Nineteenth Century

The Academy, 29 December 1900; reprinted in *Works*

In the letter written to Meynell on completing this ode, dated 24 December 1900, Thompson described it as a 'poor mechanic thing'. Yet at times during its composition, he added, 'I have felt something like faint stirrings of the forgotten power' (*Letters*, p. 217).

As, fore-announced by threat of flame and smoke,
Out of the night's lair broke
The sun among the startled stars, whose blood
Looses its slow bright flood
Beneath the radiant onset of the sun;   5
So crouches he anon,
With nostrils breathing threat of smoke and flame,
Back to the lairing night wherefrom he came.

And who is she,
With cloudy battle smoking round her feet,   10
That issues through the exit-doors of death;
And at the alternate limit of her path,
Where first her nascent footsteps troubled day,
Forgotten tumult curls itself away?
Who is she that rose   15
Tumultuous, and in tumult goes?

This is she
That rose 'mid dust of a down-tumbled world,
And dies with rumour on the air
Of preparation   20
For a more ample devastation,
And death of ancient fairness no more fair.
First when she knew the day,
The holy poets sung her on her way.
The high, clear band that takes   25
Its name from heaven-acquainted mountain-lakes;
And he
That like a star set in Italian sea;
And he that mangled by the jaws of our
Fierce London, from all frets   30
Lies balmed in Roman violets.
And other names of power,
Too recent but for worship and regret,
On whom the tears lie wet.

*

But not to these   35
She gave her heart; her heart she gave
To the blind worm that bores the mold,
Bloodless, pertinacious, cold,
Unweeting what itself upturns,
The seer and prophet of the grave.   40
It reared its head from off the earth
(Which gives it life and gave it birth)
And placed upon its eyeless head a crown,
And all the peoples in their turns
Before the blind worm bowed them down.   45
Yet, crowned beyond its due,
Working dull way by obdurate, slow degrees,
It is a thing of sightless prophecies;
And glories, past its own conceit,
Attend to crown   50
Its travail, when the mounded time is meet.
Nor measured, fit renown,
When that hour paces forth,
Shall overlook those workers of the North,
And West, those patient Darwins who forthdrew   55
From humble dust what truth they knew,
And greater than they knew, not knowing all they knew.
Yet was their knowledge in its scope a Might,
Strong and true souls to measure of their sight.
Behold the broad globe in their hands comprest,   60
As a boy kneads a pellet, till the East
Looks in the eyes o' the West;
And as guest whispers guest
That counters him at feast,
The Northern mouth   65
Leans to the attent ear of the bended South.
The fur-skinned garb justling the northern bear
Crosses the threshold where,
With linen wisp girt on,
Drowses the next-door neighbour of the sun.   70
Such their laborious worth
To change the old face of the wonted earth.

Nor were they all o' the dust; as witness may
Davy and Faraday;
And they   75
Who clomb the cars

And learned to rein the chariots of the stars;
Or who in night's dark waters dipt their hands
To sift the hid gold from its sands;
And theirs the greatest gift, who drew to light   80
By their sciential might,
The secret ladder, wherethrough all things climb
Upward from the primeval slime.

Nor less we praise
Him that with burnished tube betrays   85
The multitudinous diminutive
Recessed in virtual night
Below the surface-seas of sight;
Him whose enchanted window gives
Upon the populated ways   90
Where the shy universes live
Ambushed beyond the unapprehending gaze.
The dusted anther's globe of spiky stars;
The beetle flashing in his minute mail
Of green and golden scale;   95
And every water-drop a-sting with writhing wars.
The unnoted green scale cleaving to the moist earth's face
Behold disclosed a conjugal embrace,
And womb—
Submitting to the tomb—   100
That sprouts its lusty issue: everywhere conjoins
Either glad sex, and from unguessed-at loins
Breeds in an opulent ease
The liberal earth's increase;
Such Valentine's sweet unsurmisèd diocese.   105

Nor, dying Lady, of the sons
Whom proudly owns
Thy valedictory and difficult breath,
The least are they who followed Death
Into his obscure fastnesses,   110
Tracked to her secret lair Disease—
Under the candid-seeming and confederate Day
Venoming the air's pure lips to kiss and to betray.
Who foiled the ancient Tyrant's grey design
Unfathomed long, and brake his dusty toils,   115
Spoiling him of his spoils,

And man, the loud dull fly, loosed from his woven line.
Such triumph theirs, who at the destined term
Descried the arrow flying in the day—
The age-long, hidden germ—   120
And threw their prescient shield before its deadly way.

Thou, spacious Century!
Hast seen the Western knee
Set on the Asian neck,
The dusky Africa   125
Kneel to imperial Europe's beck;
And that refusèd head plucked to the day
Of the close-hooded Nile.
Hast seen the West for its permitted while
Stand mistress-wise and tutelar   130
To the grey nations dreaming on their days afar,
From old forgotten war
Folding hands from whence has slid disusèd rule;
The while, unprescient, in her regent school
She shapes the ample days and things to be,   135
And large new empery.
Thence Asia shall be brought to bed
Of dominations yet undreamed;
Narrow-eyed Egypt lift again the head
Whereon the far-seen crown Nilotic gleamed.   140
Thou'st seen the Saxon horde whose veins run brine,
Spawned of the salt wave, wet with the salt breeze,
Their sails combine,
Lash their proud prows together, and turn swords
Against the world's knit hordes;   145
The whelps repeat the lioness' roar athwart the windy seas.

Yet let it grieve, grey Dame,
Thy passing spirit, God wot,
Thou wast half-hearted, wishing peace, but not
The means of it. The avaricious flame   150
Thou'st fanned, which thou should'st tame:
Cluck'dst thy wide brood beneath thy mothering plumes,
And coo'dst them from their fumes,
Stretched necks provocative, and throats
Ruffled with challenging notes;   155
Yet all didst mar

Flattering the too-much-pampered Boy of War:
Whence the far-jetting engine, and the globe
In labour with her iron progeny,—
Infernal litter of sudden-whelpèd deaths,   160
Vomiting venomous breaths;
Thicker than driven dust of testy March
When the blown flood o'erswells,
The armèd parallels
Of the long nations' columned march;   165
The growl as of long surf that draweth back
Half a beach in its rattling track,
When like a tiger-cat
The angry rifle spat
Its fury in the opposing foemen's eyes;—   170
These are thy consummating victories,
For this hast thou been troubled to be wise!

And now what child is this upon thy lap,
Born in the red glow of relighted war?
That draws Bellona's pap,   175
Fierce foster-mother; dost already stare
With mimicked dark regard
And copied threat of brow whose trick it took from her?—
The twentieth of Time's loins, since that
Which in the quiet snows of Bethlehem he begat.   180
Ah! born, grey mother, in an hour ill-starred,
After the day of blood and night of fate,
Shall it survive with brow no longer marred,
Lip no more wry with hate;
With all thou hadst of good,   185
But from its blood
Washed thine heriditary ill,
Yet thy child still?

---

6 *he* the sun. **9** *And Works*: Say; *she* the nineteenth century. **14** *tumult Works*: turmoil. **25** *The high, clear band* the Lake Poets, Wordsworth, Coleridge and Southey. **27–8** Shelley. **29–31** Keats. **37** *blind worm* science. **43** *Works*: Two lines from a draft in NB 43 are added here: Thereon a name writ new, / 'Science,' erstwhile with ampler meanings known; **50** *Works*: Wait to complete. **54–5** *workers . . . Darwins* scientists. **58–9** These lines seem to mean: their knowledge was mighty and measured by the vision of strong and true souls. **77** FT note: 'Measuring the stars' orbits'. **79** FT note: 'Discovery of new stars'. **83** FT note: 'Evolution'. **93** *anther* petal. **97–102** FT note: 'The prothallus of the fern, for example; which contains in itself the two sexes, and decays as the young fern sprouts from it'. **106** no new stanza in *Works*. **127–8** omitted in *Works*. **129** *Works*: The

West for her permitted while didst see. Together with 139–40 the lines refer to the discovery of the source of the Nile and, in 1882, the British occupation of Egypt. **157** *Boy of War* the god Mars. **162–5** omitted in *Works*. **174** The Boer War. **175** *Bellona* Roman goddess of war. **178** *Works:* two lines from draft in NB 43 are added here: Young Century, born to hear / The canon talking at its infant ear. **181** *Works:* line substituted from same draft: Ah! with forthbringing such and so ill-starred.

Bethlehem

Franciscan Annals, January 1901; reprinted in *Collecteana Franciscana* (see headnote for 'Franciscus Christificatus'). Also in *MHW* under the title 'Madonna and Child'.

TLC was not aware that the poem had already been published and, according to his note, took the text from a rough draft in NB 41. This accounts for the minor but numerous variants in the *MHW* text, which is heavily edited.

Bound in a little woman's arms,
    Without a language plain;
His feet were on the turning world,
    He held the stars in rein.

His feet were on the turning globe,   5
    The stars His fingers twirled;
His cry was all for mother's milk,
    Her lap was all His world.

So narrowed to a point the whole,
    The Word was without word;   10
The Godhead asked a woman's breast,
    And unafraid she heard.

He asked not spheral lullabies,
    Nor stretched for ministrant wings;
Being God, He took with happy mouth   15
    Mild elemental things.

The maiden pearls of mother's milk
    Was food for Him who fed
Out of His hand the fledgèd worlds—
    She bare up the Godhead.   20

The Trinity nested in her lap;
    The angels' plumy laughter
At a thing far too sweet for awe
    Left their lips tender after.

Victoria

'God gave her peace.' (Tennyson)

The Academy, 26 January 1901; not reprinted

Lo, she is dead,
Our noble England's noble Head,
In whom her corporate glories all might see
Summed up in single majesty,
Like sunset on a fronting face.   5
She has fulfilled her sovereign ways.

A woman, she
Had nations at her nurturing knee;
Mother, hers too the ampler motherhood;
Virtues, the home in her imbued,   10
Went forth in royalty; formed—Queen-spouse—
To rule an Empire and her house.

She is no more,
Whose sympathy stood at every door,
The woman crowned who wept all women's tears   15
Throughout her Britain. On her bier's
Black mantle let your eyes to-day,
Women, those queenly tears repay.

Her Empire's house
Garnished and swept, just Heaven allows   20
The folding of her hands in sleep. Ah! who
Would desire for her burthens new
At the task's end? This way is best;
With a world weeping her to rest.

Pope Leo's Ode on the Opening Century

The Tablet, 26 January 1901; not reprinted
This, Thompson's translation, appeared with the Latin original on the facing page.

The noble age that nursed the noble arts
Is gone; and they may sing who have the hearts
Of public 'vantage ampler grown,
And nature's powers made known.

The dying time's commissions far more deep   5
To me touch home; at these I shudder and weep.
  In backward-gazing memory
    What blushing shames I see!

The up-rooted sceptre, and the ruler slain,
Or portents of wild license, should I 'plain?   10
  Or of the Vatican citadel
    The leaguer subtle and fell?

Where is the city that was chief among
The cities, on whose grace no bondage hung?
  The pontiff's seat, the veneration   15
    Of bygone age and nation.

Alas for laws dissociate from Awe!
What rests of faith, or honourable law?
  Rights, from the altar disallied,
    Nod, and to ruin glide.   20

Hark! how the herd of the unwisely wise
In maddened transport bend their energies
  Brute Nature's form to set on high
    For sole divinity!

The heavenly origin of our human race,   25
Senseless, they scorn against; and would abase
  —Their minds with empty shadows pleased—
    The strain of man to beast.

Alack! in what a shameful vortex toiled,
The blind force of proud impotence is turmoiled: 30
  Mortals! for ever be confest
    The Godhead's dread behest!

Who is sole Life and certain Verity,
The one straight Way to those high things to be;
  He can to longing men retrieve   35
    Sole, the years fugitive.

The pious multitudes whose holy trust
Bore them of late to Peter's sacred dust,
  'Twas He that led; no auspice vain
    That faith shall seed again.   40

Jesu, the future Who dost rule and gauge,
Prosper the courses of this cradling age,
   The froward folk, with holy goad
    Prick, to the goodlier road.

Hearten the weak young fruits of gentle peace,   45
Let wraths, and broils, and woeful wars surcease;
   Thrust down the evil workers' frauds
    Into their black abodes.

Let one mind temper kings within Thy lead,
That to Thy laws they may give hasty heed: 50
   Within one Shepherd's fold infurled,
    Let one Faith sway the world.

My course is run, I twice nine lustres have
(So Thou hast willed it) seen. Grant now the grave:
   Suffer Thy Leo's prayers obtain   55
    That he pray not in vain.

Lines to Monica Mary Meynell

Monthly Review, August 1901; reprinted in *Works*

The title in *Works*, 'To Monica after Nine Years', refers to the time that had elapsed since the incident Thompson had described in 'The Poppy' (p. 53) and which this poem recalls.

     In the land of flag-lilies,
     Where burst in golden clangours
     The joy-bells of the broom;
     You were full of willy-nillies,
     Pets, and bee-like angers: 5
     Flaming like a dusky poppy,
     In a wrathful bloom.

     You were full of sweet and sour,
     Like a dish of strawberries
     Set about with curd.   10
     In your petulant foot was power,
     In your wilful innocences,
     Your wild and fragrant word.
     O was it thou that sweetly spake,
     Or I that sweetly heard?   15
           *

Yellow were the wheat-ways,
The poppies were most red;
And all your meet and feat ways,
Your sudden bee-like snarlings,
Ah, do you remember,   20
Darling of the darlings?
Or is it but an ember,
A rusted peal of joy-bells,
Their golden buzzings dead?
Now at one, and now at two,   25
Swift to pout and swift to woo,
The maid I knew:
Still I see the duskèd tresses—
But the old angers, old caresses?
Still your eyes are autumn thunders,   30
But where are *you*, child, you?

This your beauty is a script
Writ with pencil brightest-dipt—
Oh, it is the fairest scroll
For a young, departed soul!—   35
Thus you say:
'Thrice three years ago to-day,
There was one
Shall no more beneath the sun
Darkle, fondle, featly play.   40
If to think on her be gloom,
Rejoice she has so rich a tomb!'
But there's he—
Ask thou not who it may be!—
That, until Time's boughs are bare,   45
Shall be unconsoled for her.

Cecil Rhodes

The Academy, 12 April 1902; reprinted in *Works*

C. L. Hind, editor of *The Academy*, has left a descripton of the delivery of this
obituary ode at his office:

His 'Ode on the Death of Cecil Rhodes' which I had urged him to write, was
brought to me by a bewildered Thompson when the paper should have been
going to press, in various pieces, written upon the backs of envelopes and toilet
pages, produced from various pockets. I gave him half a crown to buy food, as

in those days the Academy was his banker. I pieced the pieces of the Ode together and had them put into type. When Francis Thompson returned an hour or so later, flushed and momentarily eased in body, he read the proofs swaying (I see him now) and said in his slow, distinct enunciation, a little blurred, maybe, at that moment, 'It's all right, Hind.' It was. There was not a word to alter in it.

(C. L. Hind, Introduction to Stephen Phillips, *Christ in Hades*, John Lane, 1917, p. 42)

In this ode, Rhodes' dubious statecraft and his calculating acquisitive disposition are not bypassed. But Thompson looks deeper, to find the source for his theme in the unwavering pursuit of ideals that went well beyond mere ambition and brought no reward but the loneliness represented by the isolated grave in the Matoppo hills.

> They that mis-said
> This man yet living, praise him dead.
> And I too praise, yet not the baser things
> Wherewith the market and the tavern rings.
> Not that high things for gold, 5
> He held, were bought and sold,
> That statecraft's means approved are by the end;
> Not for all which commands
> The loud world's clapping hands,
> To which cheap press and cheaper patriots bend; 10
> But for the dreams,
> For those impossible gleams
> He half made possible; for that he was
> Visioner of vision in a most sordid day:
> This draws 15
> Back to me song long alien and astray.
>
> In dreams what did he not,
> Wider than his wide deeds? In dreams he wrought
> What the old world's long livers must in act forego.
> From the Zambesi to the Limpopo 20
> He the many-languaged land
> Took with his large compacting hand
> And pressed into a nation: 'thwart the accurst
> And lion-'larumed ways
> Where the lean-fingered Thirst 25
> Wrings at the throat, and Famine strips the bone;
> A tawny land, with sun at sullen gaze,
> And all above a cope of heated stone;

He heard the shirted miner's rough halloo
Call up the mosquèd Cairene; hearkened clear   30
The Cairene's far-off summons sounding through
The sea's long noises to the Capeman's ear.

He saw the Teuton and the Saxon grip
Hands round the warded world, and bid it rock,
While they did watch its cradle. Like a ship   35
It swung, whileas the cabined inmates slept,
Secure their peace was kept,
Such arms of warranty about them lock.
Ophir he saw, her long-ungazed-at gold,
Stirred from its deep,   40
And often-centuried sleep,
Wink at the new Sun in an English hold.
England, from Afric's swarthy loins
Drawing fecundity,
Wax to the South and North,   45
To East and West increase her puissant goings-forth,
And strike young emperies, like coins,
In her own regent effigy.
He saw the three-branched Teuton hold the sides
Of the round world, and part it as a dish   50
Whereof to each his wish
The amity of the full feast decides.

So large his dreams, so little come to act!
Who must call on the cannon to compact
The hard Dutch-stubborned land,   55
Seditious even to such a potent hand.
Who grasped and held his Ophir: held, no less,
The Northern ways, but never lived to see
The wing-foot messages
Dart from the Delta to the Southern Sea.   60
Who, confident of gold,
A leaner on the statesman's arts
And the unmartial conquests of the marts,
Died while the sound of battle round him rolled,
And rumour of battle in all nations' hearts.   65
Dying saw his life a thing
Of large beginnings; and for young
Hands yet untrained the harvesting,

Amid the iniquitous years if harvest sprung.
So in his death he sowed himself anew;   70
Cast his intents over the grave to strike
In the left world of livers living roots,
And banyan-like,
From his one tree raise up a wood of shoots.
The indestructible intents which drew   75
Their sap from him,
Thus, with a purpose grim,
Into strange lands and hostile yet he threw,
That there might be
From him throughout the earth posterity: 80
And so did he—
Like to a smouldering fire by wind-blasts swirled—
His dying embers strew to kindle all the world.

Yet not for this I praise
The ending of his strenuous days;   85
No, not alone that still
Beyond the grave stretched that imperial Will.
But that Death seems
To set the gateway wide to ampler dreams;
Yea, yet his dreams upon Matoppo hill,   90
The while the German and the Saxon see,
And seeing, wonder,
The spacious dreams take shape and be,
As at compulsion of his sleep thereunder.
Lo, young America at the Mother's knee,   95
Unlearning centuries' hate,
For love's more blest extreme;
And this is in his dream,
And sure the dream is great.
Lo, Colonies on Colonies,   100
The furred Canadian and the digger's shirt,
To the one Mother's skirt
Cling, in the lore of empire to be wise;
A hundred wheels a-turn
All to one end—that England's sons may learn   105
The glory of their sonship, the supreme
Worth that befits the heirs of such estate.
All these are in his dream,
And sure the dream is great.

*

So, to the last   110
A visionary vast,
The aspirant soul would have the body lie
Among the hills immovably exalt
As he above the crowd that haste and halt,
'Upon that hill which I   115
Called "View of All the World" '; to show thereby
That still his unappeasable desires
Beneath his feet surveyed the peoples and empires.
Dreams, haply of scant worth,
Bound by our little thumb-ring of an earth;   120
Yet an exalted thing
By the gross search for food and raimenting.
So in his own Matoppos, high, aloof,
The elements for roof,
Claiming his mountain kindred, and secure,   125
Within that sepulture
Stern like himself and unadorned,
From the loud multitude he ruled and scorned,
There let him cease from breath,—
Alone in crowded life, not lonelier in death.   130

30, 32, *mosquèd Cairene* native of Cairo, famed for its mosques; *Capeman* native of Capetown. Rhodes envisaged a communications system by rail and telegraph to link Cairo in Egypt with Capetown in the extreme south of Africa. 39 *Ophir* sometimes identified as Africa. 48 *regent Works*: recent. 49 *three-branched Teuton* Britain, Germany and the United States. 53 Rhodes' words on his deathbed were 'So little done, so much to do'. 54–6 Rhodes died just over two months before the end of the Boer War. 70–83 References to the founding of the Rhodes Scholarships, set up to enable students from the United States, Germany and the British Commonwealth to study for three years at Oxford. 73 *banyan* Indian tree whose branches send out roots that create additional trunks. 90 *Matoppo hill* According to his own wish, Rhodes was buried in a grave cut from granite on the crest of the Matoppo hills.

Dress

T. P.'s Weekly, 27 February 1903; not reprinted

Dress! Dress! Woman may bless
That consoler of life, that bliss-giver—dress!
To soften the curse, when she first felt its stress,
A merciful Providence ordered her dress.
Dressmaker and tailor may proudly profess   5
The Almighty Himself the first maker of dress.

Each sorrow that woman's soft heart can depress
At the rustle will fly of a ruinous dress;
And what is the touch of a lover's caress
To the soul-felt embrace of a too-lovely dress?   10
What man's circling arm can atone for the mess,
If the man's profane foot in the dance tear her dress?
Be her name Adelaide, Laura, Gladys, or Bess,
Her life's young ideal is dress, ah, is dress!
If she travel to Paris, Milan, Inverness,   15
She may travel without food, but not without dress.
And the beauties of Nature will fail to impress
If she cannot behold them in *comme-il-faut* dress.
What makes Miss Smith hanker to be a princess?
Unlimited titles?—unlimited dress!   20
What odds 'twixt Jane Ann and a live marchioness,
If it were not for that anti-Communist—dress?
Without gems or love-letters locked up in *duresse*,
Life's not incomplete while she's good store of dress.
What drives Lady Tattle to write for the Press?   25
She has only a dozen frocks—really no dress!
She would sooner go bald than go naked, I guess,
For lack of hair's better than lacking of dress;
And, besides, the *coiffeur* can supply her a tress,
Which, in more than one sense, is a *capital* dress.   30
When a girl sits apart with some sprig of *noblesse*,
If he should be seduced by the quiet recess
At the risk of her frock on her lips to aggress,
She's one eye on her lips and two eyes on her dress.
Nay (as climax to rhymes with an *e-double-s*),   35
When she speaks that momentous and fluttering 'Yes,'
If her front-thought's the wedding, her back-thought's the dress!
She would think Paradise an extreme poor success,
If, like Grandmother Eve, she had never a dress.
Yet one thought might make her modiste's account less,—   40
That (as *Genesis* slily contrives to express)
Into Eden at first with the devil came dress!
And this was the curse laid on man for excess—
'Thou shalt work with thy hands—and thy women shall dress.'

'Body and Sprite'

Health and Holiness, 1906; reprinted in *Works*

Thompson included these untitled lines in his monograph, *Health and Holiness*, to illustrate his argument that body and soul must work together to achieve true health and holiness. Meynell left them in their original position when he included the monograph in the prose selection in the third volume of *Works*, but they do not appear in TLC*Poems*.

'Said sprite o' me to body o' me:
    "A malison on thee, trustless creature,
That prat'st thyself mine effigy
    To them which view thy much misfeature.
My hest thou no ways slav'st aright,   5
    Though slave-service be all thy nature:
An evil thrall I have of thee,
Thou adder coiled about delight!"

'Said body o' me to sprite o' me:
    "Since bricks were wrought without straw,   10
Was never task-master like thee!
    Who art more evil of thy law
Than Egypt's sooty Mizraim—
    That beetle of an ancient dung:
Nought wrecks it thee though I in limb   15
    Wax meagre—so thy songs be sung."

'Thus each by other is mis-said,
    And answereth with like despite;
The spirit bruises body's head;
    The body fangs the heel of sprite;   20
And either hath the other's wrong.
And ye may see, that of this stour
My heavy life doth fall her flower.'

2 *malison* curse. 13 *Mizraim* grandson of Noah, and 'father' of the dark-skinned peoples of upper Egypt. 22 *stour* conflict.

To the English Martyrs

DR, April 1906; reprinted in *Works*

This ode in honour of the Catholic martyrs of the sixteenth and seventeenth centuries was Thompson's last major poem. After sending it to Meynell he wrote to him: 'One quite certain thing is, the *Dublin* might go further & fare a good deal worse. Even in my ashes, I think there is a little more fire than in any other Catholic versifier of whom I know' (*Letters*, p. 257). The final manuscript, at Ushaw College, opens with the 46 lines given here in the endnotes. They were suppressed at Meynell's insistence, probably because he attributed their exaggerations to the effects of the opium which Thompson increased during his last illness. He himself was very reluctant to cut the lines out and it should be added that they are similar to many drafts for the later odes which are haunted by fears of war and other catastrophies to come in the century ahead. When he reprinted the poem in *Works* Meynell also deleted further lines, as indicated in the endnotes below.

> Rain, rain on Tyburn tree,
> Red rain a-falling;
> Dew, dew on Tyburn tree,
> Red dew on Tyburn tree,
> And the swart bird a-calling.   5
> Thence it roots so fast and free,
> Yet it is a gaunt tree,
> Black as be
> The swart birds alone that seek,
> With red-bedabbled breast and beak,   10
> Its lank black shadow falling.
>
> The shadow lies on England now
> Of the deathly-fruited bough,
> Cold and black with malison
> Lies between the land and sun;   15
> Putting out the sun, the bough
> Shades England now!
>
> The troubled heavens do wan with care,
> And burthened with the earth's despair
> Shiver a-cold; the starvèd heaven   20
> Has want with wanting man bereaven.
> Blest fruit of the unblest bough!
> Aid the land that smote you, now!
> Which feels the sentence and the curse
> Ye died if so ye might reverse.   25

When God was stolen from out man's mouth,
Stolen was the bread; then hunger and drouth
Went to and fro; began the wail,
Struck root the poor-house and the jail.
Ere cut the dykes, let through that flood,   30
Ye writ the protest with your blood;
Against this night wherein our breath
Withers, the toiled heart perisheth,
Entered the *caveat* of your death.
Christ, in the form of His true Bride,   35
Again hung pierced and crucified,
And groaned, 'I thirst!' Not still ye stood,—
Ye had your hearts, ye had your blood;
And pouring out the eager cup,—
'The wine is weak, yet, Lord Christ, sup!'   40
Ah, blest! who bathed the parchèd Vine
With richer than His Cana-wine,
And heard, your most sharp supper past,
'Ye kept the best wine to the last!'

Ah, happy who   45
That sequestered secret knew,
How sweeter than bee-haunted dells
The blosmy blood of martyrs smells!
Who did upon the scaffold's bed,
The ceremonial steel between you, wed   50
With God's grave proxy, high and reverend Death;
Or felt about your neck, sweetly,
(While the dull horde
Saw but the unrelenting cord)
The Bridegroom's arm, and that long kiss   55
That kissed away your breath, and claimed you His.
You did, with thrift of holy gain,
Unvenoming the sting of pain,
Hive its sharp heather-honey. Ye
Had sentience of the mystery   60
To make Abaddon's hookèd wings
Buoy you up to starry things;
Pain of heart, and pain of sense,
Pain the scourge, ye taught to cleanse;
Pain the loss became possessing;   65
Pain the curse was pain the blessing.
Chains, rack, solitude—these,

Which did your soul from earth release,
Left it free to rush upon
And merge in its compulsive sun.   70
Desolated, bruised, forsaken,
Nothing taking, all things taken,
Lacerated and tormented,
The stifled soul, in naught contented,
On all hands straitened, cribbed, denied,   75
Can but fetch breath o' the Godward side.
Oh to me, give but to me
That flower of felicity,
Which on your topmost spirit ware
The difficult and snowy air   80
Of high refusal! And the heat
Of central love which fed with sweet
And holy fire i' the frozen sod
Roots that had ta'en hold on God.

Unwithering youth in you renewed   85
Those rosy waters of your blood,—
The true *fons Juventutis*—ye
Pass with conquest that Red Sea,
And stretch out your victorious hand
Over the Fair and Holy Land;   90
Compasses about
With a ninefold battle-shout,
Trumpet, and wind and clang of wings,
And a thousand fiery things,
And Heaven's triumphing spears: while far   95
Beneath go down the Egyptian war—
A loosened hillside—with brazen jar
Underneath your dreadful blood,
Into steep night. Celestial feud
Not long forbears the Tudor's brood,   100
Rule, unsoldered from his line,
See unto the Scots decline;
And the kin Scots' weird shall be
Axe, exile and infamy;
Till the German fill the room   105
Of him who gave the bloody doom.

Oh by the Church's pondering art
Late set and named upon the chart

Of her divine astronomy,
Though your influence from on high   110
Long ye shed unnoticed! Bright
New cluster in our Northern night!
Cleanse from its pain and undelight
An impotent and tarnished hymn,
Whose marish exhalations dim   115
Splendours they would transfuse! And thou
Kindle the words which blot thee now,
Over whose sacred corse unhearsed
Europe veiled her face, and cursed
The regal mantle grained in gore   120
Of Genius, Freedom, Faith and More!

   Ah, happy Fool of Christ! unawed
By familiar sanctities,
You served your Lord at holy ease.
Dear Jester in the Courts of God!   125
In whose spirit, enchanting yet,
Wisdom and love, together met,
Laughed on each other for content!
That an inward merriment,
An inviolate soul of pleasure   130
To your motions taught a measure
All your days; which tyrant king,
Nor bonds, nor any bitter thing
Could embitter or perturb;
No daughter's tears, nor more acerb,   135
A daughter's frail declension from
Thy serene example, come
Between thee and thy much content.
Nor could the last sharp argument
Turn thee from thy sweetest folly;   140
To the keen accolade and holy
Thou didst bend low a sprightly knee,
And jest Death out of gravity
As a too sad-visaged friend;
So, jocund, passing to the end   145
Of thy laughing martrydom,
And now from travel art gone home
Where, since gain of thee was given,
Surely there is more mirth in heaven!

*

Thus, in Fisher and in thee,   150
Arose the purple dynasty,
The anointed Kings of Tyburn tree;
High in act and word each one.
He that spake—and to the sun
Pointed—'I shall shortly be   155
Above yon fellow.' He too, he
No less high of speech and brave,
Whose word was: 'Though I shall have
Sharp dinner, yet I trust in Christ
To have a most sweet supper.' Priced   160
Much by men that utterance was
Of the doomed Leonidas,—
Not more exalt than these, which note
Men who thought as Shakespeare wrote.

But more lofty eloquence   165
Than is writ by poets' pens
Lives in your great deaths: O these
Have more fire than poesies!
And more ardent than all ode
The pomps and raptures of your blood!   170
By that blood ye hold in fee
This earth of England; Kings are ye,
And ye have armies—Want, and Cold,
And heavy judgements manifold
Hung in the unhappy air, and Sins   175
That the sick gorge to heave begins,
Agonies and Martyrdoms,
Love, Hope, Desire, and all that comes
From the unwatered soul of man
Gaping on God. These are the van   180
Of conquest, these obey you; these,
And all the strengths of weaknesses,
That brazen walls disbed. Your hand,
Princes, put forth to the command,
And levy upon the guilty land   185
Your saving wars; on it go down,
Black beneath God's and heaven's frown;
Your prevalent approaches make
With unsustainable Grace, and take
Captive the land that captived you;   190

To Christ enslave ye and subdue
Her so bragged freedom: for the crime
She wrought on you in antique time,
Parcel the land among you: reign,
Viceroys to your sweet Suzerain!   195
Till she shall know
This lesson in her overthrow:
Hardest servitude has he
That's gaoled in arrogant liberty;
And freedom, spacious and unflawed,   200
Who is walled about with God.

In the final MS the ode starts with the following 46 lines (the 'approach retributive' in line 2 seems to refer to the English Reformation)

Now the third year,
Since the approach retributive begun,
With shrivelling fear
And expectation, or with dull unsense
Of fat indifference,
We watch the avenging wrath
Draw downward on its unavoided path
Of the malignant sun.
Our world is venomed at the flaming heart,
That from its burning systole
Spirts a poisoned life-blood. See
The gathering contagion thence
Sick influence
Shed on the seasons, and on men
Madness of nations, plague, and famine stern,
Earthquake, and flood, and all disastrous birth,
Change, war, and steaming pestilence.

There's anarchy in heaven, and on earth
Palsy in rods of kings, that here now turn,
Now there, as turns the frighted needle, when
Heaven's mountain cracks in fire. Within
Men feel the barb, and all astound
Cry on their deities impure
For impotent cure,
Yet from the wound
Will not pluck forth the arrow, Sin.
Nature is ailing with the pest
Man, and Earth feels the vermin in her vest.
Here, in our England, men may see
And touch within the blearèd air
The palpable calamity.
The night of something is aware,
And the day has a thing to bear,
The blossoms travail to be fair.

There is an evil in the wind,
There is a trouble in the tree,
The clouds of heaven are unkind,
And with fears discomfort me,
Earth as a cowering dog hath whined,
She sees the Spirit men cannot see,
And trembles, for a thing to be.

Whence is the scourge come on us? Why,
O land, hast thou calamity?
England, England, what the root
That yields thee now so ill a fruit?
Hear, and with a blush be mute.

1 *Tyburn tree* the triple gallows at Tyburn in London on which up to 18 victims could be hanged at the same time. **6–11** Not in *Works*. **33** The sense here seems to require a bracket after Withers and another of the end of the line, or the word 'and' added after Withers. **61** *Abaddon* the destroying angel (Apoc. 9 : 11). **87** *fons Juventutis* Fountain of Youth. **88–90** *Pass . . . Fair and Holy Land* The crossing of the Red Sea by the Israelites and their arrival in the Promised Land is here taken as a sign of the blood of martyrdom leading to heaven. **91** It is difficult to know what the subject of the verb 'Compasses' is. **91–106** not in *Works*. **102** *Scots* the Stuarts. **105–6** George I on the throne of Henry VIII. **106–7** *Works:* stanza break. **107** In 1886 Pope Leo XIII bestowed the title 'Venerable' on the martyrs of England and Wales, the first stage in the process of canonisation. **121** *More* Sir Thomas More. **141** *accolade* an embrace about the neck, in particular when bestowing a knighthood. In More's case, because of the high office he had held as Lord Chancellor, the sentence of hanging was commuted to beheading. **150** *Fisher* St John Fisher, Bishop of Rochester, also executed on account of his office. **152** *The anointed Kings of Tyburn tree* According to a note on the English martyrs in *Works* there were: 'Some three hundred in all, of whom one hundred suffered at Tyburn; the first, John Houghton, Carthusian (4 May 1535), the last, Archbishop Oliver Plunkett (1 July 1681)'. **155–6** words spoken by Ralph Sherwin who, two days before his death on 1 December 1581, looked up at the sun and said to his companion, the martyr Edmund Campion: 'Ah, Father Campion, I shall soon be above yon fellow.' **158–60** On the morning of his execution John Sugar said to his companions: 'Be ye all merry, for have we not occasion of sorrow but of joy; for, although I shall have a sharp dinner, yet I trust in Jesus Christ I shall have a most sweet supper.' **162** *Leonidas* Greek king of Sparta who with three hundred companions defended the Pass of Thermopylae against the Persian army. The inscription where they fell is here ascribed to Leonidas but the author was Simonides of Ceos: 'Stranger, go tell the Lacedaemonians that we lie here, obedient to their commands' (TLC*Poems*, p. 525; see also headnote for 'Leonidas to the Three Hundred', p. 245). **183** *disbed* destroy.

The Fair Inconstant

The Nation, 6 April 1907; reprinted in *Works*

Dost thou still hope thou shalt be fair,
    When no more fair to me?
Or those that by thee taken were
    Hold their captivity?
Is this thy confidence? No, no;   5
    Trust it not; it can not be so.

But thou too late, too late shall find
    'Twas I that made thee fair;
Thy beauties never from thy mind
    But from my loving were;   10
And those delights that did thee stole
Confessed the vicinage of my soul.

The rosy reflex of my heart
    Did thy pale cheek attire;
And what I was, not what thou art,   15
    Did gazers-on admire.
Go, and too late thou shalt confess
I looked thee into loveliness!

Poems Published after Thompson's Death

IN VARIOUS JOURNALS, 1907–35

Two short poems are included here which first appeared in poetry collections rather than journals: 'Lines: to W. M.' was first printed in *Selected Poems of Francis Thompson* (1908) and 'This Is My Beloved Son' in *Halt! Who Goes There* (1916), both edited by Wilfrid Meynell.

Omnia per Ipsum, et Sine Ipso Nihil

Alice Meynell, 'Some Memories of Francis Thompson', *DR*, January 1908; reprinted in *Works* under the title 'Motto and Invocation'

The title translates: 'Everything through him and nothing without him', based on John 1 : 3: 'All things were made by him: and without him was made nothing that was made.' This poem from Thompson's last notebook, known as the Large Commonplace Book, was intended as a preface for a collection of his prose writings he hoped to publish towards the end of his life but was too ill to undertake. Meynell placed it at the end of the Preface to the third volume of *Works*, the first collection of Thompson's prose to be published.

> Pardon, O St. John Divine,
> That I change a word of thee:
> None the less, aid thou me.
> And, Siena's Catharine;
> Lofty Doctor, Augustine,   5
> Glorious penitent; and be,
> Assisi's Francis, also mine;
> Mine be Padua's Anthony;
> And that other Francis, he
> Called of Sales, Let all combine   10
> To counsel, of great charity,
> What I write; Thy wings incline,
> Ah, my Angel, o'er the line.

Last and first, O Queen Mary,
Of thy white Immaculacy,   15
If my work may profit aught,
Fill with lilies every thought.
I surmise,
What is white will then be wise.
   (To which I add)
Thomas More,   20
Teach, (thereof my need is sore)
What thou showedst well on earth—
Good writ, good wit, make goodly mirth.

1 Refers to FT's adaptation of the verse forming the title. **20–3** FT's special devotion to St Thomas More underlies these lines (cf. 'To the English Martyrs', 122–49).

In No Strange Land
'The Kingdom of God'

The Athenaeum, 8 August 1908; reprinted in *Works*

The poem is generally known by the title supplied by Meynell, taken from the subtitle in the manuscripts. When he first published it he added a note:

> The following poem, found among the unpublished papers of Francis Thompson when he died last November, he might have worked upon to remove here a defective rhyme, or there an unexpected elision. But no altered mind would he have brought to the purport of it: and the pre-vision of 'Heaven in earth, and God in man', pervading his earlier published verse, is here accented by poignantly local and personal allusions—the retrospect of those days and nights of human dereliction he spent beside the Thames and in the shadow— but all radiance to him—of Charing Cross.

From Meynell's note it appears the manucript he used was not a final text and none seems to exist. There was a fair text in the possession of Maitland Dodd, a friend of the Meynells, which is now lost. In a letter to Olivia Meynell dated February 1964, he refers to its being framed and says he will bring it on his next visit. Although it has not since been traced, he enclosed a typed copy in the letter (M). According to a note on the letter, the text in his possession was dictated by Thompson from his sickbed to Dodd's brother 'Bosie' who gave Thompson a copy. There are some changes in the text printed by Meynell but Meynell's choices appear as variants to the Dodd text in another manuscript discovered in 1991 in the EMH collection. There is no way of knowing now which of the variants in the EMH text Thompson might have used for a final version. (There is another very rough draft at BC with some very incoherent lines added, reproduced in *SHSS*, pp. 191–5.) It is clear that Meynell used the EMH text, which is also followed here with the variants chosen by him. Those appearing there and in the Dodd version are given in the endnotes. As Meynell printed the poem there are no indentations but in the EMH manuscript the second and fourth lines are indented and this format is now restored.

O world invisible, we view thee,
    O world intangible, we touch thee,
O world unknowable, we knew thee,
    Inapprehensible, we clutch thee!

Does the fish soar to find the ocean,   5
    The eagle plunge to find the air?
That we cry to the stars in motion
    If they have rumour of thee there?

Not where the wheeling systems darken,
    And our benumbed conceiving soars;   10
The drift of pinions, would we hearken,
    Beats at our own clay-shuttered doors.

The angels keep their ancient places,
    Turn but a stone and start a wing:
'Tis ye, 'tis your estrangèd faces   15
    That miss the many-splendoured thing.

But when so sad thou canst not sadder,
    Cry, and upon thy so sore loss
Shall shine the traffic of Jacob's Ladder
    Pitched betwixt Heaven and Charing Cross.   20

But in the night, my soul, my daughter,
    Cry, clinging heaven by the hems;
And lo! Christ walking on the water
    Not of Genesereth, but Thames.

3 *knew* Dodd: know. 7 *cry to* WM text: ask of. 10 *And our benumbed conceiving soars* Dodd: And fires freeze flawless to the cores. 11 *drift* Dodd: storm. 21 *But* WM text: Yea.

Lines: To W. M.

Selected Poems of Francis Thompson, ed. Wilfrid Meynell, 1908; reprinted in *Eyes of Youth*, 1910 and in *Works*, 'To W. M.'

O Tree of many branches! One thou hast
Thou barest not, but grafted'st onto thee. Now,
Should all men's thunders break on thee, and leave
Thee reft of bough and blossom, that one branch
Shall cling to thee, my Father, Brother, Friend,
Shall cling to thee, until the end of end!

Buona Notte

The Athenaeum, 10 July 1909; reprinted in *Works*

The writing of this poem can be dated by a reference to it in a letter Thompson
wrote to Canon John Carroll in the summer of 1890 (he rarely gave his letters an
exact date). 'My lines on Shelley,' he says, 'are founded on a letter given in
Trelawny's "Recollections"; a letter from Jane Williams to Shelley two days before
his death. The poem is put into the mouth of the dead Shelley, and is supposed to
be addressed by the poet's spirit to Jane while his body is tossing on the waters of
Spezzia' (*Letters*, p. 46).

When Meynell first published it he prefixed the following note, based on one
by Thompson in the manuscript: 'Jane Williams, in her last letter to Shelley,
wrote: "Why do you talk of never enjoying moments like the past? Are you going
to join your friend Plato, or do you expect that I shall do so soon? *Buona notte*."
This letter was dated July 6th—an anniversary passed this week. Shelley was
drowned on the 8th, and the following reply made by him from another world was
imagined by the late Francis Thompson.' The note has been retained in *Works* and
since, without the concluding references to recent dates.

'Ariel to Miranda':—hear
This good-night the sea-winds bear,
And let thine unacquainted ear
Take the grief for their interpreter.

Good-night; I have risen so high   5
Into slumber's rarity,
Not a dream can beat its feather
Through the unsustaining ether.
Let the sea-winds make avouch
How thunder summoned me to couch,   10
Tempest curtained me about
And turned the sun with his own hand out:

And though I toss upon my bed,
My sleep is not disquieted;
Nay, deep I sleep upon the deep, 15
And my eyes are wet, but I do not weep;
And I fell to sleep so suddenly,
That my lips are moist yet, could'st thou see—
With the good-night draught I have drunk to thee.
Thou canst not wipe them; for it was death 20
Damped my lips that has dried my breath.
A little while—it is not long,—
The salt shall be dry on them like the song.

Now know'st thou, that voice desolate
Mourning ruined joy's estate, 25
Reached thee through a closing gate.
'Goest thou to Plato?' Ah, girl, no!
It is to Pluto that I go.

28 *Pluto* the god or ruler of the Underworld.

Threatened Tears

The Athenaeum, 13 November 1909; reprinted in *Eyes of Youth* (1910) and *Works*

Do not loose those rains thy wet
Eyes, my Fair, unsurely threat
Do not, Sweet, do not so;—
Thou canst not have a single woe,
But this sad and doubtful weather 5
Overcasts us both together.
In the aspèct of those known eyes
My soul's a captain weatherwise.
Ah me! what presages it sees
In those watery Hyades. 10

10 *Hyades* constellation of seven stars which, when rising simultaneously with the sun, were said to forecast rain.

ECCLESIASTICAL BALLADS

DR, January 1910; reprinted in *Works*

When first published the following two poems were accompanied by an explanatory note: 'Late in life Francis Thompson planned out a series of *Ecclesiastical Ballads*, of which, however, only two were completed: "The Veteran of Heaven", Whose wounds were His victories, and: "The Lily of the King", the patient Church, to whom the poet foretells the miseries of the world and her own final peace.' They are printed here in the order in which they appear in the manuscripts, which is reversed in *DR* and *Works*. The punctuation in the published text varies considerably from the manuscripts as followed here.

1 Lilium Regis

The title, 'The Lily of the King', refers to the verse in the *Song of Songs* as it has been applied traditionally to the Church: 'I am the flower of the field and the lily of the valleys' (Song 2 : 1).

O Lily of the King! low lies thy silver wing,
    And long has been the hour of thy unqueening;
And thy scent of Paradise on the night-wind spills its sighs,
    Nor any take the sweets of its meaning.
O Lily of the King! speak a heavy thing,   5
    O patience, most sorrowful of daughters!
Lo, the hour is at hand for the troubling of the land,
    And red shall be the breaking of the waters.

Sit fast upon thy stalk when the blast shall with thee talk,
    With the mercies of the King for thine awning;   10
And the just understand that thine hour is at hand,
    Thine hour at hand with power in the dawning.
When the nations lie in blood, and their kings a broken wood,
    Look up, O most sorrowful of daughters!
Lift up thy head, and hark what sounds are in the dark,   15
    For His feet are coming to thee on the waters!

O Lily of the King! I shall not see, that sing,
    I shall not see the hour of thy queening!
But my song shall see, and wake like a flower that dawn-winds shake,
    And sigh with joy the odours of its meaning.   20

O Lily of the King, remember then the thing
  That this dead mouth sang; and thy daughters,
As they dance before His way, sing then in the Day
  What I sang when the Night was on the water.   5

4 *sweets Works*: secret.

2 *The Veteran of Heaven*

O Captain of the wars, whence won ye so great scars?
In what fight did ye smite, and what manner was the foe?
Was it on a day of rout they compassed thee about,
Or gat ye these adornings when ye wrought their overthrow?

''Twas on a day of rout they girded me about,   5
They wounded all my brow, and they smote me through the side:
My hand held no sword when I met their armèd horde,
And the conqueror fell down, and the conquered bruised his pride.'

What is this, unheard before, that the unarmed makes war,
And the slain hath the gain, and the victor hath the rout?   10
What wars then are these, and what the enemies,
Strange Chief, with the scars of thy conquest trenched about?

'The Prince I drave forth held the Mount of the North,
Girt with the guards of flame that roll round the pole.
I drave him with my wars from all his fortress-stars,   15
And the sea of Death divided that my march might strike its goal.

'In the keep of Northern Gard, many a great dæmonian sword
Burns as it turns round the Mount occult apart:
There is given him power and place still for some certain days,
And his Name would turn the Sun's blood back upon its heart.'   20

What is *thy* Name? O show!—'My Name ye may not know;
'Tis a going-forth with banners, and a baring of much swords:
But my titles that are high, are they not upon my thigh?—
"King of kings," are the words, "Lord of lords;"
It is written "King of kings, Lord of lords!" '   25

An editorial note in the *DR* draws attention to a source for the idea behind the poem and its metre in T. B. Macaulay's 'On the Battle of Naseby'. The resemblance is particularly noticeable in the first and second stanzas of Macaulay's poem:

> Oh! wherefore come ye forth in triumph from the North.
> With your hands, and your feet, and your raiment all red?
> And wherefore doth your rout send forth a joyous shout?
> And whence be the grapes of the wine-press which ye tread?
>
> Oh evil was the root, and bitter was the fruit,
> And crimson was the juice of the vintage which we trod,
> For we trampled on the throng of the haughty and the strong,
> Who sate in the high places, and slew the saints of God.
> (T. B. Macaulay, *Lays of Ancient Rome*)

In the published text the second and fourth lines of each verse are indented but not in the manuscript as followed here.

6 references to Christ's crown of thorns and pierced side. **13** *the Mount of the North* In addition to the possible parallel in Macaulay's poem, the North has from earliest times been associated with forces of darkness and the devil. FT's interest in this symbolism appears in several notebook entries and in his correspondence with Coventry Patmore. In the Old Testament there are references to the evil associated with the North and here he probably had the prophecy of Daniel in mind: 'And the king of the North shall come; and shall cast up a mount, and shall take the best fenced cities . . .' (Daniel 11:15). **17** *Gard DR* and *Works:* Guard; *daemonian DR* and *Works:* doemonian.

Absence

English Review, January 1910; reprinted in *Works*

The manuscript of this poem is included with the 'Ad Amicam' poems addressed to Katie King (see Part Three: 'Ad Amicam Notebook'). It is followed here, disregarding the changes in punctuation in the published text.

> When music's fading's faded,
>   And the rose's death is dead,
> And my heart is fain of tears, because
>   Mine eyes have none to shed;
>   I said, 5
> Whence shall faith be fed?
>
> Canst thou be what thou hast been?
>   No, no more what thou hast!
> Lo, all last things that I have known,
>   And all that shall be last, 10
>   Went past
> With the thing thou wast!

If the petal of this Spring be
   As of the Spring that's flown
If the thought that now as sweet is   15
   As the sweet thought overblown;
     Alone,
Canst thou be thy self gone!

To yester-rose a richer
   The rose-spray may bear;   20
Thrice-thousand fairer you may be,—
   But tears for the fair
     You were,
When you first were fair!

Know you where they have laid her,   25
   Maiden May that died?
With the loves that lived not
   Strowing her soft side?
     I cried;
Where Has-been may hide?   30

To him that waiteth, all things,
   Even death, if thou wait!
And they that part too early
   May meet again too late:—
     Ah, fate!   35
If meeting be too late!

And when the year new launchèd
   Shall from its wake extend
The blossomy foam of Summer,
   What shall I attend,   40
     My friend!
Flower of thee, my friend?

Sweet shall have its sorrow,
   The rainbow its rain,
Loving have its leaving,   45
   And bliss is of pain
     So fain,
Ah, is she bliss or pain?

Orison-Tryst

DR, April 1910; reprinted in *Works*

The autograph manuscript used by Meynell has only recently come to light and is now in a private collection. A copy in his hand is in the EMH Collection. Another longer text at BC carries the note 'corrected version', but both are fair copies and signed. The shorter text gains from its greater brevity and is followed here, with the longer one included in the endnotes. In *DR* it was prefixed by a note by Meynell: 'This hitherto unpublished poem was written by Francis Thompson after hearing from a friend, whose prayers he asked at a time of stress, that it was her habit to pray for him every morning.' Connolly added the following comment in his Notes, provided for him by Meynell: 'The friend was Mrs. Meynell, to whom he said, "Pray for me, Mrs. Meynell." She replied, "I do, Francis, every morning." He went into another room and wrote "Orison-Tryst" ' (TLC*Poems*, p. 415).

> She told me, in the morning her white thought
> Did beat to Godward, like a carrier-dove,
> My name beneath its wing, And I—how long!—
> That, (like a bubble from a water-flower
> Released as it withdraws itself up-curled 5
> Into the nightly lake), her sighèd name
> So loosened from my sleepward-sinking heart;
> And in the morning did like Phosphor set it
> To lead the vaward of my orient soul
> When it storms Heaven; and did all alone, 10
> Methought, upon the live coals of my love
> Those distillations of rich memory cast
> To feed the fumes of prayer:—Oh! I was then
> Like one who, dreaming solitude, awakes
> In sobbing from his dream; and, straining arms 15
> That ache for their own void, with sudden shock
> Takes a dear form beside him!—
>   Now, when light
> Pricks at my lids, I never rouse but think—
> 'Is't orison-time with her?'—And then my hand 20
> Presses thy letters in my pulses shook;
> Where, neighboured on my heart with those pure lines
> In amity of kindred pureness, lies
> Image of Her conceived Immaculate;
> And on the purple inward, thine,—ah! Thine 25
> O' the purple-linèd side!
>   And I do set
> Tryst with thy soul in its own Paradise;

As lovers of an earthly rate that use,
In severance, for their sweet messages   30
Some concave of a tree, and do their hearts
Enharbour in its continent heart,—I drop
My message in the hollow breast of God.
Thy name is known in Heaven; yea, Heaven is weary
With the reverberation of thy name: 35
I fill with it the gap between two sleeps,
The inter-pause of dream: hell's gates have learned
To shake in it; and their fierce forayers
Before the iterate echoing recoil,
In armèd watches when my separate soul—   40
(A war-cry in the alarums of the Night)—
Conjoins thy name with Hers Auxiliatrix.

The longer text at BC, referred to in the headnote, is as follows (brigandine in 37: coat of chain mail):

She told me, in the morning her white thought
Did beat to Godward, like a carrier-dove,
My name beneath its wing. And, I how long!—
Even as a half up-petalled water-flower
Recoiling in the nightly mere's serene   5
May loose one bubble, sinking,—I, whose heart,
As it did sink beneath the undulous sleep,
So loosened, folding, her exhalèd name;
And who at flood of prime like Phosphor set it
To lead the vaward of my orient soul   10
Against the steepy Heaven; and all alone,
Methought, those rich-distillèd memories
Cast on the fuming censer of my heart:—
Oh! I was then an uncompanioned boy,
When first his self doth try the doors of self   15
And shaking strong and stronger knows at length
Its prison; and like one betrayed that hopes
An angel of the Lord, he cries on 'Love!'
And cries in desperation of all love,
And waits to hear the silence answer him;   20
And hears from the great vaultage of his heart
The echo grown god in prophecy
Revolve on him, with all assurance, 'Love!'

Now, when the prickings of the slate-blue dawn
Fret at my lids, my heart with sudden stir   25
Bursts like a lily of the East, and shakes
A gust of fragrant prayer about my sense
Or ere the mouth begin; as if all night
The sanctities had hived there round her name.
'Somewhere,' I think, 'her lips perhaps at this hour   30
Of common words make holy alchemy,

And her voice beateth with the ebbing stars
About God's feet, for me.'
     Then, then my hand
Presses thy letters in my pulses shook;   35
Where, on the armèd outward of my heart
With that pure script divinely brigandined,
Lies, like two lilies rocked upon one wave,
The image of the Lady Immaculate,
And on the purple inward, thine,—ah! thine   40
O' the purple-linèd side!
     And I do set
Tryst with thee in thy native paradise;
As lovers of an earthly rate that use,
In severance, for the sweet messages,   45
Some concave of a tree, and their wild hearts
Enharbour in its continent heart,—I drop
My message in the hollow breast of God.
Thy name is known in Heaven; yea, Heaven is weary
With the reverberation of thy name: 50
I fill with it the gap between two sleeps,
The inter-pause of dream: hell's gates have learned
To shake in it; and their fierce forayers
Before the iterate echoing recoil,
When in armed watches my preparèd soul,   55
A war-cry in the alarums of the night,
Conjoins the sound with Hers Auxiliatrix.

4, 6 no parentheses in *DR*. **8** *Phosphor* the morning star. **9** *vaward DR*: vanward; FT used vaward elsewhere as alternative to vanguard. **24** WM added a note for this line, that it 'refers to a medal the poet, during all the years of his London life, wore round his neck. In his last illness, when he was being medically examined, he raised his frail hand to prevent its being temporarily removed; and it went with him to the grave.' **40** *separate DR*: preparate. **42** *Hers Auxiliatrix* term applied to the Blessed Virgin as intercessor for mankind.

To Daisies

English Review, July 1910; reprinted in *Works*

The manuscript is a fair copy in ink but the order of the stanzas has been re-arranged by Thompson with the use of marginal numbers. These have been followed here, as have his divisions between stanzas, which were not retained in the text as published by Meynell.

   Ah, drops of gold in whitening flame
   Burning, we know your lovely name!
   Daisies, that little children pull!
   Like all weak things, over the strong
   Ye do not know your power for wrong,   5
   And much abuse your feebleness.

Weak maids, with flutter of a dress,
Increase most heavy tyrannies;
And vengeance unto heaven cries
For multiplied injustice of dove-eyes.   10
Daisies, that little children pull,
As ye are weak, be merciful!
O hide your eyes! they are to me
Beautiful insupportably!
Or be but conscious ye are fair,   15
And I your loveliness could bear;
But being fair so without art,
Ye vex the silted memories of my heart!

As a pale ghost yearning strays,
With sundered gaze,   20
'Mid corporal presences that are
To it impalpable; such a bar
Sets you more distant than the morning star.
Such wonder is on you and amaze
I look, and marvel if I be   25
Indeed the phantom, or are ye?
The light is on your innocence
Which fell from me, and made no stays:
The fields ye still inhabit whence
My world-acquainted treading strays,—   30
The country where I did commence;
And though ye shine on me so near
So close to gross and visible sense,
Between us lies impassable year on year.

To other time and far-off place   35
Belongs your beauty: silent thus,
Though to others nought you tell,
To me your ranks are rumourous
Of an ancient miracle.
Vain does my touch your petals graze,   40
I touch you not; and though ye blossom here,
Your roots are fast in alienated days.
Ye there are anchored, while Time's stream
Has swept me past them: your white ways
And infantile delights do seem   45
To look in on me like a face

Dear and sweet, come back through dream,
With tears, because for old embrace
It has no arms. These hands did toy,
Children, with you when I was child,   50
And in each other's eyes we smiled:
Not yours, not yours the grievous-fair
Apparelling
With which you wet mine eyes; you wear,
Ah me, the garment of the grace   55
I wove you when I was a boy;
O mine, and not the year's, your stolen Spring!
And since ye wear it,
Hide your sweet selves! I cannot bear it.

For when ye break the cloven earth   60
With your young laughter and endearment,
No blossomy carillon 'tis of mirth
To me; I see my slaughtered joy
Bursting is cerement.

Ad Castitatem: De Profundis

DR, July 1910; reprinted in *Works*

The title translates as 'To Chastity: From the Depths'. When Meynell edited this poem he followed a manuscript which has now been located with the EMH Collection, a fair copy in ink and signed. He omitted 'De Profundis' from the title and deleted the first ten lines and the last four. In *Works* he added it to the 'Sight and Insight' group, where it has continued to appear since. Another fair copy, at BC, differs from this one from the fifth verse on, continuing with 10 verses not found in the EMH manuscript. This version has the title in English, 'Song to Chastity', without the added 'De Profundis'. A rough draft in NB14A, which contains drafts for *New Poems*, suggests that period for composition but it was not included with the final texts as prepared by Thompson for the publisher. The text as printed in the *DR* is clearly his final text and is followed here with the addition of the deleted lines. There is some influence from Patmore's ideas on the sanctity of human love, but Patmore could never have shared Thompson's view of virginity as not less self-fulfilling than the married state.

Out of the grisly dread of tainted nights,
Out of the horrid reek of pitchy hell,
Out of the seething of all foul delights,

Which are to me affrights;
Out of unlawful and corroding spell;   5
O Lady Chastity,
Out of all vileness which thy lucence mars,
I dare to sing to thee:
O thou whose feet are set upon the stars!
This chant floats up to thee through the infernal bars.   10

Through thee virginity endure
The stars, most integral and pure,
    And ever contemplate
    Themselves inviolate

In waters, and do love unknown   15
Beauty they dream not is their own!
    Through thee the waters bare
    Their bosoms to the air,

And with confession never done
Admit the sacerdotal sun,   20
    Absolved eternally
    By his asperging eye.

To tread the floor of lofty souls,
With thee Love mingles aureoles;
    Who walk his mountain-peak   25
    Thy sister-hand must seek.

A hymen all unguessed of men
In dreams thou givest to my ken;
    For lacking of like mate,
    Eternally frustrate: 30

Where, that the soul of either spouse
Securelier clasp in either's house,
    They never breach at all
    Their mures corporeal.

This was the secret of the great   35
And primal Paradisal state
    Which Adam and which Eve
    Might not again retrieve.

Yet hast thou toward my vision taught
A way to draw in vernal thought,   40
    Not all too far from that
    Great Paradisal state.

Which for that earthy men might wrong,
Were't uttered in this earthless song,
    Thou layest cold finger-tips   45
    Upon my histed lips.

But thou, who knowest the hidden thing
Thou hast instructed me to sing,
    Teach love the way to be
    A new virginity!   50

Do thou with thy protecting hand
Shelter the flame thy breath has fanned;
    Let my heart's reddest glow
    Be but as sun-flushed snow.

And if they say that snow is cold,   55
O Chastity, must they be told
    The hand that's chafed with snow
    Takes redoubled glow?

That extreme cold like heat doth sear?
O to this heart of love draw near,   60
    And feel how scorching rise
    Its white-cold purities!

Life, ancient and o'er-childed nurse,
To turn my thirsting mouth averse,
    Her breast embittereth   65
    With my foretaste of death.

But thou, sweet Lady Chastity,
Thou, and thy brother Love with thee,
    Upon her lap mayest still
    Sustain me, if thou will.   70

Out of the terrors of the tomb,
And unclean shapes that haunt sleep's gloom,
    Yet, yet I call on thee,—
    'Abandon thou not me!'

Now sung is all the singing of this chant. 75
Lord, Lord, be nigh unto me in my want!
For to the idols of the Gentiles I
Will never make me an hierophant,
Their false-fair gods of gold and ivory;
Which have a mouth, nor any speech thereby, 80
Save such as soundeth from the throat of hell
The aboriginal lie;
And eyes, nor any seeing in the light,—
Gods of the obscene night,
To whom the darkness is for diadem. 85
Let them that serve them be made like to them,—
Yea, like to him who fell
Shattered in Gaza, as the Hebrews tell,
Before the simple presence of the Ark.
My singing is gone out upon the dark; 90
And sleep shall thrust me back, impitiable,
To tread the fiery furnaces of dream.
Lo, from afar I mark
The menace and the bicker and the gleam!

27 *hymen* virginal membrane, **46** *histed* silenced. **78** *hierophant* pagan priest of the mystery religions. **87** *him who fell* Dagon, god of the Philistines. When the Ark of the Lord was brought into his temple, the next day his statue was found prostrate before it (1 Kings 5:2–3).

This is the most appropriate place to draw attention to a poem that has been ascribed to FT and that appeared with 'Ad Castitatem' in the *DR*, April 1910. The poem, 'Westminister Cathedral MCMX', is not listed in any collections of FT's poetry, but TLC included it in his bibliography of uncollected verse (TLC *Poems* p. 562). The contents list for that issue of the *DR* gives Thompson's name for 'Ad Castitatem' but no name for the poem which follows it. Clearly it is not by him since the date in the title is 1910 and he died in 1907.

Carmen Genesis

DR, October 1910; reprinted in *Works*

The title translates as 'A Song of Creation'. The fair copy, in ink with some corrections and signed, is at H and is reproduced here. The *DR* text divides the poem into three Parts, after the ninth and fourteenth stanzas. In addition there are minor alterations which, like the divisions, have been repeated since and are given here in the endnotes.

Sing how the uncreated Light
Moved first upon the deep and Night,
    And at its *fiat lux*
Created light unfurled, to be
God's pinions, stirred perpetually   5
    In flux and in reflux.

From light create and the vexed ooze
God shaped to potency and thews
    All things beheld, and all
Which lessen beyond human mark   10
Into the spaces man calls dark
    Because his day is small.

Far-storied, lanterned with the skies,
All nature, magic palace-wise,
    Did from the waters come: 15
The angelic singing masons knew
How many centuried centuries through
    The awful courses clomb.

The regent light his strong ordain
Then laid upon the snarling main;   20
    Shook all its wallowing girth
The shaggy brute, and did, for ire
Low bellowing in its chafed retire,
    Sullen disglut the Earth.

Meanwhile the universal light   25
Broke itself into bounds, and Night
    And Day were two, yet one:
Dividual splendour did begin
Its procreant task, and globing, spin
    In moon, and stars, and sun.   30

With interspheral counterdance
Consenting contraries advance,
   And plan is hid for plan:
In roaring harmonies would burst
The thunder's throat, the heavens uncurst   35
   Restlessly steady ran.

All Day Earth waded in the sun,
Free-bosomed, and when Night begun
   Spelled in the secret stars;
Day unto Day did utter speech,   40
Night unto Night the knowledge teach
   Barred in its golden bars.

And last man's self, the little world
Where was creation's semblance furled,
   Rose at the [hiatus] nod: 45
For the first world the moon and sun
Swung orbed; that human second one
   Was dark, and waited God.

His locks He spread upon the breeze,
His feet He lifted on the seas,   50
   Into His worlds He came:
Man made confession: 'There is Light!'
And named, while Nature to its height
   Quailed, the enormous Name.

Poet! still, still thou dost rehearse   55
In the great *fiat* of thy verse
   Creation's primal plot;
And what thy Maker in the whole
Worked, little maker, in thy soul
   Thou work'st, and men know not.   60

Thine intellect, a luminous voice,
Compulsive moves above the noise
   Of thy still-fluctuous sense;
And Song, a water-child like Earth,
Stands with feet sea-washed, a wild birth,   65
   Amid their subsidence.

Bold copyist! who dost relimn
The traits, in man's gross mind grown dim,
    Of the first Masterpiece;
Remaking all in thy one Day,   70
God give thee Sabbath to repay
    Thy sad work with full peace!

Still Nature, to the clang of doom,
Again thou bearest in thy womb:
    Thou makest all things new,   75
Elias, when thou comest! yea,
Mak'st straight the intelligential way
    For God to pace into.

His locks perturb man's eddying thought,
His feet man's surgy breast have sought,   80
    To man, His world, He came;
Man makes confession; 'there is Light;'
And names, with being to its height
    Rocked, the desired Name.

God! if not yet the royal siege   85
Of Thee, my terrible sweet Liege,
    Hath shook my soul to fall;
If, 'gainst Thy great investment, still
Some broken bands of rebel Will
    Do man the desperate wall;   90

Yet, yet, Thy graciousness! I tread
All quick through tribes of moving dead,
    Whose life's a sepulchre
Sealed with the dull stone of a heart
No angel can roll round. I start,   95
    Thy secrets lie so bare!

With beautiful importunacy
All things plead, 'We are fair!' To me
    Thy world's a morning haunt,
A bride whose zone no man hath slipt   100
But I; with baptism still bedript
    Of the prime waters' font.

---

3 *fiat lux* let there be light. **9** *beheld DR*: we see. **18** *clomb* climbed. **19** *ordain DR*:
decree. **20** *main DR*: sea. **22** *ire DR*: wrath. **23** *retire DR*: path. **45** hiatus in MS *DR*:

linking. **62** *moves DR*: moved. **70** *Remaking DR*: Remarking. **74** *DR*: Thy verse re-beareth in thy womb. **76** *Elias* Old Testament prophet who, it was believed, would return to herald the Messiah. **83** *with* MS: while. **84** *Rocked DR*: Rocks. **97** *importunacy OED* cites 16th- and 17th-century usage for pertinacity.

The House of Sorrows

DR, January 1911; reprinted in *Works*

The occasion for this poem was the assassination of Elizabeth, Empress of Austria and wife of the Emperor Francis Joseph, on 10 September 1898. While visiting Geneva she was stabbed by an Italian anarchist as she boarded a lake-steamer. Unaware that she was fatally wounded she entered the boat but died soon after while on the lake. When the poem was first published, it was prefixed by an explanatory note, part of which runs as follows:

> In the first seven stanzas the Empress herself is heard addressing first Our Lady, then the 'Dark Fool', Death, and finally the Son of Sorrows, in allusion to the griefs of her own and her husband's line—the shooting of her brother-in-law, Maximilian of Mexico, her sister's burning at the Paris Bazar de la Charité, the tragedy of the Crown Prince Rudolph, her son, and the drowning of the King of Bavaria—to name no more.

The manuscript of the poem is a fair corrected copy in ink. The fourth stanza was altered and completed by Meynell and another was added by him, after the sixth, from an earlier draft where Thompson had deleted it. The *DR* text also divides the poem into two parts with the second starting at the seventh stanza according to the number of stanzas in the present text.

> 'Of the white purity
>   They wrought my wedding-dress,
> Inwoven silverly—
>   For tears, as I do guess;
> Oh, why did they with tears inweave my marriage-dress?   5

> A girl, I did espouse
>   Destiny, Grief, and Fears;
> The lore of Austria's house
>   And its ancestral years
> I learned, and my salt eyes grew erudite in tears.   10

> Devote our tragic line!—
>   One to his rebels' aim,
> One to the ignorant brine,
>   One to the eyeless flame.
> Who should be skilled to weep but I, O Christ's dear Dame?   15

One more to fire ordain,
   One more for water keep:—
O Death [hiatus] grain
   More Austria must thou reap?
Can I have plummetless tears, that still thou bidd'st: "Weep, weep?"   20

No! thou at length with me
   Too far, dark fool, hast gone!
One costly cruelty
   Voids thy dominion:
I am drained to the utmost tear. O Rudolph, O my son!   25

Take this woof of sorrows,
   Son of all womens' tears!
I am not for the morrows,
   I am dead with the dead years.
Lo, I vest thee, Christ, with my woven tears!'   30

The Son of Weeping heard,
   The gift benignly saw;
The women's Pitier heard—
   Together, by hid law,
The life-gashed heart, the assassin's healing poniard draw.   35

Too long that consummation
   The obdurate seasons thwart,
Too long were the sharp consolation
   And her breast apart;—
The remedy of steel has gone home to her sick heart!   40

Her breast dishabited
   Revealed, her heart above,
A little blot of red,—
   Death's reverent sign to approve   45
He had sealed up that royal tomb of martyred love.

Now, Death, if thou wouldst show
   Some ruth still left in store,
Guide thou the armèd blow
   To strike one bosom more,   50
Where any blow were pity, to this it struck before!

8 *Austria's house* the house of Habsburg. 10 *erudite* in MS, pencilled below: recondite. 12
In 1866 Maximilian, Francis Joseph's brother and ruler of Mexico, was executed by Mexican

rebels. **13** King Ludwig of Bavaria, Elizabeth's cousin, was drowned in 1886, not in the sea as FT implies but in a Bavarian Lake. **14** Elizabeth's sister, the Duchesse d'Alençon, was burned to death in Paris in 1897.

16–19 *DR*:

> Give one more to the fire,
>> One more for water keep:
> O Death, wilt thou not tire?
>> Still Austria must thou reap?

25 In 1889 Rudolf, Elizabeth's only son, was found dead at his hunting lodge, Mayerling, together with Baroness Vetsera, his mistress.

Between 30–1 *DR*, Stanza from an earlier draft:

> My bridal wreath, take thou,
>> Mary! Take Thou, O Christ,
> My bridal garment! Now
>> Is all my fate sufficed,
> And, robed and garlanded, the victim sacrificed.

Cheated Elsie

Century Magazine, June 1911; reprinted in *Works*

No manuscript has been located for this poem.

> Elsie was a maiden fair
>> As the sun
>> Shone upon:
> Born to teach her swains despair
> By smiling on them every one; 5
> Born to win all hearts to her
> Just because herself had none.
> All the day she had no care,
> For she was a maiden fair
>> As the sun
>> Shone upon, 10
> Heartless as the brooks that run.
>
> All the maids, with envy tart,
> Sneering said, 'She has no heart.'
> All the youths, with bitter smart,
> Sighing said, 'She has no heart.' 15
>> Could she care
> For their sneers or their despair
> When she was a maiden fair
>> As the sun
>> Shone upon, 20
> Heartless as the brooks that run?

But one day, whenas she stood
    In a wood
Haunted by the fairy brood,
Did she view or dream she viewed,   25
    In a vision's
    Wild misprisions,
How a pedlar, dry and rude
As a crook'd branch taking flesh,
Caught the spirit in a mesh,   30
Singing of—'What is't ye lack?'
    Wizard-pack
    On twisted back,
Still he sang, 'What is't ye lack?

'Lack ye land or lack ye gold?   35
What I give, I give unsold;
Lack ye wisdom, lack ye beauty,
    To your suit he
Gives unpaid, the pedlar old!'

FAIRIES Beware! beware! the gift he gives   40
    One pays for, sweetheart, while one lives!
ELSIE What is it the maidens say
    That I lack?
PEDLAR   By this bright day!
    Can so fair a maiden lack?   45
      Maid so sweet
      Should be complete.
ELSIE Yet a thing they say I lack,
      In thy pack,—
      Pedlar, tell—   50
    Hast thou ever a heart to sell?
PEDLAR Yea, a heart I have, as tender
    As the mood of evening air.
ELSIE Name thy price!
PEDLAR   The price, by Sorrow!   55
    Only is, the heart to wear.
ELSIE Not great the price, as was my fear!
FAIRIES So cheap a price was ne'er so dear.
      Beware, beware,
      O rash and fair!   60
      The gifts he gives
    Sweetheart, one pays for while one lives.
        *

Scarce the present did she take,
When the heart began to ache.

ELSIE   Ah, what is this? Take back thy gift!   65
I had not, and I knew no lack;
Now I have, I lack forever.
FAIRIES The gifts he gives, he takes not back.
ELSIE   Ah, why the present did I take,
And knew not that a heart would ache?   70
FAIRIES Ache! and is that all thy sorrow?—
Beware, beware, a heart will break!

Against Woman Derogating from Herself

DR, April 1912; not reprinted

The poem, to which Thompson gave the title as above in the final manuscript, a
fair copy in ink, was shortened by Meynell to seven stanzas when published in the
DR under the title 'Holy Ground'. This text, constructed from a separate earlier
manuscript and a draft in NB52, is given in the endnotes. It omits the verses from
the original poem where the poet's protest at the fate of the women of the streets is
most keenly expressed, with what can be regarded as concealed references to the
street girl.

O woman! how the unclean press
    Thou sufferest ope thy sacred book;
Soiling the inmost hiddenness
    On which they should not even look!

As London's herds unpent of stye   5
    Whither they go their own stye bring;
With obscene voice and revelry
    Rending smirched Nature's vesturing.

O woman! O weak! the sacrosanct
    Keys of the holy places ye   10
To them have yielded, all unthanked,
    Who enter in unworthily.

Whose tongues with blasphemies prevail
    Against the lilies and the shrine,
Pollute the porch, and rend the veil,   15
    And make your mysteries undivine!

Their sacrilege of touch, yea, their
    Infamous jest, more infamous praise,
Ye suffer; nay, in weak despair,
    Ape, heavenly, their unheavenly ways.   20

Yourselves have to the heathen greed
    Betrayed the inaccessible Gate;
Yourselves the laughing dances lead
    Through your shamed cloisters desecrate.

When unclean aliens like to these   25
    One word had chidden from your bound,
Your chaste insulted mysteries:—
    'Avaunt, profane! 'tis holy ground!'

Since no man so uncouthly proud
    (Such sacred reverence guards the place)   30
Would but attempt speech over-loud,
    Save by the sanctioning priestess' grace.

O Woman, if the keys God gave
    Unto thy consecrating hand
Thou keptest at thy girdle; rave   35
    Who would, thy house should safely stand.

And all the good make pilgrimage
    Thither, and climbing higher and higher,
From age to every sequent age,
    Draw nigher to thee, Sweet, and nigher!   40

Not blasphemies could taint thee, Sweet,
    Not dim thy shining flesh: this thing
We fear;—thou sufferest heathen feet
    In the Gate, sealèd to the King.

The *DR* text with the title 'Holy Ground' is as follows:
    O Woman, how the sacrosanct
        Keys of the Holy Places ye
    To them have yielded, all unthanked,
        Who enter in unworthily;

    Whose tongues with blasphemies prevail
        Against the lilies of the shrine,
    Who raze the porch and rend the veil,
        And make your mysteries undivine!

You to the sacrilegious foe
  Betray the inaccessible gate;
Yourselves in laughing dances go
  Over your ramparts desecrate.

Even unclean aliens like to these
  With one chaste word you could astound
From your insulted sanctuaries:
  'Avaunt, profane, 'tis holy ground!'

For no man, so uncouth or proud,
  (Such sacred reverence guards the place)
Would venture speech even over-loud,
  Save by the sanctioning priestess' grace.

O Lady, if the keys God gave
  Into thy consecrating hand
Thou kepst but at thy girdle: rave
  Who would, thy house should safely stand;

And all the good make pilgrimage
  Thither; and climbing higher and higher,
From age to every sequent age
  Draw nigher to thee, sweet, and nigher!

Messages

The Athenaeum, 29 March 1913; reprinted in *Works*

This poem was edited by Meynell from two incomplete manuscripts of 30 and 32
lines each. The poem as published is constructed from verses taken from each and
put together in an order that differs from either. The edited text is therefore
reproduced here, the two manuscripts both being incomplete.

What shall I your true-love tell,
  Earth-forsaking maid?
What shall I your true-love tell,
  When life's spectre's laid?

'Tell him that, our side the grave,   5
  Maid may not conceive
Life should be so sad to have,
  That's so sad to leave!'

What shall I your true-love tell,
  When I come to him?   10
What shall I your true-love tell—
  Eyes growing dim!

'Tell him this, when you shall part
From a maiden pined—
That I see him with my heart,   15
Now my eyes are blind.'

Stolen Fruit of Eden-Tree

'The Schoolmaster for God'

Irish Rosary, April 1913; reprinted in *MHW*

The poem has been edited from a draft with too many variants to reproduce, and
with only a few minor exceptions the text in the *Irish Rosary* is made up from the
same variants. According to a note in the *Irish Rosary* Thompson revived the title
'The Schoolmaster for God' from an earlier essay, 'Saint John Baptist de la Salle'.
But no reference to a title appears in the drafts other than the one restored here.
When the poem was reprinted in *MHW* Connolly added stanzas 6 and 8–12 from
the draft which had not appeared in the *Irish Rosary* text. The *MHW* version is
therefore reproduced here.

The devil girned as he lurched his hoof
    Over the border-wall,
The border-wall of the guarded garth
    That is God's garth withal,
The guarded garth where the trees of God   5
    Grew seemly fair and tall.

He soused the print of a cloven dint
    On the sod beneath him kneaden;
He crunched the scent from a lily-flower
    In the lily-ranks of Eden,   10
And tare the fruitage from the tree,
    Whatso was fairest seeden.

He filled his claw; on his writhen mouth
    A smile played wry accord;
As he leaped out of the Eden-close   15
    He neighed against the Lord:—
'I trow the hint of a slit hoof-print,
    Upon this trim-kept sward,
Right plainly tells your wingèd fellows
    Have kept but evil ward!'   20

That tale was told the Master
   Ere Satan had well leaped in,
And hot-plumed came the messengers
   To bruit the later sin.
Said Uriel: 'Shall we bring him Thee,   25
   Haled hither by the chin?'
But Michael thumbed his lance's point,
   And stirred with armèd din.

The Lord made answer slow, as for
   Affair of little worth: 30
'Small luck has he with Eden-fruit,
   This robber from the North;
'Twas with My will that he brake in,
   With mine let him break forth.'

The devil had face like a twisted thing   35
   As to earth with the spoil sped he;
And sowed the seed in a plot of his own,
   Where no blest foot might be,
And fostered it fast with his own mouth's blast,
   And watered it Stygianly.   40

Then he summoned the famished sons of men
   To fruit of Paradise;
'Now feed ye of each Eden-tree,
   But and you pay my price,
And see that ye do me homage due,   45
   Who make the fruit to rise.'

And he hath cried to blinded men:
   'Hither to me, to me!
O come, ye weary, woeful souls
   That thirst and languor dree;   50
Come and drink comfort, O drink deep
   From mine enjuicèd tree!

'This is the fruit of Paradise
   Desired from the first;
O eat the fruit of Paradise   55
   Long lost to man accurst!
Be not an-hungered any more,
   Nor any more athirst!'

The fruit thereof is fair and fine,
   And golden of its blee,   60
That well the Son of God might think
   It came of Paradise-tree,
Nor deem how its root with cold Pit-fire
   Is suckled evilly.

The earthlings throng with greedy mouth   65
   To eat of that ill root;
For the Devil has gotten his criers out
   To cry the Eden-fruit.
Lord God, except Thou lift Thine arm
   Needs must be foul ensuit.   70

They ate the fruit, whose heavenly root
   'Twined in Avernian soil;
And an unsated hunger scourged
   The eater with its rod,
Which might not be appeased—for they   75
   An-hungered were of God.

And some of the devil for comfort came,
   Who them did fatly dine
Upon his remainder-store of the husks
   Which the Prodigal ate with swine;   80
From fruit to husk, and husk to fruit,
   Went others—but to pine.

Yet one by one, and more and more
   (The noblest, leading those),
Drawn by that Eden-hunger sought   85
   The Master of the close;
For He alone could sate them, in
   Whose garth the first fruit grows.

The devil groaned in himself and said:
   'I shall finish where I began: 90
I toil and toil, and I take in the end
   But the sorriest clots of man;
Must I ever house at last in the swine,
   On the filthy Gadarene plan?

'Like Peter, a fisher of men, sometimes   95
    A man to my stomach I gain;
But the most are stuff that neither stamp
    Of hell or heaven retain,
And for one that gives him his due, ten take
    The devil's name in vain.'   100

But the Master said: 'Peace, Satan; still
    I reap where thou hast sowed:
Still steal my truth, for truth like fire
    Must tend back whence it flowed;
Despite himself, the devil must be   105
    The schoolmaster for God.'

1 *girned* snarled. **7** *dint* imprint. **25** *Uriel* one of the six archangels. **40** *Stygianly* gloomily. **50** *dree* endure. **60** *blee* colour. **72** *Avernian* infernal.

This is My Beloved Son

WM, *Halt! Who goes there*, 1916; reprinted in *SHSS*, p. 25; *BHCC*, p. 49

This poem, which first appeared in a lay tract inspired by the First World War, seems to have been written soon after the death of FT's mother. This occurred the day before his twenty-first birthday, at the time when he was failing in his medical studies and probably starting his opium addiction. The title is taken from the words spoken from the cloud at the Transfiguration of Christ (Matt. 17: 5). The theme is summarised in the last two lines where the 'second death' refers to the words in Apoc. 20: 7: 'Blessed and holy is he that hath part in the first resurrection. In these the second death hath no power.' Now that the poet's mother sees him as he really is and knows all, she has suffered an agony equal to the pain of the damned although she is one of those who would otherwise be 'blessed and holy'.

Son of the womb of her,
Loved till doom of her,
Thought of the brain of her
Heart of her side:
Joyed in him, grieved in him,   5
Hoped, believed in him—
God grew fain of her,
    And she died.

Died; and horribly
Saw the mystery   10
Saw the grime of it—

That hid soul;
Saw the sear of it,
Saw the fear of it,
Saw the slime of it;   15
Saw it whole!
O mother! mother! For all the sweet John saith,
O mother, was not *this* the second death?

13–14 MS lines omitted in WM text, restored in *SHSS* and *BHCC*.

An Epigram from Ecclesiasticus

Stylus (Boston College Journal), May 1934; not reprinted

The theme here and in the next linked poem is based on the Book of Ecclesiasticus, a collection of sayings and exhortations by the son of Sirach of Jerusalem and included in the Wisdom literature of the Old Testament. In the published text the alternate readings for the last line are reproduced from the manuscript but with minor changes in the position of the variant words on the lines. Their position in the manuscript is followed here.

Two silent men: the one, 'tis said, a fool,
The other, wise as ever taught in school.
Call fool the wise, who hides his wisdom wholly;
Call wise the fool, for he but hides⎫ his folly.
                              hideth⎭

Call fool the wise who hides his wisdom wholly
                    concealeth⎫
Call wise the fool, for he conceals⎭ his folly.

The Wise Man's Answer

Stylus (Boston College Journal), May 1934; not reprinted

The note above also applies to the variants in the last line here.

Ah, Son of Sirach! Wisdom to display
To fools, is to be greater fool than they!
                    doth⎫
Ah, Son of Sirach! he who does⎭ display
Wisdom to fools, is even more fool⎫ than they!
                    greater fool⎭

Marah Amarior

Stylus (Boston College Journal), May 1934; not reprinted

The *Stylus* text reproduces the manuscript as Thompson wrote it, a fair copy in ink and signed. The title translates as 'Bitterness more bitter', 'Marah' being Hebrew for 'bitter'.

> Not love made exile hottliest sears;
>   But that brave vaunt struck to its knee,
> When faith, with contumacious tears,
>   Is taught her own mortality.
> Bitter is voiding of desire;   5
>   But more intolerable yet
> The haughty heart's most shameful ire,
>   When first it finds it can forget.

'An Homage'

Poetry, December, 1935; not reprinted

There is an untitled typescript for this poem in the EMH Collection. A title was added for publication.

> Because I feared her little frown,
>   I looked and looked, and dared not speak;
> Because I feared the very blush
>   That made the sweet-briar buds in her cheek.
> But when she let her long hair down,   5
>   Whose fire-shot smoke suffused her round,
> I gazed, like Moses on the bush,
>   And thought her face was holy ground.
>
> Be less, be less, or be more kind!
>   I wish your very comb I were,   10
> Because it every morning runs
>   Its happy fingers through your hair!
> My heat shakes flame-like in the wind
>   Of your light feet; I have, in place
> Of rise and set of stars and suns,   15
>   Coming and going of your face.

IN *THE LIFE OF FRANCIS THOMPSON* (1913)

These five poems have not been reprinted apart from extracts in *SHSS* and *BHCC*.

'With dawn and children'

No manuscript has been found for these lines, which are therefore given the title they have in *Life*, pp. 73–4. They are accompanied there by Thompson's explanatory note: 'It was my practice from the time I left college to pray for the lady whom I was destined to love—the unknown She. It is curious that even then I did not dream of praying for her whom I was destined to marry; and yet not curious: for already I previsioned that with me it would be to love, not to be loved.' The distinct references in the second stanza to the three years spent on the London streets indicate that the 'lady' came to be associated in his mind with Alice Meynell.

> With dawn and children would he run,
>   Which knew not the fool's wisdom to be sad,
>   He that had childhood sometimes to be glad,
> Before her window with the co-mate sun.
> At night his angel's wing before the Throne   5
>   Dropped (and God smiled) the unnamed name of Her:
>   Nor did she feel her destinate poet's prayer
> Asperse her from her angel's pinion.
>
> So strangely near! So far, that ere they meet,
> The boy shall traverse with his bloody feet   10
>   The mired and hungered ways, three sullen years,
> Of the fell city: and those feet shall ooze
> Crueller blood through ruinous avenues
>   Of shattered youth, made plashy by his tears!
>   As full of love as scant of poetry;   15
>   Ah! in the verse but the sender see,
>   And in the sender, but his heart, lady!

Degraded Poor

The fair copy of this poem, in ink, is in the EMH Collection. It appears in *Life*, pp. 77–8, in a footnote. It is the only one of Thompson's poems of social protest to have been published.

<blockquote>

Lo, at the first, Lord, Satan took from Thee
Wealth, Beauty, Honour, World's Felicity.
Then didst Thou say: 'Let be;
For with his leavings and neglects will I
Please Me, which he sets by,—   5
Of all disvalued, thence which all will leave Me,
And fair to none but Me, will not deceive Me.'
My simple Lord! so deeming erringly,
Thou tookest Poverty;
Who beautied with Thy kiss, laved in Thy streams,   10
'Gan then to cast forth gleams,
That all men did admire
Her modest looks, her ragged sweet attire
In which the ribboned shoe could not compete
With her clear simple feet.   15
But Satan, envying Thee Thy one ewe-lamb,
With Wealth, World's Beauty and Felicity
Was not content, till last unthought-of she
Was also his to damn.
Thine ingrate, ignorant lamb   20
He won from Thee; kissed, spurned, and made of her
This thing which qualms the air—
Vile, terrible, old,
Whereat the red blood of the Day runs cold.

</blockquote>

'Of little poets'

In *Life*, p. 270, lines 1–3, 4–6 and 12–22 are printed from the manuscript of this poem, which runs to 22 lines in a fair corrected copy, reproduced here. They suggest a spontaneous outburst of frustration at the time when Thompson was being commissioned to write his 'public' odes and was paid the dubious compliment of imitation by a number of over-ambitious versifiers.

<blockquote>

Of little poets, neither fool nor seer,
Aping the larger song, let all men hear
How weary is our heart this many days!
                    *

</blockquote>

Of bards who, feeling half the thing they say,
Say twice the thing they feel, and in such way   5
Piece out a passion; of all them whose art,
Seeking the scorn inspired and fury fine,
With 'damn' and 'hell' stuffs out the mouthing line;
O powers divine!
How weary is our heart!   10
How weary is our heart these many days!

Of bards who shriek according to the school,
Of bards who curse by precedent and rule;
Bards who will live, as daily papers trash,
In 'anthropologies of English speech;'   15
Of bards indignant in an easy-chair
(Because just so great bards before them were),
Who yet can only bring,
With all their toil,
Their kettle of verse to sing,   20
But never boil;
How weary in our heart these many days!

Epitaphium Scriptoris

The title translates as 'Epitaph for a Writer'. Contrary to the view of EM, the lines are more applicable to Coventry Patmore than to Thompson himself (*Life*, pp. 292–3; cf. 'A Captain of Song'). The manuscript is a final copy in ink, NB14.

Here lies one, who could only be heroic.
How little in the sifted judgements seems
That swelling sound of vanity! Still 'tis proved,
To be heroic is an easier thing
Than to be just and good. If any be,   5
(As are how many daily ones!) who love
With love unlofty through no lofty days
Their little simple wives, and consecrate
Dull deeds with undulled justice; such poor livers,
Though they as little look to be admired   10
As thou to admire, are of more prizeful rate
Than he, who worshipped with unmortal love
A nigh unmortal woman, and knew to take
The pricking air of snowy sacrifice.

'To each a separate loneliness'

In *Life*, pp. 296–7, these 17 lines are edited from a rough draft of 25 lines in NB BC 32, with 'loveliness' mistaken for 'loneliness'. The overall content of the manuscript is contained in the edited version reproduced here.

> To each a separate loneliness,
> Environed by Thy sole caress.
> O Christ the just, and can it be
> I am made for love, no love for me?
> Of two loves, one at least be mine;   5
> Love of earth, though I repine,
> I have not, nor, O just Christ, Thine!
> Can life miss, doubly sacrificed,
> Kiss of maid, and kiss of Christ?
> Ah, can I, doubly-wretched, miss   10
> Maid's kiss, and Thy perfect kiss?
> Not all kisses, woe is me!
> Are kissed true and holily.
> Not all clasps; there be embraces
> Add a shame-tip to the daisies.   15
> These if, O dear Christ, I have known
> Let all my loveless lips atone.

IN *THE WORKS OF FRANCIS THOMPSON* (1913)

Proemion

Proemion translates as 'Preface'. In *Works* the poem is the first in the sequence 'Love in Dian's Lap'. There is no manuscript but a typescript in the EMH Collection has the title 'Her Portrait' above 'Proemion', which appears to be an abbreviation for the first poem of the original sequence, 'Before Her Portrait in Youth', rather than the one with that title, the seventh in the sequence in both *Poems* and *Works*. It appears to have been composed about a year after Thompson gave 'Sister Songs' to the Meynells at Christmas 1892, in accordance with the reference in the second verse to the dedication to them (completed in January). Therefore it has no connection with the original sequence. In his notes Connolly says the second verse refers to the dedication of *Poems* to the Meynells, giving 1894 as the date for this poem (TLC*Poems*, p. 340). But Thompson sent the manuscript to them in the summer of 1893 and the volume was published in November. These dates do not fit with the phrase: 'When the Years last met', whereas it does fit with the gift of 'Sister Songs' and the added 'Inscription' addressed to the Meynells. The mood of this poem suggests the period of depression on account of his poetry that Thompson underwent in January 1892 (see *Letters*, pp. 73–4). Meynell published 15 verses from it in *The Athenaeum*, 12 November 1910, with the title 'Lines to Two Friends'. The verses are 2–11; 13–16; 25. But after the second verse the poem as a whole is addressed to Alice only, probably accounting for its position in *Works* at the start of 'Love in Dian's Lap'.

> *Hear, my Muses, I demand*
> *A little labour at your hand,*
>   *Ere quite is loosed our amity:*
> *A little husband out the sand*
>   *That times the gasps of Poesy!*   5
>
> O belovèd, O ye Two,
> When the Years last met, to you
>   I sent a gift exultingly.
> My song's sands, like the Year's, are few;
>   But take this last weak gift from me.   10
>
> One year ago (one year, one year!)
> I had no prescience, no, nor fear;
>   I said to Oblivion: 'Dread thou me!'
> What cared I for the mortal year?
>   I was not of its company.   15
>
> Before mine own Elect stood I,
> And said to Death: 'Not these shall die!'
>   I issued mandate royally.
> I bade Decay: 'Avoid and fly,
>   For I am fatal unto thee.'   20
>
> I sprinkled a few drops of verse,
> And said to Ruin: 'Quit thy hearse;'
>   To my Loved: 'Pale not, come with me;
> I will escort thee down the years,
>   With me thou walk'st immortally.'   25
>
> Rhyme did I as a charmed cup give,
> That who I would might drink and live.
>   'Enter,' I cried, 'Song's ark with me!'
> And knew not that a witch's sieve
>   Were built somewhat more seamanly.   30

I said unto my heart: 'Be light!
Thy grain will soon for long delight
 Oppress the future's granary:'
Poor fool! and did not hear—'This night
 They shall demand thy song of thee.'   35

Of God and you I pardon crave;
Who would save others, nor can save
 My own self from mortality:
I throw my whole songs in the grave—
 They will not fill that pit for me.   40

But thou, to whom I sing this last—
The bitterest bitterness I taste
 Is that thy children have from me
The best I had where all is waste,
 And but the crumbs were cast to thee.   45

It may be I did little wrong;
Since no notes of thy lyre belong
 To them; thou leftest them for me;
And what didst *thou* want of my song,—
 Thou, thine own immortality?   50

Ah, I would that I had yet
Given thy head one coronet
 With thine ivies to agree!
Ere thou restest where are set
 Wreaths but on the breast of thee.   55

Though what avails?—The ivies twined
By thine own hand thou must unbind,
 When there thy temples laid shall be:
'Tis haply Death's prevision kind
 That ungirt brows lie easily.   60

'*Of all thy trees thou lovest so,*
None with thee to grave shall go,
 Save the abhorrèd cypress tree.'
The abhorrèd?—Ah, I know, I know,
 The dearest follower it would be!   65

Thou would'st sweetly lie in death
The dark southerner beneath:
   We should interpret, knowing thee,—
'Here I rest' (her symbol saith),
    'And above me, Italy.'   70

But above thy English grave
Who knows if a tree shall wave?
   Save—when the far certainty
Of thy fame fulfilled is—save
    The laurel that shall spring from thee.   75

Very little carest thou
If the world no laurel-bough
   Set in thy dead hand, ah me!
But *my* heart to grieve allow
    For the fame thou shalt not see!   80

Yet my heart to grieve allow,
With the grief that grieves it now,
   Looking to futurity,
With too sure presaging how
    Fools will blind blind eyes from thee:—   85

Bitterly presaging how
Sightless death must them endow
   With sight, who gladder blind would be.
'Though our eyes be blind enow,
    Let us hide them, lest we see!'   90

I would their hearts but hardened were
In the way that I aver
   All men shall find this heart of me:
Which is so hard, thy name cut there
    Never worn or blurred can be.   95

If my song as much might say!
But in all too late a day
   I use thy name for melody;
And with the sweet theme assay
    To hide my descant's poverty.   100

When that last song gave I you,
Ye and I, beloved Two,
    Were each to each half mystery!
Now the tender veil is through;
    Unafraid the whole we see.   105

Small for you the danger was!
Statued deity but thaws
    In you to warm divinity;
Some fair defect completion flaws
    With a completing grace to me.   110

But when *I* my veiling raised—
The Milonian less were crazed
    To talk with men incarnately:
The poor goddess but appraised
    By her lacking arms would be.   115

Though Pan may have delicious throat,
'Tis hard to tolerate the goat.
    What if Pan were suddenly
To lose his singing, every note?—
    Then pity have of Pan, and me!   120

Love and Song together sing;
Song is weak and fain to cling
    About Love's shoulder wearily.
Let her voice, poor fainting thing,
    In his strong voice drownèd be!   125

In my soul's Temple seems a sound
Of unfolding wings around
    The vacant shrine of poesy:
Voices of parting songs resound:—
    'Let us go hence!' *A space let be!*   130

A space, my Muses,—I demand
This last of labours at your hand,
    Ere quite is loosed our amity:
A little stay the cruel sand
    That times the gasps of Poesy!

29–30 Witches were believed to sail about in sieves. 52–3 Dionysus, god of poetical inspiration, wore a crown of ivy. **61–3** FT has asterisk here with footnote: 'The words of Horace'. They are a rendering of Horace's lines: 'Neque harum, quas colis, arborum / Te praeter invisas cupressos/Ulla brevem dominum sequetur' (Ode XIV, Bk 2:22–4). **109–10** What might be a defect in her is a grace for him. **112** *The Milonian* the goddess Venus, so called here for the famous armless statue known as the Venus de Milo. So the poet's attempt at revealing the beauty of her he praises must be as empty as the place for the statue's missing arms. **116** *Pan* the god of the countryside, with the head and torso of a man and the lower body of a goat, who invented the shepherd's flute, the 'Pipes of Pan'.

Domus Tua

This short poem, whose title translates as 'Thy House', was included in the manuscript Thompson sent to the publisher as part of the 'Love in Dian's Lap' sequence but he then withdrew it. In *Works* it is the eighth in the Sequence. The title and theme are adapted from Psalm 25:8: 'I have loved O Lord the beauty of thy house, and the place where thy glory dwelleth.'

> A perfect Woman—Thine be laud!
> Her body is a Temple of God.
> At doom-bar dare I make avows:
> I have loved the beauty of Thy house.

'To Stars'

The manuscript for this poem, in NB BC16, is complete but with many variants and with the title 'Aestris'. The text as edited for *Works* conveys the overall theme without appreciably altering the original and is followed here in accordance with the editorial policy for these poems given in the Introduction (p. xxxii). The poem was written during Viola Meynell's slow recovery from a fall down the staircase at the Meynells' home in Palace Court. Lines 18–21 refer to this.

> You, my unrest, and Night's tranquillity,
> Bringers of peace to it, and pang to me:
> You that on heaven and on my heart cast fire,
> To heaven a purging light, my heart unpurged desire;
> Bright juts for foothold to the climbing sight　　　　5
> Which else must slip from the steep infinite;
> Reared standards which the sequent centuries
> Snatch, each from his forerunner's grasp who dies,
> To lead our forlorn hope upon the skies;
> Bells that from night's great bell-tower hang in gold,　　　10
> Whereon God rings His changes manifold;
> Meek guides and daughters to the blinded heaven
> In Oedipean, remitless wandering driven;

The burning rhetoric, quenchless oratory,
Of the magniloquent and all-suasive sky;   15
I see and feel you—but to feel and see
How two child-eyes have dulled a firmament for me.

Once did I bring her, hurt upon her bed,
Flowers we had loved together; brought, and said:—
'I plucked them; yester-morn you liked them wild.'   20
And then she laid them on my eyes, and smiled.
And now, poor Stars, your fairness is not fair,
Because I cannot gather it for her;
I cannot sheave you in my arms, and say:—
'See, sweet, you liked these yester-eve; like them for *me* today!'   25

She has no care, my Stars, of you or me;
She has no care, we tire her speedily;
She has no care, because she cannot see—
She cannot see, who sees not past her sight.
We are too high, we tire her with our height: 30
Her years are small, and ill to strain above.
She may not love us: wherefore keep we love
To her who may not love us—you and I?
And yet you thrill down towards her, even as I,
With all your golden eloquence held in mute.   35
We may not plead, we may not plead our suit;
Our wingèd love must beat against its bars:
For should she enter once within those guarding bars,
Our love would do her hurt—oh, think of that, my Stars!

12–13 reference to King Oedipus in Sophocles' plays *Oedipus the King* and *Oedipus at Colonus*. After he was blinded he went forth with his daughter to become a wanderer.

All Flesh

The title is derived from Isaiah 38 : 6: 'All flesh is grass.'

I do not need the skies'
Pomp, when I would be wise;
For pleasaunce nor to use
Heaven's champaign when I muse.
One grass-blade in its veins   5
Wisdom's whole flood contains:
Thereon my foundering mind
Odyssean fate can find.

*

O little blade, now vaunt
Thee, and be arrogant!   10
Tell the proud sun that he
Sweated in shaping thee;
Night, that she did unvest
Her mooned and argent breast
To suckle thee; Heaven fain   15
Yearned over thee in rain,
And with wide parent wing
Shadowed thee, nested thing!
Fed thee, and slaved for thy
Impotent tyranny.   20
Nature's broad thews bent
Meek for thy content.
Mastering littleness,
Which the wise heavens confess,
The frailty which doth draw   25
Magnipotence to its law;
These were, O happy one, these
Thy laughing puissances!
Be confident of thought,
Seeing that thou art naught;   30
And be thy pride thou'rt all
Delectably safe and small.
Epitomized in thee
Was the mystery
Which shakes the spheres conjoint—   35
God focussed to a point.

All thy fine mouths shout
Scorn upon dull-eyed doubt.
Impenetrable fool
Is he thou canst not school   40
To this humility
By which the angels see!
Unfathomably framed
Sister, I am not shamed,
Before the cherubin,   45
To vaunt my flesh thy kin.
My one hand thine, and one
Imprisoned in God's own,
I am as God; alas,

And such a god of grass!   50
A little root clay-caught,
A wind, a flame, a thought,
Inestimably nought.

53 *nought   Works*: naught!

Of Nature: Laud and Plaint

The final manuscript, a fair copy in ink, is included with the 'Sight and Insight' poems as prepared for publication, but was withdrawn. The *Works* text is heavily edited from this manuscript, with many deletions as shown in the endnotes. Whereas the manuscript as reproduced here runs to 228 lines, the edited text has 172. The theme is close to that of Thompson's essay 'Nature's Immortality' (*Works* 3, pp. 78–88). The poem also alludes to Wordsworth's 'Immortality Ode'.

Lo, here stand I and Nature, gaze to gaze,
And I the greater; couch thou at my feet,
Barren of heart, and beautiful of ways,
Strong to weak purpose, fair and brute-brained beast.
I am not of thy fools,   5
Who goddess thee with impious flatteries sweet,
Stolen from the little Schools
Which cheeped when that great mouth of Rydal ceased;
And gaud thee in the customary phrase
Wherewith, by purblind use,   10
Thy poor ape, woman, still is graced—
Though 'twixt your deities small be to choose,
And either service waste.
A little suffer that I try
What thou art, child, and what am I—   15
Thy younger, forward brother, subtle and small,
As thou art gross and of thy person great withal.

Behold, the child
With Nature needs not to be reconciled.
The babe that keeps the womb   20
Questions not if with love
The life distrainèd for its uses come;
Nor we demand then of
The Nature who is in us and around us,

Whose life doth compass, feed, and bound us,   25
(Thinking sufficiency,
That of the Is, it is the way to be,)
What prompteth her to bless
With gifts unknown for gifts our innocent thanklessness.
Mother unguessed is she, to whom   30
We still are in the womb;
Nor yet the Curse's working, and
The soon-delivering hand
Of sin to share the insensible kind cord.
After, a space   35
We from her yielded bosom draw the nursing grace,
And love or thanks for that less intimate boon
No more afford,
Than to the sun the milky suckling moon.
Then comes the incidental day   40
When our young mouth is weaned; and from her arms we stray.

'Tis over: not, mistake me not,
Those divine gleams forgot
Which one with a so ampler mouth hath sung;
Not of these sings   45
My weak endeavouring tongue;
But of those simpler things
Less heavenful: the unstrained integrity
Moving most natively,
As the glad customed lot   50
Of birthright privilege allows,
Through the domestic chambers of its Father's house:
The virgin hills, provoking to be trod,
The cloud, the stream, the tree,
The allowing bosom of the warm-breathed sod,   55
No alien and untemptable delight—
The wonder in a wondrous sight
Was wondrous simple, as our simple God.
Yet not düllèd daily, base,
But sweet and safe possession as our mother's face,   60
Which we not knew for sweet, but sweetly had;
For who says—'Lo, how sweet!' has first said—'Lo, how sad!'
This, not to be regained with utmost sighs,
This unconsidered birthright is made void
As Edom's, and destroyed.   65

*

Nature, thy life is with us and around us,
Feedeth and doth compass us and bound us,
Yet; but not as once thou fed'st us,
Or by the young hand led'st us.
Grown man, we now despise   70
Thee, known for woman, nor too wise;
As still the mother human
Is known for not too wise, and even woman.
We take ingrateful, for a blinded while,
Thine ignorant, sweet smile: 75
Yea, now we follow other lures,
And smiles of maidens, knowing not,
Ah Nature, they are but as yours,
And little more the meed of maidens' wooers,
When all the heaven we have of them is got.   80
Yield they their eyes unto their lovers' gaze?—
Why, so dost thou: and is their gracious favour
Doled but to draw us on through warpèd ways,
Delays behind delays,
To tempt with scent, and to deny the savour?—   85
Thou canst no less, canst sit as well content
But to be fair, and hear thy lovers' praise;
And with as sweet aspèct and debonair,
Delectably untouchèd ravishment,
Comfort thyself in their despair,   90
As any she that poets' plaudits raise.
Ah, Lady, if that vengeance were thy bent,
Woman should 'venge thee for thy scornèd smiles:
Her ways are as thy ways,
Her wiles are as thy wiles.   95

Not unlearned youth surmise,
What gay and facile-flowering cruelties
Make bended brows of tyrants clement show
To those dove-seemings of a virgin's eyes.
Seek pity of the worm that never dies,   100
And thou may'st find it, ere thou find a part
Of ruth in little heart.
And let thy feet take hold on lowest hell,
For there all mercies dwell,
Though mercies in disguise;   105
But not where laughing low,

Maids pluck the wing from men like summer-flies.
And he that to the brim,
Even for the clusters of Engeddi athirst,
With wine of asps his life hath crownèd so,   110
Which shrinking from the envenomed glow,
Like to a Venice glass hath foamed and burst;
At Nature's feet rejected casteth him,—
For cure of fiery woe
Looking upon that brazen snake,   115
As weak an idol as the woman erst,
As doomed to overthrow;
And, till from the new frenzy he awake,
Does to like foil through like wild mazes go.

No second joy; one only first and over,   120
Which all life wanders from and looks back to;
For sweet too sweet, till sweet is past recover:—
Let bitter Love, and every bitter lover
Say, Love's not bitter, if I speak not true.
The first kiss to repeat!   125
The first—'Mine only Sweet!'
Thine only sweet that sweetness, very surely,
And a sour truth thou spakest, if thou knew.
That first kiss to restore
By Nature given so frankly, taken so securely!   130
To knit again the broken chain, once more
To run and be to the Sun's bosom caught;
Over life's bended brows prevail
With laughters of the insolent nightingale,
Jocund of heart in darkness; to be taught   135
Once more the daisy's tale,
And hear each sun-smote buttercup clang bold,
A beaten gong of gold;
To call delaying Phoebus up with chanticleer;
Once more, once more to see the Dawn unfold   140
Her rosy bosom to the married Sun;
Fulfilled with his delight
Perfected in sweet fear—
Sweet fear, that trembles for sweet joy begun,
As slowly drops the swathing night,   145
And all her barèd beauty lies warm-kissed and won!
                              *

No extreme rites of penitence avail
To lighten thee of knowledge, to impart
Once more the language of the daisy's tale,
And that doctorial Art 150
Of knowing-not to thine oblivious heart!
Of all the vain
Words of man's mouth, there are no words so vain
As 'once more' and 'again!'
Hope not of Nature; she nor gives nor teaches; 155
She suffers thee to take
But what thine own hand reaches,
And can itself make sovereign for thine ache.
Ah, hope not her to heal
The ills she cannot feel, 160
Or dry with many-businessed hand the tear
Which never yet was weak
In her unfretted eyes, on her uncarkèd cheek.
O heart of Nature! did man ever hear
Thy beating once anear?— 165
Alas, it is the beating of his own!
O voice of Nature! did man ever hear
Thy yearned-for word, supposèd-dear?—
His pleading voice returns to him alone;
He hears none other tone. 170
No, no;
Take back, O poets, your praises little-wise,
Nor fool weak hearts to their unshunned distress,
Who deem that even after your device
They shall lie down in Nature's holiness: 175
For it was never so;
She has no hands to bless.
Her pontiff thou; she looks to thee,
O man; she has no use, nor asks not for thy knee,
Which but bewilders her, 180
Poor child; nor seeks thy fealty,
And those divinities thou wouldst confer.
If thou wouldst bend in prayer,
Arise, pass forth, thou must look otherwhere.
Thy travail all is null; 185
This Nature fair,
This gate is closèd, this Gate Beautiful,
No man shall go in there,

Since the Lord God did pass through it;
'Tis sealed unto the King,   190
The King Himself shall sit
Therein, with them that are His following.
Go, leave thy labour null;
Ponder this thing.

Lady divine!   195
That giv'st to men good wine,
But yet the best thou hast
And nectarous, keepest to the last,
And bring'st not forth before the Master's sign:
How few there be thereof that ever taste,   200
Quaffing in brutish haste,
Without distinction of thy great repast!
For ah, this Lady I have much miscalled,
Nor fault in her, but in thy wooing is;
And her allowèd lovers that are installed,   205
Find her right frank of her sweet heart, y-wis.
Then if thy wooing thou wouldst 'gin,
Lo here the door; straight and rough-shapen 'tis,
And scant they be that ever here make stays;
But do the lintel miss,   210
In dust of these blind days.
Knock; tarry thou and knock,
Although it seem but rock:
Here is the door where thou must enter in
To heart of Nature and of woman too,   215
And olden things made new.
Stand at the door and knock;
For it unlocked,
Shall all locked things unlock,
And win but here, thou shalt to all things win,   220
And thou no more be mocked.
For know, this Lady Nature thou hast left,
Of whom thou fear'st thee reft,
This Lady is God's daughter, and she lends
Her hand but to His friends;   225
But to her Father's friends the hand which thou wouldst win.
Then enter in;
And here is that which shall for all make mends.

---

8 *great mouth of Rydal* William Wordworth. **9** *gaud* adorn. **9–13** not in *Works*. **22** *dis-*

trainèd allocated. **26–7** We think it is enough to base our knowledge of our being on the fact that we exist. Lines not in *Works*. **32–9** not in *Works*. **32–4** general reference to the burden of original sin we take on at birth. **34** *share* cut. **42–46** FT makes clear here that unlike Wordsworth in his 'Immortality Ode', he is not going to touch on the Platonic doctrine of *anamnesis*, the idea of pre-existence: 'Our birth is but a sleep and a forgetting: The soul . . . cometh from afar . . . trailing clouds of glory . . .' **63–4** new stanza in *Works*. **65** *Edom* Jacob's eldest son, Esau, and later the land he inhabited. **76–80** not in *Works*. **79** *meed* reward. **81** (57 in *Works*) *they Works*: maids. **85** Two lines (61–2) in *Works*. **86–91** not in *Works*. **96–119** not in *Works*. **109** *Engeddi*: oasis near the Dead Sea. **112** *a Venice glass* one believed to shatter when poison was put in it. **115** *brazen snake* the brazen serpent God ordered Moses to fashion to cure the Israelites of snake bites. **116** *erst* formerly. **119** *foil* repulse. **139** *Phoebus* sun god; *chanticleer* cock. **163–4** new stanza in *Works*. **163** *uncarkèd* smooth. **165–7** not in *Works*.

'Prologue to a Pastoral'

These lines appear in *Works* 3 as a footnote to the opening passage of the essay 'Nature's Immortality', for which they form a paraphrase. According to a note by Meynell they were written as the prologue for an unfinished 'Pastoral Play', the manuscript for which is at BC. A complete manuscript of the 'Prologue' with some corrections appears on the verso of p. 61 of the manuscript of Thompson's essay on Shelley, written in 1888. The passage paraphrased clarifies the theme:

> In the days when days were fable, before the grim Tartar fled from Cathay, or the hardy Goth from the shafted Tartar; before the hardy Goth rolled on the hot Kelt, or the hot Kelt on Italy; before the wolf-cubs lolled tongues of prey, or Rhodian galleys sheered the brine, an isle there was which has passed into the dreams of men, itself
>
> > Full of sweet dreams, and health, and quiet breathing.
>
> And when the Muses talked, they named it Sicily. Was it, and is it not? Alas, where's Eden, or Taprobane? Where flows Alpheus now? You take a map (great Poetry! have they mapped Heaven?) and show me—what? The dust-heap of Italy; a thing spurned contemptuously from the toe of the Ausonian mainland; you point to it, you man of knowledge, and this, you say, is Sicily. You may be right, I know not; but it is not Sicily to me.

The essay continues to show that each of us has our secret 'Sicily', a dream-world where Paradise still exists. The line of verse is from Keats' *Endymion*.

> Ere the fierce Tartar fled Cathay,
>   The stark Goth shafted Tartary,
> The fiery Kelt the Gothic fray,—
>   And the Kelt rolled on Italy;
> Ere the wolf-cubs lolled tongues of prey,   5
> Or Rhodian galleys sheered the sea,
> An isle there was—where is't to-day?—
>   The Muses called it Sicily.

Was it, and is it not?—Aye me,
Where's Eden, or Taprobane?   10
Where now does old Simaethus flow?
    You take a map (great Poesy,
Have they mapped Heaven!) and thereon show—
    What?—the dust-heap of Italy!
The Ausonian mainland from its toe   15
    Spurns it aside contemptuously.
    And this, you say, is Sicily.
I know not, how the thing may be—
It is not Sicily to me!

10 *Taprobane* Greek name for Sri Lanka. 11 *Simaethus* the Simeto river in Sicily. 15
Ausonian Italian.

'Pastoral'

These lines form the opening for the second scene of the unfinished 'Pastoral
Play' as described in the headnote for the previous poem. They are written in
another hand, ascribed by Connolly to Monica Meynell (TLC*Poems*, p. 418).

Pan-imbued
Tempe wood,
Pretty players' sporting-place;
Tempe wood's
Solitude's   5
Everywhere a courting-place.
Kiss me, sweet
Tipsy-feet,
Though a kissed maid hath her red:
Kisses grow—   10
Trust me so—
Faster than they're gatherèd.

I will play a tune
On the pipes of ivory,
All long noon   15
Fluting of a melody;
A merry, merry, merry, merry,
Merry, merry melody.
Dance, ho! foot it so! feat fleets the melody!

Let the wise   20
   Say—Youth dies:
'Tis for pleasure's mending, Sweet!
   Kisses are
   Costlier far
That they have an ending, Sweet!   25
   Half a kiss's
   Dainty bliss is
From the day of Kiss-no-more;
   When we shall,
   Roseal   30
Lass, do this and this no more!

I will play a tune
   On the pipes of ivory;
All long noon
   Piping of a melody,—   35
A merry, merry, merry, merry
   Merry, merry melody.
Dance, ho! foot it so! feat fleets the melody!

My love must
   Be to trust,   40
While you safely fold me close:
   Yours will smile
   A kissing-while,
For the hour of hold-me-close.
   Maiden gold   45
   Clipping bold
Where the truest mintage is:
   Lips will bear
   But, I swear,
In the press their vintages!   50

So I play a tune
   On the pipes of ivory,
All long noon
   Fluting of a melody,—
A merry, merry, merry, merry   55
   Merry, merry melody.
Dance, ho! foot it so! feat fleets the melody!

Throughout, in *Works* there is no break before the refrain which the concluding lines to each stanza form. 8 *Tipsy-feet Works*: Gipsy fleet. 13 *play Works*: flute. 16 *Fluting*

Works: Piping. **32** *I will play a tune Works*: And we pipe a tune. **35** *Piping Works*: Fluting. **41** *hold me close Works*: fold me close. **51** *So I play a tune Works*: I will flute a
tune. **54** *Fluting Works*: Piping.

Past Thinking of Solomon

The quotation from the Book of Ecclesiastes at the start of the poem in *Works*
omits the phrase 'before the time of affliction come'. As there is no manuscript it is
not possible to know whether the mistake can be attibuted to Thompson but it is
unlikely considering his notable knowledge of the Bible and particularly of this
Book. The error is repeated in T L C *Poems*, p. 140.

> Remember thy Creator in the days of thy youth, before the time of
> affliction come, and the years draw nigh of which thou shalt say:
> They please me not: Before the sun, and the light, and the moon
> and the stars be darkened, and the clouds return after the rain.
>
> (Eccles. 12:1–2)

Wise-unto-hell Ecclesiast,
Who siev'dst life to the gritted last!

This thy sting, thy darkness, Mage—
Cloud upon sun, upon youth age?

Now is come a darker thing,   5
And is come a colder sting,

Unto us, who find the womb
Opes on the courtyard of the tomb.

Now in this fuliginous
City of flesh our sires for us   10

Darkly built, the sun at prime
Is hidden, and betwixt the time

Of day and night is variance none,
Who know not altern moon and sun;

Whose deposed heaven through dungeon-bars   15
Looks down blinded of its stars.

Yea, in the days of youth, God wot,
Now we say: They please me not.

Title *Solomon* the alleged author of Ecclesiastes. **3** *Mage* sage or wise man. **9** *fuliginous* dark.

Insentience

No manuscript has been found for this poem.

> O sweet is Love, and sweet is Lack!
>   But is there any charm
> When Lack from round the neck of Love
>   Drops her languid arm?
>
> Weary, I no longer love,   5
>   Weary, no more lack;
> O for a pang, that listless Loss
> Might wake, and, with a playmate's voice,
>   Call the tired Love back!

A Hollow Wood

An important reference to this poem occurs in Christopher Hassall's biography of Edward Marsh, where he writes of Marsh's friendship with the Meynells: 'An evening was spent with Alice Meynell and her husband, discussing the forthcoming edition of Francis Thompson on which they wanted Marsh's advice. While sitting in the window-seat helping Alice Meynell thread her new bead curtain Marsh expressed himself anxious to cut four lines out of the poem 'The Hollow Wood'. 'I steel myself to a sacrifice,' wrote Meynell next day, 'that I knew the poet would have sanctioned under my considered approval' (*Edward Marsh, Patron of the Arts*, 1959, pp. 213–14). That there is no adequate basis for such an observation has been made clear in the Introduction to the present edition (p. xxx). In fact, Meynell cut a further five lines from the manuscript, which is a complete fair copy as reproduced here (see endnotes).

> This is the mansion built for me
> By the sweating centuries;
> Roofed with intertwinèd tree,
> Woofed with green for my princelier ease
> Who am from loins of the centuries;   5
> Tapestried with waving dream
> And shapes of things that are or seem.
> Here I lie with my world about me
> Shadowed off from the world without me,
> Even as my thoughts embosom me   10
> From wayside humanity—
> Me who here, in my secret green,
> Toss back song for song, I ween,
> To the insolent lark in his secret blue.

A fast immure of poesy   15
Girds the precincts viewlessly,
And here can only enter who
Delight me—the pricèd few.
Come you in, and make you cheer,
It draweth toward my banquet-time: 20
Would you win to my universe?
Your thought must turn in the wards of rhyme;
Loose the chain of linkèd verse,
Stoop your knowledge, and enter here.

Here cushioned ivies you invite   25
To fall to with appetite.—
What for my viands?—
   Dainty thoughts.
What for my brows?—
   Forget-me-nots.   30
What for my feet?—
   A bath of green.
My servers?—
   Phantasies unseen.
What shall I find me for feasting-dress?—   35
Your white disusèd childlikeness.
What hid music will laugh to my calls?—
An orgie of mad bird-bacchanals.
Such meats, such music, such coronals!
From the cask which the summer sets aflow,   40
Under the roof of my raftered house,
The birds above, we below,
We carouse as they carouse.
Or have but the ear the ear within,
And you may hear, if you hold you mute,   45
You may hear, by my amulet,
The wind-like keenness of violin,
The enamelled tone of shallow flute,
And the furry richness of clarinet.
These are the things shall make you cheer,   50
If you will grace my banquet-time:
Would you win to my universe?—
Your thought must turn in the wards of rhyme;
Loose the chains of linkèd verse,
Stoop your knowledge, and enter here.   55

5–7 not in *Works*. 12–16 not in *Works*.

'A double need'

(To W—)

The only surviving manuscript is a rough draft but the poem is included here in accordance with the editorial procedure described in the Introduction. The dedication to Wilfrid Meynell clarifies the theme. Whereas in the past the poet could regard his achievement as some return for all he had received from his patron and friend, with the passing of his earlier inspiration there is now a 'double need' which has become a constant burden.

> Ah, gone the days when for undying kindness
> I still could render you undying song!
> You yet can give, but I can give no more;
> Fate, in her extreme blindness,
> Has wrought me so great wrong.   5
> I am left poor indeed;
> Gone is my sole and amends-making store,
> And I am needy with a double need.
>
> Behold that I am like a fountained nymph,
> Lacking her customed lymph,   10
> The longing parched in stone upon her mouth,
> Unwatered of its ancient plenty. She
> (Remembering her irrevocable streams,)
> A Thirst made marble, sits perpetually
> With sundered lips of still-memorial drouth.   15

10 *lymph* pure water.

Love's Varlets

The title takes the *OED* definition of 'varlet' as a 'low fellow, a rascal' and the sonnet then acts as a kind of commentary on the parable of the Pharisee and the Publican (Luke 23 : 10–14). In *Works* the alternate lines are indented, but otherwise there are only minor variants in punctuation.

> Love, he is nearer (though the moralist
> Of rule and line cry shame on me) more near
> To thee and to the heart of thee, be't wist,
> Who sins against thee, even for the dear
> Lack that he hath of thee; than who, chill-wrapt   5
> In thy light-thought-on customed livery,
> Keeps all thy laws with formal service apt,
> Save that great law to tremble and to be

Shook to his heart-strings if there do but pass
The rumour of thy pinions. Such one is   10
Thy varlet, guerdoned with the daily mass
That feed on thy remainder-meats of bliss.
  More hath he of thy bosom, whose slips of grace
  Fell through despair of thy close-gracious face.

Laus Amara Doloris

A Double Ode

The title translates as 'The Bitter Praise of Sorrow'. In *Works* there are deletions
and other changes from the final manuscript, followed here, for which see the
endnotes. A card accompanying the manuscript refers to it as a 'rough draft'
although clearly it is a final one. Presumably this was to cover the alterations made
in the text when published in *Works*. In *Works* there is no subtitle as above, nor the
divisions into 'Ode' and 'Palinode'. A palinode in an ode or song retracts that part
which has preceded it.

Ode

Implacable sweet daemon, Poetry,
What have I lost for thee!
Whose lips too sensitively well
Have shaped thy shrivelling oracle.
So much as I have lost, O world, thou hast,   5
And for thy plenty I am waste:
Ah, count, O world, my cost!
Ah, count, O world, thy gain!
For thou hast nothing gained but I have lost.
And ah, my loss is such,   10
If thou have gained as much
Thou hast even harvest of Egyptian years;
And that great overflow which gives thee grain—
The bitter Nilus of my risen tears!

I witness call the austere goddess, Pain,   15
Whose mirrored image trembles where it lies
In my confronting eyes,
If I have learned her sad and solemn scroll?
Have I neglected her high sacrifice,
Spared my heart's children from the sacred knife,   20
Or turned her customed footing from my soul?

Yea, thou pale Ashtaroth who rul'st my life,
Of my poor offspring thou hast claimed the whole.
One after one they passed at thy desire
To sacrificial sword, or sacrificial fire;   25
Save one,
Save one alone
I gave thee all, pale Dole.
One have I hid apart,
The latest-born and loveliest of my heart,   30
From thy requiring eyes.
O hope most futile of futilities!
Thine iron summons comes again,
O inevadable Pain!!
Not faithless to my pact, I yield: 'tis here,   35
That solitary and fair,
That most sweet, last, and dear;
Swerv'st thou? Behold, I swerve not:—strike, nor spare!
Not my will shudders, but my flesh,
In awful secrecy to hear   40
The wind of thy great treading sweep afresh
Athwart my face, and agitate my hair.
The ultimate unnerving dearness take,
The extreme rite of abnegation make,
And sum in one all renderings that were.   45
The agony is done,
Her footstep passes on;—
The unchilded chambers of my heart rest bare.
The love, but not the loved, remains;
As where a flower has pressed a leaf   50
The page yet keeps the trace and stains.
For thy delight, world, one more grief!
My world, one loss more for thy gains!

Palinode

Yet, yet, ye few, to whom is given   55
This weak singing, I have learned.
Ill the starry roll of heaven,
Were this all that I discerned
Or of Poetry or Pain.
Song! turn on thy hinge again!   60
Thine alternate panel showed,
Give the Ode a Palinode!

Pain, not thou an Ashtaroth,
Glutted with a bloody rite,
But the icy bath which doth   65
String the slack sinews loosened with delight.
O great Key-bearer and Keeper
Of the treasuries of God!
Wisdom's love is buried deeper
Than the arm of man can go,   70
Save thou show
First the way, and turn the sod.
Ill does the poet who
Takes the bride Joy, nor thee, pale Leah, too;
Still doth the Lord   75
To the stave Beauty add thy rigid Cord;
And when with sacrifice of costliest cost
On my heart's altar is the Eterne adored,
Thy fire from heaven consumes the holocaust.
Nay, to vicegerence o'er the wide-confined   80
And mutinous principate of man's restless mind
With thine anointing oils the singer is designed:
To that most desolate station
Thine is his deep and dolorous consecration.
Oh! when thy chrism shall dry upon my brow,   85
By that authentic sign I know
The sway is parted from this tenuous hand:
And all the wonted dreams which rankèd stand,
The high majestic state,
And cloud-consorting towers of visionary Land,   90
To some young usurpation needs must go;
And I am all unsceptred of command.
Disdiademed I wait,
To speak with sieging Death, mine enemy, in the gate.

Preceptress in the wars of God!   95
His tyros draw the unmortal sword,
And their celestial virtue exercise,
Beneath thy rigorous eyes.
Thou severe bride, with the glad suit adored
Of many a lover whose love is unto blood;   100
Every jewel in their crown
Thy lapidary hand does own;
Nor that deep jacinth of the heart can put

True lustre forth till it be cut.
Thou settest thine abode   105
A portress in the gateways of all love,
And tak'st the toll of joys; no maid is wed,
But thou dost draw the curtains of her bed.
Yea, on the brow of mother and of wife
Descends thy confirmation from above,   110
A Pentecostal flame; and love's great bread
Consecrated
Not sacramental is, but with thy leaven!
Thou pacest either frontier where our life
Marches with God's, both birth and death are given   115
Into thy lordship; those debated lands
Are subject to thy hands:
The border-warden thou of Heaven!
Yea, that same awful angel with the glaive
Which in disparadising orbit swept   120
Lintel, and pilaster, and architrave
Of Eden-gates, and forth before it drave
The primal pair, then first whose startled eyes,
With pristine drops o' the no less startled skies
Their own commingling, wept;—   125
With strange affright
Sin knew the bitter first baptismal rite.

Save through thy ministry man is not fed;
Thou uninvoked presid'st and unconfest,
The mistress of his feast: 130
From the earth we gain our bread; and like the bread
Dropt and regatherèd
By a child crost and thwart,
Whom need makes eat, though sorely weep he for't,
It tastes of dust and tears.   135

Iron Ceres of an earth where since the curse
Man has had power perverse
Beside God's good to set his evil seed!
Those shining acres of the musket-spears,
Where flame and wither with swift intercease   140
Flowers of red sleep that not the cornfield bears,
Do yield thee minatory harvest, when
Unto the seeding-time of sensual ease

Implacably succeed
The bristling issues of the sensual deed;   145
And like to meteors from a rotting fen
The fiery pennons flit o'er the stagnation
Of the world's sluggish and putrescent life,
Misleading to engulfing desolation,
And blind, retributive, unguessing strife,   150
The fatal footsteps of pursuing men.

Thy pall in purple sovereignty was dipt
Beneath the tree of Golgotha;
And from the Hand wherein the reed was clipt
Thy bare and antique sceptre thou dost draw.   155
That God-sprung Lover to thy front allows,
Fairest, the bloody honour of His brows,
The great reversion of that diadem
Which did His drenched locks hem.
For the predestinated Man of Grief,   160
O regnant Pain, to thee
His subject sway elected to enfeoff;
And from thy sad conferring to endure
The sanguine state of His investiture;
Yea, at thy hand, most sombre suzerain,   165
That dreadful crown He held in fealty;
O Queen of Calvary,
Holy and terrible, anointed Pain!

12–14 reference to the Egyptian harvests on the banks of the Nile as among the richest in the world, fertilised by the silt deposited by the flooding river each year. **20** *from Works*: to (deleted by FT in MS). **22** *Ashtaroth* Egyptian moon goddess. **23** *claimed Works*: had. **26–8** *Works* reduces to single line: All, all, save one, the sole. **30** *loveliest Works*: sweetest. **31–2** stanza break in *Works*. **34** *inevadable* unavoidable. **45–6** stanza break in *Works*. **65** *that Works*: which. **72–5** not in *Works*, which substitutes lines from an earlier draft: The poet's crown, with misty weakness tarnished, / In thy golden fire is burnished / To round with more illustrious gleam his forehead. **74** *Leah* Jacob was constrained to marry Leah, the plain elder sister of Rachel whom he loved, in accordance with ancient Jewish Law, that the elder must wed before the younger. **76** FT note: 'And I took unto me two rods: one I called Beauty, and the other I called A Cord: and I fed the flock' (Zach. 11:7). This obscure prophecy refers to shepherds' staves, here representing two ways of God's dealings with his people, one by gentle means, the other by means of punishments. **79** *holocaust* sacrifice. **80** *vicegerence* delegated power to rule. **81** *principate* state ruled by a prince. **80–7** references to holy oils used at ordinations or coronations. **87** *sway* control. **88** *which Works*: that. **96** *tyros* armed bands. **103** *jacinth* red gem. **104** *True lustre Works*: Its lustres. **113–14** stanza break in *Works*. **119** *glaive* sword. **140** *intercease* alternate pattern of cessation. **142** *minatory* threatening. **143** *seeding Works*: fallow. **146** the phenomenon of the will-o'-the-wisp, the light caused by burning methane over marshlands. **162** *enfeoff* invest. **165** *suzerain* feudal lord. **166** *fealty* obligation of loyalty to a feudal lord.

To Olivia

No manuscript has survived, but in his Introduction to *Selected Poems*, published in 1908, Meynell quoted the first two lines of this sonnet, describing it as 'some newly pencilled lines' found after Thompson's death and addressed to Olivia Meynell, 'recalling the strains of fifteen years before': that is, the period when he was writing the poems to the Meynell children.

> I fear to love thee, Sweet, because
> Love's the ambassador of loss;
> White flake of childhood, clinging so
> To my soiled raiment, thy shy snow
> At tenderest touch will shrink and go.   5
> Love me not, delightful child.
> My heart, by many snares beguiled,
> Has grown timorous and wild.
> It would fear thee not at all,
> Wert thou not so harmless-small.   10
> Because thy arrows, not yet dire,
> Are still unbarbed with destined fire,
> I fear thee more than hadst thou stood
> Full-panoplied in womanhood.

'Peace'

'On the Treaty in South Africa in 1902'

Thompson was commissioned by the *Daily Chronicle* to write an ode to mark the end of the Boer War but never completed it. The number of drafts in several notebooks as well as the separate manuscript, far from finished, testify to the difficulty he found in attempting to celebrate an occasion in which he, like many others at the time, saw little cause for rejoicing. Many of the sentiments expressed here echo those in the earlier ode 'To England'. In *Works* the text has been edited from the many variants in the manuscript. Although it is not possible to know how Thompson himself might have completed it, this text is given here in accordance with the editorial policy for *Works* as described in the Introduction. In his notes Connolly refers to a comparison in preparation between the manuscript and the published text, part of the catalogue of the BC collection which was apparently never undertaken (see Introduction, p. xxxiii; also TLC*Poems*, p. 533). The manuscript has no title or subtitle.

Peace:—as a dawn that flares
Within the brazier of the barrèd East,
Kindling the ruinous walls of storm surceased
To rent and roughened glares,
After such night when lateral wind and rain   5
Torment the to-and-fro perplexèd trees
With thwart encounter; which, of fixture strong,
Take only strength from the endurèd pain:
And throat by throat begin
The birds to make adventure of sweet din,   10
Till all the forest prosper into song:—
     Peace, even such a peace,
(O be my words an auspice!) dawns again
Upon our England, from her lethargies
Healed by that baptism of *her* cleansing pain.   15

Ended, the long endeavour of the land:
Ended, the set of manhood towards the sand
Of thirsty death; and their more deadly death,
Who brought back only what they fain had lost,
No more worth-breathing breath,—   20
Gone the laborious and use-working hand.
Ended, the patient drip of women's tears,
Which joined the patient drip of faithful blood
To make of blood and water the sore flood
That pays our conquest's costliest cost.   25
This day, if fate dispose,
Shall make firm friends from firm and firm-met foes.
And now, Lord, since Thou hast upon hell's floor
Bound, like a snoring sea, the blood-drowsed bulk of War,
Shall we not cry, on recognising knees,   30
This is Thy peace?

If, England, it be but to lay
The heavy head down, the old heavy way;
Having a space awakened and been bold
To break from them that had thee in the snare,—   35
Resume the arms of thy false Dalila, Gold,
Shameful and nowise fair:
Forget thy sons who have lain down in bed
With Dingaan and old dynasties, nor heed
The ants that build their empires overhead;   40
Forget their large in thy contracted deed,
And that thou stand'st twice-pledged to being great
For whom so many children greatly bleed,
Trusting thy greatness with their deaths: if thou,

England, incapable of proffered fate,   45
See in such deaths as these
But purchased pledges of unhindered mart,
And hirelings spent that in thy ringed estate
For some space longer now
Thou may'st add gain to gain, and take thine ease,—   50
God has made hard thy heart;
Thou hast but bought thee respite, not surcease.
Lord, this is not Thy peace!

But wilt thou, England, stand
With vigilant heart and prescient brain?—   55
Knowing there is no peace
Such as fools deem, of equal-balanced ease:—
That they who build the State
Must, like the builders of Jerusalem,
The trowel in their hand,   60
Work with the sword laid ever nigh to them.
If thou hold Honour worthy gain
At price of gold and pain;
And all thy sail and cannon somewhat more
Than the fee'd watchers of the rich man's store.   65
If thou discern the thing which all these ward
Is that imperishable thing, a Name,
And that Name, England, which alone is lord
Where myriad-armèd India owns with awe
A few white faces; uttered forth in flame   70
Where circling round the earth
Has English battle roared;
Deep in mid-forest African a Law;
That in this Name's small girth
The treasure is, thy sword and navies guard: 75
If thou wilt crop the specious sin of ease,
Whence still is War's increase,—
Proud flesh, which asks for War, the knife of God,
Save to thyself, thyself use cautery;
Wilt stay the war of all with all at odd,   80
And teach thy jarring sons
Truth innate once,—
That in the whole alone the part is blest and great.
O should this fire of war thus purge away
The inveterate stains of too-long ease,   85
And yield us back our Empire's clay
Into one shoreless State
Compact and hardened for its uses: these
No futile sounds of joyance are today;—
Lord, unrebuked we may   90
Call this Thy peace!

*

And in this day be not
Wholly forgot
They that made possible but shall not see
Our solemn jubilee.   95
Peace most to them who lie
Beneath unnative sky;
In whose still hearts is dipt
Our reconciling script:
Peace! But when shouts shall start the housetop bird,   100
Let these, that speak not, be the loudest heard!

36 *false Dalila* her seductive wiles robbed Samson of his strength (Judges 16). **39** *Dingaan* Zulu chief defeated by the Boers in 1838. **59** *builders of Jerusalem* When Jerusalem was rebuilt after the Exile, the builders were armed against their enemies (Esdras 4:16–18).

AD AMICAM: FIVE SONNETS FROM THE AD AMICAM NOTEBOOK

This sequence of five sonnets gives the title to the Ad Amicam Notebook, for a full description of which, see pp. 435–6. Like most of the contents, they were addressed to Katie King. The original manuscripts of these sonnets are at the Lilly Library, Indiana University, with photostats at BC. In addition, at BC there are rough drafts, but the final texts are followed here. There are some variants in the *Works* texts which, where more significant than punctuation, are given in the endnotes. All five sonnets are written out as printed here, but in *Works* their alternate lines are indented.

I

Dear dove, that bear'st to my sole-labouring ark
The olive-branch of so long-wishèd rest,
When the white solace glimmers through my dark
Of nearing wings, what comfort in my breast!
Oh, may that doubted day not come, not come,   5
When you shall fail, my heavenly messenger,
And drift into the distance and the doom
Of all my impermissable things that were!
Rather than so, now make the sad farewell,
While yet may be with not too-painèd pain,   10
Lest I again the acquainted tale should tell
Of sharpest loss that pays for shortest gain.
    Ah, if my heart should hear no white wings thrill
    Against its waiting window, open still.

2

In *Works* WM adds a note: 'Both in its theme and in its imagery this sonnet was written as a variation of Mrs Meynell's verses "At Night".' Her poem, given in the endnotes, is dedicated 'To W. M.'

> When from the blossoms of the noiseful day
> Unto the hive of sleep and hushèd gloom
> Throng the dim-wingèd dreams; what dreams are they
> That with the wildest honey hover home?
> Oh, they that have from many thousand thoughts   5
> Stolen the strange sweet of ever-blosmy you,
> A thousand fancies in fair-coloured knots
> Which you are inexhausted meadow to.
> Ah, what sharp heathery honey quick with pain
> Do they bring home! It holds the night awake   10
> To hear their lovely murmur in my brain,
> And Sleep's wings have a trouble for your sake.
>   Day and you dawn together: for at end,
>   With the first light breaks the first thought—'My Friend!'

6 *blosmy Works*: blossomy. The change here affects the scansion of the line. Mrs Meynell's verses read:

> Home, home from the horizon far and clear,
>   Hither the soft wings sweep;
> Flocks of the memories of the day draw near
>   The dovecote doors of sleep.
>
> Oh, which are they that come through sweetest light
>   Of all these homing birds?
> Which with the straightest and the swiftest flight?
>   Your words to me, your words!

[3] *Friend*

In the manuscript there is no number to this sonnet, which instead is given the title as above and is prefixed by the following lines from Wordsworth's Sonnet, 'O Nightingale! Thou surely art'.

> I hear a stock-dove sing or say
> Her homely tale this very day
> *   *   *   *   *
> She sang of love with quiet blending,
> Slow to begin, and never ending.

O friend, who mak'st that misspent word of 'friend'
Sweet as the low note that a summer dove
Fondles in her warm throat! And shall it end,
Because so swift on friend and friend broke love?
Lo, when all words to honour thee are spent,   5
And flung a bold stave to the old bald Time,
Telling him that he is too insolent
Who thinks to rase thee from my heart or rhyme;
Whereof to one because thou life hast given,
The other yet shall give a life to thee,   10
Such as to gain, the prowest swords have striven,
And compassed weaker immortality:
    These spent, my heart not stinteth in her breast
    Her sweet 'Friend friend!'—one note, and loves it best.

11 *prowest* proudest.

4

This sonnet is numbered 'II' in the manuscript, as a second part of the previous one.

No, no, it cannot be, it cannot be,
Because this love of close-affinèd friends
In its sweet sudden ambush toilèd me
So swift, that therefore all as swift it ends.
For swift it was, yet quiet as the birth   5
Of smoothest music in a Master's soul,
Whose mild fans lapsing as she slides to earth
Waver in the bold arms which dare control
Her from her lineal heaven; yea, it was still
As the young Moon that bares her nightly breast,   10
And smiles to see the babe Earth suck its fill.
O Halcyon! was thine auspice not of rest?
    Shall this proud verse bid after-livers:—'See,
    How friends could love for immortality.'

12 *Halcyon* fabled bird said to calm the sea in order to float its nest on the waves. 13–14 no
dramatic voice in *Works*.

[5] *Of Her Aura*

The title is omitted in *Works*, where the number has been added instead.

When that part heavenliest of all-heavenly you
First at my side did breathe its blosmy air,
What lovely wilderment alarmed me through!
On what ambrosial effluence did I fare,
And comforts Paradisal! What gales came,   5
Through ports for one divinest space ajar,
Of rankèd lilies blown into a flame
By watered banks where walks of young saints are!
One attent space, my trembling locks did rise
Swayed on the wind, in planetary wheel,   10
Of intervolving sweet societies
From wavèd vesture and from fledgèd heel
    Odorous aspersion trailing. Then, alone
    In her eyes' central glory, God took throne.

2 *blosmy Works*: blossomy. As in Sonnet 2.6 above, the change affects the scansion of this line. **9** *attent* intense.

IN *THE MAN HAS WINGS* (1957)

TWO SONNETS FROM THE AD AMICAM NOTEBOOK

The following two sonnets, addressed to Katie King, are from the Ad Amicam Notebook. (For a description of the manuscripts contained in the Notebook at the Lilly Library, Indiana, see pp. 435–6.) In his notes Connolly refers to using rough drafts rather than the final texts (*MHW*, p. 145). The completed texts, as in the Ad Amicam Notebook, are followed here. The drafts are at BC where there is now a photostat of the contents of the Ad Amicam Notebook.

1 'A bitter friend'

A bitter friend, sweet Friend, you have of me,
How rash of speech, and how unfixed of mood!
And like the sandy Holly of the Sea,
Its very flower to tender touches rude.
A fruit unlovely, and of harshest rind,   5
Is that best homage which I do profess;
And my best kind so twisted with unkind
As wounds thy hand with proffered tenderness.
For so sweet friend a bitter friend! Let be:
I am no comrade for your gentle years;   10
Save were I quite repured, and all of me
Recrystallisèd from dissolvent tears.
    Save this might be, O better thou shouldst part
    Dear Friend, from me, who canst not from my heart!

2 'Alack! my deep offence'

Alack! my deep offence is kneaded in
Even with the very stuff of poetry;
So that, sore striving with the ungracious sin,
Defeat comes hard on my best victory.
Even as a conqueror, feasting in his tent,   5
That is surprisèd by the beaten foe,
Losing the purchase of his hardiment,
From the overthrown receives his overthrow.
Enough for me the sick unfruit of toil,
And the won fight to be won o'er again;   10
But oh! I faint, when that intestine broil
Means to thee pain, my dear, and to thee pain!
    For the renewed fight I am sad and strong;
    But stand from me, lest I should do *thee* wrong!

A POETIC SEQUENCE

In *MHW* and in the final texts in ink at BC the following four poems are given the title 'A Poetic Sequence'.

1 Elijah

When the old prophet's spirit murmurèd
For famine, loneliness, necessitude,
God sent the bird far-visitant which fed
His bitter need, and his sick heart renewed.
No less to me, with spirit all o'ertasked   5
God has sent gentlest succour, and a boon
My rashest tongue as hopefully had asked
As hang petitions on the horns o' the moon.
Whence I resume my fortitude, and hold
The perilous verges of the appointed way,   10
Even to that spot predestined and foretold
Where, on a nigh-at-hand implacable day,
   (Long shown and known in what prenunciant gloom!)
   The sudden gulf goes down to dreadful doom.

3 *bird* Elijah was fed in the desert by ravens.

2 Waiting

Behold, behold!
Come hither, thaw from out their torpid cold,
My thoughts, as weeds in waters are
Congealed with severe frost; how far,
Through the cold mind's unmoving mere,   5
In rigid mockery they appear
Of the life which they have not!
It is not that thou art forgot;
But thou, a most remembered day
Of summer when shrewd skies are grey,   10
Giv'st to the too palpable chill
Contrast, not comfort, howsoe'er I will.
Ah, break my leaden broodings through
With a ray of very you!
A dream of you has wrought me wrong,   15

Wherein one smile was all your tongue;
I woke—alas, my heart frost-stricken
Only into live ache did quicken!
Like an odour whose fine fume
One weak moment doth relume   20
The ruined sun of fallen fields:
The vision parts in tears, and yields
Pang to the poor heart and brain
For a dead day dead again.

Ah, is it dead indeed! I cry;   25
Ah, is it dead, which still can die?
Or is your friendship live? then give
Its life to me, that I may live!
I trust; O help thou my untrust!
The soul stands fast, yet the heart must,   30
In soul's despite, with this thought sicken—
O is that quick, which doth not quicken?

3 *Forgoing*

The white wings come no more: out through the gloom
I look,—no, no, no more! My prayer not fell
Unanswered; she hath made a speedy doom.
Well, it was well; you have done all things well.
I do believe some tender wisdom bade   5
Your choice; I unreproaching, friend late dear,
Say *Fiat*. I am sad, that now was glad;
The last smile is o'ertaken in a tear,
Ere it had time to die, making fair weeping.
A butterfly, that brushes some dark thing   10
Some dusty splendour leaves unto its keeping;
And some good thoughts, late fallen from your wing,
  Tell what bright visitant one moment lit
  On my sad spirit, and then fled from it.

4 'So now, give o'er'

So now, give o'er; for you are lost, I see,
And this poor babe was dead even [in] its birth,
Which I had thought a young Joy born to me,
Who had no child but Sorrow: and with mirth
I gazed upon its face, nor knew it dead,   5
And in my madness vowed that it did smile;
I said: 'Dear Soul, learn laughter, leave thy shed
Sore tears, put off thy mourning weeds a while.
This is our child a space, even though it die
Hereafter; laugh a season, though it be   10
Thy tears are but sad jewels thou put'st by,
One day to wear again.' Very wan she
   Tried, doubting, unused smiles; then bowed her head:—
   'Much tears have made thee blind: this, too, is dead!'

'The solemn voice'

The manuscript is a fair copy with no significant variants. Connolly attributes the lines to Thompson's efforts to overcome his feelings towards Alice Meynell (*MHW*, pp. 145–6).

Do I not hear the solemn voice
The voice which I have heard so long,
Which says: 'Stand like a lonely tower
Amidst the grim lean life which works thee wrong.
Thrust down thy heart: teach Love himself   5
To dread the shaking of the whip,
And fold his lovely passionate wings,
Nor moan against the bitter hurt of things!'
I hear the wind drum and the long rain drip;
I keep the lonely-burning thought of thee   10
Trimmed in my lonely heart,
And all apart
It flickers in the passionate wind
Of longing; with a stern-set mind
I work and watch it patiently.   15
I have endured, and I endure,
I know it is the bitter blast
Of sacrifice which sifts the pure

Snow of the love which lofty souls'
Pained peaks enstoles;   20
I have stood fast, and I stand fast.
But O, rebuke me not if sometimes at the last
Love wakens with a shrill and piercing cry
Amid my life's wide arid sand,
Crying with power   25
No menace of the will can stay:
'O for one hour
To look again into her very eye!
O, for one vital day,
Feel the lost Eden of her very hand!'   30
O friend! that rebel cry dies down;
And I am king still in my iron crown.

Adversity

In addition to the final text in ink in the Notebook of Early Poems there is a rough
draft for this sonnet in NB46B, one of the London streets notebooks. Its theme
arises from the hours Thompson passed in the public libraries and art galleries of
the city during those years.

My soul in desolate royalty of woe
Sits diademed with sorrow as a crown,
All misery's blazing jewelry aglow
On melancholy's dim, majestic gown.
She, wont to sport unblamed with Poetry,   5
Music and Painting, boundlessly content,
Accepted playmate of the glorious three,
For only viol now has loud lament!
And Poetry sits weeping through her hair,
And Painting's eye is misty with its tears.   10
Yet am I to the dead years' riches heir;
Not wholly poor, nor bondslave to my fears.
    My spirit feeds, although my body fast,
    Amid the garnered memories of the Past.

Ecce Ancilla Domini

(National Gallery)

The title is taken from the words spoken by the Blessed Virgin to the Angel at the Annunciation: 'Behold the handmaid of the Lord'. Thompson's subtitle relates the sonnet to the painting by Rossetti of the same title, then in the National Gallery and now removed to the Tate Gallery. He came to know and love this particular painting on his frequent visits to the gallery during his years on the London streets. As well as the final text in ink in the Notebook of Early Poems, a rough draft is contained in NB45, one of the notebooks kept at that time.

This angel's feet, winged with aspiring light,
　　That kindles its own image in the floor,
His gravely noble face, serene in might
　　From gazing on the Godhead evermore;
This lily shining from the lilied land,　　　　　　　　　　5
　　Making a breath of heaven in the room;
Yon dove, whose presence tells how near at hand
　　The mystical conception of her womb:
Were *these* the things that roused from holy dreams
　　To holier waking the elected maid?　　　　　　　　　　10
Absorbed in all the great to-be she seems,
　　With pensive eyes that yet are not afraid.
　　　　Soon her low voice shall ratify heaven's will,
　　　　And hell's gate groan, and death's stern heart stand still.

A Ballad of Fair Weather

As well as the final text in ink in the Notebook of Early Poems, there are two early drafts, in NBs BC24 and 46B. In 46B the draft follows drafts of other poems and fragments grouped together with a note: 'all at present written above Dec. 1886'. That is, the time Thompson made a short visit home and heard of his father's imminent re-marriage and his sister's decision to enter an enclosed religious order. The theme and imagery connect the poem unmistakably with his reaction to these two events and the opium-induced fears they aroused on his return to the streets. For an interpretation of the symbolism and its sources see *BHCC*, pp. 77–9, 365, n. 22.

They went by the greenwood,
　　The sunny-built forest,
They went by the water
　　With hearts of the sorest;

They sought through the branches   5
   Entangled together,
The fern and the bracken
   A-flush in full feather
For death in fair weather.

They looked in the deep grass   10
   Where it was deepest;
They looked down the steep bank
   Where it was steepest;
But under the bruisèd fern
   Crushed in its feather   15
The head and the body
   Were lying together,—
Ah, death of fair weather.

'Tell me, thou perished head,
   What hand could sever thee?   20
Was it thy cruel sire
   Menacing ever thee?
Was it thy step-mother
   (Bird of ill feather!)
Snapping the stem and flower   25
   Hid them together,
To soil thus fair weather?'

'My evil step-mother,
   So witch-like in wish,
She caught all my pretty blood   30
   Up in a dish:
She took out my heart
   For a ghoul-meal together;
But peaceful my body lies
   In the fern-feather,   35
For now is fair weather.

'My father, too cruel,
   Would scorn me and beat me;
My wicked step-mother
   Would take me and eat me;   40
My sweet little sister
   Will weep through the heather,
Not knowing, down there

'Mid your clouds of dull feather,
That death brings fair weather.　　45

'But I joy me most wishful,
　　Desireless to range else,
Up here in the beautiful
　　Land of the angels;
The beautiful angels,　　50
　　All laughing together,
Fan me to sleep
　　With a gale of gold feather.
Ah, death brings fair weather!'

They have planted two willows　　55
　　To kiss one another
Where the sweet sister
　　Kisses her brother:
The silver-drooped willows
　　They mingle their feather　　60
Where they are lying
　　In sunshine together,
Asleep in fair weather,—
Dead, in fair weather.

44 *your* MS unclear; possibly 'yon'.

Une Fille de Joie

This sonnet was composed when Thompson realised he would not be able to find the street girl after her deliberate disappearance at the time of his meeting with the Meynells (see Introduction, p. xxvii, and Biographical Summary). In the Note-book of Early Poems the final text in ink of the poem is followed by 'Vox Aspasiae Reclamantis' because, according to a prefixed note, the latter's theme was close to that of 'Une Fille de Joie'. (The second poem, hitherto unpublished, appears in Part Three on pp. 454–6 with the note that Thompson wrote about the two poems.) The indentations in *MHW* do not appear in the original manuscript as reproduced here.

Hell's gates revolve around her yet alive;
To her no Christ the beautiful is nigh:
The stony world has daffed his teaching by;
'Go!' saith it; 'sin on still that you may thrive,
Let one sin be as queen for all the hive　　5

Of sins to swarm around; while I, chaste I,
In cheap immaculateness avert mine eye:—
Poor galley-slave of lust, rot in your gyve!'
This is her doom! The ways are barriered which
Should lead to the All Merciful's abode;   10
The house of penitence which Mary trod
Long since is grown an appanage of the rich:
And though she strive, yea, strive and strive, *how* strive!—
The gates of hell have shut her in alive.

3 *daffed* set aside. 8 *gyve* fetter or shackle. 12 *appanage* attribute.

'Sad Semele'

A number of Thompson's poems contain references to his memories of the street girl, but few are as explicit as this sonnet based on the union of Zeus and the mortal Semele. Although Semele was condemned to flames of divine punishment her child was saved—Dionysus the god of poetic inspiration. In consequence of his double nature as offspring of god and mortal, he bestowed a semi-divine power of creativity on his devotees. Thompson identifies the street girl as his Semele, sharing with him the birth of his poetry through her self-sacrifice. The manuscript is a final copy, a single sheet in ink, signed and, except for the last two lines, without the indentations added in *MHW*. It has no title, and the one above was supplied by Connolly.

Who clasp lost spirits, also clasp their hell;
You have clasped, and burn, sad child, sad Semele!
One half of my cup you have drunk too well,
And that's the death; the immortality
Girt in the fiery spirit flies your lip.   5
That to my deathless progeny of pain
You should be mother, bear your fellowship
I'the mortal grief, without the immortal gain!
Not only I, that these poor verses live,
A heavy vigil keep of parchèd nights;   10
But you for unborn men your pangs must give,
And wake in tears, that they may dream delights.
   What poems be, Sweet, you did never know;
   And yet are poems suckled by your woe!

Nisi Dominus

Connolly was not aware of the final text of this poem at Ushaw College, reproduced here. The version in *MHW* is a rough draft in NB14A, which is prefixed by the first verse from Psalm 126 that gives the poem its title: 'Nisi Dominus aedificaverit domum, In vanum laboraverunt qui aedificant eam.' ('Unless the Lord build the house, they labour in vain that build it.') The theme here could be based on Thompson's disillusion towards the end of his poetic career.

> Alack! how have the gates of hell prevailed
> Against this spirit, and its firm mortise failed;
> This spirit of mine; which thou and I have raised
> On secret heights where but the eagle gazed!
> In vain we pile, with our poor mortal hands,   5
> Stone upon stone, until the building stands
> Irradiate in completed purity,
> Unless the Holy One its keystone be.
> Unless the Lord have builded and have knit
> This house of aspirant spirit, is it not writ   10
> In vain we labour that have builded it?
> Like to the tower which Sennaar saw sublime,
> It rests a nayword to successive time:
> Confusion of tongues has come on us, God wot!
> And that which I would speak, thou understandest not.   15

3 *thou* could refer to WM. **12** *Sennaar* Shinar, the Babylonia of the Old Testament, traditional site of the Tower of Babel, where human pride caused its destruction and the introduction of different languages (Gen. 11:1–9)

'The Bride of God and Thee'

The manuscript, a final copy in ink, has no title. At BC it is catalogued as 'Lines to a husband and wife'.

> Of loftiest worship would'st thou know
>   The test? 'Tis when thou canst espy
> This truth: thy lady is more low
>   Than thou, and therefore is more high;
> When thy right potence of command   5
>   Thou canst retain with reverence sweet;
> And the proud secret understand,
>   To sway, duteous at her feet.

In term and lowlihead Man is crowned;
    And she, the bride of God and thee,   10
Is doubly Bride, and doubly Bound,
    And so the Man peculiarly.
Because the ruler from the ruled
    Takes rule, thou shalt take rule from her,
And yet shall rule her; nor be schooled   15
    By what the blind and fools aver.
Save Man be not God's subject, this
    Is fixed as are the roots of heaven:
Yet she's thine equal; for there is
    By place no right equality riven.   20
Or thus I paradox the thing,
    And let the wise take what I mean;—
That thou shalt rule her as her King,
    And she shall rule thee as thy Queen.
Thou art the first, the second she;   25
    Yet in thine homage be this reversed,
Knowing God doth delightedly
    With him the Last ordain the First.
These things I utter; but who doth them is
The woman's servant, for the woman's his.   30

Fragment of Hell

These lines appear in NB46B, one of the London streets notebooks. They are followed by part of the 'Nightmare of the Witch-Babies' (p. 388) and convey something of Thompson's state of mind at that time. The 'friends' could not therefore refer to the Meynells as Connolly suggests, for Thompson had not yet met them (*MHW*, p. 144).

My friends, ye weep around my bed—for me—
Weep not! pray, pray! put one life in a prayer
To hold me back, for I am going, dying,—
Oh pray! pray all! one prayer!—what can tears do?
For I sink, sink, clutch earth as in a nightmare,   5
Slipping by inches—one prayer, one, for me,
Will you not pray for me, for your own me,
Your son, your cousin, brother, friend,
Who die, who drop into eternal fires,
And cannot pray,—prayer?—I ne'er prayed myself!   10
Oh!—soul's hope! Pray!—weep, weep?—can tears quench hell?

Maria Intra Limina Aestuant

The title translates as 'The seas rage within their boundaries.'

> Not what wouldst be, in thy blind heart,
> But what God willed thee, thou art.
> Learn, darkly with the fates at strife,
> To shape thyself within thy life:
> In the traced furrow sow thy crops;   5
> Give homage to the checks and stops
> Which point thy life's set period,
> And circumstance, the goad of God.
> Believe, with spirit nigh to break,
> Believe for the believing's sake;   10
> When the thwart time its worst has done,
> There is some fruit beneath the sun;
> Some fruit there is beneath the sun.

'No Singer of His Time'

The *MHW* text has no significant variants from the manuscript in NB33, which appears to be a spontaneous expression of the frustrations of Thompson's later years. The title of *The Man Has Wings* is taken from the reference in line 25 and its context.

> Ye have denied
> Ye have denied
> Ye have denied
> Ye have denied
> Nothing at all is of august and high,   5
> Allaying man's dull dust, ye not deny:
> Ye have said: 'Go out from us, and leave our earth
> Utterly of the comfortable clay;
> Demand nought from us; let us hood our eyes
> With a strong veil of flesh, for this is wise,   10
> And but to peer forth is to pall in mirth;
> Disconsolate and hateful is your day.
> Your sights but trouble us: here in the mire,
> Hognuts we have, if hognuts we desire:
> Forth! for all comfort is in the fat clay   15
> Whence man was dug in his ignoble birth,

And all disaster is it thence to stray.'
Though sole and single be my wayfaring,
I will not be partaker in this thing.
Wherefore ye cry: 'No singer of his time,   20
Not of to-day, nor yet of any day,
He shapes aloof an ineffectual rhyme,
Nourished upon the husks of threshed-out things,
Which who will hearken? Of our fire-new world
No note has he. Pity! the man has wings   25
But all as one it were that they were furled.
His muse he will not tire
Upon the entrails of the unclean ideals
Which serve for us;
His dainty Pegasus   30
Disdains nutricious hogwash. Still he flings
His aimless flights in [hiatus] gyre,
With some fool's dream of fleshless hymeneals:—
A Bee of Maeterlinck! 'Tis a waste lyre?

But you, not I, have strayed; but you, not I,   35
Have wandered from the mighty company,
Processional
Down the unshaken ages, testifying
To that which smiles at your most vain denying;
And stands though you must fall: 40
Yea; though the whole world with one tongue deny,
Answers: 'Yet here am I!'

31 *gyre* spiral. 33 *hymeneals* songs addressed to Hymen, Roman god of marriage. 34 According to Maurice Maeterlinck's *Life of the Bee* the queen bee will only mate with the male, or drone, who can attain the altitude to which she can fly. After a few moments of ecstatic union his body disintegrates and he falls to the ground. The poet's critics regard him as one of the multitude of drones who never attain that goal. FT may here imply a further association, as Maeterlinck sees in this phenomenon an example of the 'profound idea' that 'Nature demands that the giver of life should die at the moment of giving' (*Life of the Bee*, 1901, pp. 249–50).

Genesis

The manuscript is on the verso of the last page of the manuscript of 'The Sere of the Leaf'. There are no variants in the *MHW* text.

A little brown seed, on the breezes blown,
Fell to earth in a land unknown;
Whither it drifted it knew not, nor
What was the secret its bosom bore.

No fairness was its to take men's heed,   5
Of the little brown stranger they knew no need:
Itself to itself seemed a futile birth,
And it sank or was trampled into the earth.

As it lay in earth, as it lay in earth,
Itself to itself but a futile birth,   10
With the worm and the insect for company,
Its soul grew sterile, its heart turned dry.

Frost barred the doors of its prisoning mould,
Where it lay in hunger, and dark, and cold,
And after the frost came the drenching rain,   15
Till dulled and lethargied, pained out of pain,

It recked no longer of rains that beat,
Nor the pitiless chill, nor the trampling feet;
And when hastening spring sent her voice before,
It lay in swoon, with a palsied core.   20

At length did a tender sunshine come
With fostering warmth to it, shrivelled and numb,
And the seed awoke in the earth apart
To stirrings wild, and a pang at the heart.

The new life stabbed it with jaggèd pains,   25
As when blood is rash-thawed in curdled veins;
And, like lightning crouched panting within the storm,
Its bosom was heaved by some vital form.

It struggled, foreseeing not, blindly pained,
To what were its throes and itself ordained;   30
Till at last to the very heart it split,—
And only a little shoot burst from it.

But the little shoot grew to a lusty shoot,
While the cloven seed fell from the deepening root;
While the lusty shoot opened a radiant bloom,   35
The seed rotted into an earthy tomb.

Fragrance blew wide from the beautiful flower,
And maidens bore it into their bower,
But under their tread, its mission done,
The dissolved seed felt not the rain or sun.   40

So it must be; the seed must throe,
And its heart be rent, that the flower may grow,
Be rent to the heart for the beautiful flower
That maidens cherish within their bower.

So it must be, while Fate has power,   45
To earth the seed, the blossom to bower:
The flower was meet for a maiden's mouth,
The seed brown, withered with wintry drouth.

The seed was fit but to grow the flower;
And the maid who bends lips to the blossom in bower   50
Sighs no sigh for the seed, I wis,
That never a maiden had lips to kiss.

41 *throe* struggle, agonise.

To a Wind

There are two manuscripts, one included in the Ad Amicam Notebook at the Lilly Library (photostat at BC), the other a single notebook page. There is no difference between the two except that the latter has 'of the South' added to the title and deleted. There are no variants in the *MHW* text.

Breeze that meetest *her* mouth,
    Wing unto me here!
I should know the breath you bare
    From all breath less dear.

I should know your soft fall   5
    From all gales less dear;
I should say: 'My friend's breath
    Sighs in my ear.'

Oh, from every meaner breeze
   Blowing West or South,   10
I should know the breeze had blown
   Across her fragrant mouth.

An Unamiable Child

There are earlier drafts for these lines in NBs BC12 and BC15 but the text in
MHW follows the final ink manuscript.

'A child unsweet of face or air,
Childhood's sworn amorists put her by;
Nothing to love I see in her.'
Nothing. A sad God's-truth. Nor I.
Because there is nothing to love her for,   5
Good need is it that I love her the more;
Because she's unlovesome, I needs must love
With all the love that she cannot move;
For that *you* cannot love her, you
Have left your love for me to do.   10
Nothing to love in her I see,
Except it be the very she.
They who love what all men crave,
Fearing to lose, scarce seem to have;
But never fear can overcome me   15
Lest men steal this sweet nothing from me:
Nothing to love I sweetly choose,
So, sweetly safe nothing to lose.
Because you have nothing that world's love charms,
I clasp you, child, with the whole world's arms.   20
Yet—yet—ah, if it should befall,
To have nothing, and lose it all!

De Mortuis

The title translates as 'Of the Dead'. The identity of the child whose death forms the theme of this poem is not known. The manuscript is a final corrected copy with a few minor variants in the *MHW* text.

> Yester-hour, Sweet, you were a child
>   (To me at least, so old and sad,)
> Sweet-briar buds out of April's font
>   Recent, hailed 'Sister!' and were glad.
>
> To-day, the height, whence Noah saw   5
>   A drowned world's face up-float amid
> The waters, is less old; or years
>   Sanded about the Pyramid;
>
> You are more old than aged brine
>   Which scurfed the dragon-pressed seaweed;   10
> Yet young, past antenatal bloom
>   That biggens the unseeded seed.
>
> Girl, you can lesson the white beard to-day!
>   And sedulous Science shall expound—
> A thousand peering years to be—   15
>   What your fair eyes have early found.
>
> With greater and with lesser tube
>   Are careful generations pained
> To search the bones o' the world.—Sweet child,
>   You beat your wing, and you attained!   20
>
> Yesterday's simple kneeler, now
>   Who smilest holier philosophy
> Than schools disputing! Who didst list
>   My song, the stars now hush for thee;
>
> So quick the inward music breaks   25
>   When rended is the dyke of flesh;
> So swift the fledged escaping songs
>   Mount from the broken body's mesh.

To us the crumbs of song and knowledge; you
    Sit at the high table, and are calm.   30
We munch with earth-bowed head, nor look
    Where your full feast is wreathed with palm.

Ah, wherefore do we dim-eyed race of men
    For knowledge root, and vaunt of that we know,
Since Death so great a master is,   35
    And of his teaching is not slow?

When you, child, to out-learn us all,
    Did but from our dull converse rise,
And, bedward somewhat early ere the dark,
    Let out the light, Sweet, and your eyes.   40

17 the telescope and microscope.

A Question

The manuscript is a final copy in ink and signed. This poem is not to be confused with the other of the same title, first published in *New Poems*. There are no variants in the *MHW* text. It is reprinted in *BHCC*, p. 355.

Wherefore should the singer sing,
    So his song be true?
Truth is ever old, old,
    Song ever new.

Ere the world was, was the lie,   5
    And the truth too:
But the old lie still is old,
    The old truth true.

IN *STRANGE HARP, STRANGE SYMPHONY* (1968)

Cor Meum

The title translates as 'My Heart'. Walsh says of this sonnet that 'one final manu-script is contained in a Storrington notebook'. It has not been traced and the text is given here as it appears in *SHSS*, pp. 258–9.

Unpriced of chafferers in any mart;
Most valueless and precious; What thou art
Dearly despised! I know not, and would know!
Which God has built without so poor and low
Love's crowned head cannot stoop to pass thy gate,   5
Yet within ample for thy purple state;
Too mean a cup for Midas-love to hold
Although his lips would turn thee into gold.
Tent of the Arab tale! That I can pitch
Over what rustling multitudes! yet which   10
I beat in so strait compass thou art hid.
Too great for merchandise, though kings should bid;
Too little for the beggar in the street
To heed, if thou lay naked at his naked feet.

7 King Midas' love for gold resulted in the granting of his wish that all he touched turned into it.

ON THE ANNIVERSARY OF ROSSETTI'S DEATH

Rossetti died in April 1882, so that the following spring is the probable date for this series of sonnets. Thompson later copied them into the Notebook of Early Poems, which is the text reproduced here. Although they show marked influences from Rossetti's 'Willowood', Thompson's youthful admiration gave rise to the first clear signs of the character of his own future poetry in the relationship between visual and verbal imagery that Rossetti here represents. The last one has an extra line.

I

This was the day that great, sad heart,
    That great, sad heart did beat no more,
Which nursed so long its Southern flame
    Amid our vapours dull and frore.

He said a thing in English verse,   5
   He made our English painting young,
He taught her lingering lips to speak
   As Giotto spake in Tuscan tongue.

Through voice of art and voice of song
   He uttered one same truth abroad,—   10
Through voice of art and voice of song—
   That Love below a pilgrim trod:
He said through women's eyes, 'How long!
   Love's other half's with God!'

2

He taught our English art to burn
   With colours from diviner skies,
He taught our English art to gaze
   On Nature with a learner's eyes:
That hills which look into the heaven   5
   Have their firm bases on the earth;
God paints his most angelic hues
   On vapours of a terrene birth.

This first was he in all Time's girth
   Who painted Sadness crowned and fair—   10
He only, in all Time's wide girth—
   With royal eyes and glooming hair;
In this poor day's ungod-ed dearth
   The one divine thing left to her.

3

He gave our art his poet's mind,
   He gave our North his Southern song,
He gave our verse his painter's eye,
   And Dante's soul to Shakespeare's tongue.
Sad Dante sang a flowerless love,   5
   And lost what never had been his:
He, more unhappy, knew too well
   The sweetness of the vanished kiss.

He had embraced his Beatrice,
   And tamed the plumes that soon grew cold: 10
He had embraced his Beatrice!
   And if his heart were early old,
It yearned for the remembered bliss
   Clasped in death's fleshless fold.

4

If he were weak, forgive it him;
   Be mindful only of his power:
Remember all God dowered him with,
   And how to us he gave that dower.
Kindler of colour, fiery heart   5
   Of deep, imaginative design,
He trod the vintage whence we draw
   Our modern painting's richest wine.

May God his locks with glories twine,
   Be kind to all he wrought amiss!   10
May God his locks with glories twine,
   And give him back his Beatrice.
This day the sad heart ceased to pine,
   I trust his lady's beats at his,
And two souls flame in single bliss.   15

The Owl

Drafts for this poem appear in notebooks that Thompson kept while living on the London streets, which are full of stray verses and fragments written under the influence of opium. This is one of the only two completed poems, the other being the 'Nightmare of the Witch-Babies' to follow below. Of these two only 'The Owl' was copied later into the Notebook of Early Poems, from which the present text is taken. From a note by Everard Meynell, intended for *Life* but not used, it appears likely that these two were with the poems Thompson sent to Wilfrid Meynell from the streets. The note is based on a recollection by Alice Meynell of the occasion when she first read some Thompson manuscripts, which included 'some witch-opium poems which she detested' (quoted in *SHSS*, p. 69). That he submitted poems of this kind indicates Thompson's confused state at the time, but there may have been an underlying 'cry for help' in doing so. The Owl, traditionally a messenger of death, here assumes the role of the Witch—with mythical associations between the Witch and the Wicked Stepmother (see the headnote for

'A Ballad of Fair Weather' (p. 371) for the biographical influences). The Cauldron of Nightmares with which the Witch-Owl torments her victims is a perversion of the Cauldron of Regeneration, given its best-known form in the Holy Grail. The witch-cults of the Middle Ages abound with instances of the spells and curses brewed in the Cauldron and the horrible ingredients used for the purpose. How far Thompson was familiar with these associations is uncertain, but he knew the witch-scenes in *Macbeth*, drawn largely from the same sources, and the poem identifies his own state of mind with the guilt and fear that the play exposes so mercilessly.

The Owl she has eyes that bicker and gleam,
And a hookèd foul nose, as may well beseem;
And she laughed out loud with a whooping note,
She laughed out bale from her rusty throat:
Why doth she laugh from her rusty throat?   5
She laugheth at Sleep that sleepeth not.

The Owl is the witch of the cauldron of Sleep;
And she stirs it and seethes it, whooping deep;
And she thrusts the witch-bits into it deep,
Gendering ghosts for the smoke of sleep.   10
She flings in toads from the money-dust,
And feeds it thick with dead fat of lust;
Corpse-limbs of love yet quivering new;
And blood of the thoughts that are writhing too,
Drawn from the place where the pang went through: 15
Adders of longing, and fanged regrets;
Winged lizards of terror and monstrous threats,—
Ah, horrible terrors! ah, withering threats!
And she sees with her eyes which the fires look through
Her deep-sleep cauldron reeking new;   20
And she laughs at sleep, tu-whit, tu-whoo!

And so murk is the sleep-smoke of despair,
And so awful the spectres rising there,
And so fearful they throng on the calm night air;
That were not sleep as brief as deep,   25
It were better almost to die than sleep!

The Nightmare of the Witch-Babies

This seems to have been one of the 'witch-opium poems' sent to the Meynells from the streets (for which see the headnote above, to 'The Owl') but Thompson did not copy it into the Notebook of Early Poems as he did most of the completed or near-completed poetry he wrote while on the London streets. It survives in a very faded text in NB45, from which Walsh printed twelve of the fifteen stanzas in *SHSS*, pp. 57–60. The present text therefore reproduces the notebook manuscript with the inconsistencies in punctuation that have been regularised in Walsh's version. Another very fragmentary draft in NB46B is followed by a note: 'Finished before Oct. 1886', giving a date of about a year after Thompson's arrival in London. Of all the poems and fragments dating from those years it is the most revealing of his mental anguish, expressed through imagery deriving from memories of his medical training together with his present experiences. The knights and ladies of his childhood dreams that first aroused the poet in him are transformed and entangled with hideous witch-babies, the progeny of one of the most universal archetypes of nightmare, the Witch as the Terrible Mother. For a fuller interpretation see *BHCC*, pp. 65–7.

Two witch-babies,
  Ha! Ha!
Two witch-babies,
  Ho! Ho!
A bedemon-ridden hag,   5
  With the devil pigged alone,
Begat them, laid at night
  On the bloody-rusted stone;
And they dwell within the Land
  Of the Bare Shank-Bone,   10
Where the Evil goes to and fro.
  Two witch-babies, ho, ho, ho!

A lusty knight
  Ha! Ha!
On a swart steed   15
  Ho! Ho!
Rode upon the land
  Where the silence feels alone,
Rode upon the land
  Of the Bare Shank-Bone,   20
Rode upon the Strand,
  Of the Dead Men's Groan,
Where the Evil goes to and fro.
  Two witch-babies, ho, ho, ho!

A rotten mist,   25
  Ha! Ha!
Like a dead man's flesh,
Was abhorrent in the air,
  Clung a tether to the wood
Of the wicked-looking trees,   30
  Was a scurf upon the flood;
And the reeds they were pulpy
  With blood, blood, blood!
And the clouds were a–looming low.
  Two witch-babies, ho, ho, ho!   35

No one life there!
  Ha! Ha!
No sweet life there!
  Ho! Ho!
But the long loud laugh,   40
  And the short shrill howl,
And the quick, brisk flip
  Of the hornèd owl,
As he flits right past
  With his gloomy cowl   45
Through the murkiness long and low.
  Two witch-babies, ho! ho! ho!

What is it sees he?
  Ha! Ha!
There in the frightfulness?   50
  Ho! Ho!
There he saw a maiden
  Fairest fair:
Sad were her dusk eyes,
  Long was her hair;   55
Sad were her dreaming eyes,
  Misty her hair,
And strange was her garments' flow,
  Two witch-babies, ho, ho, ho!

Swiftly he followed her,   60
  Ha! Ha!
Eagerly followed her,
  Ho! Ho!

From the rank, the greasy soil,
   Red bubbles oozed and stood;   65
Till it grew a putrid slime,
   And where'er his horse has trod,
The ground plash, plashes,
   With a wet too like to blood;
And chill terrors like a fungus grow.   70
   Two witch-babies, ho! ho! ho!

   There stayed the maiden;
      Ha! Ha!
   Shed all her beauty;
      Ho! Ho!   75
She shed her flower of beauty,
   Grew laidly, old, and dire,
Was the demon-ridden witch,
   And the consort of Hell-fire:
'Am I lovely, noble knight?   80
   See thy heart's own desire!
Now they come, come upon thee, lo!
   Two witch-babies, ho! ho! ho!'

   Into the fogginess
      Ha! Ha!   85
   Lo, she corrupted!
      Ho! Ho!
Comes there a Death
   With the looks of a witch,
And joints that creak   90
   Like a night-bird's scritch,
And a breath that smokes
   Like a smoking pitch,
And eyeless sockets a-glow.
   Two witch-babies, ho! ho! ho!   95

   Close behind it
      Ha! Ha!
   Ah! close behind it!
      Ho! Ho!
Comes there a babe   100
   Of bloated youth,
With a curdled eye
   And a snaggy tooth,

And a life—no mortal
　　Dare speak its sooth;　　　　　　　　105
And its tongue like a worm doth show.
　　Two witch-babies, ho! ho! ho!

　　Its paunch a-swollen
　　　　Ha! Ha!
　　Its life a-swollen　　　　　　　　110
　　　　Ho! Ho!
Like the [hiatus] days drowned.
　　Harsh was its hum;
And its paunch was rent
　　Like a brasten drum;　　　　　　　115
And the blubbered fat
　　From its belly doth come
With a sickening ooze—Hell made it so!
　　Two witch-babies, ho! ho! ho!

　　It leaps on his charger,　　　　　　120
　　　　Ha! Ha!
　　It clasps him right fondly,
　　　　Ho! Ho!
Its joints are about him,
　　Its breath in his bones;　　　　　　125
Its eyes glare in his,
　　And it sucks up his groans:
He [hiatus] from his horse,
　　He burns on the stones,
And his mail cracks off in a glow.　　　130
　　Two witch-babies, ho! ho! ho!

　　Its tooth in his shoulder,
　　　　Ha! Ha!
　　His skin dully champing.
　　　　Ho! Ho!　　　　　　　　135
　　Slimed like a snail
　　With that loathly thing,
His own self writhed him
　　With shuddering;
His gaze grew dark,　　　　　　　140
　　And his soul took wing
While his breath still kept its flow.
　　Two witch-babies, ho! ho! ho!

Hist! Hist! a gloominess!
   Ha! Ha!   145
Hist! Hist! a *something*!
   Ho! Ho!
Away with a scream
   The swart steed flew—
The evil shadows   150
   Those ghastly two
And a [hiatus] slime kneaded
   With sanguine dew
Into that dread slime below.
   Two witch-babies, ho! ho! ho!   155

Two witch-babies,
   Ha! Ha!
Two witch-babies,
   Ho! Ho!
The elder hath a name,   160
   And the name of it is Lust;
And the name of that its brother
   Ah, its name is Lust's Disgust!
They are ever in a land
   Where the sun is dead with rust,   165
So the scummy [?] mist thickens below:
   Woe, for the witch-babies, woe! woe! woe!

There, where corruption
   Alone doth grow,
There still the Evil   170
   Goes to and fro:
It is formless, nameless, vague,
   It is dread made palpable;
None can paint its face, for none
   Who behold it live to tell: 175
'Tis a shadow on the earth
   Of the awful nether-hell;
It is nightmare—God made it so!
Shun the land, and shun the woman,
   Shun the wicked spell;   180
     Two witch-babies, woe! woe! woe!

Between **27** and **28** Ho! Ho! - missing. **105** *sooth* truth. **115** *brasten* burst.

'A moment unforgot'

In the manuscript these 22 lines appear to constitute a complete poem in fair copy form, although Walsh regards them as 'a fragment' (*SHSS*, p. 156). But as they are included in the BC manuscripts of the Ad Amicam poems (see pp. 435–6) he is correct in assuming that they were addressed to Katie King, probably at the time when Thompson first became aware that, on his side, their relationship was to be more than friendship.

A moment unforgot!
A space our converse sunk its wing, but not
The inward converse that still grew;
And like two glowworm-lights that mix their hue,
The liquid sphere which clothed her spread its fine   5
And mantling verge until it blent with mine.
Even as the downward sun that to a hill
Floats, while the air doth thrill
With much expectance, and for peace is still;
The orb at length, ah see!   10
Resting upon the peak, most sensibly
Trembles, as does a bubble touching gound;
And in the spirit of its light breathed round
The extreme height
Becomes invisible, and with the light   15
One substance, and is sucked into the sun:—
Her emanation so with mine grew one,
Consentient, interfused, and we became
A single effluence in a double frame,
One being distinct in two, and yet the same;   20
I felt the touch of state primordial,
I knew the Paradise before the Fall.

PART THREE

UNPUBLISHED POEMS

SEPARATE MANUSCRIPTS

Wild-Flower

The manuscript is a fair copy, signed and in ink. According to a note by Meynell it was 'written to the young daughter of his landlady at Pantasaph'. That is, it was intended as part of the 'Narrow Vessel' sequence in *New Poems*, addressed to Maggie Brien. Thompson probably decided to omit it partly on account of its length but mainly because it expresses the underlying theme of the sequence more clearly and therefore could have caused pain to Maggie and her family. Lines 1–4, 8–12, 17–18 and 21–3 are quoted in *SHSS*, pp. 129–33.

A little gift to me you gave,
And for your meed a poem crave.
　　You do not know how much you ask,
You will not know how much you have.

Such hard words here to try you! oh,　　　　　　5
I see you frown, and read, and sew!
　　But if you know they mean, 'I love you,'
What matter all you do not know?

Brown eyes! that laughed in fair amaze
To learn your beauty from my gaze;　　　　　　10
　　Yet would not trust the too glad tidings
Until my mouth sware to the praise!

Age has some conscience taught my tongue,
It would not flatter you to your wrong,
　　Dear girl; but ah, I fear mine eyes　　　　　15
Are babblers still, unlearned and young!

Yours is a pretty trick and sweet
To love your namesake *marguerite*;
　　Which but the country children gather,
The men pass by with lumpish feet.　　　　　　20

Only some poet, chancing through
These meads, has looks which cleave unto
　　The childlike face and golden heart
Of the wild *marguerite* and you.

You care not for me much. Well, drink   25
Was mine once from the exhaustless brink
    Of love's own fount. Now I can take
Your cup, and call it good, I think.

One thought of mine has nobler art
Of love, than all your little heart;   30
    Which God made shallow, for he knew
Your days in joy should have small part.

And so I love you more than can
You, dearest dear, love any man.
    To your strait clod-walled days, the boon   35
Of love's fine sense were cruel ban.

What hardest heart could wish it you?
Nay, do, poor child, as children do—
    Love me as long as the whole space
Between two playthings leaveth you.   40

Love me one vast hour, more or less,
Till a lost kerchief's wept distress
    Void the weak pang; love me almost
As sweetly, Sweet! as a new dress.

Yes, play the vagrant too! for still   45
The child from knee to knee strays, till
    The first-forsaken pardon it
With half a laugh and all his will.

I never made my heart your law,
Nor would possess you, whom I saw—   50
    Nought wishing what you could not gauge—
Chafe me with your disdain, love, awe.

So bungler's luck, or Providence,
Bringeth yourself to my defence
    Against yourself; where I, perchance,   55
Should slip in the just trick of fence.

Willed you, the spoil 'tis odds you'd lift;
For poets, with heavenly unthrift,
    Exult to give themselves where but
Themselves can price the wasteful gift.   60

'Fine love!' you'd say; 'Can I love him
That cares not where I love?' Wild whim
    It were, to adore a maid who cannot
Love out six kisses' *interim*!

Nay, but you my deep-bended glance   65
Foil with insentient countenance,
    And absent eyes unknowing. Whence
I know you know it with joyance.

Then my gaze mocks, and the smiles grow
Just at your mouth-tip, and you glow.   70
    Love-fashions, surely?—Pest on it!
But you would love ten dozen so!

How should you feel love's verity,
Unto which hope and memory
    The very flower and sap are; you,   75
Who nor remember nor foresee?

O, I love all you'd have me, quite,
Foolish one! To my dizziest might,
    I grant, no; yet perchance as much
As you may bear without affright.   80

With love so past your compassing
You count it but a little thing.
    With love you shall not know again—
You do not know it now—I sing;

With love beyond your own kin's love,   85
Of threads too fine for your sight wove;
    With love enough to make me sad
Seeing you have no skill thereof;

With love enough to let you make
My lips smile and my heart half ache,   90
    When you grow tired, and pout, because
The toy's too strong for you to break.

2 *for your meed* in return

'Well, love I have'

Like 'Wild-Flower' this untitled poem was almost certainly intended originally for the 'Narrow Vessel' sequence. There is a draft in a separate manuscript, but in NB20A there is a fair copy, with some minor corrections, which is followed here.

Well, love I have, which all girls dream,
    But not the love I dreamèd;
And is it that I wrongly dreamed,
    Or love not what it seemèd?

For love should be a pretty thing,—   5
    A kiss, a ruffled curl,
The laugh that makes a boyish arm
    A light weight for a girl.

When that a girl must keep the house
    And dust and clean all day,   10
What should she take a lover for
    But a sun-bright holiday?

The shaping of a new dress,
    And what the neighbours say,
These make a maiden's business,   15
    She goes to love for play.

As if there were not trouble enough!
    I do not think it right
That any man should make of love
    A thing that's half affright!   20

Oh, the old days when love I lacked,
    Happy to know not lack!
And could I leave him, or he me,
    And laugh the old days back!

Then what was it I loved him for,   25
    If loving so dismayed me?
I did not want to love at all,
    He followed, plagued, and made me!

Alas, this love's a fretful thing,
   Of which I fain would clear me;—   30
To sigh for him when he is far,
   And fly him when he's near me!

All in my dreams pursue his kiss,
   And quake to see it coming;
When laugh & jest would bring me to't   35
   Native as bees to homing!

(Ah child, this heavy golden shower
   Seems to crave golden answer:
A light love's the right love
   To which a maid would dance her.   40

For little love asks least of love,
   And oh, a girl's heart's small;
And lover's love best liketh her
   When it is none at all.)

Love Divided against Itself

The present text is from a copy (by BMB) of the original manuscript at M which has since been lost. The only reference to the poem is in *BHCC*, p. 235, where lines 55–9 and 91–102 are quoted. The manuscript was a fair text and provides the fullest surviving account of Thompson's love for Alice Meynell. The poem also describes its sublimation and can be dated with confidence to the period during 1885–6 when the struggle was at its height. At that time his friendship with Coventry Patmore meant that Patmore's much more outspoken love for Alice forced Thompson into a confrontation with his own submerged desires. The Patmorean style and form of the poem are therefore of special significance.

Whence is it, Lady, that I never stand
   Upon the verges of my promised land,
     That honeyed region of all-heavenly you,
   But by some undivinable command
   Some hapless ordinance, a wandering elf   5
       I am driven forth anew
   To pace the desert of mine arid self?
   Too true to trueness! other it might prove,
    Were I less loved, or were you less kind,
   Were you less pure in soul, or I in love,   10

Were I less white of will, or you of mind!
This love is as the Indian drug, and makes,
To him who once the wild enchantment takes,
    Your heart's soft pulses a soul-shaking sound,
And all your beauty too immortal-fair   15
        For mortal sight to bear,
    Your eyes a light to trouble and astound.
Ah! your near-fairness seems a thing at which
Seraphs might wish the golden flecks forgiven
      Dusting their wings from star-y-paven Heaven   20
And blush for soilure from immortal ground.
I am most poor, because you are too rich!
  Thou art the mere horizon of my life,
      Where earth and heaven meet, and whereunto
        I, ever journeying, am never near;   25
          And that old fable of the Hesperian tree
          Authentic is in thee,
O mother, lady, and untainted wife!
  Whose beauty breeds desire for ever new,
      And ever-unfamiliared holy fear;   30
        And is unto the pure
        Both dragon and allure,
    Watched by its own accessibility.
Teach me to think thee less, or think me more,
For who is bold with that he does adore?   35
Ah! teach me to be proud, or do thou be
Less threatening in thy humility!
For this, which hardies me and doth reprove
      Which bids me fly to thee and fly thee,
Yea, from thine awful fairness to remove,   40
      Yet with a net of fire entrails me by thee;
This writ of habitance and banishment,
This hopelessness just missing high content,
      Alike is love, is love!

Allay love with some frown, that I may drink   45
    And from the draft not shrink!
For if thy love have lowlied me and bowed,
It may be that thy frown had made me proud!
To touch thee I do tremble, and again
'Tis tremor from thy contact to refrain.   50
    Thy speech so tender is and low,
I fear to jar on it with passion's noise,

But, like a lily on a water, so
My heart is rocked upon thine undulant voice.
For ever to that heart mine angel says,— 55
     'Ah! desperate of grace!
How dare'st thou to our fellowship advance?
Canst thou behold how greatly she doth glance,
Nor to thy very marrow know distress
Of her too perturbating gentilesse? 60
She looks so mild and gracious, thou must die
     Of complete clemency!
Her eyes give such kind hope, thou must not dare
    But utterly despair!
How shall thy grosser flesh unshrivelled stand 65
     The effluence of her hand?
How shall thy spirit endure the keen degrees
     Of her frore purities?
Yet if the contact of her body so
     Thou dread, weak thing, to know, 70
What if at thine unlocking touch thou find,
Fool, the more sufferest contact of her mind?
What if her spirit rend its dykes, and thou—
Unsteady 'gainst the hallowed overflow—
Sink in the heady and essential stress 75
     Of extreme happiness?
What soul may be to stem that deep inured
     Of purity repured?
Ah! if who read within a sorcerer's book
   Faint at the coming of an evil thing, 80
Ah! how shalt thou, rash necromancer, brook
   The dizzying beat of an Uranian wing?'
Thus to mine ear the mystical rebuke.
And so, by an immitigable law,
   This labouring love is proved with child of Fear; 85
      In strange antiphony,
      Unintermittably,
   The love that bids 'Come near,'
Is answered by the love that menaces, 'Withdraw!'

   O Guardian, that through unpermutable days 90
   Marvellest upon the unpermutable Ways,
   What is this mystery of fearful mildness,
      This dreadful undefiledness?
     *

'Child! in the end of ending, so shalt thou,
Before the Grace of grace, the Fair of fair,   95
Feel to the roots of thy flame-winnowed hair
The archetypal longing and despair!
    So, little one, as now,
At the supportless pity of those Eyes
    Ah! clayey heart, ah! how,   100
    How shalt thou agonise!
And at that smile which says, "I love, forgive,"
How shalt thou wish there were no way to live,
Or that He would permit thee to despair!
Oh! earthquake in thy soul as a rocked city,   105
    That thou shouldst meed such pity!
Oh! that He were less clement, or less fair!
Oh! pang that not the unaltered heart can know,
    To be forgiven so.
Thus shall thy spirit roll to meet the sea   110
Of that horizonless Divinity;
And so recoil before the influxes
Of keen impitiable Love shall seize
And prey on each inusèd pride and lust
    Even as fire on rust;   115
So shalt thou sicken with desires that make
The cicatrices of thine old sins ache,
And flee Him, all for his enamouring sake
    (Shamed by thine own desires),
    To purgatorial fires.   120
Nay, and that fire, deterging and divine,
  Is but His love, which tortures more and more
    From dross the virgin ore.
For as this lady's love yields unmeant pain,
    Through thine own integral stain,   125
Though she of naught but tenderness is fain;
So the high Love where thou shalt lie immersed
Avoidless searcheth out each smirch accursed,
Assimilating thee with sharp constraint,
    Not of His choice, but thine,   130
And thine is to thyself the cruelty,
Since where dross is, flame may not but refine.
    Till thou be fiercely healed,
    And in the dreadful blast
Of that dear vengeance utterly annealed,—   135

Yea, yea, from that amorous furnace, unattaint,
And juster in His replica recast,
  His angels draw thee, a new-moulded Saint,
Gracing the sempiterne arcades above,
    To the clear-rosy veins steeped burningly   140
      In live and bickering love.

  Lo! thus God by thy lady lessoneth thee;
And with thy heart's red seal he inly seals
    This writ which He reveals!'

12 *Indian drug* FT: 'i.e. haschish'. 26 *Hesperian tree* tree of golden apples guarded by the daughters of Hesperia which Hercules was ordered to obtain as one of his twelve labours. 32 *dragon and allure* allusion to the dragon which also guarded the tree. 38 *reprove* strengthen. 41 *entrails* entwine. 68 *frore* frozen.

Between 82–3 Here the following lines are deleted from the manuscript: (naphaline: naphthaline, an inflammable distillate of coal-tar):
    And oh! what fierce concussion needs must shake
      Thy frame, if thou shouldst take,
    Into the exhalations that arise
    From thy love-heated heart in naphaline wise,
    The naked light, foolhardy, of her spirit?

84 *immitigable law* law that cannot be altered, or mitigated. 90 *unpermutable* unalterable. 106 *meed* merit. 113 *impitiable* from impiteous: pitiless. 114 *inusèd* useless, wasted. 117 *cicatrices* scars. 135 *annealed* toughened by being first heated then cooled; hence forgiven, associated especially with sacramental confession. 139 *sempiterne* eternal.

An Allegory
(Of Poetic Composition)

The manuscript of this poem, in ink and signed, was included with the texts prepared for publication in *New Poems* but was not published then or later.

    Close-curtained in a genial night
    Of safe yet unapparent light,
    In pale-poppied meads of dream
    Saintly with pathoses extreme,
    His own bliss-essenced flesh for bed,   5
    The poet to himself is wed.
    What fleet-vanned raptures him enwheel
    You that hear must almost feel.
    His angel lights the roseal torch
    Wherein Love's grosser wing would scorch;   10

And met in vibrant, long embrace
Whence not that angel turns his face,
The nuptial clasp of Heart and Soul
Languors enwrap, ardours enroll.

Yet, as with less immortal nights,   15
'Tis first as much pang as delights.
Till rehearsed bliss the Sentience coy
Season to quick and exigent joy,
She sighs against the ambrosial rights
And thrice-fanned sweets of her keen Boy: 20
Wishfully loath, aversely fain,
She takes with tears the charmèd toy—
Pain in the having, had not, pain;
And would not throe, and yet would gain.

But soon grown apt for amorous fit,   25
Inured the Spirit to admit,
With wifely boldness plumes her charms;
Recoils from nothing exquisite,
Provokes the annihilating trance,
And sickens with untold alarms   30
Unless her god is in her arms:
All's ended, if he should remit
Or he's but slack in dalliance.
But 'tis a thing I have heard told,
That gods grow strange, when girls grow bold: 35
If this be so, best left unsaid,
When poets with themselves are wed.

4 *pathoses* invented word, from Greek *pathos*: passion exciting pity or sadness (*OED*). 9 *roseal* glowing, derived from roseate: rose-coloured. 24 *throe* agonise.

Canticum Novum

The title, 'A New Song', is based on the Biblical sources that provide the main inspiration for the poem's prophetic theme (e.g. 'Sing ye to the Lord a new canticle', Psalms 95, 97). In allegorical form it expresses Thompson's predicament when he came to realise that the message he had set out to convey through his poetry was beyond his fading powers. And even if they should return, the message itself was not to be understood by his generation (see Introduction). This theme is, however, combined with extended descriptions of cosmic warfare, at once prophetic of the future for the world and expressing his personal 'psychomachia' or battle of the soul. Throughout, classical and Biblical allusions interact as the principal sources for the imagery, reflecting Thompson's intimate knowledge of both. Above 1.8 he has written the note: 'this *was* said to me,' referring ahead to 1.14 and the words: 'Poetry . . . should have its roots in hell,* and lift its branches toward heaven.' These words are quoted from Coventry Patmore's review of *Poems* (in the *Fortnightly Review*, January 1894) where Patmore had urged the younger poet to probe deeper into the mysteries of pagan symbolism and their influences on Christianity that were his own chief preoccupation. The repudiation of Patmore's ideas here gives the rest of the poem its direction at the time when Thompson was coming to realise he would be unequal to his poetic role as he had come to understand it. The 'new song' he is called upon to communicate to a future generation will have to draw on the universal symbolic levels of human experience and he fears he is unequal to such a challenge. He draws on the rhythms of the Old Testament prophets and the psalms, and he also makes use of the Anglo-Saxon metre he had used for 'A Judgment in Heaven'; to which can be added a not inconsiderable debt to Blake's 'Prophetic Books', which in turn look to scriptural sources for inspiration.

There are two manuscripts. One is completed but with corrections and the other incomplete. In addition there is a rough draft and a typescript. The completed manuscript, in ink and signed, is at the State University of New York at Buffalo and is the text followed here. It starts and ends with Latin quotations as given below. Thompson gives the attributions except for the short extracts following Psalm 88, which have been added for convenience. Translations are provided in the endnotes, with references to the particular verses he selected to quote. With the complete manuscript is a rough and incomplete pencil draft. The second manuscript, at BC, is also in ink, and contains only the first 60 lines, with none of the accompanying quotations. But this manuscript gives corrections which are on the Buffalo text and appears to have been copied from it as a later version but left unfinished. The typescript has come to light with the discovery of the EMH Collection. It follows the Buffalo text, with the corrections as in the BC manuscript, and there are some typing errors. It contains none of the preliminary quotations but the extract from Ezekiel is added at the end, where Thompson's name is typed. The paper bears on the reverse side of each page the address at 28 Orchard Street where the Meynells were living during Thompson's later years but it is impossible to tell whether it dates from before or after his death. 'Canticum Novum' appears in a list of completed poems he intended for the fourth volume of poetry he began to plan but took no further. A partial list of the contents for this volume, including the present poem, appears on a detached notebook cover in the EMH Collection. It is therefore possible that the typescript was made for him during his lifetime with publication in view. There is no evidence that he could type himself. Brackets, parentheses and asterisks are as in the manuscript.

Deus, laudem meam ne tacueris:* quia os peccatoris et os dolosi super me apertum est. Locuti sunt adversum me lingua dolosa et sermonibus odii circumdederunt me:* et expugnaverunt me gratis. Pro eo ut me diligerent, detrahebant mihi:* ego autem orabam. Et posuerunt adversum me mala pro bonis,* et odium pro dilectione mea. Constitue super eum peccatorem:* et diabolus stet a dextris suis . . . persecutus est hominem inopem et mendicum . . . Et induit maledictionem sicut vestimentum,* et intravit sicut aqua in interiora ejus, et sicut oleum in ossibus suis. Fiat ei sicut vestimentum quo operitur:* et sicut zona qua semper praecingitur. Hoc opus eorum, qui detrahunt mihi apud Dominum:* et qui loquuntur mala adversus animam meam. Et tu, Domine, Domine, fac mecum propter nomen tuum* quia suavis est misericordia tua. Libera me, quia egenus et pauper ego sum:* et cor meum conturbatum est intra me. Sicut umbra cum declinat, ablatus sum:* et excussus sum sicut locustae . . . Adjuva me, Domine Deus meus:* salvum me fac secundum misericordiam tuam. Et sciant quia manus tua haec:* et tu, Domine, fecisti eam . . . Qui insurgunt in me confundantur; servus autem tuus laetabitur. Induantur qui detrahunt mihi, pudore:* et operiantur sicut diploide confusione sua. Confitebor Domino nimis in ore meo:* et in medio multorum laudabo eum. Quia astitit a dextris pauperis,* ut salvum faceret a persequentibus animam meam.

(Psalm 108: 1–6, 17, 18–23, 26–31)

Provocaverunt eum in diis alienis:* et in abominationibus ad iracundiam concitaverunt. Immolaverunt daemoniis et non Deo,* diis, quos ignorabant . . . Juxta est dies perditionis,* et adesse festinant tempora. Judicabit Dominus populum suum,* et in servis suis miserebitur.

(Canticle of Moses, Deut. 32: 16–17, 35–6)

Domine, Deus salutis meae:* in die clamavi et nocte coram te . . . Quia repleta est malis anima mea:* et vita mea inferno appropinquavit. Aestimatus sum cum descendentibus in lacum:* factus sum sicut homo sine adjutorio . . . posuerunt me in lacu inferiori:* in tenebrosis et in umbra mortis. Super me confirmatus est furor tuus:* et omnes fluctus tuos induxisti super me. Longe fecisti notos meos a me:* posuerunt me abominationem sibi. Traditus sum et non egrediebar:* oculi mei languerunt prae inopia. Clamavi ad te, Domine, tota die:* expandi ad te manus meas . . . In me transierunt irae tuae:* et terrores tui conturbaverunt me. Circumdederunt me sicut aqua tota die:* circumdederunt me simul. Elongasti a me amicum et proximum,* et notos meos a miseria.

(Psalm 87: 2, 4–5, 7–10, 17–19)

Misericordias Domini* in aeternum cantabo. In generationem et generationem* annuntiabo veritatem tuam in ore meo . . . Quoniam quis in nubibus aequabitur Domino:* similis erit Deo in filiis Dei? . . . Domine Deus virtutum, quis similis tibi?* potens es, Domine, et veritas tua in circuitu tuo. Tu dominaris potestati maris:* motum autem fluctuum ejus tu mitigas. Tu humiliasti sicut vulneratum, superbum:* in bracchio virtutis tuae dispersisti inimicos tuos. Tui sunt coeli et tua est terra, orbem terrae et plenitudinem ejus tu fundasti:* Aquilonem et mare tu creasti. Thabor et Hermon in nomine tuo exultabunt:* tuum bracchium cum potentia.

(Psalm 88: 1–2, 7, 8–14)

Posuit me desolatam: tota die maerore confectam.   (Lam. 1: 13)

Facies mea intumuit a fletu, et palpebrae meae caligaverunt.   (Job 16: 17)

Quo abiit dilectus tuus, o pulcherrima mulierum? Quo dilectus tuus decli-
navit? . . . Vadam ad montem myrrhiae, et ad collam thuris.

(Song 5: 17, 4: 6)

Sing, all ye Angels, to the Lord of Angels;* sing, O Saintdom, to the
    Lord of Saints!
All ye worlds of the Lord in your paces,* sing to Him like a host upon
    the march!
For the enemies of my soul have gone back before His face;* and I am
    dropped from the jaws of hell.
I am left like a kid that the lion hath dropped,* when the quarrels of the
    Hunter whirr round him.
The deep-mouthed thunder, that is hound of God,* bays at the heel of
    the earth;   5
And the earth is quaked in its courses,* it shudders to its profound-
    laired heart.
So the wrath of the Lord hath barked at them;* and they have fled Him
    down the ways of Night.

What said the wicked to Thy singer,* who sang a little song,
Who sang a little song,* in the tabernacle of his heart;
A little fluting, like a throstle in a thicket,* in the tabernacle of his
    heart?—   10
'Open thy lips for a haughtier song,* that the gates of the world may
    tremble in it.
I will seat thee on the tripod of the elder gods,* and thy mouth shall be
    made an oracle;
If thou wilt but listen to my counsels,* and bow to the gods of the abyss.
[Poetry,' (saith the wicked), 'should have its roots in hell,* and lift its
    branches towards heaven.']
So hast Thou taught me, O my God?* So, O Holy and True?   15
Or is it the voice of Lucifer,* Prince of the Powers of the Air?
'Hast thou seen aught like to my flowers, O My son?* groweth their
    like in Gehenna?
Yet they reach not down unto hell,* nor take their fingers deep hold on
    earth.
Shall the tree which is rooted in the earth* rise as nigh or as swift unto
    heaven,
As that which leapeth from the clefts of the hills,* which I talk to with
    the whispers of My mouth?'   20
*

['In the land of Dis is a singing,* in the land of Dis,' (saith the wicked);
Happy is he in dreams who heareth it, for its notes are as quiring
     flames.
In the land of Dis are singers,* mighty on their harps of iron;
Cyclopean the strings of their harps of iron,* whence they beat a dread-
     forged harmony:
They shall teach thee in dreams Plutonian music,* of the secret things
     of the Abyss.   25
Thy song shall go forth as the trampling of armies,* with the blare of
     the trumpets of Erebus;
Thy words shall be banners set in array,* emblazed with aboriginal
     meanings;
Thy song shall be Alpha and Omega,* the beginning of things and the
     end.']
[But] Thou art Alpha and Omega,* the beginning of things and the end!
And the Erebean wisdom* is but a parcel of Thine.   30
[I have gathered the blossoms of hell,* that I may know them from the
     flowers of Thy Paradise;
I have hearkened the oracle of the Chasm,* that I may discern its voice
     from Thine.
Can all the harpings of those harps of iron* compare with Thy lyre
     Paradisal,
With the thousand-chorded music* that Thou sweepest from the souls
     of Thine Angels?]
Draw close, O close, the pavilion of my heart,* where I may sing Thee
     untroubled of Avernus!   35

Therefore were those hosts gathered against me,* and winded down
     the ways of the Night.
As the tempest, marching from the North,* blows his foreboding
     trumpets,
And his sulphurous battalia* hangs on the darkened hill.
So were they gathered against me,* their forms colossal vagueness,
Or known but by the beams of their lances,* as the mariner sees the
     ice-peaks   40
At distance glance from clouds* in the Hyperborean main.
Their stormy banners were like falls of Acheron,* to enhance their
     baleful splendour;
And the dreadful mass of their enridgèd spears,* like pines when the
     wind is on Pilatus,
Restlessly heaved in their coming,* with tumultuous clang and glare.
They girt all the ways of Night,* they sat down to the leaguer of my
     soul: 45

As a city in an earthquake,* so rocked my battlemented soul;
And through the breach of its ramparts they entered in,* by night,
    when the watchers slept.
But I fled into my heart as one flieth to a citadel,* that falls not when
    the city goes down.
'Look forth toward the verges of the Night,* O Hope, lone watcher
    from the tower;
What on the verges of the Night?'—'Smoke from the bivouacs of
    hell.'   50
Strait drew their lines about me;* thick flew their archery of fire.
'Look forth toward the verges of the Night,* O Hope, lone watcher
    from the tower;
What on the verges of the Night?'*—'Innumerable boding of birds.'
Straiter drew their lines about me;* thicker flew their archery of fire.
'Look forth toward the verges of the Night,* O Hope, wan watcher
    from the tower;   55
What on the verges of the Night?'*—'I see not, for assaulting wings.'
And my heart was mutinous with famine:* my mouth had sick gust of
    death.
'Look forth toward the verges of the Night:* look forth yet once ere we
    fall!'
'Like lightning far off at sea,* cometh somewhat up from the horizon.'
Yet a little while, O heart, stand hard:* for surely this is the battle of
    the Lord!   60
From wing to wing grew the Night inflamed,* like the reaches of a
    phosphored haven;
And the burning war rolled up and onward,* like sand when ye vex a
    pool.
As insects of the hearth when ye light a candle,* so ran to and fro the
    leaguer.
But the battle of the Lord came down like lava,* that confoundeth a city
    of the plain:
And the great Avernian legions* were like leaves on the floor of the
    forest,   65
Like leaves on the floor of the forest,* when the whirlblast whirls them
    in its laughter.
They were hewn in the streets of my soul,* its byways were throttled
    with their ruin;
[In my hands have they left their standard,* even the Abomination of
    Desolation.
Which shall be planted in the Holy Places,* when the Name of the
    Beast hath waxed strong.]

Lock fast the gates of Hell,* when they have sucked back the cohorts
    they vomited; 70
Lock well the infernal gates,* there shall be raiding to their very lintel.
And the gauntleted hand of Michael* shall smite on the ports of the
    Abyss!

Behold, O Lord, a mystery, for Thou too art among the simple ones,
And makest bricks where is no straw,* and wisdom is scandalized at
    Thy ways!
A dove the struggleth with a serpent,* and striketh him with the
    striking of its beak. 75
Who is he that setteth doves against serpents?* Tell us, that we may
    laugh him to scorn.
It is the Lord God of knowledge, it is the Lord God Magnipotent;*
    that holdeth the stars in His leash.
For behold again, from those intervolved folds* the dove flutters
    ruffled and trembling;
Tremulous, torn, yet uncrushed;* but the snake through-pierced to the
    spine!
Not the great brawn of Saul* hast Thou raised up against Gath 80
With brigandine and morion,* and amply-orbèd shield,
And anlace girding in fall;* but the shepherd and the pebbles from the
    stream.

'Go forth, O dove, from My ark,* and look upon the face of the
    waters!'
'O dove, that comest back from looking upon the waters,* what are the
    tidings of thy beak?'
'The floods are rising, the floods are high in anger,* they are in the
    courts of the Holy Places!' 85
'Come back, My Dove, to the windows of Mine ark, my dove that
    wentest forth over the waters.
Bring back no olive branch, but a sword,* because of the day of My
    deluge;
The new deluge that shall cover the earth;* whose floods are not of
    water, but of blood.'
Hadst Thou none of Thy Cherubim, O my God,* who might go forth
    about this thing?
Whose pinions dispread are as twin firmaments;* do they sit with
    folded vans? 90
Whose minds are hollowed for grievous wisdom,* neither does it
    crumble their hearts.

For the wings of a dove are little,* and they faint for flying over many
waters;

For the breast of a dove is tender,* and with heavy wisdom does it travail like a first-filled womb.

I am weary as a child that wanders in the night;* neither find I firm rest
for my foot.

'Are thy wings weary, little dove?* yet thou wentest but a brief way
over the deep.   95

And on My breath wentest thou forth:* could it not upstay thee?

On My wrist, little dove, is thy perch:* who art aweary with looking on
many waters.

Cry to My people, though thy voice is low:* cry to them the words of
My mouth.'

I will cry to Thy people, though my voice be low:* though my voice be
low, and none hearken.

Go up into His ark, whom the Lord hath chosen:* go up into His ark
while is time.   100

Harken to the dove that is wounded:* that is very weary of voice and
wing.

For not I speak, but the Lord:* Who needeth not the thunder for His
trumpet,

Who putteth not the thunder to His lips,* when His voice goeth forth
among His people.

The voice of the Lord upon the waters:* the majesty of the Lord upon
the waters of blood.

The mountains shall be troubled in their strength:* the nations shall
be broken like forests in flood-time.   105

He shall sow the earth with wars to its margents:* terrible are Thy
works, O Mighty One!

In the bending of His bow shall armies be scattered:* He shall melt
their bucklers in His wrath.

But the citizens of the Lord shall exult before His flood:* He shall
make them to inhabit upon the waters.

Not we, O my God, shall fear;* who have turned from the mystery of
iniquity.

The stars toss, the stars toss,* like a multitude with torches,   110

The stars toss like a multitude with torches,* before the way of the
Lord.

'Our hour is at hand with power,' say Thine enemies;* 'let us arise and
feed upon much flesh.'

But He sitteth in the tent of His firmament and taunteth you:* to His
weaklings He hath given your counsels.

From the hand of a little child shall go forth the thunderbolt:* a boy
 shall loose the levin from its slips!

Among the peoples I will sing Thee, whom Thou hast made safe:*
 I will fashion Thee a canticle before the nations.   115
For Thou hast hushed my heart like a mighty water:* my soul is a fal-
 chion in Thy sheath.
Whereto wilt Thou lift me, O my God,* and what is the stroke Thou
 shalt strike with me?
Surely not for nothing hast Thou tempered my soul,* in fire and in
 running tears.
But Thou hoodest mine eyes like a falcon,* that I prey not till Thou
 point me the quarry.
[Stay me, and break me, and bit me;* that I tremble not when Thou
 bridle me for war.]   120
Is Thy like in hell, O Magnipotent?* can Lucifer unsceptre Thee of
 state?
Are the keys of Thy suns at his girdle?* will they open to the summoning of his horn?
Can he marshal the spread ensigns of Thy winds?* doth he know the
 march-word of Thy worlds?
The sea, that dims with its cloudy breath* the azure casement of Thine
 heaven,
Doth it not lick the ground before Thy treading?* hast Thou not
 fettered it to the deep?   125
Thou stampest Thy foot, and the winds crawl to it:* they whine for the
 rebuke of Thine eye:
The thunder, that heaveth heaven with his back,* knoweth the voice of
 his Keeper;
Thou chokest heaven's nostrils with the smoke of tempest:* Thou
 breathest, and it is loosed as a fume;
Thine over-seeded worlds* burst like a fruit of fire.
Thou art Gardener of the unmeted deep,* where no man planteth
 nor gathereth,   130
And its blosmy savannahs are undulous alone,* for the plumes of Thy
 great Sea-Angels;
The tidal leafage of Thy forests* hath ebb and flow like the main;
Thou givest Thine earth soil like flesh,* and mountains like a mighty
 carapace.
As the moon draweth the waters,* so Thou the generations of man.
Six thousand years of man hast Thou wrapped athwart Thy face,*
 yet Thy countenance is relucent as at the Prime,   135

Yet Thy face is nor hidden nor dimmed from us,* we see Thy counte-
    nance as at the Prime.
At the touch of Thy finger the mountain flames,* and the ships on the
    seas of night behold it:
As the water with animalcules,* Thou hast laden Thine air with
    Angels,
Yea, its ooze is impregnate with Spirits,* as the ooze of the brine with
    salt.
Thy morning goeth forth like chariots to battle,* and Thine evening
    like a train from the sanctuary;   140
Thou dippest the clouds in Thy vats:* Thy planets cling like children
    to Thy garment,
Thy planets like children run round Thee,* that take hold by the ves-
    ture of their Sire:
With Thy lightning Thou cleavest heaven as with a share,* and hast
    harvest of the coerule calm;
Thou strewest Thy floor with stars, Lord, as with rushes;* the meteors
    nuzzle their noses in Thine hand.
Who is like to God? Declare, O hell;* and thy thrones burn sullenlier
    red.   145
Declare, O coiled Worm* in the kernel of the mouldered earth!

Si speculator viderit gladium venientem, et non insonuerit buccina: et
populus se non custodierit veneritque gladius et tulerit de eis animam: ille
quidem in iniquitate sua captus est; sanguinem autem ejus de manu specu-
latoris requiram. Et tu, fili hominis, speculatorem dedi te domui Israel:
audiens ergo ex ore meo sermonem, annuntiabis eis ex me. Si me dicente
ad impium: Impie, morte morieris: non fueris locutus, ut se custodiat impius a via sua: ipse impius in iniquitate sua morietur, sanguinem autem
ejus de manu tua requiram. Sin autem annuntiante te ad impium ut a viis
suis convertatur, non fuerit conversus a via sua: ipse in iniquitate sua
morietur: porro tu animam tuam liberasti.   (Ezek. 33: 6–9)

TRANSLATIONS OF PRELIMINARY TEXTS

O God, be not thou silent in my praise: for the mouth of the wicked and the
mouth of the deceitful man is opened against me. They have spoken against me
with evil tongues: and they have compassed me about with words of hatred: and
have fought against me without cause. Instead of making me a return of love, they
detracted me; but I gave myself to prayer. And they repaid me evil for good: and
hatred for my love. Set thou a sinner over him: and may the devil sit at his right
hand . . . Persecuted the poor man and the beggar . . . And he put on cursing like
a garment: and it went in like water into his entrails, and like oil into his bones.
May it be unto him like a garment which covereth him; and like a girdle with

which he is girded continually. This is the work of them who detract me before the Lord: and who speak evils against my soul. But thou, O Lord, do with me for thy name's sake: because thy mercy is sweet. Do thou deliver me, for I am poor and needy, and my heart is troubled within me. I am taken away like the shadow when it declineth: and I am shaken off as locusts . . . Help me, O Lord my God: save me according to thy mercy. And let them know that this is thy hand: and that thou, O Lord, hast done it . . . Let them that rise up against me be confounded: but thy servant shall rejoice. Let them that detract me be clothed with shame: and let them be covered with their confusion as with a double cloak. I will give great thanks to the Lord with my mouth: and in the midst of mercy I will praise him. Because he hath stood at the right hand of the poor, to save my soul from persecu-tion.   (Psalm 108: 1–6, 17, 18, 23, 26–31)

They provoked him by strange gods, and stirred him up to anger, with their abominations. They sacrificed to devils and not to God: to gods whom they knew not . . . The day of destruction is at hand, and the time makes haste to come. The Lord will judge his people, and will have mercy on his servants.
                                        (Canticle of Moses, Deut. 32: 16–17, 35–6)

O Lord, the God of my salvation: I have cried in the day and in the night before thee . . . For my soul is filled with evils: and my life draws nigh to hell. I am counted among them that go down to the pit: I am become as a man without help . . . They have laid me in the lower pit: in the dark places, and in the shadow of death. Thy wrath is strong over me: and all thy waves thou hast brought in upon me. Thou hast put away my acquaintance far from me: they have set me an abom-ination to themselves. I was delivered up, and came not forth: my eyes languished through poverty. All the day I cried to thee, O Lord: I stretched out my hands to thee . . . Thy wrath hath come upon me: and thy terrors have troubled me. They have come round about me like water all the day: they have compassed me about altogether. Friend and neighbour thou hast put far from me: and my acquain-tance, because of misery.   (Psalm 87: 2, 4–5, 7–10, 17–19)

The mercies of the Lord I will sing for ever. I will show forth thy truth with my mouth to generation and generation . . . For who in the clouds can be compared to the Lord: or who among the sons of God shall be like to God? . . . O Lord God of hosts, who is like to thee? Thou art mighty, O Lord, and thy truth is round about thee. Thou rulest the power of the sea: and appeasest the motion of the waves thereof. Thou hast humbled the proud one, as one that is slain: with the arm of thy strength thou hast scattered thy enemies. Thine are the heavens, and thine is the earth: the world and the fullness thereof thou hast founded. The north and the sea thou hast created. Thabor and Hermon shall rejoice in thy name. Thy arm is with might.   (Psalm 88: 1–2, 7, 8–14)

He hath made me desolate and spent with sorrow all the day long.   (Lam. 1: 13)

My face is swollen with weeping, and my eyelids are dim.   (Job 16: 17)

Whither is thy beloved gone O most beautiful among women? Whither is thy beloved turned aside? . . . I will go to the mountain of myrrh, and to the hill of frankincense.   (Song 5: 17, 4: 6)

TRANSLATION OF CONCLUDING TEXT

And if the watchman sees the sword coming, and sound not the trumpet: and the people look not to themselves, and the sword come, and cut off a soul from among them: he indeed is taken away in his iniquity; but I will require his blood at the hand of the watchman. So thou, O son of man, I have made thee a watchman to the house of Israel: therefore thou shalt hear the word from my mouth, and shalt tell it them from me. When I say to the wicked: O wicked man, thou shalt surely die: if thou dost not speak to warn the wicked man from his way: that wicked man shall die in his iniquity, but I will require his blood at thy hand. But if thou tell the wicked man, that he may be converted from his ways, and he be not converted from his way: he shall die in his iniquity: but thou hast delivered thy soul.

(Ezek. 33: 6–9)

4 *quarrels* arrows. **14** See headnote for FT's note on this line. **21** *Dis* Hades, or the Underworld. **24** *Cyclopean* The Cyclops were mythical giants often associated with thunderbolts. **26** *Erebus* the dark entrance to the Underworld. **35** *Avernus* lake associated with entry to the Underworld. **38** *battalia* brigade. **41** *Hyperborean* descriptive of the legendary land of plenty and sunshine beyond the reach of the north wind. **42** *falls of Acheron* waterfalls on the river of the Underworld. **43** *Pilatus* Swiss mountain traditionally associated with the suicide of Pontius Pliate. See also note to l. 98 of 'Ode to the Setting Sun'. **45–69** passage recalling the theme of 'Psychomachia' or 'Battle of the Soul'. FT would have been familiar with the best-known version by Prudentius, the fourth-century Spanish pioneer of Christian literature **45** *leaguer* siege. **53** *boding of birds* flight of birds used as a form of prophecy. **64** The BC MS ends here. **68–9** Imagery here derives from Daniel 12: 11 and Matt. 24: 15. **72** *Michael* the archangel who triumphed over the fallen archangel Lucifer. **80–2** The heavy armour of King Saul is contrasted with the pebble and sling with which David slew the giant warrior Goliath (1 Kings 17: 38–50). **82** *anlace girding* and dagger hanging at the waist. **83–8** The dove that Noah sent out from the Ark, to look for dry land appearing after the Flood, returned with an olive branch in her beak. Her release over the waters and return to the Ark as a place of safety symbolises the poet-prophet who has been sent to bear a message that cannot survive the flood-tide of the contemporary world. **99–101** The poet-prophet returns to the Ark, traditional symbol for the Church. **116** *falchion* curved sword. **130** *unmeted* boundless, immeasurable. **133** *carapace* covering shell of the tortoise. **138** *animalcules* microscopic creatures. **121–46** The concluding passage on the cosmic grandeur of the created world draws on numerous Biblical passages, notably Job 38, 39; Psalm 103.

The New Woman: The New Which Is the Old

This is the first of the two poems Thompson prepared for *New Poems* as 'The New Woman', but only the second, 'The After Woman', was published (pp. 139). The unpublished poem exists in two manuscripts. One forms part of the manuscript for the two poems prepared for *New Poems;* the other is a separate manuscript. This second one has been used here. The prefixed quotations do not contain the deletions that occur in the first, and it generally appears to be the more considered text. The quotations are given here as Thompson copied them. There appears to be no precise origin for the first extract, which follows the general title 'The New Woman' and precedes the title for this poem, 'The New Which Is the

Old'. A possible source is suggested with the translation in the endnotes. The poem is in effect a series of loosely connected reflections on these passages, taken mainly from the Office of Matins for Holy Saturday.

Ceciderunt simul Tria, Tria simul resurgent. Et Tria Aqua signantur: mulier, corpus, natura. Et Tria unum: et unum hoc mulier. Mulier enim corpus; mulier natura . . .

Quomodo obscurantum est aurum, mutatus est color optimus, dispersi sunt lapides sanctuarii in capite omnium platearum? Filii Sion inclyti, et amicti auro primo: quomodo reputati sunt in vasa testea, opus manum figuli?   (Lam. 4: 1–2)

Recordare, Domine, quid acciderit nobis: intuere, et respice opprobrium nostrum. Hereditas nostra versa est ad alienos: domus nostrae ad extraneos . . . Aegypto dedimus manum, et Assyrus, ut saturaremur pane . . . Servi dominati sunt nostri: non fuit qui redimeret de manu eorum.
                                                                    (Lam. 5: 1–2, 6, 8)

Bonum est praestolari cum silentio salutare Dei. Bonum est viro, cum portaverit jugum ab adolescentia sua. Sedebit solitarius, et tacebit: quia levarit super se.   (Lam. 3: 26–8)

Funes ceciderunt mihi in praeclaris: etenim hereditas mea praeclara est mihi. Benedicam Dominum qui tribuit mihi intellectum.   (Psalm 15: 6–7)

O God, whose ancient miracles we see shining even in our own days; since that which by the power of Thy right hand thou didst confer upon one people by delivering them from Egyptian persecution, Thou dost operate by the water of regeneration for the salvation of the gentiles: grant that the fullness of the whole world may pass over to the children of Abraham, and the dignity of Israelites.

(Prayer for the Fourth Prophecy of the Office, based on Exodus 14, 15)

> Well ye exult, O ancient Eva's daughters,
> So high in flood are the death-dealing Waters!
> Regard, All Seeing, our disgrace!
> How are the stones o' the holy place
> Scattered at head, O Lord of every square!   5
> The gold o'erdusted, the fine colour changed;
> The many have ranged
> After each lying soothsayer
> Which spake to them the things that were
> In their own hearts. How are the prime   10
> Of Sion, whom Thou hast instoled
> In Thine authentic gold,

By the false horde
In the extravagant time
Reputed with the earthen vessels, Lord!   15
Wisdom is taken away from age;
The stranger hath our heritage;
And the slave sceptres it, elate,
Over our unregarded state.
'While yet,' our teachers cry, 'the stones have we,   20
What shall ye for the Sanctuary?
Since stones which nothing build are still
Stones;—build ye with them each man what he will.'
To Egypt, and
To Assyria, have we given the hand,   25
If haply they may cram our mouths with bread;
Full-dieted
With science of the finest-bolted dust;
Putting our trust
In reason crafty to o'ersilver rust;   30
Guerdoned with each foul plague that ever banned
The God-smote heathen in a heathen land,
Until our spots obscene
Would rot the deluge, ere it washed us clean:
While wheels on its appointed path—   35
And the blind eyes mark not
The dreadful shadow all the landscape blot—
In ever-narrowing gyres, the great day of Thy wrath.

Yet see I must—
Although with heart at ache, and feet   40
That labour on adust
In storm-precurring heat—
The lightning travailing in the tempest's womb
That harbingers the fuller ray;
After the whirling besom of the doom   45
Thy Mercy riding on its foreswept way,
And the still voice, Lord, of Thy gentle Day.
Good is it to wait mute
Of Thy salvation, Lord, the sure ensuit;
And well is it with such an one   50
That from his youth hath felt Thy yoke severe,
Which Thou no ways hast suffered him to shun;
And better who hath reached such term

That on himself the weight austere
He hath attainèd to confirm.   55
Sole shall he sit, and hold his peace,
Fastening his heart on what his eye foresees:
He, with reproaches saturate,
While all the bacchanal people jeer
At his uncomraded estate,   60
And joyfully themselves forefate
To their hugged ruin,—for present ease
Shall no whit bate
His mournful hope, and solemn cheer.

Yea, so: in days of evil chance,   65
High yet is mine inheritance;
Blest He who taught, in a dark land,
Mine eyes to see, my heart to understand.
But ah! Who madest me not only seer,
But singer, shall I then transgress   70
Thy law writ here,
Which bids me expect and hold my peace,
If my tongue chant the thing mine eye foresees,
And Thy sweet End show darkly clear?
When my song cloistral is no less   75
Against the feet of foolishness
Than mine enclosèd heart?—Nay, sure
In a most azure-sanctuaried and pure
Annunciation may this verse
The message mystical rehearse   80
Once by an angel utterèd,
And, save by angels, half its promise unread.
Ah, well may poet's earthlier voice reword
To earth the *Ave* dully heard,
And this song Gabriel-like reverse   85
To blessing its prime-uttered curse!
And she, the aloft and regal She,
Shall my large auspice surety,
Round whom the twinèd months are set
And burnished for a carcanet: 90
Who on this Easter roseal,
Flaming for her festival,
(Being bringer of the earth's Desire,
That from her Night hath took the world with fire),
Of untiar'd Ishtar and her wanèd house   95

This right and native title hath,
Girt with conquest on her brows,—

Light and Lady of the Path

Destroying and preserving Water!   100
By the death and life you gave
When deluge brake through heaven's wide dam;
By the Egyptian mystic wave
Which waked the song of Miriam;
O Eva's daughter!   105
Your children be
These woes, O Bitterness of the Sea!
Do you, made sweet,
Bear on your beautiful sea-feet
Glad tidings out of Sion! We wait,   110
Gate of the desert called Sin:—
Time is. Be lifted up, O Gate,
And let the King of Glory in!

TRANSLATIONS OF PRELIMINARY TEXTS

Three things have fallen at the same time, three at the same time will rise. And the three are signed with water: the woman, the body and nature. And the three are one: and this one is the woman. For the woman is body, the woman nature . . .
(For possible source for paraphrase here see 1 John 5: 7)

How is the gold become dim, the finest colour is changed, the stones of the sanctuary are scattered in the top of every street? The noble sons of Sion, and they that were clothed with the best gold: how are they esteemed as earthen vessels, the work of the potter's hands?   (Lam. 4: 1–2)

Remember, O Lord, what is come upon us: consider and behold our reproach. Our inheritance is turned to aliens: our house to strangers . . . We have given our hand to Egypt, and to the Assyrians, that we might be satisfied with bread . . . Servants have ruled over us: there was none to redeem us out of their hand.
(Lam. 5: 1–2, 6, 8)

It is good to wait with silence, for the salvation of God. It is good for a man, when he has borne the yoke from his youth. He shall sit solitary, and hold his peace: because he hath taken it upon himself.   (Lam. 3: 26–8)

The lines are fallen to me in goodly places: for my inheritance is goodly to me. I will bless the Lord, who hath given me understanding.   (Psalm 15: 6–7)

31–4 reference to the seven plagues of Egypt (Exodus 7–12). 42 *precurring* foretelling. 49 *ensuit* outcome, effect. 84–6 The Angel Gabriel's salutation (*Ave*) to the Virgin Mary reverses the name of Eva, the first woman. 88 *auspice surety* confirm a prophecy. 90 *carcanet* crown. 95 *Ishtar* Egyptian goddess now displaced by the Virgin Mary. 100–1 reference to the Flood. 103–4 reference to the crossing of the Red Sea by the Israelites and Miriam's subsequent song of triumph (Exodus 14; 15: 20–2).

Stellis Matutinis Humanis

The title translates as 'To the Human Morning Stars'. The poem was composed as part of Thompson's preparatory work for a fourth volume of poetry, to be called 'First Fruits and Aftermath'. The project did not get beyond the early stages as he was already suffering the symptoms that led to his last illness. The manuscript is in ink and signed, the poem prefixed with the following 'Explanation': 'All my poems to children (with one exception made for a special reason), I would purpose, should they be published during my life and under my supervision, to draw together in a special section towards the end of the book. That section would have the ensuing allegorical title and motto from Shelley; and then would follow a dedicatory poem to children in general, which would further show the meaning of the title. In form and manner following.' The excepted poem would have been 'Sister Songs', on account of its length. The allegorical title was to be 'In the Gardens of Phosphorus' (the morning star) and the motto from Shelley's 'The Cloud':

> *From my wings are shaken the dews that waken*
> *The sweet buds everyone,*
> *When rocked to rest on their mother's breast.*

The dedicatory poem was 'Stellis Matutinis Humanis'.

Stars of the Morning
Why have ye fallen from heaven?
Leaving your brother above you,
Phosphor, to look down and love you:
Stars have drifted, a golden snow-storm,   5
West in slow storm,
The fiery snow of the stars is riven;
Phosphor only the sunrise scorning
Thaws i' the morning,
Last frail flake of a fall o'erdriven.   10
And I below, as he above you,
Ask, for we love you,
Stars of the Morning!
Why have ye fallen from heaven?

What the ambrosial   15
Clarities meet to be food for you?
Foam of the Milky Way?
Suck of the sun that is bosom of day?
The Pleiads in cup prest? Moonbeams curded?
Oh! the ungirded   20
Peaks of Titania's breast were too rude for you!
Heady dew such as the bacchanal, social
Fairies with roseal

Spices inflame were a drink to be brewed for you!
Nuzzlers in mire, snouters in clay, 25
  Can we purvey
  Essence ambrosial,
Balms that were meet to be food for you?

  Ah! but a hill is
Laden with virginal snows! 30
Twin are the peaks of it, twin
Fountains that rise from therein!
Mother's bosom has water bright for you,
  Pure and white for you
As the winters from which it flows. 35
There, as a doe feeds among lilies,
  Sweet and still is
Your soft feeding, tender does!
Paradise fledglings, heirless to sin,
  Young seraphin, 40
  Where Eden rill is
Might change for your mounts of snows!

  Very rich is
  The drink your lips
  Draw from that argent 45
  Fountain exquisite,
  Seemly wroughten
  In lucent rondure
   By Messer God.
  Sorrow that witches, 50
  Joys that eclipse,
  Dear loves mix in it,
  For your mouth's margent;
  Tears that conjure,
  And holy thought, in 55
   Its woman's flood.
  All mortality
  Given to your mouth in it!
  God's immortality
  Slaked His drouth in it, 60
   Seasoned so for the bitter Rood.
O fallen from heaven! for your human passion
Ye must be seasoned in self-same fashion,

Stars of the Morning!
Nothing scorning   65
  The self-same food.

Childhood! irised symbol of
Covenant of forgiving loves!
God's light from woman's tears
Re-creates you through the years.   70
At your shining did surcease
Wrath of God, man's agonies.
Children! sure your framing is
Paradisal sweet caprice,
Our smiling, God's sport,   75
A tender toy of Heaven's court;
And thereat on Eden sod,
Certes, it is May with God.
Antidotes to that prime Curse
Of the stricken universe,   80
Man,—weak nature's tyrant, fair
Virgin earth's deflowerer.

Snatches of the primal Eden!
Golden fruitage that is seeden
From the unslimèd unforbidden   85
Trees of Paradise, or e'er
The old Snake was coilèd there;
Or ever Eve's envenomed tooth
Fettered the world's lusty youth,
'Stilled the death into the mouth   90
Of the adder, and the eyes
Of the lovely-gazing plant
Which canopied her nightly haunt,
And the aconite's duskèd dyes;
And herbs and men grew poisonous-wise.   95

O warm from off the lap of God!
Fire unto the agèd blood
Of gran'dam earth, and unto me
All I am and hope to be!
Mirror of this spirit toiled   100
In a body spent and foiled;

Take these songs which have arisen
From its ineradible prison,
As a captive bird may sing
To its fellows on the wing;   105
Chanting, to your fetterless age,
Of the bird within the cage.

19 *Pleiads* the seven daughters of Atlas who were transformed into the constellation of stars known by this name. 21 *Titania* queen of the fairies. 36–8 For the image of the doe feeding among lilies cf. Song 4:5. 48 *lucent rondure* shining circle. 92–3 *lovely gazing plant . . . nightly haunt* FT note: the nightshade. 103 *ineradible* immoveable.

Sufficit Unum

The title translates as 'One is Enough'. The manuscript is a fair copy in ink in NB BC14. With it are final drafts for several 'Narrow Vessel' poems, for which this one may have been originally intended.

The throstle has a many notes,
    The stock-dove has but one
Yet one the thing they both have said,
    When the song's done.

Why sing thee, Sweet, a thousand notes?   5
    Take the one in lieu;—
'Love, I love thee!' One's enough,
    When the one's true.

Why kiss thee five-fold kisses, Fair,
    When the one's complete?   10
Nay, keep bliss single. One's enough
    For perfect sweet.

Why clasp a score of sharp farewells,
    Now you steal, pure thief,
Your rich self from me? One's enough   15
    For divine grief.

A Ballad of the Baralong

The manuscript of this poem is in ink and signed, a fair text that Thompson may have considered for publication in order to draw attention to an incident that he rightly felt should not be forgotten. His keen interest in the Boer War was largely confined to the privacy of his notebooks, where many fragments dealing with the subject are caustically critical of some aspect of the British side.

In 1899 the Boers besieged Mafeking, including the *stadt* or native town of the African Baralong tribe as well as the British garrison under the leadership of Colonel Baden-Powell. He took an unprecedented step in arming three hundred of the Africans to help with the defence, apart from employing some seven hundred more in other capacities. On 12 May 1900 the Boer leader, Sarel Eloff, attacked Mafeking at what seemed its most vulnerable part, the African township. But it was the Baralong counter-attack that trapped the Boers and so saved the day for the British. Yet despite their bravery they received hardly any official recognition from Baden-Powell, and the relief fund raised in Britain for the victims of the siege was used by him exclusively for the benefit of the white inhabitants. The incident has, as Thompson feared, gone largely unnoticed since. The most notable exception has provided the information given here and for the endnotes: Thomas Pakenham, *The Boer War* (1979), pp. 402–18.

> The Baralongs are sore in need
>   Who right well did deserve:
> A little gift of your gold, England,
>   A little gift will serve!
>
> Harken the deeds of the Baralong,   5
>   Which he did in Mafeking town;
> When the flames went up with the breaking dawn,
>   And the Boer ranks came down.
>
> Hear the help that to England gave
>   The Baralong ready and true:—   10
> England, what will you do for him,
>   That did so much for you?
>
> 'Why guns a-growl from yonder East
>   So long or e'er the dawn?
> Why sings us up before the day   15
>   This hasty bullet-spawn?'
>
> 'Yon barking dogs,' said Baden-Powell,
>   'I hold a sorry jest;
> They knock against our Eastern gate,
>   But they'll visit us in the West.'   20

And he spake over true a thing,
    Although in guise of jest.
When like a crouching lion came
    With stealth the tawny dawn, a flame
    Made answer in the West.   25

Was never a man in Mafeking
    But his was sore dismay,
When he knew the foe had broken in
    Where the native quarter lay!

At their head young Eloff,   30
    Of Kruger's kindred, stood;
At his heels the foreigners
    That hate the Saxon blood.

'Twas shot and steel, and hunt at heel,
    And 'Shoot the Rooineks down!'   35
'Now call up them that follow us,
    And we have Mafeking town!'

How say ye to that, ye Baralongs,
    On whom the foe hath broke?
Many a son hath the Boer slain,   40
    Will ye now yield stroke for stroke?

The Baralong is brown as earth,
    Not of our Saxon white;
But his hue was the brave English red,
    When he bled in England's fight!   45

The Boers had broken in before,
    The Boers came on behind;
'Twixt them behind and them before
    Swiftly the Baralongs lined.

'Twas long rank dun, and levelled gun,   50
    And sweet the rifles' crack!
It was the dusky Baralong
    Cried—'Stand! and beat them back!'

The Boer went back from the Baralong,
   For the brown ranks stood most stout: 55
Then they cried: 'Now ye have won in,
   Pray your God ye win out!'

They turned on them that to win in
   Had found an easy thing;
But to win out, they might not do't,   60
   For the Baralong balls had sting.

Baralongs, and Englishmen,
   And they of the Colony,
With *crick! crack!* here, and *spit! zip!* there,
   They would not let them be.   65

Englishmen, and Baralongs,
   And men of the Colony,
Where they might spy a Boer head,
There they whizzed in the burning lead,
   That stung like an angry bee.   70

It was sunrise when they began,
   Sundown when they did rest;
He that came in to Mafeking
   Was no untended guest!

It was sunrise when they did rest,   75
   Sundown when they began;
For the lean earth was an-hungered
   To feed on flesh of man.

'Enough!' cried out young Eloff,
   'We yield us well,' he said.   80
'We fain would fare on Christian food,—
   We have fared full on lead!'

They led them then to Baden-Powell,
   With joyance and with shout;
Who had found our gates might open in,   85
   But did not open out.

'Welcome,' quoth Baden-Powell,
　'Brave guests to share our cup:
Hasty was your morning-call,
　But I trow you'll stay to sup!'　　　　　　　90

This was the deed of the Baralong,
　Which he did in Mafeking town;
When the fires went up with the breaking dawn,
　And the Boer ranks came down.

This was the aid to England　　　　　　　95
　Of the Baralong ready and true:
He gave his blood, he saved the town,—
England, answer, from city to down,
　What will *you* give him, you?

31 *Kruger's kindred* Sarel Eloff was the grandson of Paul Kruger, the President of the Boers. **35** *Rooinecks* nickname, 'Rednecks', for the British. **36–7** At first it looked as if the victory would be easily won by the Boers. **40–1** The Baralong had their own reason for revenge on the Boers, who had murdered a number of refugees from the *stadt*, including women and children, when the Baralong had been forced to leave Mafeking on account of the food shortage. **63, 67** *Colony* Cape Colony, whose inhabitants fought on the British side. **72–3** Eloff surrendered the same evening as the battle, 12 May.

Threat of French Invasion

The final manuscript of this poem, in ink and signed, is at the Humanities Research Center, Austin, Texas. There are two drafts at BC, in NBs 8A and 122. In a letter accompanying the manuscript Meynell wrote that 'The Fashoda incident was the occasion of the verse.' This dates the poem to 1898 when a French force in Africa took possession of Fashoda, a village on the Upper Nile claimed by the English. Settlement was reached, but not before relations between the two countries became seriously strained. Among drafts for Thompson's later odes for public occasions there are many passages on the country's passing greatness similar to the main theme here.

Hearest thou, Lady of Western waters, the mock which thy mockers
　　have cried?—
That the Gallic cock shall strike his spur in thy toothless lion's hide?
Summon the servant forces, which the Powers have enfeoffed to thee
Who set thy chair in the salty ooze, chained below the chains of the sea.

＊

Whistle the winds that they observe thee, which mangled the sail of
    Spain;   5
Shall they not harken thy word and serve thee, child of the ancient
    main?
Call to the East wind, call to the West wind, with power to the South and
    the North,
That they fledge the heels of thy snorting keels when the smoke from
    their nostrils goeth forth.

Lift up thy voice to the clouds thy kindred, till their ranking angers form
In the imminent verges, the swiftness unhinderèd, and prevalent
    approaches of storm.   10
They shall pass as a herd of the pampas pass, and the foe shall be riven
    and flee,
Thrust down under their hooves of thunder,—for are they not foaled of
    thy lineal sea?

Lay thy hand on the strong sea-horses; shall they not heed thy frown?
Shall they not fight for thee in their courses, that trod the galleons down?
Shall they not render their backs to bear thee, and leap to thy regent
    call,   15
That tossed of old from their stormy necks the alien hand of the mount-
    ing Gaul?

At the threat of France—in the rustling flaw as the leaves of yester-
    year—
The dead dust stirs on Cressy, is restless on Poitier,
Like dogs that dream of the chase, thy heroes move in their shroudless
    bed;
And a hundred victories trouble at root the tremulous grass of the fields
    they fed.   20

Is thy heart less quick, O England, than grasses and dust of men?
Or art thou dulled with age, nor hear'st the loud hunt gird thy den?
Or deem'st the bruit of thy voice alone will startle thy foes from the field?
Arise, and fashion anew thine arms, and look thou well to thine outworn
    shield!

If the term of thy years have found thee, choose mighty ways to fall!   25
Die with thy victories drawn around thee, Caesar-like, for pall!
At the base of thine ancient greatness if the nations lay thee dead,
They cannot take and they shall not shake the clinging laurel from thy
    head!

17 *flaw* gust of wind

Gilboa

These lines probably express ideas that occurred to Thompson while he was working on a fragmentary verse play, *Saul*. They remain elusive, although an anonymous attempt at explanation has been appended to the single manuscript page at a late date, in typescript. The note reads: 'In this unpublished poem the love referred to in the first line might well be David's with which he strove to counter Saul's hatred. But he lost "the last and crowning fight" when Saul, defeated by the Philistines with whom David was then allied, "took his sword and fell upon it" (1 Kings 31:4). The scene of Saul's last battle and death was Mount Gilboa, or Gelboe. There may be a suggestion of David's lament for Saul in "this song—the last" (2 Kings 1). It would seem to be David who was "well quit", in the end, because of his persevering love.'

> Love, foredoomèd opposite!
> 'Gainst his sin's oft-encountered might
> Lost the last and crowning fight.
>
> On the field he stood alone,
> Stood and groaned Saul's heavy groan,   5
> Smote, and fell self-overthrown.
>
> Yet, as Roland's spirit past
> In the loud death of a blast,
> So Love in this song—the last.
>
> All is done. You are well quit.   10
> All is loved, as is most fit.
> Let what is writ be what is writ.

7–8 cryptic reference to 'The Song of Roland' when Roland chooses to die rather than sound the horn that would bring aid against his betrayer.

A Ballad of Charity

The manuscript for this poem is in two parts, both in ink and signed at the end of the second part. Until *c.* 1976 lines 1–82 were at BC and lines 83–121 at M. Since then the two have been joined to form the complete poem at BC. In *Life* the following lines are quoted: 89–92, 97–100, 105–8, 119–20. The variants in these quotes indicate that Everard Meynell was not using the final text but taking it from drafts in several notebooks. In addition he refers to the poem as 'unfinished' and gives it an incorrect title, 'A Ballad of Judgement' (*Life*, p. 292). Thompson uses the ballad form here to experiment with a double theme, one aspect alternating with the other in alternate lines. Some of his punctuation has been regularised.

The humour is similar to the occasional verse of his later years, with its underlying criticism of religious and social attitudes. In this sense, the medieval setting
does not 'date' this more considered poem.

Friar Peter thundered in St Gudule's
    (A preacher preaching from God's own writ)
Of charity after the heart of the Schools,
    (Shall preach clean crooked from God's good wit.)

How the kindly gifts of man to man,   5
    Save but they be purely done for God.
With man have end as they began.
    (And burgher John he hearkened awed.)

Lowly, he said, was their altar-plate,
    (Far meeter your grapes in God's blood ran)   10
Right poor for the Highest to take His state.
    (Than crushed in a cup for your light leman.)

'I will get me' said John, 'a quaint chalice
    (Carven over with fair device)
And give it the Church for my soul's bliss;   15
    That God may know me in Paradise.'

But as homeward he passed, one 'Hail!' him bade;
    (Shall not the blossom think on the bee?)
He thought on the friends he had meant to glad:
    And the chalice sublimed in that flushed thought free.   20

So he gathered them unto him, brimmed them a cup
    (Gold honey immingled in ooze o' the vine.)
Whose beads from his heart trembled gleaming up.
    (Gold love melting at bosom o' the wine.)

Yet the mass-cup's Blood remained true as It   25
    (Scant his reck perhaps—who may tell?—)
That seasoned Iscariot's throat or the Pit.
    (Though His cup be carved to a fair marvel.)

'Unfinished the church-walls! Not one face'
    (Friar Peter thus: John hears devoutly.)   30
'To show how the devilkin imps grimace!'
    ('This time for my soul!' said John right stoutly.)

'But woe's me, then, for each winsome wean,
  (Franz, Trudchen, and all, in wistful dule!)
And their new playthings that should have been!'   35
  (And it grew to the hallow tide of Yule.)

So he gave their wish, on the mouth so soft
  (Alack! for the rede of St. Gudule's!)
Kissing them, as he kissed them oft.
  (And Charity after the heart of the Schools!)   40

Friar Peter preached, as he preached before;
  (Who would get them their Paradise-wear?)
Precious the Host, the church-copes poor.
  (What robe too rich for a Christ-bearer?)

Far better such robes, than satin and sheen   45
  ('A cope!' thinks conscious John, 'gold-decked')
For your peacock dames to prink them and preen.
  ('That never a wearer may genuflect.')

But he passed in street a merchant's shop;
  (Turned him—'By maiden Mary's snood!')   50
And his heart glowed rose through the filming cope.
  ('The mantle I promised wife Ermentrude!')

He clasped it on her; and her mouth soft,
  (The mantle in most lovely wise)
Stooping, kissed, as he kissed it oft,   55
  (Figured as all with flag-lilies.)

'Dead?' quo' Friar Peter, 'I heard the toll.'
  (Had he done for the glory of the Lord's house)
'Good husband, father? Yea, rest his soul!'
  (What he did for friend, and child, and spouse!)   60

'To friends, the poor, kind? H'm, 'm,—well!'
  (Some charity, see you, is guerdoned here.)
'But "Judge not," saith Scripture. 'Tis hard to tell.'
  (In sleep, that night, his eyes saw clear.)

He saw the burgher with humbled eyes   65
  (The spirit that guarded him piloteth.)
Go in to the Father of Paradise.
  (With the spirit in Heaven's tongue Life, ours Death.)

The angels a–play on its fields of summer
  *(Their mad wings rippled his guides' cymars)*70
Looked up from their sport at the passing comer,
  (As they pelted each other with handfuls of stars.)

'For the drink thou gavest Me, John, good grace!'
  (The wind knows not when it sows a seed.)
'Good thanks for My feet thou did'st embrace!'75
  (Of its kiss to the lily it has no heed.)

'Good thanks for the gift wherewith erewhile'
  (Scents the flower its odorousness?)
'Thou madest My young Jesus smile.'
  *(That your heart leaps up for it, what does it guess?)*80

'Good thanks for the mantle, servant John.'
  (Fire its robe on the torch shall throw)
'Thou has clasped my daughter Mary upon.'
  (Nor deem you swathèd red in the glow.)

'O when with a mantle, Lord God,' said John,85
  (I wot he was a man astound!)
'Have I clothed the Lady Mary on?'
  (In the new Air wist he not his tongue's sound.)

'O when did I give Thee drink erewhile,
  *Or when embrace Thine awful feet?*90
What gifts give for my Prince Christ's smile,
  (Who am a guest here most unmeet?)'

'In the love-cup mingled for brethren thine'
  (Brother to brother of gift is free.)
'My lips had gust of the altar-wine.'95
  (Yet no father crieth, 'Why gav'st not me?')

'If but a toy gladden His little brothers,'
  (A touch in caress to a child's hair given)
'My Jesus' hands are filled as with prayers.'
  *(Fondles to music all strings of Heaven.)*100

'When thou clothed'st, of love, her I made with thee one,'
  (See, Mary's mantle, with its device,)
'Thou clothed'st the Queen of spouses on.'
  (Live flickering things like flag-lilies!)

'When thou kissedst thy wife and fair weans sweet,   105
   Their eyes are fair in My sight as thine,
I felt the embraces on My feet.
   Lovely their locks in thy sight, and Mine.'

'My finger tinctured the eyes, and spun
   Were the locks at My daughter Mary's wheel: 110
Liked'st our art? 'Tis well, dear John!
   Who like his work, to the Master kneel.'

For that mantle he's gotten from Queen Mary
The maid-moon badge of her own meinie;
For the gift that made his weans' hands clap,   115
She has set the Christ-boy into his lap;
For his friends' good gladness in that love-cup,—
'Dip thy hand in My heart and sup!'
For his sweet-kissed wife, (Friar Peter trow'th),
God kissed him on the blissful mouth.   120

3 *Schools* medieval forerunners of universities. 12 *leman* sweetheart. 33 *wean* small child. 34 *dule* woe. 38 *rede* advice. 50 *snood* hair band. 70 *cymars* loose garments. 119 *trow'th* please note.

POEMS FROM THE AD AMICAM NOTEBOOK

This is the notebook in which Thompson wrote fair copies of the poems he addressed to Katie King, written mainly in 1896 during his last months at Pantasaph. They comprised a sequence of poems he called 'De Amicitia'—On Friendship—and further sonnets and poems. To these he added others, either at that time or, more probably, later. They are not addressed to her and may have been included with the fourth volume of poems in mind. The notebook does not survive in its complete form: the contents, comprising 17 poems, have been divided between the collections at BC, H and the Lilly Library, Indiana University. While it was still intact, but at an unrecorded date, a photostat was made of the complete contents and this is now at BC. It must have been made before 1941, the date of the revised edition of TLCPoems, for in his notes Connolly refers to the photostat at BC and to the original notebook then still at M. He also refers to a catalogue of the complete Thompson Collection at BC which was to include a section on the photostat, but there is no record of such a catalogue at BC (TLCPoems, p. 541.)

Apart from the five hitherto unpublished poems now printed here, notebook contains five sonnets published in *Works* with the collective title 'Ad Amicam', two others published in *MHW*, and the following five poems which, already published, appear earlier in this volume: 'Marriage in Two Moods', 'Body and Sprite', 'To a Wind', 'Absence', and 'Elevaverunt Flumina'.

Meynell added a note to the original notebook, also at the Lilly Library, describing how the friendship between Thompson and Katie King arose when she joined the Meynell household to look after their children. He continues: 'Francis was very disappointed that somehow the verses he wrote to Katie did not answer to his wishes & hopes. On the back of this page is pasted part of one of many letters he wrote about what he feared was their failure to give pleasure to her or to us.' If Thompson wrote 'many letters' on the subject, only the one to which Meynell refers has survived, severely mutilated, together with another quoted below. In the 'Ad Amicam' letter referred to by Meynell, Thompson also wrote:

> The poems were, in fact, a kind of poetic diary; or rather a poetic substitute for letters. They were more akin to Shakespeare's sonnets than to the 'Vita Nuova' or 'Love in Dian's Lap' (so far as you can liken them). Better still, you might compare them with 'A Narrow Vessel', which has the same (or a similar) character of casual poetic diary. They were strictly incidental expressions of personal and subjective feeling, nowise idealisations of a woman (save indirectly). They were little safety-valves through which my momentary self escaped, not attempted eulogies of her. (To this there is one exception, the long terminal 'Nocturns', where precisely I recognise real failure.) To bring them into relation with 'Love in Dian's Lap' is to prejudge failure, because their standard is so alien, so much lower, and more casual and subjective in kind. I do not think they have much left for a second reading, which is a partial defect, cutting them off in substantial character from the best of my work . . . of their nature and poetic species—above all, if you come to read them in print, you may revise your present view that they are failures. With the exception which I have noted, I am not myself able to feel that they are unsuccessful in their preconceived kind. So far I feel impelled to dissent from your judgment, for once. 'Absence', in particular, seems to me to be what I meant it to be. But I may, of course, be wrong, and you right . . . Anyway, I have done what I wanted . . .
>
> (*Letters*, pp. 211–12)

In contrast to Thompson's polite concession to Meynell's negative view here, his own view is more clearly given in an earlier letter written soon after Meynell first saw the poems: 'O Wilfrid, I do think they are rather, *rather* beautiful. I may be quite wrong, but it does seem to me that they are good. I did not guess that they were so good as they *seem*. I never had the courage to look at them when my projected volume became hopeless, fearing they were poor, until now, when I was obliged to do so. If I am right it is a crime they cannot be published' (*Letters*, p. 206). Thompson is referring to the fourth volume of poetry, proposed but not undertaken. Meynell's view would have been at least partly influenced by his fear lest, in the event of their publication, the poems to Katie would suggest the relationship was more than friendship on both sides.

Prologue
The Singer Saith of His Song

This poem appears to have been intended as the prologue to the fourth volume of poems rather than to the poems addressed to Katie King. The original manuscript is at H. Stanzas 1, 3 and 13 appear in *Works* under the same title. 'She' in this poem is the personification of Thompson's poetic inspiration.

> The touches of your modern speech
>   Perplex her unacquainted tongue;
> There seems through all her songs a sound
>   Of falling tears. She is not young;
>
> Antique and strange from ruined suns   5
>   And ghosts of moons forgotten; and
> Beholds with eyes uncomforted
>   New faces, and another land.
>
> Within her eyes profound arcane
>   Resides the glory of her dreams;   10
> Behind her secret cloud of hair
>   She sees the Is beyond the Seems.
>
> Upon the battlements of sleep
>   She hears the wind-shook flag of dream
> Fume in the wind that shakes it: hears   15
>   Rather than sees, with lids that seem
>
> Snows that half-hide the violet,
>   And tremble t'ward a thaw. She hath
> Thence her regard of patientness
>   When her eyes ope on life, her death.   20
>
> She speaketh but of things forgot,
>   Undesired, which ye will not hear,
> Fearing to hear: your fear is vain,
>   She hath shut up for a far year
>
> The Song;—to you a moan o' the sea,   25
>   Dumb with a distant thing unsaid
> And said; which yet, ye wot not how,
>   Your souls hark, and are burthenèd.

What gifts her gifts are? Tears for weeping,
   And she will give you sighs to sigh,   30
And you shall hear the burthened bosom
   That waits upon the seeing eye:

Shall learn the bitter heart of honey,
   Shall learn the sleepless core of sleep,
And know of sweet, that your tears therefore   35
   Be more unslakeable when ye weep.

And when, for griefs ye now can grieve not,
   For many deaths, no more can die,
The secret of it all and guerdon
   Ye then shall find, I trust,—and I.   40

For, saith she, whose mouth is Truth's mouth,
   Of this thing is your great gain;—
That the boon of one sole hour
   Can assuage a year of bane.

Strengthless, with inner heart of strength,   45
   Much sour, with little sweet for leaven,
Her feet have taken hold on hell,
   Her eyes have taken hold on heaven;

Her heart sole-towered in her steep spirit,
   Somewhat sweet is she, somewhat wan;   50
And she sings the songs of Sion,
   By the streams of Babylon.

And the singing that she singeth
   Lacks celestial serene breath;
For still it keeps an under-droning   55
   Sombrous hiss o' the snakes of Death:

Like the pipe Athene fashioned,
   Tried, and cast upon the grass.
Pallas! teach her breath composèd,
   Who hath too much of Marsyas!   60

---

1 *your Works*: man's. **15** *Fume* chafe. **39** *guerdon* recompense. **51–2** The Israelites were held captive in Babylon from 587 to 538 BC. **57–60** reference to the arrogance of Marsyas, a satyr who, on finding the flute discarded by the goddess Athene, challenged the god Apollo to a musical contest in which he was defeated and punished for his presumption by being flayed alive.

A Lost Friend

This title in the manuscript is preceded by the general title 'De Amicitia. A Sequence of Poems'. The Ad Amicam Notebook manuscript of this poem is at the Lilly Library but at BC there is a fair copy with only a few minor variants and, at the start, the date 'July 27, '96'. Before the concluding Postscript is the date 'July 31'. The dates were omitted from the final copy for the notebook, but they provide an accurate context for the poem and its composition. The first date refers to the day Thompson left London, after a short visit to the Meynells, to return to Pantasaph, when he was deliberately prevented from seeing Katie King before his departure. A few days later he received a consolatory letter from Katie and added the Postscript with the second date. For fuller details of the circumstances see *BHCC*, pp. 258–9, where the first three verses are printed. The third also appears in *SHSS*, p. 157.

From height, and cold, and mist I fell,
　　With furlèd wing; and on my way
What waited me, and what befell—
The silence at Song's heart can only say.

The height and mist again are mine;　　　　　5
　　And all my sad and secret things
No song can utter, but the fine
Trembling subsidence of Song's aching strings.

The hill looks with a colder brow;
　　The silence I have made my choice　　　　10
Is doubly silent, having now
The irreparable silence of her voice.

With her dear countenance, dear my friend,
　　She suns her children most sweetly;
While in my heart's poor cot I tend　　　　　15
A fretful memory, with its ailing cry.

And all my light of all my ways
　　Burns from one crushed bud of a rose,
Which keeps the life of sundered days
Swathed in its damask and distainèd glows.　　20

Therein she has shut up a power
　　Which, at aspéct alone and small,
Can make her eyes, for one sole hour,
Turn all to blossom and to miracle.

Know you whereof 'tis redolent?—   25
    Its smell is youth, and most glad grace,
    And one fine essence that is blent
From fragrance of her most soul-sweetened face.

    And with its scent there breathe to me
    A thousand odours of a wood   30
    Wherein no greener thing could be
Than was the effluence of her vernal mood.

    'Friend should be sweet to match, in sooth,
    Such sweet remembrance!'—Then I end:—
    'Nay, the remembrance, by my truth,   35
Had need be sweet, to match so sweet a friend.'

    Ah, Song! and has she taught thee so,
    Traitress, to prate of her to me?
    Yea, thou and I were two, we know,
Now, in our solemn consort, we are three.   40

Postscript to the Foregoing; after Receipt of a Letter.

    Lost, did I call her?—Nay;
    She hath found out a way
    That we in severance are bound,
    And she, being lost, is then most found.
    Yea, to lose her, by her dear spells,   5
    Makes me more rich than gain of any else!

22 *at aspéct* in appearance. **27** *blent* mingled.

Alone
Canst Thou Be to Thyself Gone

The Ad Amicam Notebook manuscript of this poem is at the Lilly Library.

To yester-rose a richer
  The rose-spray may bear;
Thrice thousand fairer you may be,—
  But tears for the fair
    You were,   5
When you first were fair!

Know you where they have laid her,
  Maiden May that died?
With the loves that lived not
  Strowing her soft side?   10
    I cried;
Where Has-been may hide?

To him that waiteth, all things,
  Even death, if thou wait!
And they that part too early   15
  May meet again too late:—
    Ah, fate!
If meeting be too late!

And when the year new-launchèd
  Shall from its wake extend   20
The blossomy foam of Summer,
  What shall I attend,
    My friend!
Flower of thee, my friend?

Sweet shall have its sorrow,   25
  The rainbow its rain,
Loving have its leaving,
  And bliss is of pain
    So fain,
Ah, is she bliss or pain?   30

Nocturns of My Friend

The Ad Amicam Notebook manuscript of this poem is at the Lilly Library. The last two stanzas are quoted in *Life*, p. 295; the first two with the last four, in *SHSS*, pp. 172–3. The first and last stanzas were published as a separate poem in *Works* with the title 'Of my Friend', but with no reference to their origin. This led Connolly to assume they were addressed to Alice Meynell and he made a mistaken connection between them and an observation by Thompson relating to 'In Her Paths' (*Letters*, p. 83 and note, p. 84; for the mistaken comment by Connolly see TLC*Poems*, p. 551). For Thompson's own view of the poem see the Introduction to this section, p. 436.

The moonlight cloud of her invisible beauty
　　Shook from the torrent glory of her soul
In aëry spray, hangs round her; love grows duty,
　　　If you that angel-populous aureole
　　　　Have the glad dower to feel;　　　　　　5
　　　　As all our longings kneel
To the intense and cherub-wingèd stole
Orbing a painted Saint: and through control
　　　　Of this sweet faint
　　　　　Veil, my unguessing Saint　　　　　10
Celestial ministrations sheds which heal.

'Tis undulous with her undulating mood;
　　Love, pity, tenderness dissolve in it
Like honey in bright wine; and so imbued,
　　　It is a thing for Jovian breathing fit,　　　　15
　　　　That gods might have of her
　　　　Both cup and cupbearer,
Immortal drink in chalice exquisite!
Her most meteorous thought do burn and flit
　　　　In lovely clear　　　　　　　　　　20
　　　　Ascent through that felt sphere,
Nor need they words, 'tis thought unrobed and bare.

Like the fledged spirit from an utmost star
　　This heavenly effluence she can dart from her;
Nor sablest brooding glooms obdurate are　　　25
　　　But that so blest aspersion them can scare,
　　　　As fly the murky crew
　　　　From holy-water dew.

But of this presence, which out-beauties far
Her gracious form, unwinnowed flesh doth bar   30
    The sense from most;
    They feel not that fair ghost,
Sacred and secret, poet, for only you!

Most sad, lost, pined, I yet for this good grace
    Thank God; my friend, for me too dear a prize,   35
Bereft from me by waste and lonely space,
    Given like boon heaven, to all less-valuing eyes,
    Though all but I taste free
    Her sweet society,
Her fairest Fairness can no way devise   40
To them; thereof they shall not even surmise;
    For them the glows,
    The touch, the grace o' the rose,
Her fragrance sealed and claustral is for me!

Nay, but her friendship, is not that too mine   45
    Apart and singular? Save a poet's heart,
Can that religion stoop unto a shrine
    Where with due purple state it is confessed?
    He but affords, but he
    Its hidden deity   50
A mountain-fane exalt and manifest,
Where in his cloud-girt nature it may rest.
    Through him alone
    Its possible is known,
Its flag is streamed on wind-swift poesy,   55

It may be as a power which in the mind
    Kindles all births that are most fair and true;
It may be as a fostering cloud to bind
    The spirit's peaks with blossoms ever new,
    With petals Paradisal   60
    Passing our dull devisal,
To which the fallen earth had bid adieu.
And the precipitant songs which from it drew
    Their taintless food,
    Tell to man's wormy brood   65
Of the pure source, beyond the swarm's surmisal.
        *

It may be an apocalypse infinite
   Of whelming mercy to the soul forlorn,
Even as with thunders and with shocks of light
   The burning inundation of the dawn,   70
      When dyking night is riven,
      Submerges the shook heaven:
Or like the poet's image which doth smite
Sudden in one things diverse to gross sight.
      What may it be?   75
      All the divinity
To which, in our earth's tongue, no name but She is given.

The stars, those islanded and burning peaks
   Vomiting golden lava; every wind
Whose fountain o'er the arch of heaven breaks   80
   And falls back whence it rose; how shall the mind
      For sorrow find amend
      In aught that these can lend?
With sun and moon as pebbles spurned behind,
Term in interminable glory find,   85
      Save it can sink
      Homing from heaven's dim brink,
And feel its feet take hold on its safe friend?

See I not folded in my whitest thought
   Her presence, as the fuchsia's pale shut sheath   90
Dawns with the tinging bud? Ah, know we not
   The sea-thing with its precious ooze doth wreathe
      The worthless particle
      Which frets it in its shell?
I, fretted so with things of pain and death,   95
Impearlèd them with song; but now the breath
      Of thoughts which flow
      From her, doth softly blow
O'er my heart's pendulous harp, that answers well!

Is she not as the heaven from which my wave   100
   Assumes all beauty that she gazes on,
Which she, unwitting what she is and gave,
   Beholds for mine, and dreams not 'tis her own?
      The rainbow which appears
      Cast on my mortal tears,   105

Covenanting the rest through her made known?
The Ark, where He Who sits therein is shown
    By the intense
    Pure effluence
And shining cloud that with her going veers?   110

Yea, was she not (ah, infamy of *was!*)
  In that pure converse where we met and knew,
Rose to my root, Effect unto my Cause
    Wherein my bodiless thoughts incarnate grew,
    And in aspect and form   115
    Gazed back upon me, warm,
Palpable, a creation young and new
That did take breath and motion, and indue
    The living, fair
    Raiment of radiant Her,   120
A lovelier Song than language could inform?

Ah, perfect Poet then only, when I set
  My songs in beauty in her face, and felt
Their refluence on me in the tide that met
    Me from her emanation, and did melt   125
    Into mine, confluent,
    Antiphonally blent!
Were we not then a music that could belt
Infinity, to which the world had knelt,
    If it could throw   130
    Slough of slimed flesh, and grow
Of the prime tongueless tongue intelligent!

Has she not given the flowers the odorous air
  Which from her sphere she breathes, and like dew
Of fire is spilled from her most fragrant hair?   135
    Does not their sweet remember her, as two
    Lovers a perfume frail,
    Not of themselves, exhale,
Which from each other's converse they renew?
Earth is a censer in her hands, which do   140
    Sway thence sweet ooze
    Past the wrought flowers-de-luce
Of the stars' golden sanctuary-rail!
       *

She in light motion, like a cloud unbound
   From the main vapour by the tetchy wind,   145
Sandals her feet with gladness; and the ground
    Leaps to her tread, and the trees would unwind
       Their knitted roots, and spring,
       To see so brave a thing!
As straight, as brave, as swift, her unconfined   150
Thoughts fearless tread along her springy mind.
       O, to be sad
       Beside her, leave the bad!
Whoso hath soul of good, his heart must sing!

Read in her eyes, whoso hath soul of good!   155
    For like the babe within the lotus-flower,
So is her childhood in her womanhood
    Clear symbolled by their sweet wise innocent power.
       The fool shall in his folly
       The child herefrom read wholly;   160
Nor see there, cloistered 'gainst its fitting hour,
Grave, tender, prudent, all the woman's dower
       And this I add:—
       Ye comfortless and sad,
Therein is healing, for those wells are holy.   165

But of that thing which verse can not enscroll,
    To which all these lead up by winding ways,
The very keep and donjon of the whole,
    Which all these mean, and does their purple praise
       Both justify and crown,   170
       What song shall give renown?
Lend me the sound of fragrance, or, a space,
The word that silence hath, nor ever says!
       Then were the merit
       Of her sole-sealèd spirit   175
For ever shown, and ever more unknown!

Whence comes the consummation of all peace,
    And dignity past fools to comprehend,
In that dear favour she for me decrees,
    Sealed by the daily-dullèd name of Friend,   180
       Debased with what alloy,
       And each knave's cheapened toy.

This from her mouth doth sweet with sweetness mend,
This in her presence is its own white end.
      Fame counts past fame   185
      The splendour of this name;
This is calm deep of unperturbèd joy.

Now, friend, short sweet out-sweetening sharpest woes,
   In wintry cold a little, little flame,—
So much to me that little! Here I close   190
   This errant song, O pardon its much blame!
      Now my grey day grows bright
      A little ere the night,
Let after-livers who may love my name,
And gauge the price I paid for dear-bought fame,   195
      Know that at end,
      Pain was well paid, sweet Friend,
Pain was well paid, which brought me to your sight!

End of Sequence

1 Against this line FT has added a note: 'This is said of her *Aura*, or atmosphere about her body.' The idea of an emanation from the body as its spiritual counterpart characterises several of FT's love poems, notably the fifth Ad Amicam sonnet published in *Works*. **104–10** There are two separate images here, linked by the associations with Covenant. The covenant made between God and Noah is symbolised by the rainbow, the continuation of which is the 'shining cloud' that covered the Ark of the Covenant during the years that the Israelites wandered in the desert. **156** The ancient Egyptians portrayed the Creator born from the heart of the lotus flower.

Earth Plains

Fragment from a Designed Poem

The Ad Amicam manuscript of this poem is at the Lilly Library. Although it is described as only part of a proposed poem Thompson still regarded it as complete enough to include with the other finished poems in this notebook. Its mood indicates that it was copied into the notebook at a later date than the rest of the contents: in his last years his oppressive gloom for the state of the world and its future was underlined by his own physical sufferings. There are many fragmentary poems in the later notebooks with similar themes, which here he carried further than the rest. As with others of his later poems on the impending disasters of the twentieth century, this one suggests a premonition of the effects of man's misuse of the natural world. The last seven lines appear in *BHCC*, p. 334.

My flesh grows old, my flesh grows old in pain,
My bones are full of trouble
And leaden-weighed despair;
The superincumbence of the enormous years
Heavy hangs upon me,   5
And all its billows heave above my head:
In my great pulses dull the fires;
My heart grows hard for misery,
There is no pause from pain.

Lo, how my scabbèd ulcers issue fire,   10
The earthquake kennels in me, and doth rend
My tortured womb; man burrows in my flesh
A pestering nit, and vexes me for harvest,
Which I with labour yield; with labour bear
All composts which the powers of heat and cold,   15
Of fire and spirituous seething, work and forge
Restless and fierce within me: nor this worst.
Not worst the snow which nips, the fiery spume
Which agues me, nor aught of natural wrong;
But full-sinned man that doth his poison vent   20
I' the loathing air, and with contagion damned
Infect me to the marrow: I am plagued and plastered
With this disease called man, not to be cured,
A vermin from my robes not to be shook,
A venom in my blood. Great God, a deluge,   25
A second draught to purge me of mankind!

Woe is me, my tyrant!
I bear to him in pain
Corn, and wine, and oil;
He giveth me for guerdon   30
Poison and contagion.
Even of man, of lethal man,
Lo, behold me sick,
Fevered, unhealèd,
Dying!   35
My flesh grows old, my flesh grows old in pain,
There is no rest at all from ills,
There is no space from sorrow,
There is no pause from pain!

POEMS FROM THE NOTEBOOK
OF EARLY POEMS

While Thompson was at Storrington, from February 1889 until March 1890, he made fair copies of the poems he had written up to that time of which he had record or which he could recall. For most there are rough drafts in notebooks which, it is possible to deduce from their tattered condition and from other entries, were being used while he was living on the streets: but there is no way of knowing which of these notebooks may also have been in use earlier. They are all in a very damaged condition and in many places now barely legible. No earlier notebooks survive, apart from the Ushaw College Notebook (see Part Four). This Notebook of Early Poems, in which Thompson made his fair copies, is a small account-book where every page is closely covered with the copperplate handwriting that he often used for completed texts in his early years and which is similar to the writing in the Ushaw College Notebook. For lack of space, he substituted the ampersand in many places but, as this was the only reason, it has not been retained in the texts here. The poems would have been composed between the date he left Ushaw in 1877 and his arrival at Storrington; that is, while he was at Owens College from 1878 to 1885 and then during the three years on the London streets. Of the notebook's 32 poems, the following have been published: 'Not Even in Dream', 'The Owl', 'The Lily Maiden', 'In the Garden', 'Ecce Ancilla Domini', 'Adversity', 'A Ballad of Fair Weather', and 'Une Fille de Joie'. The first appeared in *ME*, December 1888, the second in *SHSS*, and the rest in *MHW*. Except for 'The Lily Maiden' and 'In the Garden' they are included elsewhere in the present volume. A selection from the unpublished poems has been made here in the order in which they were copied into the notebook. Those omitted are either unfinished or show little or no sign of future promise.

If

If I be sweet in those sweet eyes
   Wherein I sweet would be,
Take all the eyes of all the skies,
   There are but two for me!

If I be blest with those sweet hands   5
   Wherewith I blest would be,
Take all the hands of all the lands,
   There are but two for me!

If I were fed with that sweet voice
   Which Music made for me,   10
Take all the words of all the birds,
   And let my one song be.

If I were kissed with those sweet lips
  Which make Love shake to see,
Take all the flowers of all the bowers,   15
  Leave my twin-flower to me.

If I were loved with that deep soul
  Which Mary smiles to see,—
O shadows of the trees of Heaven,
  How near you seem to me!   20

Alone

Amabam amare, nec quod amarem habebam, et quaerebam quid
amarem, amans amare.

(St Augustine, *Confessions* [FT])

This quotation is taken from a passage in St Augustine's *Confessions*, Book 3,
para. 1: 'Nondum amabam et amare amabam et secretiore indigentia oderam me
minus indigentem. Quaerebam quid amarem, amans amare . . .' 'I was not yet in
love, but I was in love with love, and from the very depth of my need hated myself
for not more keenly feeling the need. I sought some object to love, since I was thus
in love with loving . . .' (*The Confessions of Saint Augustine*, trans. F. J. Sheed, 1943,
p. 39).

  There is a rough draft of this poem in NB45, one of the notebooks dating from
the London streets years. At the time Thompson would have quoted St Augustine
from memory, accounting for the error in the text. The last three verses and parts
of the sixth and seventh appear in *BHCC*, p. 92.

I sat me down upon the sands of Time,
Beside Life's ocean, changing in its chime;
And loneliness and silence companied me.

I said, 'Where art thou, lady of my life?'
I cried, 'Where art thou, O my unknown wife?   5
Come hither, then, hither and sit by me.

'Lo thou! I sit alone upon these sands;
Alone I sit and stretch out empty hands;
Come, fill these aching hands and come to me.'

Life's sea drew up upon the sands of Time,   10
Death's bird alone shrieked answer to my rhyme,
And no fair woman rose and came to me.

I longed for Love that with his noise of wings
Scareth the black bird Death and all its things,
To bring my lady in his hand to me.   15

I said, 'When comest thou, O Love? I wait.
Or art thou far or near, for thou art late:
Out of the caverned future come to me.'

Oh, Love came out, and sat upon the sands;
Oh, Love came out, and clapped his shining hands;   20
Oh, Love came out, and sat, and laughed at me.

He said, 'Behold, I have thee in my net!
Me dost thou love, and canst not me forget;
And thou shalt have no other love than me.

'Thou shalt behold the glitter of my wings,   25
And groan thee for the yearning that it brings;
But thou shalt have no other love than me!'

And Love sits there and claps his shining hands,
Oh, Love sits there, and laughs upon the sands!
And all my heart is hungered within me.   30

Night and Fate

Part of an early draft for the poem in NB45 appears in *BHCC*, p. 86.

Yon stellèd lights with all the stars between
Are grown a nightly figure for my fate:
'Twixt me and all my hopes there intervene
(Remote or vanished) glooms forlornly great.
It is my life that mocks my sorrowing sight,—   5
Stars, and between me and the stars, the night.

Could I forget! Forget? – Ah, yes, forget!
Forget the care, the trouble, and the strife;
Forget joy, grief; the aidance and the let;
Forget the love that was not for a life: 10
Forget that in forgetting was regret;
Forget the thought which calleth memory wife:
Forget these seemings, Is and false Is Not;
Forget myself, and be myself forgot!

9 *the aidance and the let* support and obstruction.

Lost

The reference to 'this dim place of books' may be to the library in Manchester which Thompson frequented while at Owens College. But it is more likely to be to one of the libraries in London where he spent much of his time while on the streets, or the bookshop where he was employed for a few months after his arrival in London. Unlike most of these poems, this one seems to speak of an actual experience, a chance encounter in a library or the bookshop.

I thought I had found at last the one woman
    For whom my soul was searching through the world;
The one whose tender light my heart might hymn in,
    For whom my flag of fight might be unfurled.
Of this me thought I, for her sweetest sake   5
    I might behie myself to work, not dream;
Who, knowing me unbeautiful, would take
    Me for her gentle sweetness, as I deem,
Seeing my love in its imperfectness.
    So long I watched for her with her sweet looks   10
To enter like a sudden star and bless
    With brightness for me this dim place of books.
But now I think she will not come again.
    She never cared for me. Oh! not as I,
Oh! not as I! or thou wouldst surely pain   15
    Thy heart with searching for me achingly.
I would I had not known, or, having known thee,
    Could be as if I had not known! Lost prize,
Wouldst thou had never spoken, never shown me
    The deep, uncharted waters of thine eyes!   20
Thinking of which, the waters of my soul
    Turn salt with bitter longings. Thy soft voice
Still runs through all the crannies dark with dole
    Of my scarred spirit, but alas! its noise
Seems full of parting. Henceforth thou must be   25
    A ghost within the house of memory!

A Ballad

The fourth stanza appears in *BHCC*, p. 74.

It was a knight rode wearily
   Down to a wood.
O knight, you cannot ride too fast
To see your true love ere day be past!
It was a knight rode wearily   5
   Down to a wood.

It was a maid sat lingeringly
   Out on a wall,
O maiden, and will you listen long
For hoofs from the wood ere evensong?   10
It was a maid sat lingeringly
   Out on a wall.

It was a steed ran riderlessly
   Under the wood.
O steed, you could not ride so fast through the wood 15
As the pale horse and its rider could!
It was a steed ran riderlessly
   Under the wood.

It was a stream ran bloodily
   Under the wall.   20
O stream, you cannot run too red
To tell a maid her widowhead!
It was a stream ran bloodily
   Under the wall.

It was a heart brake heavily   25
   Under its vest!
O heart, you cannot break too fast
Till her soul to her own dear soul be past!
Farewell, poor heart rent heavily
   Under thy vest!   30

After Love's End

These lines would seem to refer to Thompson's relationship with the street girl during his last six months on the London streets. The first stanza appears in *BHCC*, p. 91.

> We lay in sleep, I think, in sleep
>   Together, she and I;
> And each were conscious in our sleep
>   O' the other's breathing nigh.
> What came of it? the touch of lip   5
>   (In dream), the twine of arms, the lock
> Of wills? these things are dim, and slip
>   Our memories since we woke:
>   None knows, nor she nor I.
>
> To dream and to forget our dream   10
>   Is but the common lot of sleep;
> To dream, and to forget our dream,
>   And then to weep, to weep!
> Was never dreamed a fairer dream,
>   Nor ever sweeter dream forgot,   15
> None wept with softer tears, I deem,
>   Than this, which now is not.
>   Keep peace: the lot of sleep!

Vox Aspasiae Reclamantis

The title can be translated as 'Aspasia's voice of protest'. Aspasia was a highly intelligent and educated woman, a friend of Socrates but also the mistress of Pericles. In the notebook this poem follows 'Une Fille de Joie', published in *MHW* (see Part Two, pp. 373–4), where there is also a note by Thompson in which he says that: ' "Une Fille de Joie" brings to my recollection one of my juvenile efforts. As it is almost the sole relic of my pre-Rossettian days which I can recollect, I think I shall write it down as a curiosity, while I recollect it. Not that it is much worse, I daresay, than many of the previous things in this motley collection.' By 'pre-Rossettian days' he means before writing 'On the Anniver-sary of Rossetti's Death' (pp. 384–6). 'Une Fille de Joie' and the present poem share a similar theme and it is clear that even before his experiences in London he was aware of the sad fate of many of the women of the streets whom he must have come across during his years of medical training at Owens College.

Restless, restless, ill at ease!
   No quitting my thoughts by any stealth;
In pride of this beauty and youth of mine
   Sick for the lack of the spirit's health.
     No wealth,   5
     None, none,
Can bid the smirch from my soul begone,
Set there by you, man! The brand inhuman
Which sears the woman within the woman.

It fades from man like a breath from steel,   10
   It stabs our fame with a deadly knife:
Ye smile at a man—'tis the sin of youth;
   In woman ye make it the sin of life!
     Vain strife!
     Long woe!   15
Ah! can it be? Ah! is it so?
It is so, alas! and our life may pass,
But the brand will follow us under the grass!

I met a child in the street today,
   A fairy child with a winsome face: 20
I tell you, I knew not I had a heart,
   But something stirred here, in its place.
     Sweet face!
     I dared not do,
Or else I had hugged it and kissed it too;   25
Crushed and caressed on my parched, pained breast
That callow Love from another's nest!

What is this yearning? for love, for love?
   If ever I knew it, I have forgot.
Love! from men, who but woo us to leave?   30
   Love! from the gods, who heed us not?
     What, what?
     Vain pain!
A sick girl's longing, beyond attain.
Ay me! Ay me! There scarce can be   35
A soul in the land that loveth me!

Whom shall I turn to from men? The gods?
   Carven ivory, graven stone!

What is yonder Olympian Zeus
   That he should have me when I make moan?   40
      Oft I groan!
      But cold, cold,
Cold in their ivory, cold in their gold,
The gods are dumb, we may go or come,
And our hearts may ache till our hearts are numb!   45

No! Let me snatch the Maenad's wreath,
   And live for the glow of the passing hour,
Pericles waits at the door without—
   If I cannot have love, I can have power.
      Leaf and flower   50
      Into the cup
I cast ye, and drain the mad draught up:
For life, the dream, will fairest seem
Through the crimson veil of the wine-light's gleam!

46 *Maenad* devotee of Dionysus, the god of wine.

The Marriage of Cana

The Gospel incident on which this poem is based is generally referred to as 'The Marriage (or Wedding) at Cana' (John 2:1–11). Thompson prefixed it with the following note: 'A striking example of the "double facet" sonnet (i.e. showing in octave & sestet the two aspects of a single idea) . . . I took an image from the octave for "Paganism".' The image to which he refers, adapted for his essay 'Paganism Old and New', is the transfer of 'faithful Love' from Jove's to Jehovah's child. The essay was included with the poems Thompson sent to *ME* while on the streets so the poem would have been written during those years. Its mood also suggests the bitterness of much of his notebook poetry then and later, recognised by Connolly in a note on the back cover of the notebook: 'This double-facet sonnet shows Thompson's queer humour and the secret bitterness of which he never rid himself.'

At Cana's marriage-feast Christ sat and smiled,
Blessing the work which Paradise began;
And, grafting woman on the hardier man
Proclaimed true marriage just and undefiled,
And faithful Love Jehovah's, not Jove's child: 5
Whence he may scorn the cynic's censuring ban
Who, taking woman for this mortal span,
Makes earth the gladder by a simple child.
      *

But yet the story has another side
Too little by the multitude descried.   10
The Lord declared his thought by that his carriage,
(Transmitted to us for a warning sign,)
That any man who ventured upon marriage
Could not go through it without much wine!

Lui et Moi

The title translates as 'He and I'. The references to the 'hills' and 'the toil that
tills' suggest the Owens College years for this poem. Thompson's home in
Ashton-under-Lyne is very close to the foothills of the Pennines. But the poem's
sense of growing isolation could apply throughout his earlier years. Stanzas 3–6
appear in *BHCC*, pp. 42–3.

To you the joys, to me the ills;
    To you the commerce of the heart;
    To me the life that lives apart,
And the lone outlook of the hills.

To me the thought that feeds and kills,   5
    To you the joys of kind with kind;
    To you the gardens of the mind,
To me the toil that tills.

The sign that sends me out from men,
    The sign that seals my life apart,   10
    That sign is written in my heart,
And on my brow for all may ken.

They cannot read it, one in ten,
    Know but this is not one of them;
    And look askance, as beasts contemn   15
Their fellow-beast that breaks the pen.

Just some few women may you cull
    Who say 'This boy is strange, and thus
    He cannot be as one of us;
Wherefore we should be pitiful:'   20

O women! though you asked the skull
    Of Death to speak a bitter truth,
    It could say nought more full of sooth
Than *that*,—'We should be pitiful!'

[The next two stanzas follow on but appear as if they are from a second part of the poem, either lost or never developed. They conclude the contents of the notebook.]

> I only showed to her my heart—
>   She looked, and knew not what it was;
>   It was no more to her than straws
> Which quiver when the gusts upstart.
>
> He looked her to him half in game;   5
>   Said lightly, 'Give to me thy heart!'
>   But said 'Set me thy life apart;'
> But said, 'Come'—and she came!

OCCASIONAL NOTEBOOK POETRY ·

The notebooks are full of fragmentary poems, from which the following four have been selected as more finished than most. They convey the mood of much of the rest and in addition provide examples of Thompson's method of composition as described in the Introduction (p. xxx). His use of the ampersand is retained and all brackets and parentheses are also part of his text.

'The rich, who with intention pure'

These lines from NB47A are typical of the kind of bitter social criticism found in the notebooks at all periods but more especially in Thompson's later years. They reflect the lasting influence from his years on the London streets, which he did not generally allow to appear in verse intended for publication. An edited version of the text appears in *BHCC*, p. 301.

> The rich, who with intention pure
> Amuse⎫ themselves to help the poor;
> Enjoy ⎭
> Loving the gospel ordinance,
> All night, to clothe the naked, dance;
> To aid the widow go to balls,
> and flirt to succour hospitals
> [All for the widow go to balls,   [carnivals]
> For needy widows
> And flirt in aid of hospitals;]
> To educate the fatherless

Array themselves in fancy dress;
[Array themselves in fancy-dress
To educate the fatherless]
[Do cake-walks for the fatherless,
And for the infirm wear fancy-dress.;   *or*
For indigence wear fancy-dress,
And cake-walk for the fatherless;]
To feed the hungry drink champagne,
And have good times for those in pain;⎱
                         the insane ⎰
[And waltz like mad for the insane;]
   mazurk
To keep the old and out-of-work;⎱
All to assist the out-of-work   ⎰
And feed on fowl & *consommé*   *entrée*
To give the poor soup once-a-day:
[And gobble some six courses up
To give the starving rich pea-soup;   *or,*
And fish, & joint, & *entrée* gobble
To give pea-soup to those in trouble;]
Bedeck themselves with gold & jewel
To give dames petticoats & fuel;
With paint and rouge their cheeks bedizen
In aid of those discharged from prison;
And have a time that's really sweet
For sake of wretches on the street
To keep young women from the street;
                         every
Coquette ⎰with zeal at many a fête
         ⎱ unselfishly at fêtes
To rescue ⎰the unfortunate;
         ⎱ poor unfortunates;
Then feel⎱ (if they have not been bored)
   say⎰
That 'Charity's its own reward.'
'Charity is its own reward.'
Virtue's indeed its own reward.

That happiness is one with virtue.
[Then gladly own, when all is done,
Virtue and happiness are one.
Then own, in an unstinted measure,
That charity is a true pleasure].

'Wilt thou, feasting in thy purple state'

The text for these lines, in NB BC20, is very rough but written with comparatively few variants, as if composed in a fit of sudden inspiration. They comprise a
separate poem but appear among the drafts for the 'Victorian Ode', written for the
Diamond Jubilee of 1897 (pp. 259–65). When Thompson was writing his commissioned odes in his later years, in the privacy of his notebooks he often added
fierce condemnations of contemporary society, of which these lines are an
example. Lines 1–15 appear in *BHCC*, p. 275.

> —Wilt thou, feasting in thy purple state,
> Police the festering Lazarus from thy gate?
> So, all the inns are full: hast thou for Christ
> No stable? Shall the ox be stalled & fed,
> The race-horse delicately pamperèd,
> He, in the outer street, bit by the surly wind,
> Not find
> Necessitous bread?
> Shall all thy charity be picked & nice
> And only then sufficed
> Clean-washed of sin & vermin in thine eyes?
> Alas, this modern Christ,
> Guilty & dirty, stinks against thy sense
> Of wholesome & neat-handed poverty.
> If, after thy 'deserving', recompense
> Were meted out to thee,
> Where were thy linen fine & bravery?
>   England
> Treat them according to thy power
> Greatly to give,
> Not their right to receive;
> Let hunger make their right; lest God to thee
> Reckon 'deserving,' in thine own improvident hour.
> Keep the great heart, O Land, to guard thine own,
> And feed thine own;
> Lest the long glories wither round thy throne.
>   Shrivel

'Omar, you sang the roses & the wine'

The lines are from NB BC18. Here Thompson's caustic wit is directed to those
who would transform the sensuous beauty of the *Rubaiyat of Omar Khayyam* by

giving it a 'mystical' interpretation more acceptable to contemporary sensibilities. It is notable, also, that he is ahead of his time in his view of the *Song of Songs* as a sensuous love poem no less than a celebration of mystical love.

> Omar, you sang the roses & the wine,
> The singing girl, the swinging tavern sign;
>   Shame on the pedant who would make our Sage
> A moon-struck mystic or a deep divine!
>
> They do to you as scribes & priests have done   5
> To that great Song of golden Solomon;
>   They read their dogma on your rosy page,
> For they are saints; but, Omar, you were none.

Favoured of Heaven

In the manuscript Thompson's title for this poem follows the last line. It is a fair copy but with corrections and alternatives, written on a single detached notebook page. Thompson here contrasts two varieties of 'favouritism'.

> From rich men's trouble & the poor's;
> Health, to acquire & to enjoy
> That I acquire without annoy;
> But enough struggle for delight
> I' the hurly-burly of the fight:—
> Whence I thank God by day & night,
> Being His & Fortune's favourite.
>
> Woman's love I have asked—my clasp
>   slips
> It slipped, as water flees the grasp;
> Much I loved children—& no child
> Smiles on me as on them I smiled;
> Wealth I sought not—well I prove
> It loves not them who it not love;
> Health I desired,—but ah me, health
> Fled me, like woman & like wealth;
> Struggle & care alone have sought
> And clung to me, whom I loved⎱ not:
>   sought⎰
> Whence I thanked Him, Who said—'My own,
> We two alone, we two alone!'

LIGHT VERSE

Thompson's later notebooks contain many drafts and a few completed fair copies of humorous verse, often in doggerel and apparently written for his own amusement. What appears to have fascinated him about this genre is the word play, for which he developed a not inconsiderable skill. As he was writing to amuse himself he had no reason to shape and finish the poems, which can run on to too great a length, often in a succession of the puns that were now his way of exploring the resources of the language. The manuscripts are fair copies, either separate sheets or detached notebook pages, placed together in the Thompson collection at BC under the title 'Light Verse'.

Sidereal Musings

The *OED* definition of 'sidereal' is 'of the constellations or fixed stars'. Thompson takes these stars as the focal point for 'musings' that allow him to range through the realm of the classical pantheon. In his study of ancient mythologies he had in some respects been ahead of his time: his ability to laugh at such studies is no less unusual. But his goddesses have their earthly counterparts in the 'New Women' of the early feminist movement, at which he directs a humorous cynicism.

A modest poet must perforce
Blush at the profligate discourse
Of your mythologists, who handle
The gods' affairs with so much scandal,
And all the Olympian club-tattle   5
Much like their Pall Mall brethren prattle.
The ones on earth no character,
And the others none in heaven spare:
Till ladies might make question nice,
When they've the *entrée* of the skies   10
If they may put, no honour missed,
The gods upon their visiting-list.
The heavens, 'tis plain, for prudent ladies,
Must scarce less shady be than Hades,
Society's so strangely mixed   15
'Mong stars of habits loose or fixed;
So that a dubious point arises,
If one translated to the skies is
More for his virtues or his vices.
Some for virginity there sit,   20
And others for the lack of it;

Juno, good lady, in that place
Will not so much as show her face,
Although that counterfeit, that pale
Cheat Dian, fears not to unveil,   25
Though the old rascal *roué* Jupiter,
Of doubtful stars flaunts such a troop at her.
Some will have Mars there for his bravery;
Ye are wrong, say others; there's more knavery:
He's set there for that open, heinous   30
Affair of his with Madam Venus;
To hint a man does oftentime
To fame through the divorce-court climb.
Nay, then, I have you at a dead-lock—
Andromeda's there to further wedlock;   35
Maidenhood brought her the sea-monster,
But marriage in the heaven ensconced her.
Quick the New Woman: 'Every day
Our sex does prove it t'other way:
From maidenhood our heaven arises,   40
And marriage to the monster ties us.'

Madam, I never of my knowledge
Argued with any of your college,
And fear you'd chant as doleful a psalm in
The skies, if one may trust the Brahmin;   45
Where the same matrimonial sin does
Obtain, as witness the wise Hindoos,
Who the bright Pleiads all aver
To be contract to the Great Bear.
But troth, the Hindoo's made to vex you all   50
Where question is of matters sexual,
Who limns the Virgin in a chariot
With lion harnessed there to carry it;
To show he lion's heart must summon
That yokes himself unto a woman.   55
And truly, it is very plain, a
Like thought beset the Lord at Cana;
The man who faced the marriage-twine,
He held, must need have of much wine.
So the Lord cast deep sleep on Adam,   60
Ere from his bone He shaped a Madam,
(Whence, as some gifted have had shown 'em,
Woman e'er since is held man's *bonum*),

Which some interpreters sophistic a-
Ver should be reckoned *verba mystica*,   65
And *somnum mentis* understood—
A thesis which they thus make good:
That men their wives still use to take,
When least their judgments are awake.

But to return from this *excursus*,—   70
Deep cogitation must immerse us
(When the skies populated we see
With thieves, gallants, and ladies easy),
Whether there are, to tell truth even,
More sinners damned to hell or heaven.   75
St. George I can descry nowhere,
Then what, pray, makes the dragon there?
     What none e'er doubted of to hint—
Man could not be with heaven content,
Not find therein his proper level,   80
Till he had introduced the devil.
     But why is't Libra in the skies is,
Which can nor virtues have nor vices?
     The Scales are there, let none admire,
For the same reason as the Lyre.   85
Justice and Poesy in the sky
Are set this truth to signify—
That heaven may find in them some worth,
But there's no use for them on earth.
'Tis true, though unfamiliar,   90
The stars our Upper Chamber are,
Where we promote the things we love
To honour and be ridded of.
     The things we love
To honour and be ridded of?   95
Prythee, on this ground how came Mars
To get his head among the stars?
     Venus' gallant? Remember late
Some very eminent men of state,
Of whom their honouring country did   100
For much like reason make it rid.
     How Virgo then?—Oh, sir, your pardon;
My blushes it were somewhat hard on
To show i' the category how
Virginity you must allow!   105

But faith, my tender conscience fears
To scandal more the starry peers,
Inquire, like virtuous democrat,
How title came to this and that;
Besides, I have my trepidations 110
Lest they refuse their inspirations,
When I some choicer matter write would
Than makes for a right bardic knighthood.

22 *Juno* often regarded as the protectress of women, of whom the myths recount no scandal. 25 *Dian* goddess of the hunt, whose chief characteristic was her resistance to any form of love-making. 26 *Jupiter* king of the gods and lover of many goddesses and mortals: in Greek, Zeus. 28–31 *Mars . . . Venus* The illicit union of the god of war and the goddess of love has had a constant appeal for poets and artists. 35 *Andromeda* When she was about to be sacrificed to the sea monster who would otherwise devastate her father's land, she was saved by Perseus, who later married her. After her death she was transformed into a star. 47–9 FT has a footnote: 'Hindoo mysticism represents the Seven Pleiades as the brides of the Seven Rishis—which latter constellation is our Ursa Major.' 57–9 Cf. 'The Marriage of Cana' (pp. 456–7) for the same idea. 63 *bonum* good. 65 *verba mystica* mystical words. 66 *somnum mentis* sleep of the mind. 70 *excursus* aside. 82 *Libra* the heavenly scales of justice. 91–101 It is not known to which British statesman, 'kicked upstairs' to the House of Lords, Thompson is referring. 110–13 The poet does not want to offend those on high for fear that he might miss out on similar (highly dubious) honours.

A Ballad of the Boer(ing) War

Thompson's criticism of the Boer War and doubt of the outcome appear in many of the fragments written in the privacy of his notebooks. The only two poems he completed on the subject are 'A Ballad of the Baralong' (pp. 426–9) and this 'Ballad' where, despite its much lighter mood and often tedious puns, the last three stanzas hint at a similar criticism. As with 'Baralong', here the information in the endnotes has been largely supplied by Thomas Pakenham.

O Mr. Bull, to hold war's trumps,
    Whenas war's trumps are blown,—
If you would open Kruger's eyes,
    Pray do not shut your own!

Or else you'll rue, as nearly you 5
    Did at the Drift called Rorke's;
And you may have to pass between
    Dutch-metal Caudine Forks,—
Like Lord Cornwallis, with the Yank-
    -Ee men who deal in porks. 10

For Tommy A. (historians say
   Who're worthy of belief)
Is mostly full of valour, when
   He's also full of beef.
He does not care for potted boots,   15
His appetite in no way suits
   Fried pockethandkerchief.

And if the commissariat
   Go wrong instead of right,
While he is like baked meat all day,   20
   And frozen meat all night,
His stomach is so large for food
   'Tis very small for fight.

It is a thing I have been told
   (And it is fearful news),   25
That if you march troops off their feet
   Their flesh they'll likewise lose,
And then their heads, and then lay down
   Their arms,—which *must* confuse.

Summon our turbaned lancers up   30
   To these Batavian wars,
Who—broiled in towns which end in -pore—
   Thus sweat in all their -pores;
For since they're used to stick at pigs,
   They will not stick at Boers.   35

Call up our Bisley volunteers
   To prove they can shoot lead
Without reclining on their backs—
   A pose discredited;
In war it mayn't make men dead shots,   40
   It might make men shot dead;
But 'tis the very thing for those
   Who fight at home in bed.

Call up our officers so keen
   On riding hell-for-leather,   45
So versed in slang and vintages;
   These birds of chosen feather,
The nation knows, in war or peace,
   Will make a mess together.

After the mess comes Tommy in 50
    To clear, the staunch and strong;
To clear the table or the name,
    And put to rights the wrong:
Whoever muddles job or brain,
    He helps, and holds his tongue. 55

Alas! poor wight, he has to fight
    In lee of stones and banks,
Upon his stomach, till you'd think,
    To look upon such pranks,
Frogs, banished from commissioned breasts, 60
    Had crawled into the ranks.

And then such clouds of khaki dirt
    Food, water, mouth encrust,
It seems the curse that's laid on him
    Is like the Serpent's, just,— 65
For all his days to go upon
    His belly, and eat dust.

The missionaries say he shuns
    Intoxication's sin,—
But yet, alas! so many traps 70
    The Dutch have caught him in,
'Tis sadly clear he was, I fear,
    Ensnared by Hollands gin.

Then, should a shell of melinite
    But chance to come too near, 75
If not in liquor, yet he dies
    In half-and-half, I fear,
And yet (strange contradiction!) has
    To go without his bier.

It were some consolation if 80
    The busy doctor-men
His poor remains would piously
    In stoppered vessels pen:
Though not exempt from jars, he would
    Be in high spirits then. 85

De Wet ne'er covered so much ground
　　As he does now; and he's
Just like a famous actor, in
　　His multiple decease,—
For he appears in many parts,   90
　　Though not in one same piece.

Now had he been a cricketer,
　　He had been spared these dumps,
Nor got his leg before the ball
　　Upon a ground that bumps;   95
But there was too much break on it,
　　And so it split his stumps.

Ah! who that missile vile dispatched
　　From Creusot or from Krupp,
To pour its iron contents in   100
　　Poor Tommy's bitter cup?
For, like a bank, it came to smash,
　　And then it broke him up.

Ah, think of Lyddite's dreadful might,
　　And think how bad it smells!   105
And think what horrid verdant hue
　　It prints on all it fells;
Till they are green as ocean is,
　　And likewise floored with shells.

Some other Tommy left, perhaps,   110
　　A widow in Calcutty,
Though all her life she'll be a black,
　　She cannot be a Suttee.
And ah! his eyes are glazed, for on
　　His leg we see the puttie!   115

Give me Majuba! By the Boer
　　Untimely visited,
You turn your back on him, with scorn
　　Of people so low-bred,
Which is the gentlemanly way   120
　　To cut your foeman dead.

And, Mr. Bull! though honour be
    A jewel and what else,
It is a pearl one would not seek
    Among so many shells: 125
Give me, for war with swelling roars,
    The Park with roaring swells!

Make glorious wars (the phrase might now
    Be left to the Mikado),
And, John, prepare to meet the bill   130
    For two years' glory, pray do!
A bleeding land mayn't touch you much,
    A bleeding pocket may do!

You trust to the war-public, who
    'Rule Britain' loud at home;   135
But howsoever you may beat
    The bold recruiting-drum,
'War publics,' with but one reverse
Of 'war' (I think this neat and terse),
    'Raw publics' will become.   140

And oh, Sir Alfred Milner, please,
    When all the fighting's done,
Instruct the pious Boer-men
    Some wholesome texts to con,—
To ponder well the last of Paul,   145
    Likewise the first of John!

1 *Mr. Bull* John Bull. 3 *Kruger* Paul Kruger, President of the Transvaal 1881–1901. 6 *Drift called Rorke's* Rorke's Drift was a British post that had been besieged unsuccessfully by the Zulus in the Zulu War of 1879. 8 *Caudine Forks* an Italian mountain pass where a Roman army was defeated in 321 BC. 9 *Cornwallis* surrendered at Yorktown in the American War of Independence. 11 *Tommy A.* the British soldier—Tommy Atkins. 30 *turbaned lancers* Indian cavalry. 31 *Batavian* Dutch. 36–8 One posture used by target shooters at Bisley, the home of the sport, involved lying on one's back and propping the rifle up on one's knees. 60 *Frogs* frogging on officers' tunics. 74 *melinite* an explosive. 77 *half-and-half* mixture of mild and bitter beer. 86 *De Wet* Christian De Wet was the Boer leader in the guerrilla war of 1900–2: he was never captured. 99 *Creusot, Krupp:* the two firms, French and German, that sold artillery to the Boers. Creusots were nicknamed 'Long Toms'. 104 *Lyddite* an explosive. 113 *Suttee* Hindu widow who immolates herself on her husband's funeral pyre. 114–15 a play upon the glazier's use of putty and the puttees worn by British soldiers, wrapped round their legs. 116 *Majuba* the battle that concluded the first Boer War of 1880–1 with a defeat for the British. 141 *Sir Alfred Milner* British High Commissioner in South Africa who helped precipitate the War in 1899. 145–6 *last of Paul . . . first of John* St Paul's 'last' letter is to Philemon, where he pleads on behalf of a slave for love and compassion. The 'first' letter of St John is likewise an appeal for love and fellowship among those who share the name of Christian.

A Tick Lunch

The subject here is a curiosity today in two respects—marking the opening of the first self-service snack bar in London and the introduction of the 'free gift' as advertisement. The poem also shows Thompson's knowledge of the cockney dialect, which he never forgot from his years on the London streets. He prefixed the poem with a note: 'According to a recent statement in the "Daily Mail", American "quick-lunch" bars are to be started in London. The customers will serve themselves, while on certain days the management will distribute among them gold watches and other souvenirs.'

Leavin' a 'Quick-Lunch' 'e was lagged,
    My pore old pal, Job Vickars:
'Is lunch it 'ad been 'ad on tick,
    And 'e was 'ad on tickers.

Sal was with 'im, to 'elp take care   5
    Of watches or of lockets:
'I'll share your pickin's, Job,' she said,
    'Particlarly of pockets.'

'E saw they 'ad 'im: 'Come,' 'e said,
    'What counts against me, squarely?'   10
'Our counts,' they said, 'concern your "dukes;" '
    'E grinned; 'goodbye, my girlie.'

'E pinched Sal on her little cheek,
    Then on her little chin-chin:
The copper says: 'Your ruin comes,   15
    My man, from cheek and pinchin'.'

With that 'e slipped the bracelets on,
    And marched 'im to the station;
A warnin' 'im 'e better 'ad
    Not make no observation.   20

'Least observed, least you let out,' says
    The copper with a frown:
'For though as 'ow you've been took up,
    Yet you will be took down.'

'Your 'ead is all as I observe,'   25
    Says Job, 'this blessed minute,—
A 'armless observation, for
    It aint got nothing in it.'

Now when Job came into the court,
   All on 'is best be'avour,   30
'Is Worship's face by no means pre-
   Possessed 'im in 'is favour.

The witnesses they said as Job
   Indulged in several 'Scotches,'
Two veal-and-'ams, three sandwiches,   35
   And 'alf-a-dozen watches;

Two di'mond pins; with 'ankerchers
   Had lib. (in which 'e tied 'em);
Five ladies' purses, and likewise
   Promiskyus chink inside 'em.   40

All which 'e 'ad on tick—leastways
   It slipped 'is mind to pay for it.
'Is Worship, then 'e ups and asks
   What Job 'ad got to say for it.

Job says 'e asked if 'Elp yourself'   45
   Was rules, as people swears;
And souvenirs and watches was
   Give out to customers.

'They told me, "Yuss," ' says Job, 'and so
   I 'elped my blankin' self   50
(Bein' a rule-abidin' man)
   To 'alf the blankin' shelf.

'Your Worship, but the Manager
   (Through various occupation)
Forgot them watch and souvenirs   55
   Which was my expectation.

'Your Worship, so I 'elped myself
   To whatsomede'er might prove anear—
I 'elped myself to watches gold
   And various kinds of souvenir.   60

'Them watches as they nabbed from me
   (Your Worship, 'ark, if you've an ear)
Them di'mond pins, and other things,
   Was just a blanky souvenir!'

'Is Worship said as Managers   65
    Should not leave honest blokes
To 'elp theirselves to souvenirs
    Belongin' other folks.

'But I myself will make amends
    For honest hopes so marred: 70
Accept' says 'e, 'a souvenir
    From me,—eighteen months 'ard.

'Adoo, adoo; remember me.'
    'Remember thee?' says Job:
'Adds-hooks! while memory 'olds 'er seat   75
    In this subtracted globe!'

1 *lagged* arrested. 11 *dukes* FT note: 'fingers'. 16 *pinchin'* FT note: 'stealing'. 17 *bracelets* handcuffs. 24 *took down* sentenced to be imprisoned. 35 *veal-and-'ams* meat pies. 38 *Had lib.* (i.e. *ad libitum*) as many as he liked. 40 *chink* coins. 72 a sentence of eighteen months' hard labour. 75 *Adds-hooks* gadzooks, God's hooks (oath).

'Doris Biggs'

Although the manuscript is a fair copy in ink and signed, it has no title. Verses 1–4 are quoted by Viola Meynell in *Francis Thompson and Wilfrid Meynell* (1952) pp. 158–9. Verses 4–5 are quoted in *BHCC*, pp. 322–3.

Now Doris Biggs was a pretty maid
    Who dealt in the fish-line,
And so she hooked young William Higgs
    Of the Pike and Gudgeon sign.

But soon she loved another man,   5
    Who worked at the Red Earl,
And was engaged again, for she
    Was an engaging girl.

Poor William sought her where she plied
    A brisk fish-mongering trade,   10
Unheedful of his woes, because
    She was a sell-fish maid.

'O Doris Biggs, how can you thus
   Pursue your finny sales?
The time has been, alas! you weighed   15
   Me in quite other scales.'

Said she, 'They say I fished for you.'
   (She gave a bitter look),
'And hooked you; but if so, you now
   Can go—and take your hook.'   20

'Too well you know that I am fast
   To you, both hook-and-I;
But why you treat me thus I know—
   You've other fish to fry!

'Had I but taken my own hook   25
   Before yours did allure me!
By love though like a herring dried,
   Alack! you will not cure me!

'No doubt you think me a poor sole
   Because I fell so flat: 30
Why did I nibble at your bait—
   Ah, what white bait was that!

'But you shall find that I have teeth,
   You hard, inconstant lady!'
Said she, 'You know, my dear, I've had   35
   A bite of you already!

'Although you are a dry fish, yet
   You get too wet, O Bill!
Too like a fish you are, in that
   You have more than one gill.   40

'And if I hooked you, Bill, you're not
   The sort of fish I wished you;
I find I cannot stomach you,
   Although I've tried,—and dished you.

'For while you are so often "fresh,"   45
   'Tis not from sea, but malt;
And though you're in a pickle now,
   You are not worth your salt.'

He drew forth a torn handkerchief
    At hearing of her jeers;   50
And took all full of tears his wipe,
    And his full wipe of tears.

'I never would have thought of you
    Had I known (useless wish!)
That though you fished your only love,   55
    You only loved your fish.

'If I must be a banished man
    To pay for lovers' sins,
For old association's sake
    I'll live among the Finns.   60

''Mid heavy size of heaving whales
    I'll mourn my hapless suit;
For you are false, O Doris Biggs,
    Yea, false from head to foot!

'Behind the counter to and fro,   65
    Fish-prices you repeat,
Till your very head is a figure-head,
    And your feet are counter-feet.

'And ah! these golden locks I praised,—
    If truth's in gossip's tongue,   70
'Tis seen the gods must love you well,
    For, Doris, you dye young!

'Oh, I believe astrology,
    'Tis destiny prevails,
And my evil stars are the Fishes, with   75
    The Virgin and the Scales!

'Farewell, farewell, my useless plea,
    I see you do but palter;
Though I cannot bring you to the priest,
    You'll bring me to the halter!'   80

So he put poison in her plaice,
    Which shortly did prevail.
The jury found, which sat on her,
That like a mermaid, when laid bare
    Hers was a fishy tale.   85

The stern judge said to William,
   'Your wish at length you've got;
For you shall have a parson, and
   We'll tie for you the knot.'

Said Bill, 'You've made a pretty catch;   90
   But you're all wrong—for why?
You think that I would tie the knot,
   But I would not the tie.

'And O, your Warship, please reflect,
   'Twill be the same thing still,   95
Instead of settling my account
   If you discharge this Bill.'

But ah! no more to hold by hope,
   Advised that judge so grim;
So they tried ('twas but a letter's change)   100
   If rope would hold by him.

Now, as it chanced, the rope gave way,
   But they bade him not repine,
For the nearest cord to hand they'd take
Instead, and that one did not break,   105
   For *it* was a *fish-line*.

But when his last act finished, with
   A drop-scene and a pit,
He still did kick against his fate,
   Though he'd no ground for it.   110

A head-stone and a stone above
   Her chest marked Doris' bed;
To show the hardness of her heart,
   And likewise of her head.

They carved the Early Christian Fish   115
   On the stone worth many a guinea;
And the motto they put over her—
   In French—was 'tout est *finny*.'

---

20 *take your hook* depart (cockney slang). **40** *gill* a measure of spirits. **51** *wipe* handkerchief. **78** *palter* equivocate. **97** *discharge* dismiss; *Bill* written accusation of crime. **108** *drop-scene* theatrical scenery; *pit* seating area in a theatre.

PART FOUR

Cricket Verse

In his later years, Thompson's lifelong love of cricket led him to write several poems on matches and players he had known; in addition, there are unfinished poems scattered through the later notebooks. His special loyalty to his Lancashire background was always a central theme, with many references to the Red Rose that is the symbol for the Lancashire teams. The best introduction to his cricket verse is provided by himself in a late notebook entry (NB35).

> I attained a considerable critical apprehension of the supreme English game by watching the play of its finest masters; while I was assisted, no little, to perceive something of its technique by my own practical experience as a zealous, if necessarily occasional and trumpery amateur. A local match on a Saturday afternoon will open a youth's eyes to the merits of a Wyatt or a Barlow . . . Knowing the ordinary difficulties he can appreciate with a new vividness the extraordinary difficulties, and the extraordinary skill which meets them, in the great players he watches. So, not presuming to call himself a cricketer, he becomes a connoisseur in cricketers: at least within certain modest limits. Such is my case. For several years, living within distance O[ld] T[rafford] Ground, where successively played each year the chief cricketers of England . . .

Rime O'Bat of O My Sky-Em

The poem is a parody of Edward FitzGerald's *Rubaiyat of Omar Khayyam* and, as such, also an example of Thompson's capacity for humorous verse. It was first published by E.V. Lucas in his article 'Francis Thompson's Cricket Verse' (*Cornhill Magazine*, July–December 1908). The poems and extracts in that article were reprinted in his *One Day and Another* (1909). Lucas added his own notes and observations to the poems, some of which are of doubtful reliability. But his comment on this poem is valid when he says of the theme that it 'quickly became individual and human . . . a new and independent thing in cricket verse'. No manuscript has been traced.

I

Wake! For the Ruddy Ball has taken flight
That scatters the slow Wicket of the Night;
    And the swift Batsman of the Dawn has driven
Against the Star-spiked Rails a fiery Smite.

Wake, my Beloved! take the Bat that clears
The sluggish Liver, and Dyspeptics cheers;
    To-morrow? Why, to-morrow I may be
Myself with Hambledon and all its Peers.

5

To-day a score of Batsmen brings, you say?
Yes, but where leaves the Bats of Yesterday?   10
     And this same summer day that brings a Knight
May take the Grace and Ranjitsinjh away.

Willsher the famed is gone with all his 'throws,'
And Alfred's six-Foot-Reach where no man knows;
     And Hornby—that great hitter—his own Son   15
Plays in his place, yet recks not the Red Rose.

And Silver Billy, Fuller Pilch and Small,
Alike the pigmy Briggs and Ulyett tall,
     Have swung their Bats an hour or two before,
But none played out the last and silent Ball.   20

Well, let them Perish! What have we to do
With Gilbert Grace the Great, or that Hindu?
     Let Hurst and Spooner slog them as they list,
On Warren bowl his 'snorter'; care not you!

With me along the Strip of Herbage strown,   25
That is not laid or watered, rolled or sown,
     Where name of Lord's and Oval is forgot,
And peace to Nicholas on his bomb-girt Throne.

A level Wicket, as the Ground allow,
A driving Bat, a lively Ball, and thou   30
     Before me bowling on the Cricket-pitch—
O Cricket-pitch were Paradise enow!

II

I listened where the Grass was shaven small,
And heard the Bat that groaned against the Ball:
     'Thou pitchest Here and There, and Left and Right,   35
Nor deem I where the Spot thou next may'st Fall.

Forward I play, and Back, and Left and Right,
And overthrown at once, or stay till Night:
     But this I know, where nothing else I know,
The last is Thine, how so the Bat shall smite.   40

This thing is sure, where nothing else is sure,
The boldest Bat may but a Space endure;
    And he who One or who a Hundred hits
Falleth at ending to thy Force or Lure.

Wherefore am I allotted but a Day 45
To taste Delight, and make so brief a stay;
    For meed of all my Labour laid aside,
Ended alike the Player and the Play.

Behold, there is an Arm behind the Ball,
Not the Bat's Stroke of its own Striking all; 50
    And who the Gamesters, to what end the Game,
I think thereof our Willing is but small.

Against the Attack and Twist of Circumstance
Though I oppose Defence and shifty Glance,
    What Power gives Nerve to me, and what Assaults,— 55
This is the Riddle. Let dull Bats cry "Chance."

Is there a Foe that [domineers] the Ball?
And one that Shapes and wields us Willows all?
    Be patient if Thy Creature in Thy Hand
Break, and the so-long-guarded Wicket fall!' 60

Thus spoke the Bat. Perchance a foolish Speech
And wooden, for a Bat has straightened Reach:
    Yet thought I, I had heard Philosophers
Prate much on this wise, and aspire to Teach.

Ah, let us take our Stand, and play the Game, 65
But rather for the Cause than for the Fame;
    Albeit right evil is the Ground, and we
Know our defence thereon will be but lame.

O Love, if thou and I could but Conspire
Against this Pitch of Life, so false with Mire, 70
    Would we not Doctor it afresh, and then
Roll it out smoother to the Bat's Desire.

---

8 *Hambledon* the Hampshire village where cricket first became a recognised sport, *c.* 1750. 11 *Knight* Albert E. Knight (1872–1946). Cricket historian, author of *The Complete Cricketer* (1906). 12 *Grace* Dr W. G. Grace (1848–1915). Most famous of all

cricketers, dominated the game 1871–1900; played for Gloucestershire (1870–99) and England (1880–99). *Ranjitsinjh* (1872–1933) Indian prince and outstanding batsman, played for Sussex (1895–1902) and England (1896–1902). **13** *Willsher* Edgar Willsher (1828–85), a renowned bowler, played for Kent. **14** *Alfred* Alfred Myn (1807–61). Played for Kent (1834–59) and Sussex (1839–47) as the greatest all-rounder of his day. **15** *Hornby* A. N. Hornby (1847–1925). Played for Lancashire (1867–99) and England (1878–84). Brilliant fielder and noted Rugby player. His son, A. H. Hornby, played for Lancashire (1899–1914). **17** *Silver Billy* nickname for William Beldam (1766–1862). Played for Surrey (1801–17), Hampshire (1805–7) and Kent (1806). Regarded as best batsman of his time at the end of the Hambledon period. *Fuller Pilch* (1804–70). Played for Norfolk (1820–36), Kent (1836–54), Hampshire (1842–5), Surrey (1830–44) and Sussex (1840–2). Famous as a batsman. *Small* J. Small (1737–1826). Played for Hampshire (1773–98). Original member of the Hambledon Club. **18** *pigmy Briggs* John Briggs (1862–1902). Played for Lancashire (1879–1900) and England (1884–99). Called 'Boy' Briggs because he was only 5ft 5in. tall, and made his debut at age 16. *Ulyett* George Ulyatt (1851–98). Played for Yorkshire (1873–93) and England (1876–90). At his death he was regarded as the best batsman Yorkshire had produced. **22** *Grace, Hindu* see note to 12 above. **23** *Hurst* must refer to C. S. Hurst who was playing for Uppingham as a schoolboy and did not play for a county until after FT's death. *Spooner* R. H. Spooner (1880–1961). Played for Lancashire (1899–1921) and England (1905–12). Known as a stylish batsman and a Rugby player. **24** *Warren* T. H. Warren (1859–1936). Played for Leicestershire (1882–5). A fast bowler. **27** *Lord's and Oval* international cricket grounds in London and county grounds for Middlesex and Surrey respectively. **58** *Willows* Good cricket bats are made from willow wood. **71** *Doctor* Doctor W. G. Grace (see note to 12 above).

Middlesex v. Yorkshire: May 28–31, 1899

E. V. Lucas (see headnote above) quotes two lengthy extracts from the following poem, lines 32–40 and 59 to the end. But as the whole manuscript has survived at H it is followed here. It is a detailed description of one of the most famous matches played at Lord's at the end of the nineteenth century. Like most of Thompson's cricket verse it was not meant for publication: as Lucas says, 'it was merely a versified memorandum of the match for the writer's own amusement'. But as such it is a good example of another facet of Thompson's work.

<blockquote>
White sprinkle a-glitter 'gainst the sun,
With dark-clad silence gazing on,
Whence thunders break in unison,
Lo, what gusts shall in the shine be done!
Unbeaten South, unbeaten North,   5
On Lord's field come to the battle forth;
Unbeaten North goes down, ah me!
For a poor two hundred and some three,
Before the potent-to-overturn
Dread-bowling Trott, and Roche, and Hearne.   10
Five Middlesex wickets fallen, too,
</blockquote>

For none too many, if none so few:
For the days are as batsmen love, pitch good
Whereon to make firm the stubborn wood.
Now, the second day, I who sing   15
Watch what the fortune of cricket shall bring—
Fortune of cricket, sterner far
Than is the partial fortune of war.
A Warner, who all month has slept,
By such shall ye at bay be kept,   20
Ye men of Yorkshire? For ye have too
O'erturners of wickets not a few.
Alas! this so-long-slumbrous-Warner
Has our best bowling in a corner;
Retires, with hundred, and fifty more,   25
'Midst clapping and loud-throated roar.
But he is gone, with roar and claps;
Now, say, are ended our evil haps,
Thou Hawke, who stand'st with fallen chaps?
Alack! to Trott M'Gregor comes forth,   30
Last state is worse than thy first, O North!
For Trott, who also month-long kept
Inert, as the batsman in him slept,
Wakes, and with tumult of his waking
The many-girded ground is shaking!   35
With rolling claps and clamour, as soar
Fours after fours, and ever four!
Bowls Rhodes, bowls Jackson, Hague bowls, Hurst,—
To him the last is as the first:
West-end tent or pavilion-rail,   40
He lashes them home with a thresher's flail.
Says Hawke: 'I would give the half I've got
To him who made yon devil's bird Trott!'
So spake, in the out-field where he stands,
My lord, with his clenchèd teeth and hands.   45
But, for fuming smother and vicious grin,
His men stay out, and those men stay in.
All the long noon, under the sun,
Those men hit out, and those men hit on,
And never are, but his side *is*—done.   50
Ha! Trott at last a chance has lent
In the long-field yonder,—sure heavenly-sent—
Sail down left of pavilion-tent.

By all the——angels, the slave has dropped it!
Be Nemesis thanked, his hand has copped it!   55
As he shakes on the grass his fingers bloody,
Thinks Hawke: 'I would it were all in your body!
Your blind bat-blink, my beauty gay,
Will cost us seventy runs today!'
Trott keeps them trotting, till his d——d score   60
Is just one hundred, sixty, and four,—
The highest tally this match has scored,
And the century fourth is long up on the board.
Thank heaven, the fellow's grown reckless now,
Jumps and slogs at them anyhow: 65
Two narrow shaves, amid frenzied howl
Of jubilant people, and lordly growl;
Till a clinker tingles in Brown's left hand—
Good Brown! you have snapped the infernal stand!
The last two wickets go tedious down,   70
And my lord strides off with his teeth and frown.

6 *Lord's field* Lord's cricket ground. 10 *Trott* could be one of two brothers, G. H. S. Trott (1866–1917) or A. E. Trott (1873–1914). They were Australian and both were bowlers who played for Australia in England. *Roche* W. Roche (1871–1950). Australian bowler who played for Australia and then for Middlesex and England. *Hearne* F. Hearne (1858–1949). All-rounder who played for Kent (1879–89) before emigrating to South Africa. 19 *Warner* Sir P. F. Warner (1873–1963), knighted in 1937 for his services to cricket. 29 *Hawke* Hon. M. B. Hawke (1860–1938). Played for Yorkshire (1881–1911); President of Yorkshire from 1898 until his death and a major influence on the game in the county. 30 *M'Gregor* G. Macgregor (1869–1919). Played for Middlesex (1892–1907). 38 *Rhodes* W. Rhodes (1877–1973). Played for Yorkshire (1898–1930). One of the greatest of all bowlers. *Jackson* Rt Hon. Sir F. S. Jackson (1870–1947). Played for Yorkshire (1890–1907); captained England, brilliant all-rounder.— *Hague* S. Haigh (1871–1921). Played for Yorkshire, outstanding bowler. *Hurst* doubtful reference: C. S. Hurst, the only cricketer of note with the name, did not start playing until after FT's death. 68 *Brown* At the time there were two cricketers of the same name, J. T. Brown. Here the reference is probably to the bowler who played for Yorkshire (1897–1903).

'A Rhapsodist at Lords'

The first three stanzas were published by E. V. Lucas in 'Francis Thompson's Cricket Verse' (see headnote for 'Rime O'Bat of O My Sky-Em', p. 479). They were reprinted in *Life* (p. 40) and the first was reprinted again in *Works* under the title 'At Lords'. The fourth stanza was quoted independently of the rest by Everard Meynell in 'The Notebooks of Francis Thompson', *DR*, January 1917 (see

Introduction, p. xxxii). In the EMH Collection there are notebook drafts for the whole poem with many variants. This is E. V. Lucas's description of the match that forms the theme of the poem:

> The match in question was played at Old Trafford on July 25, 26, 27, 1878, when the poet was eighteen . . . It was an historic contest, for the two counties had never before met. The fame of the Graces was such that 16,000 people were present on the Saturday, the third day—of whom, by the way, 2,000 did not pay but took the ground by storm. The result was a draw, a little in Lancashire's favour, after a very determined fight interrupted now and then by rain. It was eminently Hornby and Barlow's match. In the first innings the amateur made only 5, but Barlow went right through it, his wicket falling last for 40. In the second innings Hornby was at his best, making with incredible dash 100 out of 156 while he was in, Barlow supporting him while he made 80 of them.

It is little I repair to the matches of the Southron folk,
    Though my own red roses there may blow;
It is little I repair to the matches of the Southron folk,
    Though the red roses crest the caps I know.
For the field is full of shades as I near the shadowy coast,   5
And a ghostly batsman plays to the bowling of a ghost,
And I look through my tears on a soundless clapping host
    As the run-stealers flicker to and fro,
        To and fro.
    O my Hornby and my Barlow long ago!   10

It is Glo'ster coming North, the irresistible,
    The Sire of the Graces, long ago!
It is Gloucestershire up North, the irresistible,
    And new-arisen Lancashire the foe!
A Shire so young that has scarce impressed its traces,   15
Ah, how shall it stand before all resistless Graces?
O little red rose, their bats are as maces
    To beat thee down, this summer long ago!

This day of seventy-eight they are come up North against thee,
    This day of seventy-eight, long ago!   20
The champion of the centuries, he cometh up against thee,
    With his brethren, every one a famous foe!
The long-whiskered Doctor, that laugheth rules to scorn,
While the bowler, pitched against him, bans the day that he was born;
And G.F. with his science makes the fairest length forlorn;   25
    They are come up from the West to work thee woe!

Somewhere still ye bide among my long-lost Northern faces,
　　My heroes of the past, they tell me so!
Somewhere still ye bide in my long-lost Northern places,
　　But dead to me with youth, long ago.　　　　　　　　　　　　30
I mind me of your staunchness as I near the shadowy water,
O Stonewall, and the look of your little fair-haired daughter;
(But the years have done upon you all the unassuagable slaughter)
　　As the run-stealers flicker to and fro,
　　　　To and fro,　　　　　　　　　　　　　　　　　　　　35
　　O my Monkey and my Stonewall long ago!

10 *Hornby* A. N. Hornby (1847–1925). Played for Lancashire (1867–99) and for many years partnered *Barlow* R. E. Barlow (1851–1919). Played for Lancashire (1871–91). **12** *Sire of the Graces* W. G. Grace; (see 'Rime O'Bat . . .' 12n.). **23** *Doctor* W. G. Grace. **25** *G.F.* G. F. Grace (1850–80). Brother of W. G. Grace, played for Gloucestershire (1870–80). **32** *Stonewall* R. E. Barlow, known as a 'stonewaller' as a batsman although a brilliant fielder. **36** *Monkey* nickname for Hornby.

'The little Red Rose shall be pale at last'

These lines were published in *Life*, p. 45. According to Everard Meynell the reference in the last line is to the area in London known as Marylebone. As Thompson made his way late at night from the Meynells' home to his lodgings he would pass through this area and often compose poetry as he went: 'The following lines he wrote out for me and posted in the early hours after such a journey (p. 45) But see also the endnote below.

　　The little Red Rose shall be pale at last.
　　　　What made it red but the June wind's sigh?
　　And Brearley's ball that he bowls so fast?
　　　　It shall sink in the dust of the late July!

　　The pride of the North shall droop at last;　　　　　　　　5
　　　　What made her proud but the Tyl-des-lie?
　　An Austral ball shall be bowled full fast,
　　　　And baffle his bat and pass it by.

　　The Rose once wounded shall snap at last.
　　　　The Rose long bleeding it shall not die.　　　　　　　10
　　This song is secret. Mine ear it passed
　　　　In a wind from the field of Le-Bone-Marie.

3 *Brearley* W. Brearley (1876–1937). Noted as a fast bowler, played for Lancashire

(1902–11) and England (1905–12). **6** *Tyl-des-lie* J. T. Tyldesley (1873–1930). Played for Lancashire (1895–1923). **12** *field of Le-Bone-Marie* see headnote for EM's interpretation. FT probably intended a double meaning in a reference to Lord's cricket ground, the home of the Marylebone Cricket Club (the MCC) in St John's Wood, to the north of Marylebone.

'Sons, who have sucked stern nature forth'

These verses were included with the cricket poems in *Life* (pp. 41–2)as a further example of the elegiac mood of Thompson's cricket verse.

Sons, who have sucked stern nature forth
From the milk of our firm-breasted north!
Stubborn and stark in whatever field,
Stand, sons of the Red Rose, who may not yield!

Gone is Pattison's lovely style,   5
Not the name of him lingers awhile.
   O Lancashire Red Rose, O Lancashire Red Rose!
   The men who fostered thee, no man knows.
   Many bow to thy present shows,
   But greater far have I seen thee, my Rose!   10

Thy batting Steels, D.G., H.B.,
Dost thou forget? And him, A.G.,
Bat superb, of slows the prince,
Father of all slow bowlers since?

Yet, though Sugg, Eccles, Ward, Tyldesley play   15
The part of a great, a vanished day,
By this may ye know, and long may ye know,
Our Rose; it is greatest when hope is low.

   The Lancashire Red Rose, O the Lancashire Red Rose!
   We love the hue on her cheek that shows: 20
   And it never shall blanch, come the world as foes,
   For dipt in our hearts is the Lancashire Red Rose!

5 *Pattison* It seems likely that FT is referring to W. S. Patteson (1854–1939), who played for Lancashire (1874–82). **11–12** *batting Steels* ... A. G. D. Q. Steel (1856–1933), played for Lancashire (1876–87); H. B. Steel (1862–1911), played for Lancashire (1883–96), noted as a powerful batsman; A. G. Steel (1858–1914), played for Lancashire (1877–93) and for England (1880–8) and as captain four times. **15** *Sugg* F. H. D. Sugg (1862–1933).

Played for Lancashire (1887–99); a brilliant fielder. *Eccles* A. Eccles (1876–1919). Played for Lancashire (1898–1907). *Ward* A. Ward (1865–1939). Played for Lancashire (1889–1904). *Tyldesley* J. T. Tyldesley (1873–1930). Played for Lancashire (1895–1923).

Dies Iræ, Dies Illa

(*July 16, '98; More Park and Old Trafford*)

Thompson's title here can be rendered as 'The Day of Judgement, the Day is near.' The lines were published by Everard Meynell in his article 'The Notebooks of Francis Thompson' (see headnote for 'A Rhapsodist at Lords', pp. 484–5). As he points out, here Thompson's loyalty to his northern background even includes praise for Lancashire's rivals in the Yorkshire cricket teams, whose symbol is the White Rose.

> Woe is me, fair White Rose!
>   It is a bitter stead,
> That thou should'st fall unto false Southron,
>   And not to thy Sister Red!
>
> Woe is me, my Red, Red Rose!   5
>   Woe and shameful plight,
> When the Red Rose falls to the South blast
>   And not to the Rose of White!
>
> When Red Rose met White on Bramall grass
> And turned not back from each other; alas,   10
> Had the Red Rose smote the White Rose,
>   Or the White Rose smote the Red,
> Or ever bent to the soft Southron,
>   The stubborn Northern Head!
>
> O Red Rose, O White Rose,   15
>   Set you but side by side,
> And bring against you the leaguèd South,
>   You might their shock abide;
> Yea, bring against you the banded South,
>   With all their strength allied.   20
>   My White Rose, my Red Rose
> Could smite their puissance i' the mouth!

9 *Bramall grass* Bramall Lane, the cricket ground in Sheffield, Yorkshire.

Juvenile Poems

FROM THE USHAW COLLEGE NOTEBOOK

These nine poems were written during the years 1870–7 when Thompson was at Ushaw College. They are carefully copied into the notebook known as the Ushaw College Notebook. The following five were published in an article on his schooldays by A. Wilkinson and H. K. Mann, 'Francis Thompson: A Tribute from His Schoolfellows', (*Ushaw Magazine*, March 1908): 'Lamente forre Stephanon', 'Song of the Neglected Poet', 'Finchale', 'Dirge of Douglas', and 'A Song of Homildon'. Eight out of the nine poems in the notebook ('Lamente forre Stephanon' omitted) were published in *Youthful Verses of Francis Thompson*, (privately printed, Preston 1928). The notebook manuscripts have provided the texts: the only variants in the published texts are minor changes in punctuation.

Lamente forre Stephanon

This poem was also printed in *Life*, p. 28. According to Everard Meynell it was written for a master at the college who was sick, and he quotes it as an example of the light-hearted verse that Thompson enjoyed writing from the first.

> Come listenne to mie roundelaie,
>   Come droppe the brinie tear with me,
> Forre Stephanon is gone awaye,
>   And longe awaye perchance wille be!
>   Our friendde hee is sicke,   5
>   Gone to takke physicke,
>   Al in the infirmarie.
>
> Swart was hys dresse as the blacke, blacke nyghte,
>   Whenne the moon dothe not lyghte uppe the waye;
> And hys voice was hoarse as the gruffe Northe winde,   10
>   Whenne hee swirleth the snowe awaye.
>   Our friendde hee is sicke,
>   Gone to takke physicke,
>   Al in the infirmarie.

Eyn hee hadde lyke to a hawke,   15
　　Soothe I saye, so sharpe was hee,
That hee e'en mought see you talke,
　　Whenne you talkynge did not bee.
　　　　Our friendde hee is sicke,
　　　　Gone to takke physicke,   20
　　　　Al in the infirmarie.

We ne'er schalle see hys lyke agenne,
　　We ne'er agenne hys lyke schalle see,
Searche amonge al Englyshe menne,
　　You ne'er will fynde the lyke of hee.   25
　　　　Our friendde hee is sicke,
　　　　Gone to takke physicke,
　　　　Al in the infirmarie.

Song of the Neglected Poet

The poem is printed below as it appears in the manuscript. In the published text it is divided into four-line stanzas.

Still, be still within my breast, thou ever, ever wailing heart,
Hush; O hush within my bosom, beating, beating heart of mine!
Lay aside thy useless grief and brood not o'er thy aching smart,
Wherefore but for sick hearts' healing came down poetry divine?
Mourn not, Soul, o'er hopes departed, efforts spent, and spent in
　　　vain,   5
On a glorious strife we entered, and 'twas for a priceless stake;
Well 'twas foughten, well we've struggled, and, though all our hopes
　　　are slain,
Yet, my Soul, we have a treasure not the banded world can take.
Poesy, that glorious treasure! Poesy, my own for e'er!
Mine and thine, my Soul, for ever, ours though all else may be gone; 10
Like the Sun it shone upon us when our life began so fair,
Like the Moon it stays to cheer us now our night is almost done.
Think, my soul, how we were happy with it in the days of yore,
When upon the golden mountains we saw throned the mighty Sun,
When the gracious Moon at nighttime taught us deep and mystic lore, 15
And the holy, wise old forests spoke to us and us alone,

When the streamlet tinkled gladness all to us and none beside,
When for us the sweet birds flooded air with gurgling rapture wild;
When there was no living creature that would from our presence glide,
For they knew the Poet brother unto Nature's every child.   20
Yes, I loved them! And not least I loved to look on Ocean's face,
When he lay in peace sublime and evening's shades were stealing on,
When his child, the King of Light, from heaven stooped to his
          embrace,
And his locks were tangled with the golden tresses of the Sun.
Such thoughts, Soul, are now our treasures, such the joys that we have
          left;   25
O my Soul, and who shall dare to call us wretched and forlorn?
What though honours, riches, pleasures, human hopes, all,—all are
          left?
'Midst the past years' garnered memories we can laugh the world to
          scorn.

The Storming of Corinth

Now streamed the boding crescent on the wind;
Serried, and dark, and eager poured behind
The turbaned multitudes of Turkish war,
Scenting the destined slaughter from afar.
As when amidst the burning Ethiop land   5
The locust-swarms, innumerous as the sand,
Whir onwards on the desert's parching blast
Hide the strong sun and bare the country past,
And falling still, and still advancing more,
Pass, dealing ruin, to the ocean's shore,—   10
So countless, so destructive, rushed to fight
The Turkish hosts, resistless in their might.

Far other stood upon the crumbling wall
The Christians left to meet that tempest's fall.
How few, and yet how faithful! Battered, worn,   15
Their armour hacked and stained, their plumes all torn.

Lyric to have been inserted in 'Helias'

The first stanza is reprinted in *SHSS*, p. 15, and the third in *BHCC*, p. 35 and the fourth in *Life*, p. 29. 'Helias' was an unwritten poem.

My window is open for thee, sweet love,
   My window is open for thee,
The bindweed rope on the tree doth move,
   As the breezes come and flee;
Wert thou here, wert thou here, I would cast away fear,   5
   And descend to the garden to thee.

For my heart craves still for love, sweet life,
   And my thought to seek thee flies;
Though the moon like a silver dove, sweet life,
   Broods in tender light o'er the skies,   10
And the stars shine bright, in my heart there is night
   For the want of the light of thine eyes,
Of thy face more fair than the silver moon,
   And the starlike light of thine eyes.

And so, my casement is wide,   15
   And there comes into my room
From the copse by the basement's side
   The lilac's sweet perfume,
The rich geranium scent,
   And the breath of the rose in bloom;   20
'Tis the spirit of love from heaven lent
   That floats into my room,
'Tis the spirit of love from the heaven above
   Floats on the wings of that soft perfume.

The laden laburnum stoops   25
   In clusters gold as thy hair,
The maiden lily droops
   The fairest where all are fair,
The thick-massed fuchsias show
   In red and in white,—thy hue!   30
In a pendant cloud they spread and glow
   Of crimson, and white, and blue,
In hanging showers they droop their flowers
Of crimson and white, and crimson and blue.

*

But thou art alone my beautiful,   35
    The darling, the joy of my soul!
And here have I stood in the night-air's lull
    While into my heart there stole
A whisper, a thought with joy full-fraught,
    Which made that sick heart whole.   40

For I said, 'Perchance my darling
    Stands out in her garden tonight,
And the sleeping flowers around her
    Have opened their eyes at the sight,
And the wren and the thrush have looked out from the bush,   45
    For oh well, and oh well they know
Her footfalls so light, so soft, so faint,
That the harebell she trod on sprang up without taint,
    And the violet scarce bent low.'

And I lean far out of my window,   50
    Thinking, sweet, of thee,
And a message I say to the winds that play
    On the garden and over the lea:
'Breathe low, soft winds,
    Waft these from me,   55
To her whom well you know to tell
    Waft these from me.'

But see where the dawn breaks yonder
    And the light runs over the skies:
Too long was't delayed, too long have I stayed,   60
    Now by that brighter light of thine eyes
I will come with the speed of wonder
    And take thee by surprise!
For our night is gone, our night is done,
    Our night is over and flies,   65
Our night is away, mount, mount, fair sun,
    Shine out where my true love lies;
For the pale moon slopes, now arise, bright hopes,
    Bright dawning hopes arise!
Now the morn's bird crows, and the daisy opes,   70
    Now the marigolds ope their eyes:
Come away, come away, my darling,
    Come away where thy true-love sighs,

Come away, come away, my light, my day,
    Where the heart of thy true-love sighs   75
To be joined to thy heart, never, never to part,
    To be joined by unending ties,
To be bound to thy heart, never, never to part,
    By the bond of a love that shall never more start,
Till Death shall come with his fatal dart,   80
    And the one heart withers and dies.

Finchale

I sing the tale that which once hath been
And is no longer, what my mind has seen
In quiet musing, but a vision torn
From the dim past, ere yet the shade forlorn
Of desolation settled on the land,   5
When all yet dreamed not of the spoiler's hand.
I sing the past. Ye fair wise sisterhood,
From whose bright hands comes aught of joy or good
Which singer yet has sung, make quick my thought.
And thou, O Pan, whose dwelling must be sought   10
Deep in some vast-grown forest, where the trees
Are wet with cold, large dew, [hiatus] in the breeze
Where hangs dark moss in rain-steeped tresses long,
Aid me, O aid, to body forth in song
A scene as fair as thou in all thy days   15
Hast gazed upon, or ever yet wilt gaze.

Full in a spot which the glad sunlight laves
There spreads a wood, whose undulating waves
Of foliage thick shine in the moving light
Which shifts from tree to tree along their height: 20
And on one side a bright chill stream runs by,
From which sometimes a salmon will shoot high
—A bar of light—the spray from off it thrown
Makes transient rainbows in the morning sun,
Then sinks with pleasant pattering—   25

Spring

The rugged Winter, cold in snow and gloom,
Has fled reluctant to his northern home:
Merrily, lightly, trips in blithesome Spring,
The woods are stirring, meadows, hedgerows ring.
The glorious sky spreads boundless overhead,   5
Flecked with bright clouds, the East yet faintly red;
The wavy hills are laughing in the sun,
The changeful beams along their summits run,
And chequer them with tracks of shade and light,
One square deep shade, the rest all silvery white,   10
Another yellow, green, or russet-brown,
And so the shadows chase each other down.

War

Hark, heard ye not the echoing clang of arms,
The trumpet's summoning, and the drum's alarums?
Lo! countless squadrons crowd the glittering plain,
The exulting charger snorts, and tugs the rein,
The soaring banners flout the clouded sky,   5
The cannon roars, the trembling hills reply,
Thick-thronging thousands shake the gory ground,
And fallen hundreds lie in death around.
Say, whence arise these scenes of blood and woe,
From what dread source do all these evils flow?   10
War, only War! the cause of misery
From snow-capped Andes to the Chinese Sea:
War, only War, has been to wretched man
A baneful curse since first the world began.
Not only War is ruin to the small,   15
His very favourites fare the worst of all.

Dirge of Douglas

Let no ruthful burying song
Lament the Earl of Douglas,
But let his praises loud and long
Echo the rocks and hills among,
Poured from the lips of warriors strong   5
The doughty Earl of Douglas!

Well the Southrons know his might,
The dreadful Chief of Douglas!
The English yeomen turnèd white
When he saw the flaming homesteads' light   10
Gird with a fiery ring the night,—
''Tis the Black Earl James of Douglas!'

There was not a man on English ground
But feared the Earl of Douglas!
There was not a heart in England found   15
From the basest churl to the monarch crowned,
But hated as hell the very sound
Of the awful name of Douglas!

But the Southron kite it knew full well
The roll of the drum and the long low swell   20
Of the clarion sounding the English knell
That told the march of Douglas:
And the wolf that howls as she battens on dead
Loveth the hand that oft hath fed
Herself and her cubs with a banquet red,   25
The weighty hand of Douglas!

Long from afar will look the kite
For the gleaming spears of Douglas!
Long, long the wolf may strain her sight
To see the banner of Scotland's fight   30
Tossing adown the mountain's height
Proclaim the march of Douglas!

Bear him to his grave with a warlike pace,
Sing no sad requiem o'er him;
The mightest he of all his race,   35

He is gone, and none can fill his place!
Let the champion lie in his warrior's grave
Where his forefathers lay before him.

And it shall ring from pole to pole,
This burying of Douglas!   40
For villages shall burn, and the drums shall roll,
And the clangour of arms his knell shall toll,
And the shriek of many a parting soul
Shall sing the Dirge of Douglas!

A Song of Homildon

The Battle of Homildon Hill, at which the Scots were defeated by the English
under the Earl of Northumberland and his son Harry Hotspur, took place in 1402.

Now every man from hill and plain
Follow the banner of Percy,
For into Northumberland, trampling o'er slain,
The doughty Earl Douglas hath forayed amain,
And scorneth all ruth and mercy!   5

Hotspur hath girded his harness on,
And plucked his sword from his scabbard;
He led his army to Homildon,
There, ere the ruddy morn be done,
The lion must yield to the libbard.   10

5 *ruth* pity. 10 *libbard* leopard.

Index of Titles

Where a poem has a headnote starting on a previous page, the page number given below will be for that page.

Index of First Lines